Wellness, Wellbeing and Tourism

ASPECTS OF TOURISM

Series Editors: **Chris Cooper** (*Leeds Beckett University, UK*), **C. Michael Hall** (*University of Canterbury, New Zealand*) and **Dallen J. Timothy** (*Arizona State University, USA*)

Aspects of Tourism is an innovative, multifaceted series, which comprises authoritative reference handbooks on global tourism regions, research volumes, texts and monographs. It is designed to provide readers with the latest thinking on tourism worldwide and in so doing will push back the frontiers of tourism knowledge. The series also introduces a new generation of international tourism authors writing on leading edge topics.

The volumes are authoritative, readable and user-friendly, providing accessible sources for further research. Books in the series are commissioned to probe the relationship between tourism and cognate subject areas such as strategy, development, retailing, sport and environmental studies. The publisher and series editors welcome proposals from writers with projects on the above topics.

All books in this series are externally peer-reviewed.

Full details of all the books in this series and of all our other publications can be found on http://www.channelviewpublications.com, or by writing to Channel View Publications, BLOCK, The Fairfax, Pithay Ct, Bristol, BS1 3BN, UK.

The policy of Multilingual Matters/Channel View Publications is to use papers that are natural, renewable and recyclable products, made from wood grown in sustainable forests. In the manufacturing process of our books, and to further support our policy, preference is given to printers that have FSC and PEFC Chain of Custody certification. The FSC and/or PEFC logos will appear on those books where full certification has been granted to the printer concerned.

ASPECTS OF TOURISM: 102

Wellness, Wellbeing and Tourism

Theories, Models and Emerging Paradigms

Edited by

Ranjana Tiwari, Catheryn Khoo and Timothy J. Lee

CHANNEL VIEW PUBLICATIONS
Bristol • Jackson

DOI https://doi.org/10.21832/TIWARI9677
Library of Congress Cataloging in Publication Data
A catalog record for this book is available from the Library of Congress.
Names: Tiwari, Ranjana, editor | Khoo, Catheryn, editor | Lee, Timothy, editor
Title: Wellness, Wellbeing and Tourism: Theories, Models and Emerging Paradigms/Edited by Ranjana Tiwari, Catheryn Khoo and Timothy J. Lee.
Description: Jackson, TN: Channel View Publications, [2026] | Series: Aspects of Tourism: 102 | Includes bibliographical references and index. | Summary: 'This book explores the relationship between wellness, wellbeing and tourism, offering a framework to understand how these domains contribute to sustainable global development. It examines how traditional practices, indigenous knowledge and community engagement enhance experiences while raising concerns about authenticity and commodification' – Provided by publisher.
Identifiers: LCCN 2025026894 (print) | LCCN 2025026895 (ebook) | ISBN 9781845419677 hbk | ISBN 9781845419684 pdf | ISBN 9781845419691 epub
Subjects: LCSH: Medical tourism – Conflicts and trends | Travel – Health aspects | Tourists – Health and hygiene | Health resorts | Health promotion
Classification: LCC RA793.5 .W45 2026 (print) | LCC RA793.5 (ebook) | DDC 362.1 – dc23/eng/20250825
LC record available at https://lccn.loc.gov/2025026894
LC ebook record available at https://lccn.loc.gov/2025026895

British Library Cataloguing in Publication Data
A catalogue entry for this book is available from the British Library.

ISBN-13: 978-1-84541-967-7 (hbk)

Channel View Publications
UK: BLOCK, The Fairfax, Pithay Ct, Bristol, BS1 3BN, UK.
USA: Ingram, Jackson, TN, USA.

Authorised Representative: Easy Access System Europe - Mustamäe tee 50, 10621 Tallinn, Estonia, gpsr.requests@easproject.com.

Website: https://www.channelviewpublications.com
X: Channel_View
Bluesky: @multi-ling-mat.bsky.social
Facebook: https://www.facebook.com/channelviewpublications
Blog: https://www.channelviewpublications.wordpress.com

Typeset by Riverside Publishing Solutions.

Contents

Contributors vii

Foreword xix

Preface xxi

1 A Global Perspective on the Rising Nexus of Wellness, Wellbeing and Tourism 1
Ranjana Tiwari and Catheryn Khoo

Theme 1: Cultural and Communal Dimensions of Wellness, Wellbeing and Tourism

2 Community Wellbeing through Culinary Preservation: An Exploratory Study of Kongunadu's Heritage 9
Amalan E., L. Jenifar and V. Sarath Chandrar

3 Integrating Indigenous Cuisine Knowledge into Modern Wellbeing Practices: A Case of Malawi, Southern Africa 28
Natasha Mashura Runganga

4 Balancing Minds and Lives: Student Awareness and Wellbeing through Wellness Programmes in Private Higher Education 48
Willy Hannes Engelbrecht and Susanna Cornelia (Corné) Engelbrecht

5 Wellness Tourism and Pastoral Culture: Exploring their Symbiotic Relationship 61
Aditi Choudhary and Mahima Gopalkrishna

6 Exploring New Trends in Health Diets in Wellness Tourism: An Investigation of the Key Attributes of the Chinese Wellness Tourist 80
Yuchen Ti, Timothy J. Lee and Jing Zhuo

Theme 2: Innovation and Technology in Wellness, Wellbeing and Tourism

7 Exploring Innovations in Tourism, Wellbeing and Sustainability through the Intersection of Neurosciences and Computing 99
Altair Sancho-Pivoto, Carla Fraga and Patrick Moratori

8 Co-Designing Transformative Wellbeing Tourism Experiences for Japanese Tourists to Finland 117
Kelsey M. Johansen and Henna Konu

9 Enhancing Wellness Tourism with Calligraphy-Based Mindfulness Therapy 137
Mayumi Hieda and Malcolm Cooper

Theme 3: Wellness Tourism Destination Development and Management

10 The Prospects of Ethno-Botanical Wellness Tourism through a Destination Stewardship Approach: Evidence from India 155
Sushma Maligi and Jagadeesh Kivudanavar

11 Thermal Tourism in Europe: Exploring the Wellness Dimension 175
Dália Liberato, Joana A. Quintela, Paulo Neto, Pedro Liberato and Filipa Brandão

12 How Can Health and Wellness Tourism Boost Regional Development? Unhais da Serra, Portugal: A Potential Answer 191
Mónica Brito, Margarida Mota and Paulo Nossa

13 Developing a Sustainable Tourism Energy Therapy Model in Nature: A Case Study of Mount Sabalan 216
Sonia Azhari and Mohammad Alizadeh

14 Synthesizing Insights and Charting Future Directions in Wellness, Wellbeing and Tourism 236
Ranjana Tiwari and Timothy J. Lee

Index 244

Contributors

The Editors

Ranjana Tiwari is a wellbeing expert, a Harvard-certified higher education instructor, and a tourism case writing trainer. A gold medallist in her postgraduate studies (awarded for securing the highest academic distinction in her studies in tourism management), Dr Tiwari holds a PhD in tourist destination image and attributes. She is currently a senior lecturer at Sunway Business School, Malaysia. Her research achievements include receiving the prestigious University Grant Commission (India) Junior Research Fellowship Award in Tourism Management & Administration. She was also recognized by the European Foundation for Management Development (EFMD) in the Family Business category of their case writing competition. Dr Tiwari is actively involved in academia and in industry circles. She serves on the editorial board of *Tourism Management Perspectives* and the *International Journal of Tourism Research*. She is a Guest Editor for special issues in the *Tourism Recreation Research* and the *International Journal of Spa and Wellness*. Additionally, she is the lead editor (with M. Scerri and C. Lee) of the book *Teaching Cases in Tourism & Hospitality (with cartoon illustrations)*. Her professional affiliations include membership of the Women's Indian Chamber of Commerce & Industry (WICCI) and the REGENERA Regenerative Luxury Hotels Association. Her published research includes papers, book chapters and case studies in various international and national journals. Her primary teaching and research interests encompass wellbeing, positive psychology in tourism, wellness tourism, and destination image.

Catheryn Khoo is a distinguished scholar in the field of tourism and hospitality and is editor-in-chief of the leading journal, *Tourism Management Perspectives*. As #thetourismprofessor, she is renowned for her comprehensive research portfolio and significant contributions to the industry. As a consultant to the United Nations World Tourism Organization (UNWTO) and the Asian Development Bank, she drives pioneering research on positive tourism outcomes. Her research focus is on marginalized voices in tourism, adopting an Asian postcolonial lens. Professor Khoo acts as a consultant for governments and tourism businesses. Notably, she was the lead author of the influential UNWTO *Regional Report on Women in Tourism* and co-authored the 2019 UNWTO *Global Report on Women in Tourism*. Her research has appeared in more than 100 international publications. A strong advocate for gender equality in tourism, she founded Women Academics in Tourism (WAiT), advises World Women Tourism, and is a member of the advisory board of the International Tourism and Investment Conference. Professor Khoo's scholarship has won her numerous awards, including the US-based Stevie Awards for Social Changemaker of the Year 2024 and *Travel Weekly's* Women in Travel Award for Sustainable Practices Champion 2023.

Timothy J. Lee is a professor at the Macau University of Science and Technology (MUST) in Macao, China. He holds an MSc and a PhD in hospitality and tourism management from the University of Surrey, UK. He held professorships in Australia and Japan before moving to Macau and has been invited more than 100 times to give special lectures or keynote speeches in 20 countries. Professor Lee is the editor-in-chief of the prestigious *International Journal of Tourism Research*. He has published more than 330 research papers in academic journals, books and conference proceedings (including 120 in SSCI ranked journals and 130 in A* or A in ABDC ranked journals). His research interests include wellness/health tourism, food tourism, cultural heritage tourism, and tourism/leisure/hospitality development that incorporates regional branding or values. He is the founding organizer of the two biennial conferences: GLOSITH (Global Congress of Special Interest Tourism & Hospitality, www.glosith.net) and ICOHOTH (International Congress of Health-Oriented Tourism & Hospitality, www.icohoth.org). His website can be found at proftimothylee.org.

The Contributors (chapter order)

Beáta Szablics is an international expert in travel product development and a dedicated advocate for various wellbeing disciplines. The main focus of her work has been on reshaping the tourism landscape by embedding principles of holistic wellbeing, and slow and restorative travel in global innovations. She lends critical insight into the book's relevance and potential impact across academic and industry contexts. Beáta is a tourism and hospitality business advisor and nature-based wellbeing guide with a passion for designing transformative experiences and supporting others in their professional and personal journeys.

Amalan E is a dedicated researcher and academic professional specializing in the fields of tourism and hospitality. Currently, he serves as coordinator of the Department of Tourism & Hotel Management at KLE Society's S. Nijalingappa College Bengaluru, India, where he is instrumental in shaping the next generation of tourism and hospitality professionals.

Amalan is currently pursuing his PhD at Madurai Kamaraj University, Madurai, focusing on the theme of food tourism, a field that aligns with his passion for exploring the connections between culinary heritage and travel. His research explores how food experiences shape tourism and contribute to cultural preservation and economic growth. Throughout his career, Amalan has participated actively in national and international conferences, presenting and publishing articles that contribute valuable insights to the tourism and hospitality sectors. His work is recognized for its relevance and application to industry practices, and he is committed to advancing knowledge in his field through continuous research and collaboration.

L. Jenifar is currently pursuing a doctorate in tourism and travel management at Government Arts College, Coimbatore, India. He is a dedicated academic and industry expert with a rich background in tourism studies. He holds an MBA in tourism and travel management from the Indian Institute of Tourism and Travel Management, Gwalior, India, and he successfully attained UGC-NET three times in Tourism Administration & Management. His academic journey began with a BA LLB (BABL) degree from Tamil Nadu Dr Ambedkar Law University, Chennai, reflecting his diverse educational foundations. Professionally, he serves as an assistant professor in the Department of Tourism Studies at Madras Christian College, Chennai. His prior experience includes heading the Department of Tourism and Travel Management at Cherraan's Arts Science College, Kangayam, India and he has undertaken similar roles at prestigious institutions across Tamil Nadu. His commitment to advancing tourism education and research has been recognized through a number of awards, including that of 'Best Head of Department' by the Global Multidisciplinary Research & Academic Foundation (GMRAF) in 2022, and he has received accolades for his presentations at national and international conferences.

His research interests include digital preservation methods for cultural heritage, the role of mobile applications in tourism, and studies on medical tourism. As an active contributor to seminars, workshops and faculty development programs, he is also a mentor for the Bureau of Indian Standards and a resource person for various national webinars. His multilingual skills, legal knowledge, and leadership qualities distinguish him as a versatile professional in tourism academia and research.

V. Sarath Chandrar is a distinguished professional in tourism and hospitality management, with an extensive background in both academia and industry. He completed his undergraduate degree in engineering from Anna University (2007–2011) and subsequently earned a postgraduate diploma in management (PGDM) in tourism and travel management from the Indian Institute of Tourism and Travel Management, Bhubaneswar, India (2012–2014). He further qualified with the UGC-NET in tourism administration and management in 2018.

Currently pursuing a PhD in tourism and hospitality management at the Central University of Tamil Nadu, Sarath's published research includes articles focusing on the role of artificial intelligence in enhancing heritage and cultural tourism destinations. His academic roles have included serving as Guest Faculty in Tourism and Hospitality Management at the Central University of Tamil Nadu. Currently he is a teaching associate at the Indian Institute of Tourism and Travel Management (IITTM), Nellore, where he continues his contributions.

As a project associate for the Ministry of Tourism's Swachhta Action Plan (2017–2019), he organized more than 120 programs across Tamil Nadu, Telangana and Puducherry, raising awareness of cleanliness and tourism among students, stakeholders and tourists. His role as a customer agent with Air India Air Transport Services Ltd (2014–2017) and as a tourism assistant with the Indian Railway Catering and Tourism Corporation (IRCTC) highlighted his operational expertise, including the coordination of cultural programs like Kasi Tamil Sangam and Saurashtra Tamil Sangam.

In 2021, he founded the Madras Institute of Tourism Studies in Coimbatore, reinforcing his commitment to advancing tourism education and contributing significantly to the field.

Natasha Mashura Runganga is an early-stage researcher currently employed as a lecturer for the Bachelor of Culinary Arts degree program at Mzuzu University in Malawi. Her major areas of research focus on the consumption of Indigenous foods, the benefits of consuming Indigenous foods, waste management in kitchens, and conserving culture through food and community tourism.

Recently, Natasha has developed a new interest in wellness studies, manifest most recently in her authorship of Chapter 3 of this volume. Reflecting on her journey since joining the hospitality industry in 2006, she is happy to be imparting knowledge through real industry experiences to young industry prospects. She is delighted to be one of the pioneer lecturers to teach culinary art degrees in Malawi, graduating the first cohort of students in 2023: 'Teaching is exciting as it has opened my mind to the countless possibilities that exist in the academic field'. As a researcher, she looks forward to uncovering new knowledge and collaborating with other global researchers to share ideas.

Willy Hannes Engelbrecht is a senior lecturer and programme coordinator in the School of Management Sciences at North-West University, South Africa. He has been in the higher education industry for more than 12 years and has occupied various academic, managerial and leadership positions at both public and private higher education institutions locally and internationally. Willy obtained his PhD in tourism management from North-West University in 2015, and completed a Master's in education at the University of Johannesburg in 2021. He has teaching experience in both undergraduate and postgraduate programmes and actively participates in research projects. His research publications have appeared in both national and international journals and he has contributed to conferences and to chapters in textbooks related to tourism, marketing, supply chain, teaching and learning, and higher education management. Willy has also co-edited six textbooks over the past four years. He acts as an external examiner for master's and doctoral theses and as an external reviewer for both national and international academic journals. Willy served a second term as Scientific Chair for the SAPHE Conference and is assistant editor for the *Independent Journal of Teaching and Learning* (IJTL), which is a fully open access online journal. He serves on various academic advisory boards for higher educational institutions in South Africa and has also been appointed an Institutional Audit Panel member and programme accreditation reviewer by the Council on Higher Education (CHE).

Susanna Cornelia (Corné) Engelbrecht boasts a diverse career spanning academia and educational management, with more than 10 years of lecturing and management experience. Notable roles include senior lecturer and head of the tourism department at North-West University (NWU), and head of academics at the International Hotel School. She served as an assistant professor at Woosong University's School of Hospitality Management (SIHOM) in South Korea, where she chaired the academic committee. As learning and teaching and quality assurance manager at the Invictus Education Group, her current expertise focuses on tourism and hospitality management and education. With qualifications including a BCom, BCom Honours, MCom, a PhD in tourism management and a postgraduate diploma in higher education, she was honored with the Vice-Chancellor's Medal Award for being the Best Master of Commerce Student in the Faculty of Commerce at North-West University. As a member of the Golden Key International Honour Society, Corné actively contributes to research, publications, and academic supervision within the field.

Aditi Choudhary is an academician and consultant specializing in sustainable tourism. She holds a doctorate in sustainable tourism and has devoted her career to voicing sustainability and responsible tourism practices. A gold medallist throughout her education, Dr Choudhary's 19 years of experience reflects a diverse portfolio. As a full-time faculty member at the Indian Institute of Tourism and Travel Management (IITTM), she plays a crucial role in molding the future of sustainable tourism. She was a Nodal Officer at the Central Nodal Agency for

Sustainable Tourism under the Ministry of Tourism, Government of India. Notably, Dr Choudhary holds a Higher Education Teaching Certificate from Harvard's Derek Bok Center for Teaching and Learning, further demonstrating her dedication to continuous professional development. She is also a recipient of the Korea Partnership Initiative for Sustainable Tourism's prestigious International ODA Action Plan competition. She holds a certificate in Sustainable Tourism Destination Management from Cornell University. Dr Aditi Choudhary is a leading advocate for sustainable tourism practices in India and beyond.

Mahima Gopalkrishna is a tourism researcher and consultant specializing in sustainable and rural tourism development. She holds a Master's degree in economics and communication with a focus on international tourism from Università della Svizzera italiana, Switzerland. As a senior research analyst at Geostat Informatics, Mahima currently leads a state-wide rural tourism project for the Uttar Pradesh Tourism Department, emphasizing community empowerment and sustainable tourism practices. She previously served as a project associate for the Ministry of Tourism's Central Nodal Agency for Sustainable Tourism, where she was instrumental in policy implementation, sensitization workshops, and social media campaigns to raise awareness of sustainable tourism. Her collaborative work with the Market Research Division, Ministry of Tourism, and the Indian Institute of Tourism and Travel Management (IITTM) includes developing India's first pastoral tourism model, designed to uplift pastoral communities through tourism as a sustainable livelihood. She is co-author (with Aditi Choudhary) of 'Tides of Change: The Story of Lakshadweep Tourism' published in *Tourism Cases* (2024).

Yuchen Ti was a chef instructor of the Florida International University Marriott Tianjin China Program. She obtained her Master's degree in hospitality and tourism management from Florida International University in 2013 and obtained her professional diploma in culinary arts from Ferrandi Paris in 2015. Yuchen is a PhD candidate in hospitality and tourism management at Macau University of Science and Technology. She has five years' experience in Europe in fine dining restaurants such as Restaurant Café de la Paix in Paris and the 3-star Michelin restaurant Guy Savoy. Yuchen also holds the WSET Level 2 certificate in wines and spirits, awarded by the Wine & Spirit Education Trust (WSET) in China in 2020.

Jing Zhuo was awarded a Master's degree in risk management from the University of New South Wales, Australia. He completed his Bachelor's degree in hospitality management from Florida International University (FIU). He currently works as a teaching assistant in the Faculty of Hospitality Management at Florida International University at the TUC–FIU (Tianjin University of Commerce–Florida International

University) campus in Tianjin, China. His research interests include health and wellness tourism, food tourism, and creative tourism.

Altair Sancho-Pivoto holds a PhD in geography from the Federal University of Minas Gerais (IGC/UFMG, 2016), and an MA in social ecology from the Federal University of Rio de Janeiro (EICOS/UFRJ, 2007). He graduated in tourism from the Federal University of Juiz de Fora (UFJF) in 2004. He is currently a professor in the Department of Tourism and a permanent professor of the graduate program in geography at UFJF. He is a coordinator of the Research Center of Tourism, Territory and Social Environmental Development at UFJF, and develops academic and university extension studies with an emphasis on geography of tourism; territorial planning and protected areas; ecotourism; sustainability; tourism, wellbeing, and neurosciences; social environmental, rural and community development. He is a member of the Tourism Research Group: Neurosciences and Computing (certified by UFJF).

Carla Fraga holds a DSc and MSc in transportation engineering from the Federal University of Rio de Janeiro (UFRJ) and is a specialist in neuroscience and applied psychology at Mackenzie Presbyterian University. She holds a Bachelor of Tourism degree from the Federal University of Juiz de Fora (UFJF) where she is currently an associate professor in the Department of Tourism, focusing on teaching, research and university extension courses in tourism, transportation, neurosciences and computing. She heads the Tourism Research Group: Neurosciences and Computing (certified by UFJF).

Patrick Moratori holds a BSc in computer science from the Federal University of Juiz de Fora (UFJF) and an MSc from the Federal University of Rio de Janeiro (UFRJ), specializing in computational intelligence, evolutionary algorithms, control systems, robotics and games. His PhD and postdoctoral research at the University of Nottingham further advanced his expertise in applied computing for industry, affective computing, neuroscience, cognition, modeling and simulation. Currently, he is a lecturer at Fluminense Federal University, Brazil, focusing on teaching and research in fuzzy logic and data analysis. He is an external collaborator of the Tourism Research Group: Neurosciences and Computing (certified by UFJF).

Kelsey M. Johansen is a postdoctoral researcher at the University of Eastern Finland Business School where she is also a member of the UEF Water Research Community. She specializes in the ways in which bluespaces, trails, and virtual nature experiences create amenity, experiential, economic, and societal value – for individuals, businesses, communities, and society as a whole – through their contribution to recreation, wellbeing and tourism. As a broadly trained social scientist, she focuses on projects that activate community assets to develop sustainable recreation and tourism products and engages in knowledge mobilization and translation within and across sectors using a community-centered, service-focused, and solution-oriented lens.

Henna Konu is an associate professor at the University of Eastern Finland Business School, focusing on examining nature-based tourism business. Her research interests are nature connectedness in nature-based tourism experiences; sustainability in tourism firms; designing experiential tourism services; and tourism as a part of the bioeconomy, with specialties in: wellbeing tourism, nature-based tourism, wellbeing from nature, experience design, experiential services, customer involvement, qualitative methods, responsible tourism, sustainable tourism, eco-labels and schemes, carbon offsetting models in tourism, and cultural ecosystem services.

Mayumi Hieda, MA, is a clinical psychologist based in Oita Prefecture, Japan. She is a member of the Japanese Association of Clinical Psychologists. From 2008 to 2012 she was the inaugural clinical psychologist at a psychiatric hospital in Beppu City. From 2012 until 2013 she was employed by the Beppu City Council in the Children and Family division. She is a member of the Oita Prefecture Suicide Prevention Network, a prefectural HIV counsellor, and a member of the counselling room in Beppu University. From 2013 to 2019 she was employed at a gynaecological hospital in Oita as their infertility counsellor. Since 2019 she has been a school psychologist and has established her own clinic, Mental Care Space NECO, in Beppu. She specializes in counselling, teaching courses in psychology to individual clients and groups, psychotherapy, mindfulness, anger management consultation and treatment, and calligraphy therapy.

Malcolm Cooper PhD LLM was born in Wellington, New Zealand. Since 2003 he has lived in Beppu, Japan, where he is Emeritus Professor at Ritsumeikan Asia Pacific University and Nagasaki University. He was the Inaugural Vice President for International Relations and Research at APU (2005–2012), and taught a range of tourism and hospitality management and business management subjects. Previously, he taught and held management positions at universities in Australia, New Zealand, Sri Lanka and the United Kingdom. He has also worked in the areas of city planning and tourism policy for federal, state and local governments in Australia and New Zealand. At other times he has been a private planning consultant and a tourism education consultant to the governments of Dubai, Sri Lanka, China and Vietnam. He is a recipient of the Australian Centennial Medal, a Fellow of the Planning Institute of Australia, and has published more than 200 books and papers, specializing in tourism development, health and wellness tourism, medical tourism, events management, and environmental impact.

Sushma Maligi is currently an associate of the Department of Tourism Studies, Karnatak University's Karnatak Arts College, Dharwad, Karnataka, India. She holds graduate and postgraduate degrees in tourism administration from Karnatak University. She has been the recipient of a Junior Research Fellowship (JRF) twice from the University Grants Commission (UGC) and holds a PhD in sustainable beach destination development from IGNOU. She has eight years teaching experience and three years' experience in industry (tourism and hospitality) in industry. She also holds a certificate in Food Safety, Aviation Management and Art of Heritage Interpretation to aid teaching. She is actively involved with strategic tie-ups and industrial associations, with central agencies like India Tourism, the Airports Authority of India and with international organizations like the International Centre of Responsible Tourism (ICRT Global), to facilitate industrial exposure and lifelong learning opportunities. Her research interests lie in sustainable beach tourism, responsible and regenerative tourism, tourism education, cultural heritage and related aspects. She is a member of the International Coastal and Marine Tourism Society, New Zealand.

Jagadeesh Kivudanavar is professor and head of the Department of Studies and Research in History & Archaeology and Department of Tourism Studies, Karnatak University, Dharwad, Karnataka, India. He holds an MPhil and PhD in history from Karnatak University and also holds a postgraduate diploma in epigraphy and a diploma in tourism studies from IGNOU. In his 22 years of service, he has authored 35 books and has published more than 45 research papers in reputed journals. He has completed a major research project from the UGC, New Delhi. He has been instrumental in elevating learning through industrial and organizational MoUs. He has to his administrative credit successful designing of professional courses in tourism and hospitality offered by the public university in Karnataka. He is a key Panel Member in Tourism Policy 2020–2025 for the Government of Karnataka. He is a member of a number of university boards and academic bodies. His research interest lies in ancient, medieval and modern history along with cultural studies.

Dália Liberato holds a PhD in tourism management and planning and a Master's in the management and planning of inland and health tourism, from the University of Vigo, Spain. She is an associate professor at the Tourism and Leisure Department, School of Hospitality and Tourism, Polytechnic Institute of Porto, Portugal, where she teaches several curricular units in tourism at the undergraduate and Master's levels. Currently, she coordinates the tourist activities management degree and the Master's in sustainable hospitality and tourism management in the same school (ESHT-P. PORTO). Her main research interests are tourism destination planning and management and regional development, tourism management, tourism planning, border tourism, creative tourism, wine and gastronomy tourism, and e-tourism. She is also involved in applied research and consultancy projects in tourism and leisure and is a member of organizing and scientific committees of international conferences. She is the author or co-author of more than 50 book chapters and articles published in international journals and in international conference proceedings.

Joana A. Quintela is an assistant professor at Universidade Portucalense (UPT), Portugal, teaching in the Department of Tourism, Heritage and Culture. She collaborates with Portucalense Business School as coordinator of the Short Master - Sommelier and Global Wine Market. She holds a European doctorate in tourism from the University of Aveiro, Portugal. Throughout her professional career, she has held various operational and management positions in the hospitality sector in Portugal and abroad. She has combined these roles with those of trainer, internship coordinator and consultant in tourism and hotel management, collaborating with various companies in the sector.

She is an integrated member of REMIT – Research on Economics, Management, and Information Technologies (UPT) and collaborator of CICEE – Research Centre in Business & Economics (UAL). She has participated in international conferences, contributed to book chapters and authored a number of scientific articles in leading international journals, and has written opinion pieces to specialised tourism publications. She is international coordinator and researcher responsible for various ERASMUS+ projects. Her research interests centre on tourism and hospitality, the quality of services, with particular emphasis on health and wellness tourism, marketing and sustainability.

Paulo Neto holds a Master's degree in tourism management from the School of Hospitality and Tourism, Polytechnic Institute of Porto, Portugal. He is a researcher in tourism, with a particular interest in the area of thermalism. He is a professional in the tourism and travel sector.

Pedro Liberato holds a PhD in tourism management and planning, from the University of Vigo, Spain. He is an associate professor in the Tourism and Leisure Department of the School of Hospitality and Tourism, Polytechnic Institute of Porto, Portugal. where he teaches several curricular units in tourism at the undergraduate and Master's levels. Currently, he coordinates the tourism management Master's degree in the Tourism and Leisure Department at the same school (ESHT-P. PORTO). His main research interests are tourism marketing, digital marketing, tourism planning, creative tourism, e-tourism, and smart destinations. He is involved in applied research and consultancy projects in tourism and leisure and is a member of the organizing and scientific committees of international conferences. He is the author or co-author of more than 50 book chapters and articles published in international journals and international conference proceedings.

Filipa Brandão holds a PhD in tourism and a Master's degree in tourism management and development from the University of Aveiro, Portugal. She is an assistant professor in the Department of Economics, Management, Industrial Engineering and Tourism (DEGEIT) at the University of Aveiro, where she teaches various curricular units in tourism at the undergraduate, Master's and doctoral level. She is a member of the Research Unit on 'Governance, Competitiveness and Public Policies' at the University of Aveiro (GOVCOPP-UA), director of the Master's degree in tourism management and planning, and associate editor of the *Journal of Tourism & Development*. She is the author or co-author of a number of books, book chapters, and her articles have been published in international journals. She is also involved in applied research and consultancy projects in the field of tourism and leisure and is a member of the organizing and scientific committees of international conferences. Her research and scientific work focus on innovation in tourism, regional development, social network analysis, planning and management of tourist destinations.

Mónica Brito holds a PhD in tourism, leisure and culture (2013). She is an assistant professor in the Department of Sociology, University of Évora, Portugal, where she is also is a researcher at the Interdisciplinary Centre for History, Culture and Societies (CIDEHUS) and at the Centre of Studies in Geography and Spatial Planning (CEGOT). Her research interests focus on blue tourism, health and wellness tourism, tourism planning, sustainable tourism, and innovation and entrepreneurship in tourism.

Margarida Mota has a degree in economics (2017), a Master's degree in financial economics (2019) and a Master's degree in tourism, territory and heritage (2022) from the University of Coimbra, Portugal. She also has a postgraduate degree in administration and public policies (2025) from the Universidade Aberta (UAb), Portugal. Between 2021 and 2023, she worked as project and funding manager for the Estrela Geopark Association, the organization that manages the classification of Serra da Estrela as a UNESCO Global Geopark. Her Master's thesis focused on measuring and evaluating the importance of health and wellness tourism in the regional economy and the development of the Estrela UNESCO Global Geopark territory.

Paulo Nossa holds a PhD (2005) in human geography from the University of Minho, Portugal. He is an assistant professor in the Department of Geography and Tourism at the University of Coimbra, Portugal, and a researcher at the Centre for Geography and Spatial Planning Studies at that university. He has participated in seven research projects, acting as the principal investigator for two of them. His academic work has focused on health policies, with a particular emphasis on the complex interrelationships between health, territory and demographic ageing. He served as the coordinator of the HIV/AIDS Prevention Unit from 2003 to 2005 at the Ministry of Health. He is currently engaged in research into the demographic processes of ageing and the social determinants of health.

Sonia Azhari is a PhD student in tourism management at Allameh Tabatabai University, Tehran, Iran, in the Faculty of Management. Her thesis is entitled 'Development Patter of Eco-therapy Tourism Destinations'. The major focus of her work is on sustainable tourism and how to build sustainable destinations through strategic tourism planning and strategic environmental planning. She is the author of articles in the fields of: the social capacity of accepting tourism in the rural areas, designing the pattern of ecotourism development, assessment of social carrying capacity, management solutions of world heritage sites, cultural tourism, the key to the development of world peace, the role of tourists' experience on environmentally responsible behavior. Sonia is Tourism Marketing and Advertising Expert in Iran's Ministry of Cultural Heritage and Tourism. She also works as a university lecturer in the field of tourism at Mohaghegh Ardabili University of Ardabil, Iran.

Mohammad Alizadeh is an assistant professor in the Department of Iranian Studies at Vali-e-Asr University of Rafsanjan, Iran. He holds a Bachelor's degree in geography from Tabriz University and a Master's degree in geography and tourism planning from the University of Tehran. He received his doctorate from Allameh Tabatabai University, with a thesis titled 'Explanation of Conceptual Models for Spatial Tourism Evolution in Gateway Destinations'. Dr Alizadeh has published numerous articles on various tourism topics, including ecotourism, tourism development, geotourism, Q-methodology analysis in tourism, and film tourism. His research focuses on the sustainability of tourism destinations, investigating social tolerance capacity, and developing sustainability and passage destination models in rural tourism. The majority of his work is in the field of tourism geography, and has been published in scientific and specialized journals. He also serves as director of the journal *Tourism Management Studies of the Smart Era*.

Foreword

In recent years, the intersections of wellness, wellbeing and tourism have gained significant attention, not merely as trending concepts but also as critical pillars reshaping the way we understand travel, community, ecosystems and human flourishing. As societies grapple with rising health challenges and socioenvironmental pressures, tourism has begun to emerge not merely as a vehicle for leisure but also as a potential platform for individual renewal, nature restoration and community resilience. *Wellness, Wellbeing and Tourism: Theories, Models and Emerging Paradigms* arrives at a pivotal moment, offering a comprehensive and thoughtful examination of how tourism practices are evolving in tandem with our deepening awareness of holistic health, sustainability, regeneration and experiential innovation.

This volume brings together a diverse array of perspectives, showcasing empirical research, theoretical reflections, and emerging practices from across the globe. The contributors offer a wide-ranging exploration of how wellness and wellbeing are conceptualized, experienced and operationalized within tourism contexts. Their collective work illuminates the ways in which health-oriented and wellness tourism is not only shaped by cultural, social and environmental factors but also acts as a catalyst for innovation in destination development.

What makes this collection stand out is not only its academic rigor but also its thematic depth, diversity and real-world implications. The chapters offer valuable insights into the experiences of individuals and communities engaged in wellness tourism, as well as critical analyses of the models and frameworks that underpin its development. From local heritage and indigenous knowledge systems to emerging technologies and sustainable planning strategies, the book demonstrates the richness of wellness tourism as a field of study and practice. The interdisciplinary nature of this volume, alongside its geographic and methodological diversity, enhances its value as a foundational resource that may inform future interventions in the field. Collectively, the voices in this book chart new pathways for how we understand, design and deliver health and wellbeing through tourism. The editors have curated a truly global, multidisciplinary dialogue that will resonate with academics, policymakers, practitioners and students alike.

As someone whose professional trajectory has bridged the domains of tourism development and wellbeing advocacy, I recognize the pressing need for integrative work such as this edition. It responds to the growing demand for tourism experiences that are intentional, ethical, and oriented toward long-term individual, societal and nature-positive benefits. As we continue to navigate global challenges – from mental health crises to ecological instability – the fusion of wellness, wellbeing and tourism has never been more essential.

I am honored to write the foreword to this volume and I commend the editors and contributors for their thoughtful and forward-looking work. This book will undoubtedly serve as a valuable resource for anyone seeking to engage more deeply with the intersections of health, wellness, wellbeing and tourism. It is my hope that it will inspire further dialogue, research and innovation in support of a tourism future that is more human-centered, more nature-centered, and more sustainable.

Beáta Szablics
Basel, May 2025

Preface

Namaste and thank you for your interest in this book.

This book was inspired by the vibrant discussions and exchange of ideas among participants at the 3rd International Congress of Health-Oriented Tourism & Hospitality (ICoHOTH), held at Thammasat University, Bangkok, 8–10 September 2023. The conference served as a pivotal gathering, yet even its dynamic environment could not fully encompass the wealth of insights, research, and perspectives emerging from scholars working on the evolving field of wellness tourism. All three editors of this volume were involved in the conference in three different ways: the first contributed as a presenter, the second delivered the keynote address, and the third served as the conference chair. These diverse engagements provided us with a multifaceted understanding of the field, enabling us to curate this book as a platform to extend the conversation beyond the conference. This volume not only continues the important dialogue initiated at the conference but also stands as a legacy of the evolving research and scholarship in wellness tourism, reflecting its growing significance and impact in contemporary tourism studies.

It is also the aim of this book to expand on the conference theme, which focused on health-oriented tourism and hospitality. As the conference participants also brought to attention other pressing concerns, such as food and sustainability, this book seeks to build on the momentum of those discussions, offering a continued exploration of the theoretical, methodological and practical dimensions of wellness, wellbeing and tourism, reflecting the diverse and globalized context in which they operate today.

Ranjana Tiwari
Catheryn Khoo
Timothy Lee

1 A Global Perspective on the Rising Nexus of Wellness, Wellbeing and Tourism

Ranjana Tiwari and Catheryn Khoo

The convergence of wellness and wellbeing with tourism is not a recent phenomenon. Historically, travel has been linked to healing, relaxation, and self-discovery – from ancient Roman bathhouses to ayurveda retreats in India and Zen meditation in Japan. Today, the wellness tourism sector has evolved into a $800 billion industry, with travelers seeking experiences that foster self-care, mindfulness, and rejuvenation. The motivations behind wellness tourism vary, ranging from medical treatments and spa therapies to nature-based retreats, cultural immersion, and adventure travel.

This chapter provides a comprehensive framework for understanding the synergies between wellness, wellbeing, tourism, and sustainability, offering insights into how this interconnected ecosystem is shaping the future of global sustainable development. Throughout this book, the terms wellness and wellbeing are used deliberately to reflect their distinct yet interrelated meanings. While these concepts are often used interchangeably in casual discourse, they represent different dimensions of health and quality of life. Figure 1.1 depicts the interrelation of wellness, wellbeing, tourism, and sustainability. Understanding their nuanced differences is essential for exploring their roles in tourism, sustainability, and global development.

Wellness in this book refers to an active, self-directed pursuit of health and vitality through various practices, lifestyles, and interventions. It is a dynamic process that individuals engage in to enhance their physical, mental, emotional, and spiritual health. *Wellbeing*, on the other hand, is a broader and more holistic concept that reflects an individual's overall life satisfaction, happiness and fulfillment. In this book, wellbeing is considered in relation to community welfare, mental resilience, economic

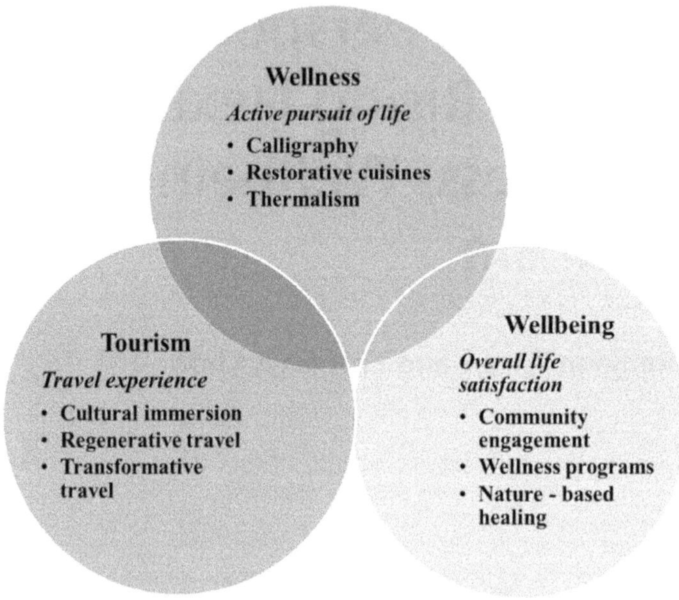

Figure 1.1 Framework of the nexus of wellness, wellbeing, tourism, and sustainability
Source: Ranjana Tiwari and Catheryn Khoo.

stability and environmental sustainability. It encompasses not only personal health but also social, economic, and environmental factors. While wellness is an essential component of wellbeing, wellbeing extends beyond individual health to encompass societal and environmental wellbeing.

Therefore, in this book when discussing wellness, we emphasize travel experiences designed to promote personal wellbeing, such as thermal tourism, activities like calligraphy, fitness getaways, and holistic healing practices. Moreover, discussions of wellbeing focus on experiences that enhance overall quality of life – such as engaging in wellness programs, cultural immersion, nature-based healing, or socially responsible travel.

To begin understanding the breadth and depth of wellness, wellbeing and tourism scholarship in this book, we invite readers to consider several key theoretical and conceptual foundations.

Holistic Health Models: These models highlight the interconnectedness of physical, mental, and spiritual wellbeing. Wellness tourism often draws from these models to create experiences that offer comprehensive health benefits. In this book, Choudhary and Gopal (Chapter 5) present in detail Dunn's High-Level Wellness Model to investigate the non-bovine milk and pastoralist lifestyles for promoting a balanced and proactive approach to health. Similarly, Runganga (Chapter 3) operationalizes PERMA wellbeing theory to demonstrate how traditional practices contribute to emotional and relational wellbeing, critical elements in holistic health. Further, using the 6-dimension model of wellness, Engelbrecht and Engelbrecht (Chapter 4) assess students' awareness of wellness programs in private higher education institutions. Liberato and her colleagues Quintela, Neto, Brandão and Liberato (Chapter 11) introduce the concept of classical thermalism using the framework of traditional thermal tourism in Europe, noting a shift from conventional curative practices to a holistic wellness approach that includes mental, physical and emotional wellbeing. Collectively, these chapters emphasize the multifaceted nature of wellness, yet they also reveal the tensions between traditional practices and modern wellness frameworks.

Cultural Integration: The adaptation of traditional cultural practices into modern wellness tourism raises important questions about authenticity and cultural respect. This framework examines how these practices are adapted and presented within a global tourism context. In this book, Amalan and his colleagues Jenifar and Chandar (Chapter 2) discuss how the Kongunadu region's culinary heritage aligns with holistic models by emphasizing the importance of cultural wellbeing and community engagement in promoting overall health. Similarly, in her chapter, Runganga (Chapter 3) sheds light on Malawi's indigenous cuisine knowledge and demonstrates how traditional practices contribute to emotional and relational wellbeing, which are critical elements in holistic health. Choudhary and Gopal (Chapter 5) discussed the traditional lifestyle of pastoralists, rooted in the harmony of nature, while aiming to enrich wellness tourism by incorporating cultural, environmental, and traditional knowledge systems, fostering a comprehensive view of wellbeing that transcends physical health alone. Together, these contributions highlight the importance of preserving cultural authenticity and respecting traditional knowledge, while also showing how these practices can enhance the wellness experience for modern tourists. This intersection of tradition and innovation encourages a deeper understanding of wellness that transcends geographical and cultural boundaries. While diverse traditions and contemporary approaches offer the potential for enriched wellness experiences, they also raise critical questions about the commodification of cultural practices and the risk of diluting their original intent. This juxtaposition challenges stakeholders to navigate carefully the balance between authenticity and commercialization in crafting wellness offerings that truly address all dimensions of health without compromising cultural integrity.

Sustainable Tourism: As wellness tourism grows, addressing its impact on the environment and local communities becomes crucial. Theories of sustainable tourism emphasize the need to balance economic benefits with environmental protection and cultural preservation. In Chapter 13, Azhari and Alizadeh present the Sustainable Model of Energy Therapy Tourism and put forth a foundational relationship between wellness and spiritual tourism within the context of Energy Therapy Tourism. Furthermore, Maligi and Kivudanavar (Chapter 10) employ the Destination Stewardship Framework to propose a model for ethno-botanical wellness tourism, integrating environmental stewardship and community empowerment. Although these ideas are still in their early stages and may be considered premature for journal publication, they are pivotal in shaping the future of theory development. The conceptualization of these models represents the essential groundwork in the iterative process of theory formation, laying the foundation for future academic inquiry and refinement within sustainable wellness tourism.

Consumer Behavior: Understanding the motivations and preferences of wellness tourists is key. Theories in consumer behavior explore why travelers seek authenticity, personalized experiences, and holistic health benefits. Johansen and Konu (Chapter 8) explore the sustainable business models employed by SaimaaLife, a wellness business in southeastern Finland, and its Japanese collaborators. Moreover, Hieda and Cooper (Chapter 9) demonstrate how calligraphy practices with mindfulness techniques can be used for wellness tourists and the destination. Sancho-Pivoto and his colleagues Fraga and Moratori (Chapter 7) delve into the intricate convergence of neuroscience and computing, particularly emphasizing affective computing showcasing the potential benefits for planners and managers. Collectively, these contributions emphasize the interdisciplinary nature of wellness tourism, where insights from behavioral sciences, technology, and cultural traditions converge to shape the future of tourism experiences tailored to evolving consumer desires.

This book could have been organized in various ways. After much deliberation, we have chosen to do so around three central themes.

- Theme 1: Cultural and Communal Dimensions of Wellness, Wellbeing and Tourism
- Theme 2: Innovation and Technology in Wellness, Wellbeing and Tourism
- Theme 3: Wellness Tourism Destination Development and Management

These themes were selected because they not only represent the most critical and emerging areas within wellness, wellbeing and tourism, but they also allow for a comprehensive exploration of the three important macro-level dimensions: cultural, technological, and sustainable. By organizing the chapters in this way, we aim to provide a holistic understanding of the nexus between wellness, wellbeing and tourism, reflecting its complexity and the multidisciplinary perspectives.

1.1 Theme 1: Cultural and Communal Dimensions of Wellness, Wellbeing and Tourism

Theme 1 examines how wellness tourism relates to cultural and communal practices. Under this theme, we feature the preservation of culinary traditions in Kongunadu by Amalan and his colleagues Jenifar,

Chandrar (Chapter 2); the incorporation of Indigenous knowledge into modern wellness practices in Malawi by Runganga (Chapter 3); and the impact of wellness programs on the wellbeing of students by Engelbrecht and Engelbrecht (Chapter 4). This theme also embraces the relationship between wellness tourism and pastoral cultures by Choudhary and Gopal (Chapter 5); and new health diet trends among Chinese wellness tourists, showcasing the evolving nature of wellness tourism by Ti, Lee and Zhuo (Chapter 6), highlighting the cultural influences that shape contemporary wellness experiences.

A critical observation here is that while these contributions celebrate the integration of traditional knowledge into wellness tourism, they also raise the challenge of ensuring these cultural practices are not commodified or diluted in the process. As wellness tourism increasingly seeks to incorporate local traditions, the tension between cultural preservation and the demand of a global market remains a key issue for the sustainability and authenticity of these experiences.

1.2 Theme 2: Innovation and Technology in Wellness, Wellbeing and Tourism

Theme 2 explores how technological advancements and new practices enhance wellness tourism. Topics include the integration of neurosciences and computing into tourism and wellbeing by Sancho-Pivoto and his colleagues Fraga and Moratori (Chapter 7); designing transformative wellness experiences for Japanese tourists by Johansen and Konu (Chapter 8); and using calligraphy-based mindfulness therapy by Hieda and Cooper (Chapter 9).

To this end, our own critical observation within this theme is that while technological innovations and new practices hold the potential to enrich wellness experiences, they also pose questions about the authenticity and accessibility of these offerings. As wellness tourism adapts to technological trends, it is essential to consider how these innovations might inadvertently create barriers to entry for certain demographics or lead to a homogenization of wellness experiences, thereby diluting the very essence of what makes wellness tourism diverse and culturally significant.

1.3 Theme 3: Wellness Tourism Destination Development and Management

Theme 3 focuses on the role of wellness tourism in regional development and sustainability. It covers the potential for wellness tourism to stimulate regional development in places like Unhais da Serra, Portugal by Brito, Mota and Nossa (Chapter 12); the role of ethno-botanical practices in India by Maligi and Kivudanavar (Chapter 10); and the exploration of thermal tourism in Europe by Liberato, Quintela,

Neto, Liberato and Brandão (Chapter 11). Case studies, such as the development of energy therapy tourism at Sabalan Mountain by Azhari and Alizadeh (Chapter 13), illustrate how wellness tourism contributes to sustainable growth.

While wellness and wellbeing present significant opportunities for regional tourism development, the long-term impacts on local communities and environments require careful examination. As wellness tourism expands, there is a risk that it may inadvertently lead to the commodification of local cultures and natural resources, challenging the very sustainability it seeks to promote. Therefore, it is essential to establish frameworks that prioritize ethical practices and ensure that the benefits of wellness and wellbeing tourism activities and practices are equitably shared among stakeholders, in order to enable a sustainable model for future growth. This, we readily acknowledge, is much easier said or written about than implemented in the practical sense.

In conclusion, we are pleased that this book has fulfilled its aim of providing scholars with a platform to explore and examine their own insights and contributions to the field of wellness, wellbeing and tourism. We are pleased to curate a volume on wellness, wellbeing and tourism that engages with discussions on culture, technology, and sustainability. Through the three thematic areas – cultural and communal dimensions; innovation and technology; and destination development and management – this volume brings forth the multidisciplinary nature of wellness tourism and its potential to promote wellbeing, cultural preservation, and regional growth. By engaging with these discussions, the book not only highlights current trends: it also lays a foundation for future research and development in this evolving field.

Theme 1
Cultural and Communal Dimensions of Wellness, Wellbeing and Tourism

2 Community Wellbeing through Culinary Preservation: An Exploratory Study of Kongunadu's Heritage

Amalan E., L. Jenifar and V. Sarath Chandrar

2.1 Introduction

The globalization of tourism has increased concern about the potential impact on local cuisines (Mak *et al.*, 2012). When local dishes are altered to accommodate the tastes of tourists, there is a risk that the unique cultural significance of the cuisine may be compromised. It is essential to recognize the delicate balance between showcasing local cuisine to visitors and preserving its authenticity and cultural integrity. Therefore, it is necessary to implement measures to safeguard the genuine essence of local dishes while also promoting them to a wider audience. Kongunadu, a culturally rich region in Tamil Nadu, India, is celebrated for its diverse and distinctive culinary heritage. The traditional foods of Kongunadu are more than just a source of sustenance: they are a vital expression of the region's history, local biodiversity, and communal identity (Venkatachalapathi & Paulsamy, 2016). These culinary practices, passed down through generations, embody a wealth of knowledge and skills that contribute significantly to the cultural wellbeing of the community. However, in the face of rapid modernization, globalization, and evolving dietary preferences, these treasured food traditions are increasingly at risk (Alexander & Leo, 2019).

The significance of protecting culinary traditions to enhance community wellbeing cannot be overstated. Culinary traditions play a crucial role in preserving cultural identity, fostering community cohesion, and promoting sustainable local economies (Mathew, 2024). The erosion of these traditions not only diminishes cultural diversity but also leads to the loss of valuable culinary knowledge and skills. It is crucial to understand the challenges and to identify the opportunities for preserving the culinary heritage of Kongunadu in order to ensure its continuation for future generations (Chera, 2020).

This exploratory study aims to address this critical issue by examining the challenges and opportunities associated with protecting Kongunadu's culinary traditions. Applying thematic analysis to the secondary data from a wide range of sources, including academic literature, government reports, historical texts, and digital archives, this research seeks to provide a comprehensive overview of the current state of Kongunadu's culinary traditions. By synthesizing insights from these diverse sources, the study aims to highlight the key obstacles hindering preservation efforts and to identify viable strategies and opportunities for safeguarding these culinary practices for the community wellbeing of the Kongunadu (Sugasini *et al.*, 2018).

The objectives of this study are twofold: firstly, to explore the major challenges faced in the preservation of Kongunadu's culinary heritage; and secondly, to uncover the potential opportunities and strategies that can be leveraged to protect and promote these traditions. Ultimately, this research aspires to contribute valuable knowledge to the field of cultural preservation and to support efforts aimed at maintaining the culinary practices and traditions of Kongunadu to enhance community wellbeing.

2.2 Literature Review

2.2.1 Wellbeing

Wellbeing is a comprehensive and multifaceted concept encompassing various aspects of an individual's life, contributing to overall happiness and quality of life (Yamaguchi & Oshima, 2024). It is generally divided into physical, mental, emotional, and social wellbeing, each playing a critical role in a person's overall health and contentment (Chen, 2019). Physical wellbeing refers to the body's condition and how well it functions. It includes regular physical activity, a balanced diet, sufficient sleep, and no disease or disability. Maintaining physical health is fundamental, as it forms the foundation for other dimensions of wellbeing (Mosko & Delach, 2021).

2.2.2 Local cuisine and community wellbeing

Local cuisine significantly enhances the wellbeing of a community by reinforcing cultural identity (Wali *et al.*, 2017), facilitating economic benefits and cultural transmission (Tsai, 2016), and fostering community cohesion (Zhang *et al.*, 2019). The flavors, ingredients, and cooking techniques unique to a region embody the history, traditions, and values of its people. Preserving and promoting local culinary traditions are vital in enhancing cultural wellbeing and fostering a sense of belonging, pride, and continuity within communities (Chen, 2019). Grimaldi *et al.* (2019) say that each traditional dish serves as a living repository of cultural heritage, preserving age-old practices and knowledge that tells a story of its origins, influenced by geography, climate, and historical events (Mosko & Delach, 2021).

Furthermore, as a component of cultural wellbeing, sharing traditional meals strengthens social ties and fosters a sense of community (Giampiccoli & Kalis, 2012). Festivals, family gatherings, and communal feasts focused on local cuisine provide opportunities for social interaction, thus enhancing emotional and social wellbeing (Yozukmaz *et al.*, 2020). These occasions allow people to connect with their cultural roots and reinforce communal bonds, promoting social harmony and a collective identity leading to cultural wellbeing (Chen, 2019). Moreover, preserving and promoting local cuisine can drive economic growth (Bessière, 2013) and sustainability (Chen *et al.*, 2022). Culinary tourism, food festivals, and local markets showcase regional specialties, attracting visitors and boosting local economies. Supporting local farmers, artisans, and chefs who produce and prepare traditional foods creates livelihoods and encourages sustainable agricultural practices (Andrieu & Batat, 2019).

Further, as an essential component of tourism, local cuisine plays a significant role in shaping the overall visitor experience (Zhang *et al.*, 2019), offering insight into local traditions (Giampiccoli *et al.*, 2020), and providing a platform for sustainability (Ocampo *et al.*, 2021); and it emphasizes a holistic approach to wellbeing (Batat *et al.*, 2019). By valorizing local food practices, cultural tourism encourages communities to maintain and celebrate their culinary traditions, contributing to cultural sustainability. Incorporating indigenous culinary traditions into cultural tourism brings about several advantages, but it is crucial to acknowledge and tackle the possible obstacles. Leakey *et al.* (2022) state that the commercial exploitation of native foods may result in their transformation into commodities, potentially causing a loss of their genuine character and identity.

2.2.3 Local cuisine and heritage reservation

Local cuisine is a vital aspect of cultural heritage, reflecting a community's history, traditions, and identity. Preserving local culinary practices is essential to maintaining cultural diversity and ensuring that traditional knowledge is passed down to future generations (Prasetyo *et al.*, 2022). Local cuisine encompasses a region's unique culinary ingredients, cooking methods, and culinary traditions. These elements are often deeply rooted in the local environment, agricultural practices, and historical influences (Wondirad *et al.*, 2021). For instance,

Kongunadu's cuisine in Tamil Nadu, India, is known for its use of millets, pulses, and native spices, reflecting the region's agrarian lifestyle and rich biodiversity. Preserving such culinary traditions helps maintain a tangible connection to the past, offering insights into the community's way of life, values, and social structures (Andrieu & Batat, 2019).

Preserving the heritage of local cuisine is a multifaceted endeavor that encompasses the thorough documentation of recipes, cooking techniques, and food-related customs specific to a particular region or community (Cook, 2024). This preservation effort involves the meticulous recording of traditional culinary practices through various means, such as written records (Askarno, 2020), oral histories (Filipiak-Florkiewicz *et al.*, 2022), digital archives (Mac Con Iomaire & Nic Philibín, 2022), and immersive experiences (Kokkranikal & Carabelli, 2024). By capturing and documenting these culinary traditions, communities can effectively safeguard their cultural heritage against the pressures of modernization and globalization (Maffei, 2012), which frequently contribute to the decline of time-honored practices and the loss of intangible cultural heritage (Cook, 2024).

Timothy and Pena (2015) argued that promoting local cuisine through culinary tourism, food festivals, and cooking classes can foster cultural pride and awareness (Chen, 2019). These initiatives help preserve traditional knowledge and create economic opportunities for local farmers, chefs, and artisans (Aulet *et al.*, 2019). For example, culinary tourism can attract visitors interested in experiencing authentic regional dishes, thereby supporting local businesses and encouraging the sustainable use of indigenous ingredients (Mosko & Delach, 2021). Moreover, preserving local cuisine is incredibly important, not just for cultural reasons but also for its potential health benefits. Traditional diets are often based on a balance of nutritious and wholesome ingredients, which can contribute to improved public health outcomes (Cena & Calder, 2020). Therefore, Andrieu and Batat (2019) suggested that, by reviving and promoting these traditional diets, communities can work towards countering the rise of diet-related diseases often associated with consuming modern processed foods.

2.3 Method

2.3.1 Research context

As shown in Figure 2.1 (see p. 16), Kongunadu boasts a rich historical tapestry and distinctive culinary heritage. Historically, Kongunadu was a vibrant cultural and trading hub, influenced by diverse dynasties such as the Cheras, Cholas, and Pandyas, each contributing to the region's unique cultural mosaic. This rich history is reflected in the region's culinary practices, which are marked by a blend of local ingredients, traditional cooking methods, and age-old recipes passed down through generations (Alexander & Leo, 2019). Kongunadu cuisine derives its name from the 'Kogunadu belt', comprising regions like Coimbatore, Pollachi, Salem, Karur, Avinashi, Mettur, Tiruppur, and Palani, whose culinary traditions are unique and rooted in their region. *Kongu* literally translates as 'border', and because a lot of these places share borders with the states of Kerala and Karnataka, culinary influences drawn from these states feature prominently in Kongunadu dishes.

The cuisine of Kongunadu is characterized by its use of indigenous ingredients such as millets, lentils, native vegetables, and an array of spices often sourced locally. Unique cooking techniques, like mud pots and slow-cooking methods, preserve the nutritional value and enhance the flavors of the dishes. Signature dishes such as *Kari Kuzhambu* (spicy mutton curry), *Kambu Sadam* (pearl millet rice), and *Arisi Paruppu Sadam* (rice and lentils), *Vazhapoovada* (made from banana flower), *Manikaram* spicy *vadagam* curry (made from holy basil and betel nut leaves), a tangy sherbet called *Nannari*, *Thenga Paal* (sweet hot milk made of jaggery, coconut, and cotton seeds), *Ulundu Kali* (a sweet dish made out of jaggery, gingelly oil, and black gram), *Kachayam* (dessert made from jaggery and rice), *Ragi Pakoda* (a crunchy snack made from ragi flour) and *Pori Urundai* (puffed rice balls), exemplify the region's culinary diversity and deep-rooted traditions (Anjana & Paulsamy, 2016).

Kongunadu's culinary practices involve food preparation and community and family bonding, with recipes often shared and meals enjoyed collectively. This culinary heritage is integral to the region's cultural identity and communal wellbeing, making its preservation all the more critical in the face of modern challenges and changing lifestyles (Amalan & Anitha, 2023).

Several studies and reports provide valuable insights into Kongunadu's rich culinary heritage, highlighting its cultural significance and the challenges faced in contemporary times. Academic research has explored the historical evolution of Kongunadu cuisine, tracing its roots to ancient agrarian practices and geographical diversity. These studies underscore the role of culinary traditions in preserving cultural identity and fostering community cohesion (Dillette *et al.*, 2021). Government reports and surveys have documented the diversity of dishes and cooking techniques prevalent in Kongunadu. These reports often emphasize the need for sustainable practices to safeguard local ingredients and traditional cooking methods. They highlight the economic potential of culinary tourism as a means to promote cultural preservation while stimulating local economies (Tiusanen, 2021).

Historical texts and ethnographic studies further deepen our understanding of Kongunadu's culinary heritage. They detail the rituals and social customs associated with food preparation and consumption, illustrating how culinary practices are intertwined with the region's everyday life and festive occasions (Singh, 2024). Digital archives and online repositories also contribute to preserving Kongunadu's culinary traditions by digitizing historical recipes, culinary manuscripts, and oral histories. These resources serve as valuable knowledge repositories, accessible for researchers, educators, and culinary enthusiasts alike (Sweeney, 2022).

Existing studies and reports on Kongunadu's culinary heritage paint a nuanced picture of its cultural significance and challenges in the modern era. They provide a foundation for identifying key preservation strategies and opportunities, emphasizing the importance of community engagement, policy support, and technological innovation in safeguarding this invaluable aspect of Kongunadu's cultural wellness (Yasmeen *et al.*, 2024).

2.3.2 Methodology and data collection

Using a conceptual research approach grounded in secondary data analysis, this exploratory study aims to investigate the challenges and prospects in protecting Kongunadu's culinary practices and to identify those factors that lead to community wellbeing. The research methodology encompasses a comprehensive review of existing literature, including academic papers, government reports, historical texts, and digital archives, to provide an in-depth understanding of the current state and potential future of Kongunadu's culinary traditions (Susmitha *et al.*, 2024). These sources provide a rich and diverse data set to understand the challenges and opportunities related to Kongunadu's culinary cultural wellness (Amalan & Anitha, 2023).

2.3.2.1 Literature review process

To ensure a thorough understanding of the subject, the literature review was conducted using a carefully selected set of keywords related to the preservation of traditional foods and cultural wellbeing. The primary keywords used in the search included Kongunadu cuisine, traditional foods of Tamil Nadu, culinary heritage preservation, food preservation methods, cultural sustainability, and traditional food systems. Variations of these terms and related synonyms were also incorporated to broaden the scope of the search.

The review spanned literature published between 2000 and March 2024, allowing the study to incorporate both recent trends and historical perspectives on the culinary heritage of Kongunadu. By focusing on this timeframe, the review captured contemporary discussions on preservation methods, while also considering earlier works related to the region's food culture.

The databases accessed for the literature review included Google Scholar, JSTOR, Science Direct, Taylor & Francis, and Wiley Online Library. And the regional resources such as the Tamil Nadu Digital Library were consulted to obtain local and historical information relevant to the study. These databases provided a diverse array of sources, from peer-reviewed academic journals to government reports and archival documents.

2.3.2.2 Article selection and review

An initial search yielded approximately 150 articles, reports, and documents. These were screened based on relevance to the research topic and the credibility of the sources. After a preliminary evaluation, 65 articles were shortlisted for detailed review. Finally, 40 articles were selected for inclusion in the study based on their direct relevance to key themes such as the preservation of traditional foods, cultural wellbeing, and the specific focus on Kongunadu or similar regional cuisines. Articles that were too general, lacked academic rigor, or were unrelated to Kongunadu or food preservation were excluded from the review.

2.3.2.3 Inclusion criteria for selecting articles

The inclusion criteria for selecting articles were:

- Studies focused on the preservation of traditional foods and culinary heritage, particularly in the context of Tamil Nadu and Kongunadu.
- Papers addressing the cultural significance of food in community wellbeing.
- Research published in reputable, peer-reviewed journals, government publications, and academic archives.
- Articles providing insights into challenges and opportunities for the preservation of traditional food systems.

The data were analyzed using content and thematic analysis. This involved identifying and examining recurring themes and patterns within the textual data to understand the key factors influencing the preservation of culinary heritage (Ahmad & Salim, 2023). The data were then categorized into themes such as the impacts of modernization and globalization, community involvement, and policy support, to organize information and draw meaningful conclusions (Ahmad & Salim, 2023). Additionally, triangulation of data sources ensures the reliability and validity of the findings. By cross-referencing data from multiple sources, the study aims to provide a comprehensive and robust understanding of the challenges associated with and the prospects of Kongunadu's culinary practices leading to cultural wellbeing (Yang & Cao, 2022).

2.4 Findings

The thematic analysis reveals several key themes that underscore the multifaceted nature of culinary preservation in the Kongunadu community (Figure 2.1). One prominent theme is the 'integration of traditional

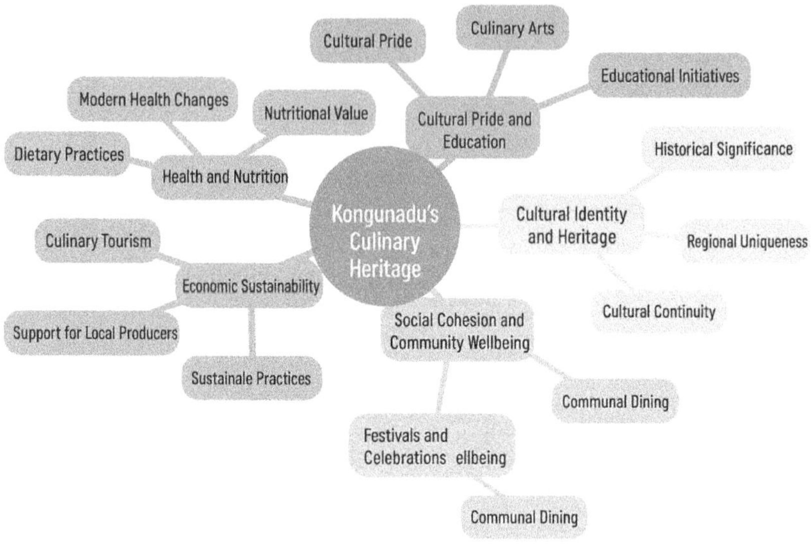

Figure 2.1 Thematic analysis of secondary texts related to Kongunadu's culinary heritage

culinary practices into modern contexts', highlighting the importance of adapting and maintaining heritage recipes while addressing contemporary dietary needs. Another significant theme is 'the role of community engagement in preserving culinary heritage', emphasizing the need for local involvement in documenting and promoting traditional foods. The analysis also identifies 'the impact of globalization and modernization on traditional culinary practices', exploring how modern food trends and fast-food culture pose challenges to maintaining culinary traditions.

The theme of 'educational initiatives' emerges, focusing on incorporating local culinary knowledge into school curricula and training programs to foster appreciation among younger generations. Lastly, the theme of 'digital and technological innovations' is crucial, as it points to the potential of digital platforms and social media in documenting, sharing, and promoting traditional culinary practices on a global scale. These themes collectively illustrate the complex interplay between tradition and modernity, emphasizing the need for multifaceted strategies to ensure the preservation and continued relevance of Kongunadu's culinary heritage. The themes that emerged are organized into three broad areas:

(1) Local cuisine and community wellbeing.
(2) Challenges in preserving the local cuisine of Kongunadu.
(3) Opportunities and strategies for safeguarding and promoting these culinary traditions.

2.4.1 Local cuisine and community wellbeing

2.4.1.1 Local cuisine and cultural identity

Culinary practices represent a multifaceted concept that encompasses more than just the preparation and consumption of food. It entails the health implications of different cuisines, traditional food's cultural and social significance, and the economic aspects of food production and distribution. A deep understanding of culinary practices is crucial for research aimed at safeguarding the overall wellbeing and cultural heritage of the Kongunadu community. These time-honored traditions play a crucial role in maintaining the unique cultural heritage of the region, contributing to its rich tapestry of customs and culinary practices. The transmission of traditional culinary knowledge from one generation to the next serves as an essential method of preserving cultural heritage. This passing down of expertise not only safeguards the richness of cultural traditions but also ensures their continued relevance in today's society, thereby improving the cultural identity of the community.

2.4.1.2 Community and social cohesion

The traditional culinary practices of Kongunadu play a significant role in fostering strong community bonds and social cohesion. From the text analysis, it is noted that communal activities such as festivals, communal cooking, and shared meals have been deeply ingrained in the social fabric of the region from time immemorial. These practices not only promote a sense of belonging among the community members but also contribute to the formation of a collective identity, hence promoting social cohesion.

Moreover, culinary festivals and events hold the potential to further strengthen community ties by providing opportunities for meaningful interactions and shared experiences while cooking or sharing local cuisines. By doing so, these events not only enhance community spirit but also can attract visitors, contributing to the overall vibrancy of the community.

2.4.1.3 Health and nutrition

Traditional diets have long emphasized the importance of a well-rounded intake of locally sourced, seasonal, and nutrient-rich ingredients. By prioritizing the consumption of wholesome, traditional food, we can promote culinary wellness and improve the overall health and nutrition of the community. Culinary wellness focuses on the holistic wellbeing of individuals, integrating physical health with cultural and emotional wellbeing. This approach encourages a deeper connection to food and a greater appreciation for its role in fostering a healthy lifestyle.

Analysis of the text highlighted the significant role of local cuisine in promoting health and nutrition. Some traditional Kongunadu cuisines have been mentioned in the research context.

2.4.1.4 Economic sustainability

Analysis of the text underscores the critical significance of safeguarding and promoting local cuisine as a means of bolstering the local economy and fostering community wellbeing. Extensive research (block references from the literature review) indicates that traditional culinary practices are pivotal in driving the local economy forward by attracting culinary tourism and advocating for local food items. This economic impetus not only serves as a driving force for preserving culinary heritage but also paves the way for the advancement of local communities. Furthermore, by encouraging the cultivation and trade of traditional foods, valuable economic opportunities are created for local farmers, chefs, and artisans, contributing to the community's overall wellbeing.

2.4.1.5 Environmental sustainability

Upon delving into the text analysis, it became evident that ancient culinary customs of Kongunadu often revolve around sustainable farming practices, such as permaculture and agroforestry, which support biodiversity and soil health. Additionally, these traditions emphasize environmentally friendly cooking methods, such as using locally-sourced ingredients and minimizing food waste. Promoting these time-honored practices not only honors culinary heritage but also contributes significantly to long-term environmental sustainability by reducing carbon emissions and supporting ecosystem health.

According to the analysis, the residents of Kongunadu believe that safeguarding traditional food systems is essential for preserving local biodiversity. Traditional diets in the region typically consist of a wide variety of Indigenous crops and animal species, which are integral to the local ecosystem.

2.4.2 Challenges in preserving the local cuisine of Kongunadu

2.4.2.1 Modernization and globalization

Analysis of the existing data reveals that the local community of Kongunadu is currently grappling with the significant challenges of modernization and globalization. As a result of these trends, traditional culinary practices within the community are facing erosion. Moreover, the younger generation is increasingly drawn to fast food and global cuisines, often at the expense of traditional dishes. This shift not only diminishes the transmission of culinary knowledge but also threatens the authenticity and continuity of Kongunadu's culinary heritage (Muthukumaran *et al.*, 2024).

2.4.2.2 Economic pressures

The economic pressures of modern times have significantly influenced how food is produced and consumed. As a result, there has been a shift towards commercializing food production, which has led to a preference for mass-produced and standardized food items at the expense of artisanal and traditional foods.

Furthermore, the commercialization of food production and distribution impacts significantly traditional food producers by altering the competitive landscape, potentially reducing their market share and profitability. This shift also affects consumer behavior by diminishing the demand for locally sourced and handmade foods, as larger commercial operations often offer lower prices and greater convenience. As a result, traditional food producers face challenges in maintaining their relevance and economic viability in this changing market environment (Aruljothi & Ramaswamy, 2019).

2.4.2.3 Environmental challenges

The data also reveal that climate change and unsustainable agricultural practices are affecting the availability of Indigenous ingredients that are essential for traditional Kongunadu recipes. This is making it increasingly challenging to find and use these important ingredients in the region's traditional dishes. Moreover, the cultivation of traditional crops has been significantly affected by shifts in weather patterns and land use. These changes have led to disruptions in the growth and availability of key ingredients, posing a challenge to preserving and practicing authentic culinary traditions (Anjana & Paulsamy, 2016).

2.4.2.4 Lack of documentation and education

Another significant challenge identified in the thematic analysis was the considerable absence of organized documentation and educational efforts centered on preserving Kongunadu's culinary heritage. The lack of comprehensive records and dedicated educational programs poses a significant risk to the preservation of traditional recipes and cooking techniques. Without proper documentation and educational initiatives, there is a real danger of losing valuable elements of Kongunadu's culinary heritage (Muthukumaran, *et al.*, 2024).

2.4.3 Opportunities and strategies for safeguarding and promoting these culinary traditions

2.4.3.1 Digital documentation and dissemination

In order to preserve and protect the local cuisines of Kongunadu, one emerging theme that has gained traction is the utilization of digital technology to document and share traditional recipes and cooking techniques. Leveraging digital platforms presents a significant opportunity to create online repositories and digital archives. By doing so, the stakeholders can ensure that this valuable knowledge is preserved for future generations and made easily accessible to them to document and share (Perumal & Rathika, 2022).

2.4.3.2 Promoting culinary tourism

Another theme that gained attention was promoting culinary tourism. Food and tourism festivals also offer a promising avenue for preserving Kongunadu's culinary heritage. The region can generate economic benefits by showcasing traditional dishes and cooking methods to tourists while raising awareness and appreciation of its unique culinary practices (Muthukumaran *et al*., 2024).

2.4.3.3 Community engagement and education

Culinary literacy includes educating younger generations about their culinary heritage and fostering a sense of pride and identity. Educational programs can integrate traditional food practices into the curriculum, ensuring cultural continuity.

Engaging local communities through culinary festivals, workshops, and cooking classes can revive interest in traditional foods. Educational programs in schools incorporating local culinary traditions can ensure that younger generations grow up with an appreciation of their heritage. Moreover, raising awareness about the value of traditional foods and culinary practices can engage the broader public and garner support for preservation efforts (Muthukumaran *et al*., 2024).

2.4.3.4 Supportive policies and sustainable agriculture

Another theme is preserving the unique local cuisine of Kongunadu and how the government has to take the measures to preserve Kongunadu cuisine. The government must offer support through the development and implementation of policies that not only promote sustainable agriculture but also provide funding for initiatives to preserve this culinary heritage. Such initiatives are crucial in ensuring that the rich and diverse gastronomic traditions of Kongunadu are safeguarded for future generations. Furthermore, encouraging the cultivation of traditional crops, such as heirloom tomatoes, millets, and heritage grains, and supporting local farmers through initiatives such as farmer's markets and fair-trade agreements (Singh & Tiwari, 2014), can contribute to maintaining the availability of indigenous ingredients. This can help preserve culinary traditions and biodiversity while supporting local economies (Perumal & Rathika, 2022).

2.5 Discussion

The study aimed to identify and analyze the primary challenges facing the preservation of Kongunadu's culinary heritage and to explore the potential opportunities and strategies for safeguarding and promoting these culinary traditions for overall community wellbeing. Figures 2.2 and 2.3 depict the customary cuisine prepared for communal festivals, served on a banana leaf due to its cultural significance.

Figure 2.2 Kongu chicken biryani with *raitha*

Figure 2.3 *ArisimparuppuSadham*, potato *poriyal*, *aval pongal* and lemon black tea

Many findings of this study align with earlier research on the importance of culinary heritage in cultural wellbeing. Previous works, such as those by Chera (2020) and Venkatachalapathi and Paulsamy (2016), highlight the deep connection between traditional foods and cultural identity. Chera (2020) emphasized the role of women in preserving Tamil culinary traditions, suggesting that culinary practices are integral to cultural and social wellbeing. Similarly, Venkatachalapathi and Paulsamy (2016) documented the use of wild medicinal mushrooms in Kongunadu, demonstrating the rich bio-cultural diversity of the region.

Like Anjana and Paulsamy (2016), this study has also noted the importance of educational initiatives in preserving culinary heritage. They advocated incorporating ethno-botanical knowledge into school curricula. This study reinforces their findings by suggesting that integrating local culinary traditions into education can foster cultural pride and continuity among younger generations.

While there is a consensus on the significance of culinary preservation, this study also highlights emerging challenges not as prominently addressed in previous works. For instance, the impact of globalization and modernization on traditional culinary practices is more pronounced in this study. Previous research, such as that by Sugasini *et al.* (2018), mainly concentrated on documenting traditional uses of spices and ingredients while not extensively addressing the threats posed by contemporary food trends and fast-food culture.

This study identifies urbanization as a significant challenge, contrasting with earlier works that did not emphasize the shift from rural to urban living and its impact on food habits. The decline in traditional farming practices and the preference for high-yield crops over indigenous varieties are critical issues affecting the availability of essential ingredients for Kongunadu cuisine. This is a relatively new perspective, expanding on the agricultural focus seen in studies like Aruna *et al.* (2015) documenting the sustainable use of edible plants by tribal communities.

This study's emphasis on the role of technology in culinary preservation represents a forward-looking approach not extensively covered in earlier research. While past studies have acknowledged the importance of documentation (Muthukumaran *et al.*, 2024), this study suggests using digital platforms and social media to engage broader audiences and promote culinary heritage actively. Additionally, the call for robust policy support and economic incentives aligns with recent discussions in the field but offers a more detailed strategy. Previous works have suggested the need for governmental and institutional support (Perumal & Rathika, 2022). However, this study goes further by proposing specific measures such as grants, subsidies, and the promotion of culinary tourism to bolster preservation efforts.

This study underscores the necessity of community engagement in preserving culinary heritage, echoing the sentiments of earlier research by Muthuswamy and Esakki (2024). However, it diverges by proposing more structured community-driven initiatives, such as local archives and food festivals, which were not the focal point of previous studies. The emphasis on creating comprehensive records and organizing events to revive interest in traditional foods suggests a proactive approach to cultural preservation.

2.6 Implications

This study has several managerial implications. It encourages community members to document traditional recipes, cooking techniques, and food-related stories by establishing local archives or digital repositories to preserve and share this valuable information (Muthukumaran *et al.*, 2024). Furthermore, hosting local food festivals and cooking workshops can celebrate and teach traditional culinary practices, reigniting interest and transmitting culinary knowledge to younger generations (Muthukumaran *et al.*, 2024). Additionally, it proposes the establishment of community gardens and small-scale farms to cultivate traditional crops and herbs essential to Kongunadu cuisine, ensuring the availability of Indigenous ingredients (Perumal & Rathika, 2022)

It is also suggested that local culinary traditions be integrated into school curricula to teach students about their heritage. This can include cooking and food history courses highlighting Kongunadu's culinary practices (Anjana & Paulsamy, 2016). The study promotes academic research on Kongunadu's culinary heritage and encourages collaborations with local historians, chefs, and cultural experts to study and advocate for traditional foods (Perumal & Rathika, 2022).

It is also recommended that policies be formulated and enforced to aid in preserving culinary heritage by offering grants and subsidies to local farmers, artisans, and cultural organizations dedicated to maintaining traditional foods and practices (Muthukumaran *et al.*, 2024). Additionally, it is recommended that the government and other stakeholders invest in infrastructure and marketing to boost culinary tourism, emphasizing Kongunadu's unique food heritage in tourism campaigns to attract visitors and drive economic growth (Perumal & Rathika, 2022).

It is further recommended that projects be initiated to document and safeguard traditional culinary knowledge by working with local communities to develop detailed records of recipes, cooking techniques, and their cultural significance (Anjana & Paulsamy, 2016). Additionally, it would be beneficial to conduct campaigns to increase awareness of the importance of preserving culinary heritage and to advocate for policies and initiatives that support cultural conservation (Muthukumaran *et al.*, 2024).

It would also be beneficial to leverage influencer marketing and create new recipes that build upon traditional Kongunadu ingredients and techniques, showcasing these dishes in restaurants and through media channels to enhance recognition and appreciation of Kongunadu cuisine (Chera, 2020; Tiwari, 2021). At the restaurant and hotel, the trained chefs could provide training programs and mentorship for aspiring chefs and home cooks to master traditional cooking methods, helping to preserve and perpetuate these culinary practices (Muthukumaran *et al*., 2024).

Another implication is for NGOs, the government, and other tourism departments to develop digital platforms to showcase collections of traditional recipes, cooking videos, and cultural narratives related to Kongunadu cuisine, ensuring this content is accessible to a worldwide audience (Perumal & Rathika, 2022). And it is further recommended to leverage social media to distribute stories, recipes, and cooking demonstrations, engaging with audiences through interactive content to stimulate interest and involvement in preserving culinary heritage (Muthukumaran *et al*., 2024).

Finally, inviting tourists to participate in culinary tours, workshops, and festivals that celebrate Kongunadu's food heritage would be beneficial. This approach will boost local economies and enhance visitors' understanding and appreciation of the culture (Perumal & Rathika, 2022). Furthermore, it will support local farmers, artisans, and food producers through the purchasing of traditional and locally produced food items, which will help sustain the livelihoods of those dedicated to preserving traditional practices (Anjana & Paulsamy, 2016).

2.7 Limitations and Future Work

This exploratory study primarily relies on secondary data sources such as academic articles, historical records, and existing reports, which may limit the depth of insight into contemporary practices and culinary preservation in Kongunadu. The diverse cultural influences and variations within Kongunadu might not be fully captured, suggesting a need for more focused research in specific areas. Additionally, the study may not account for recent developments or changes in culinary practices due to the rapidly evolving nature of cultural trends. Resource and funding constraints also pose limitations, potentially affecting the scope of research activities, including access to archives, field visits, and collaboration with local experts.

Future research should integrate primary methods, like field surveys and interviews with local experts, to gain deeper insights into preserving Kongunadu's culinary heritage. Focused regional studies could address local variations and challenges, while longitudinal research might track changes in culinary practices over time. Embracing digital tools for creating archives and interactive platforms can enhance preservation efforts. Collaborative projects with cultural organizations and academic institutions can develop comprehensive strategies and evaluating the impact of these initiatives on community wellbeing, economic benefits, and cultural pride will help refine and demonstrate their effectiveness.

References

Ahmad, A. and Salim, S. (2023) Exploring viewership patterns and engagement levels of Malayalam political satire shows' audience: A quantitative survey & SPSS analysis. *Global Media Journal* 21 (63), 1–9.

Amalan, E. and Anitha, G. (2023) Traditional foods: A value addition at tourism destinations. *Emerging Aspects of Redefined Tourism & Hospitality* 5, 73–87.

Andrieu, J. and Batat, W. (2019) TV cuisine therapy through narrative cooking programs: How does culinary journalism contribute to food pleasure and wellbeing? In W. Batat (ed.) *Food and Experiential Marketing* (pp. 57–70). Routledge.

Anjana, P.R. and Paulsamy, S. (2016) Evaluation of ethnobotanical plants used by the Malamuthans tribal community in the Medappara Forest, Western Ghats of Kerala. *Kongunadu Research Journal* 3 (2), 17–44.

Aruljothi, C. and Ramaswamy, S. (2019) *Pilgrimage Tourism: Socio-economic Analysis*. MJP Publishers.

Aruna, R., Nithyapriya, J., Ramachandran, V.S., Gopakumar, K. and Ramaswamy, R.S. (2015) A study on the sustainable utilization of edible plants by Irular tribes of Anaikatty, Western Ghats, India. *Research Journal of Pharmacognosy and Phytochemistry* 7 (2), 95–100.

Askarno, A. (2020) Efforts to preserve public interest in traditional culinary products in order to improve the community's economy. *Devotion: Journal of Research and Community Service* 1 (2), 51–58.

Aulet, S., Dolors, V.C. and Joaquim, M. (2019) Community development through gastronomic tourism. In S.K. Dixit (ed.) *The Routledge Handbook of Gastronomic Tourism* (pp. 232–241). Routledge.

Batat, W., Peter, P.C., Moscato, E.M., Castro, I.A., Chan, S., Chugani, S. and Muldrow, A. (2019) The experiential pleasure of food: A savoring journey to food wellbeing. *Journal of Business Research* 100, 392–399.

Bessière, J. (2013) 'Heritagisation', a challenge for tourism promotion and regional development: An example of food heritage. *Journal of Heritage Tourism* 8 (4), 275–291.

Cena, H. and Calder, P.C. (2020) Defining a healthy diet: Evidence for the role of contemporary dietary patterns in health and disease. *Nutrients* 12 (2), 334.

Chen, N.N. (2019) Cultural pleasures of eating and healing: Contributions to food wellbeing. In W. Batat (ed.) *Food and Experiential Marketing* (pp. 71–80). Routledge.

Chen, Y.C., Lee, C.S., Tsui, P.L. and Chiang, M.C. (2022) The application of the analytic hierarchy process approach to the inheritance of local delicious food culture and development of sustainable innovations. *Agronomy* 12 (3), 660.

Chera, M. (2020) Tamil traditions: Women cooking and eating for heritage and health in South India. Doctoral thesis in Anthropology, Indiana University.

Cook, S. (2024) The communal table: A wholistic perspective on food and social development. Master's thesis, Liberty University.

Dillette, A.K., Douglas, A.C. and Andrzejewski, C. (2021) Dimensions of holistic wellness as a result of international wellness tourism experiences. *Current Issues in Tourism* 24 (6), 794–810.

Filipiak-Florkiewicz, A., Topolska, K. and Florkiewicz, A. (2022) Regional gastronomy and the preservation of culinary heritage. In J. Hernik, M. Walczycka, E. Sankowski and B.J. Harris (eds) *Cultural Heritage – Possibilities for Land-Centered Societal Development* (pp. 95–112). Springer International.

Giampiccoli, A. and Kalis, J.H. (2012) Tourism, food, and culture: Community-based tourism, local food, and community development in Mpondoland. *Culture, Agriculture, Food and Environment* 34 (2), 101–123.

Giampiccoli, A., Mzobanzi Mnguni, E. and Dłużewska, A. (2020) Local food, community-based tourism and wellbeing: Connecting tourists and hosts. *Czasopismo Geograficzne* 91 (1– 2), 249–268.

Grimaldi, P., Fassino, G. and Porporato, D. (2019) *Culture, Heritage, Identity and Food. A Methodological Approach*. Franco Angeli.

Kokkranikal, J. and Carabelli, E. (2024) Gastronomy tourism experiences: The cooking classes of Cinque Terre. *Tourism Recreation Research* 49 (1), 161–172.

Leakey, R.R., Tientcheu Avana, M.L., Awazi, N.P., Assogbadjo, A.E., Mabhaudhi, T., Hendre, P.S., ... and Manda, L. (2022) The future of food: Domestication and commercialization of indigenous food crops in Africa over the third decade (2012–2021). *Sustainability* 14 (4), 2355.

Mac Con Iomaire, M. and Nic Philibín, C. (2022) Exploring the food-related intangible cultural heritage of *Bealtaine* (May Day) within the Irish Folklore Commission's schools' collection digital archive. *Etudes irlandaises* 47 (1), 15–32.

Maffei, M.C. (2012) Culinary traditions as cultural intangible heritage and expressions of cultural diversity. In S. Borelli and F. Lenzerini (eds) *Cultural Heritage, Cultural Rights, Cultural Diversity* (pp. 223–249). Brill.

Mak, A.H., Lumbers, M. and Eves, A. (2012) Globalisation and food consumption in tourism. *Annals of Tourism Research* 39 (1), 171–196.

Mathew, E. (2024) Globalization and local flavours: The impact of modern food production on traditional cuisine and culinary heritage preservation. *International Journal for Multidimensional Research Perspectives* 2 (7), 61–78.

Mosko, J.E. and Delach, M.J. (2021) Cooking, creativity, and well-being: An integration of quantitative and qualitative methods. *The Journal of Creative Behavior* 55 (2), 348–361.

Muthukumaran, M., Parveen, M. and Velavan, S.V. (2024) Survey of the beneficial flowers available in Coimbatore District, Tamil Nadu, India. *Plant Science Today* 11 (1), 366–376.

Muthuswamy, V.V. and Esakki, S. (2024) Exploring sustainable cultural preservation: Strategies, challenges, and community engagement in heritage conservation efforts. *Rita Revista Indexada de Textos Acadêmicos* 21 (1), 129–146.

Ocampo, J.C.C., Marshall, M., Wellton, L. and Jonsson, I.M. (2021) When sustainable cuisine imaginaries become unsustainable: Storage and preservation practices in Swedish restaurants. *International Journal of Gastronomy and Food Science* 24, 100353.

Perumal, S.B. and Rathika, K. (2022) Communities: Ethnic groups and their cultural diversities. *NeuroQuantology* 20 (11), 9691.

Prasetyo, A.H., Saga, P.A., Mokodongan, T. and Turgarini, D. (2022) Preservation of traditional and local foods of Blora regency as a gastronomic tourist attraction. *The Journal Gastronomy Tourism* 9 (2), 68–81.

Singh, A. and Tiwari, R. (2014) Sustainable rural development through tourism practices: A case study of Ranakpur, Rajasthan. *Pacific Business Review International* 7 (5), 31–36.

Singh, D., Choudhary, M.K., Dudi, A., Kumar, C., Tetarwal, A.S., Kuri, B.R. ... and Singh, R.K. (2023) Ensuring food and nutritional security in the arid climate of Rajasthan, India: Culturally rich foods of the Thar Desert – The case of Panchkutta. *Human Ecology* 51 (2), 347–356.

Singh, M. (2024) Exploring the intersection of nutrition, gastronomy, and sustainability: A comprehensive review of contemporary food trends, dietary practices, and future directions in culinary health. *International Journal for Multidimensional Research Perspectives* 2 (1), 14–30.

Sugasini, D., Yalagala, P.C., Kavitha, B., Kasthuri, T., Vijayalakshmi, Y., Kumar, P.K. and Kumar, S. (2018) Indian culinary ethnic spices uses in foods are palate of paradise. *Acta Scientific Nutritional Health* 2 (8), 22–28.

Susmitha, P., Kapoor, M., Keerthana, D., Naimuddin, S.K. and Srivastava, S. (2024) Unlocking nutritional potential: Multi-omics strategies for enhancing millet nutritional traits. *Journal of Advances in Biology & Biotechnology* 27 (6), 131–149.

Sweeney, A. (2022) Making a chef's heart sing! The role of positive health and wellbeing – Moving towards a positive health framework for culinary arts education. *Dublin Gastronomy Symposium*. https://doi.org/10.21427/z8r6-bv06.

Timothy, D.J. and Pena, M. (2015) Food festivals and heritage awareness. In D.J. Timothy (ed.) *Heritage Cuisines: Traditions, Identities and Tourism* (pp. 148–165). Routledge.

Tiusanen, K. (2021) Fulfilling the self through food in wellness blogs: Governing the healthy subject. *European Journal of Cultural Studies* 24 (6), 1382–1400.

Tiwari, R. (2021) Residents' perception of the role of local cuisine as a tourism product in destination marketing. *Journal of Hospitality Application & Research* 16 (2), 45–62.

Tsai, C.T. (2016) Memorable tourist experiences and place attachment when consuming local food. *International Journal of Tourism Research* 18 (6), 536–548.

Venkatachalapathi, A. and Paulsamy, S. (2016) Exploration of wild medicinal mushroom species in Walayar valley, the Southern Western Ghats of Coimbatore District Tamil Nadu. *Mycosphere* 7 (2), 118–130.

Wali, A., Alvira, D., Tallman, P.S., Ravikumar, A. and Macedo, M.O. (2017) A new approach to conservation: Using community empowerment for sustainable wellbeing. *Ecology & Society* 22 (4).

Wondirad, A., Kebete, Y. and Li, Y. (2021) Culinary tourism as a driver of regional economic development and socio-cultural revitalization: Evidence from Amhara National Regional State, Ethiopia. *Journal of Destination Marketing & Management* 19, 100482.

Yamaguchi, S. and Oshima, H. (2024) Analysis of the relationship between residential environment and multifaceted wellbeing. *International Journal of Community Wellbeing*, 1–23.

Yang, L. and Cao, K. (2022) Cultural ecosystem services research progress and future prospects: A review. *Sustainability* 14 (19), 11845.

Yasmeen, B., Iftikhar, I. and Fischer, F. (2024) Culinary comfort: Understanding the connection between food and wellbeing. *Nutrients* 16 (12), 1865.

Yozukmaz, N., Bertan, S. and Alkaya, S. (2020) Festivals' social impacts and emotional solidarity. *International Journal of Event and Festival Management* 11 (2), 239–253.

Zhang, T., Chen, J. and Hu, B. (2019) Authenticity, quality, and loyalty: Local food and sustainable tourism experience. *Sustainability* 11 (12), 3437.

3 Integrating Indigenous Cuisine Knowledge into Modern Wellbeing Practices: A Case of Malawi, Southern Africa

Natasha Mashura Runganga

3.1 Introduction

Food has remained one of the key features that unites people and is an expression of identity within a society through cooking practices and consumption. Indigenous foods also form part of the intangible cultural heritage (Mac Con Iomaire & Nic Philibín, 2022). Wijaya (2019) states that food plays an important role in people's lives and wellness, and it has been recognized as an expression of identity and culture. Over the years, Indigenous cuisines have been getting much attention as people are now reverting to traditional dishes. Indigenous cuisine knowledge plays a critical role in society as it serves as a means of continuity and preservation of the culture (Manyozo, 2018). The continuity of Indigenous cuisines is maintained through the Indigenous knowledge of the communities being passed on through generations, and it plays a pivotal role in promoting wellbeing among societies.

Wellbeing covers various dimensions of life that contribute to overall satisfaction amongst people living in a society and that improve the quality of life. There are a lot of aspects that make people flourish, including positive emotions, engagement with life, a sense of purpose and meaning, and fulfilling relationships with others (Seligman, 2018). Engaging in cultural practices in societies can bring a sense of belonging and fulfillment. Preserving culture in its original form gives people a sense of purpose and can emerge through different forms, which involve dressing, language, eating habits, and cuisines (Fieldhouse, 2013).

In many African societies culinary traditions have, over the years, been diluted through modernization and globalization. In some societies, engaging in Indigenous foods is associated with archaicness. Gewa *et al.* (2023) stated that the consumption of Indigenous foods in Kenya has decreased over the years. Indigenous foods are seen as old-fashioned because the older generation prepares such foods while the younger generation has access to an extensive range of modern food. However, according to Mbhenyane (2017), most people regard traditional foods as the healthiest, as they can be consumed without worrying about health complications. Presently, consuming Indigenous foods (IF) is promoted in an effort to reduce the prevalence of diet-related disease (Maudrie *et al.*, 2021). Indigenous foods are foods that originate in the region, are culturally acceptable, adapted to local climatic conditions, and have been consumed traditionally by the inhabitants, as opposed to exotic foods that have been introduced from other regions of the world (Kesa *et al.*, 2023). In South Africa, the elderly in Indigenous communities are keener to utilize Indigenous foods to improve their nutritional status and as a way to connect with their forefathers (Masuku & Bhengu, 2021). Kasimba *et al.* (2019) postulate that there is a lot of nutrition transition due to globalization and urbanization and they mention that nutrition transition has given rise to people experiencing considerable health consequences such as obesity and non-communicable disease. Penafiel *et al.* (2019) agree that traditional foods contribute to the total daily dietary requirements of the human body. Moreover, the Indigenous peoples of northwestern North America are turning to their Indigenous foods to revitalize their original foods (Joseph & Turner, 2020).

Indigenous knowledge needs to be preserved to ensure the continuity of Indigenous food practices among societies (Okoye & Oni, 2017). Health and wellbeing are closely linked to Indigenous cuisines and, therefore, the integration of Indigenous cuisine knowledge has had an impact upon modern wellbeing practices (Farmer & Cotter, 2021). Even in tourist destinations, Björk and Kauppinen-Räisänen (2016) noted that tourists often seek the authenticity of local food before visiting a destination, significantly impacting travel satisfaction.

Over the years, studies have focused on the Indigenous knowledge of food systems. However, the extant literature suggests that not much attention has been given to how the preservation of these culinary traditions impacts the wellbeing of Indigenous communities (Coté, 2016; Kuhnlein, 2015; Oloko *et al.*, 2024). This chapter explores how the integration of Indigenous cuisine knowledge amongst Malawi societies has impacted the modern wellbeing practices guided by the PERMA (Positive Emotion, Engagement, Relationships, Meaning, and Accomplishment) model. The consumption of food at gatherings signifies unity, and this brings a sense of togetherness (Marovelli, 2019). At gatherings such as funerals, it is a must that people should eat, because eating food is a cultural practice that brings a sense of belongingness and wellbeing, but, if one does not eat, then one day they may have a funeral at their place and people may decide not to eat. As such, perseveration of traditional cuisines and culture amongst societies can contribute to positive emotions, engagement, relationships, meaning, and accomplishment (Peng *et al.*, 2023), which are the critical elements of flourishing according to the PERMA model. In Malawi societies, food plays a role in nourishing and it has a cultural significance, forming an integral part of community identity and social solidity. This chapter uses the Northern and Central Region of Malawi as a case study to validate the PERMA model of overall wellbeing and happiness.

3.2 Literature Review

The PERMA model, developed by Martin Seligman (2011), provides a comprehensive framework for understanding the factors contributing to an individual's wellbeing and happiness. This literature review combines existing research on the impact of Indigenous knowledge on wellness and the overall wellbeing of societies through Indigenous cuisines.

3.2.1 Indigenous cuisine knowledge and wellbeing

Knowledge of Indigenous cuisines is one of the critical issues amongst societies because it brings people of the same culture together. Cuisines are one of the key aspects of identity, and knowledge of a society's Indigenous cuisines helps individuals identify themselves, bringing a sense of connection. In Indigenous communities, there are some cultural practices in the food consumed and the preparation methods that have been identified as nurturing the body and the wellbeing of people, and this knowledge has been passed through generations. Bisai *et al.* (2023) note that tribal communities are closely connected to nature and its resources, and this connection is reflected in their simple and respectful approach to food. Indigenous communities consider it important to have available all the nutrients that Indigenous people require, and nutrition issues in Indigenous societies are considered one of the most important aspects of maintaining good health and wellness. However, over the years, some people have been shying away from traditional practices that are informed by Indigenous knowledge as it is regarded as an old way of doing things and is deemed to have less legitimacy and potency.

Indigenous cuisines over the years have proved to be crucial in promoting wellness and health within communities. Ramos-Molina *et al.* (2019) agree that traditional foods contribute to the total daily dietary requirements of the human body. Knowledge of Indigenous cuisines, inherited from forefathers, can bring connection, culture healing, health impacts and positive wellbeing within societies as it incorporates agricultural activities into food preparation. In community-based research on integrating Indigenous methodologies into nutrition research in the Aboriginal and non-Aboriginal people in Australia, it was noted that the revitalization of cultural practices related to native foods brings cultural healing, which can positively impact the community's health and wellbeing (Lopes *et al.*, 2024).

The food sovereignty movement restores traditional Indigenous food ways and practices while reducing community reliance on highly processed and nutritionally poor foods (Takaidza, 2023). A knowledge of traditional cuisines helps communities reclaim their traditional food practices, thereby improving their nutritional intake and fostering a sense of identity and cultural continuity. For example, the use of traditional African vegetables has been recognized for its potential to enhance food security and nutritional health, particularly in the face of climate change (Takaidza, 2023).

Kuhnlein and Chotiboriboon (2022) noted that the continuity of traditional practices is essential and includes encouraging new ideas and expressions of culture with food, including Indigenous cuisines with biodiverse species and preparation techniques. It has been noted that due to urbanization, people are faced with the challenges of living in two worlds – the Indigenous and the non-Indigenous – that are in constant tension with each other, with the latter having more power in shaping the former (Sultana *et al.*, 2018). This tension can affect people's wellbeing in society, as maintained by psychologist Martin Seligman (2011). Sharing knowledge within a society helps individuals have a sense of meaning and purpose, which is essential for wellbeing. This involves feeling that one's life is meaningful, having goals and values that align with personal beliefs, and positively impacting society.

From 1819 through the 1970s the United States established and supported Indian boarding schools across the nation, designed to culturally assimilate Indigenous children into the local culture. However, the boarding schools ended up disrupting and destroying cultural knowledge and its transmission across generations, hurt the ability of Elders to step into their important role as key knowledge holders, and left a lasting impact on the health of Indigenous communities through subsequent rates of diabetes, obesity, cardiovascular disease, and depression (Demientieff *et al.*, 2023). That incident illustrates that, if the knowledge system is disturbed, it may give rise to disturbances in the wellbeing of people because people cannot be separated from their culture, which includes Indigenous cuisines. The transmission of traditional food knowledge across generations is vital for maintaining the health and wellness of Indigenous peoples. This knowledge encompasses not just the preparation and consumption of food but also the ecological relationships that sustain these food systems (Jernigan *et al.*, 2023). Indigenous cuisines are integral to the wellbeing of societies, particularly for Indigenous communities, as they embody cultural identity, promote health, and foster economic sustainability. The relationship between traditional food practices and community wellness is multifaceted, encompassing aspects of food sovereignty, cultural heritage, and social cohesion.

3.2.2 Intersections between the PERMA model of wellness and Indigenous knowledge of cuisine

Seligman (2011) proposed that Positive Emotion, Engagement, Relationships, Meaning, and Accomplishment (PERMA) are the key elements contributing to lasting wellbeing. Wellbeing is about feelings of positivity, happiness, joy and comfort, or a lack thereof. Integrating Indigenous cuisine knowledge into modern wellbeing practices is considered social wellbeing, in which people in society engage and relationships are formed through the understanding of Indigenous cuisines. Engagement refers to fully deploying skills and attention for a challenging task, leading to a gratifying experience known as flow (Keating & Heslin, 2015). Indigenous cuisines in some cases are not easy in preparation: they require so much attention to detail and one has to fully engage with their whole spirit in the preparation. Spiritual wellbeing considers a higher sense of meaning and purpose, or a greater good, and as communities engage on issues of cuisines that are passed on from generation to generation it goes beyond the individual. Connecting with others through knowledge of cuisines can help people to feel close to other people, and to feel valued for who they are in societies that share a common understanding where food is concerned. Martela and Pessi (2018) stated that finding meaning in life involves making connections, and the way people understand the world is shaped by the social, cultural, and societal frameworks that have been learned. This helps to derive purpose and meaning from belonging to something larger than oneself.

The PERMA model was built upon distinct domains; researchers have noted overlaps and intersections between these domains (Goodman *et al.*, 2018). This study explores integrating Indigenous cuisine knowledge into the modern wellbeing practices of societies. Older community members impart wisdom to the younger generation, which evokes a profound sense of pride and fulfillment (Blumenkrantz, 2016). Passing down time-honored traditions and knowledge, which have been carefully preserved over centuries, strengthens the bonds between generations and ensures that cultural heritage remains vibrant (Kumar & Lakshminarayana, 2024). This transfer of wisdom can profoundly enrich an individual's life, infusing it with greater significance and purpose as

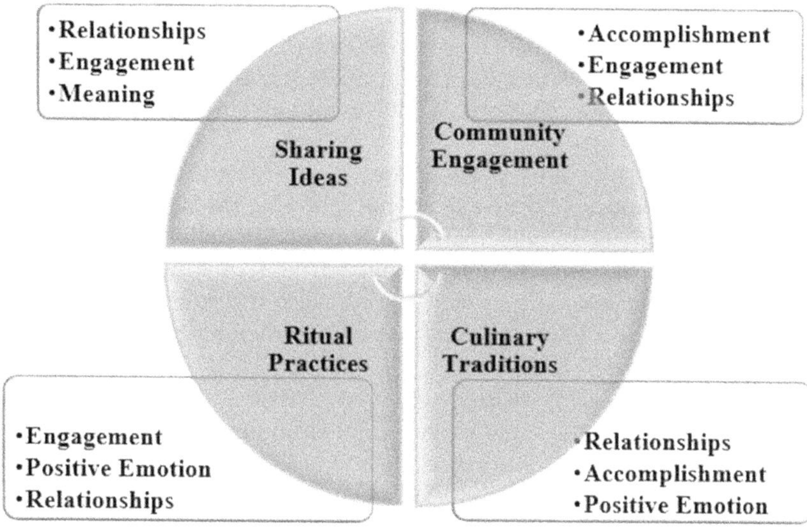

Figure 3.1 Intersections between the PERMA model and Indigenous knowledge of cuisine

they become part of a living legacy, but existing research has not fully explored the potential influence of Indigenous culinary knowledge on holistic wellbeing, leaving a gap in our understanding of how these traditional practices contribute to overall health and harmony.

Figure 3.1 illustrates the intersections between the PERMA model of wellbeing and Indigenous knowledge of cuisine. The PERMA model includes five elements essential to human flourishing: Positive Emotion, Engagement, Relationships, Meaning, and Accomplishment. These elements are integrated with four key aspects of Indigenous culinary knowledge: Sharing Ideas, Community Engagement, Culinary Traditions, and Ritual Practices. The circular design and overlapping sections suggest that these elements are interrelated and collectively contribute to holistic wellbeing through the lens of Indigenous culinary practices. The 'Sharing Ideas' quadrant is linked to Relationships, Engagement, and Meaning, highlighting how sharing culinary knowledge fosters connections and a sense of purpose. Indigenous knowledge of cuisine encompasses traditional food practices, cooking techniques, and culinary wisdom passed down through generations within Indigenous communities. Indigenous knowledge of cuisines in a community is deeply rooted in culture, years of studying the environment, and the rich history of the people of that community.

The 'Community Engagement' quadrant is strongly associated with Accomplishment, Engagement, and Relationships, emphasizing the communal aspects of culinary traditions and their role in achieving collective goals. Moyo *et al.* (2016) stated that Indigenous cuisine makes a nation different from other nations and unifies people in that nation. The act of coming together to prepare and share a meal, the sense of accomplishment in creating something delicious, and the unity it brings to a community are all part of the communal aspects of culinary traditions.

The quadrant, 'Culinary Traditions,' is connected to Relationships, Accomplishments, and Positive Emotion, reflecting the significant role of traditional practices in contributing to emotional wellbeing and social bonds. Sharing ideas in the form of recipes and cooking methods can give Elders a purpose as they will engage with the younger generation to ensure that the knowledge is passed on to other generations, thereby contributing to the PERMA model.

The last quadrant, 'Ritual Practices,' aligns with Engagement, Positive Emotion, and Relationships, underlining the importance of rituals in creating positive experiences and reinforcing relationships. In the Indigenous societies of Malawi, some traditional rituals are performed, and food is involved. Indigenous cuisines are used, which brings positive emotions and fosters relationships in the community. For example, in the installation of the chief, food is prepared and eaten as a community. Recipe-sharing and cooking lessons among societies can bring the Elders a sense of accomplishment and positive emotion.

3.3 Method

This chapter discusses the use of a qualitative approach to explore the role of Indigenous knowledge in impacting the overall wellbeing of society in Malawi. It focuses on integrating Indigenous cuisine knowledge into modern wellbeing practices and understanding from a respondent's point of view. Malawi is divided into three regions: Southern, Central, and Northern. Maize is a staple in other neighbouring countries as well as in Malawi. However, specific accompaniments and preparation methods differ as eating habits vary by region due to differences in locally available resources, cultural practices, and economic activities in that region. Some aspects of Malawian eating habits are distinctive, as traditional festivals or community gatherings centre around specific foods.

3.3.1 Participant selection

Thirty participants were purposively selected from urban and rural settings in the northern region and central region of Malawi to capture diverse perspectives on Indigenous cuisines. The purposive sampling technique was used because it allowed the researcher to focus on individuals who provided rich, detailed, and relevant information about Indigenous cuisines and how they are being integrated into modern wellbeing practices. In some rural communities, vernacular language was used, and the data were translated. Most of the participants were elderly custodians of Indigenous knowledge of cuisines and had seen how things have evolved over time. Restaurant owners, including chefs, add value to the research by providing popular Indigenous menus and how their patrons review them based on wellness issues. To ensure participant confidentiality and facilitate efficient data management, each participant in this study was allocated a number.

3.3.2 Data collection

Data were collected through semi-structured interviews and observations. Interviews were conducted with Indigenous food vendors, herbalists, culinary custodians, restaurant owners, Indigenous food specialists and chefs as they were appropriate in revealing how community members perceive the integration of traditional cuisine into modern practices, including their thoughts on its relevance, challenges, and potential benefits. The interviews were conducted in English and Chichewa (a Bantu language spoken in Malawi), and the data were later translated into English. Telephone interviews were also conducted with participants who could not make time for face-to-face interviews. Observations were conducted to shed light on community ties and wellbeing in social and cultural contexts such as communal gatherings and traditional food preparation (in both the restaurants and communities). Secondary data were gathered from books, research papers, and websites on Indigenous cuisine and wellbeing

3.3.3 Data analysis

Data were analyzed thematically. Recorded interviews are transcribed verbatim to create a text-based data set that can be analyzed. The researcher read through the transcripts and observation notes to become familiar with the content. Similar codes were grouped to form broader themes. Identified themes were reviewed and refined to ensure they accurately represent the data.

3.4 Findings and Discussions

Table 3.1 summarizes the details of the 30 study participants, while Table 3.2 summarizes the interview questions. The interviews were conducted in English and Chichewa, and the data were later translated into English. Telephone interviews were also conducted with participants who could not make time for face-to-face interviews. Content analysis was used to analyze the data gathered and align the data with the key features of the PERMA model of wellbeing.

Table 3.1 List of interviewees

Selection number	Indigenous community	Participant occupation	Gender	Age Group/ Age (years)
Participant 1	Mzuzu Community	Indigenous-ingredients vendor	Female	22
Participant 2		Indigenous-ingredients vendor	Female	45
Participant 3		Herbalist	Male	38
Participant 4		Indigenous-food specialist	Female	46
Participant 5		Indigenous-food restaurant owner	Male	50–55
Participant 6		Traditional medicine and food vendor	Female	47
Participant 7		Herbalist	Female	62
Participant 8		Indigenous-food restaurant owner	Female	62
Participant 9		Culinary custodian	Female	65–70
Participant 10		Culinary custodian /Elder	Female	65–70
Participant 11	Karonga community	Indigenous-food restaurant owner	Male	35–40
Participant 12		Chef	Female	41
Participant 13		Indigenous-food specialist	Female	48
Participant 14		Indigenous-food specialist	Male	55
Participant 15		Herbalist	Female	52
Participant 16		Indigenous-food street vendor	Female	30
Participant 17		Culinary custodian /Elder	Male	40–45
Participant 18		Restaurant owner	Female	40–45
Participant 19		Restaurant owner	Female	40–45
Participant 20		Chef	Female	30–35
Participant 21		Indigenous-food vendor	Female	40–45
Participant 22		Indigenous-food vendor	Female	40–45
Participant 23	Nkhata Bay community	Chef	Male	45
Participant 24		Chef	Male	35–40
Participant 25		Herbalist	Female	40
Participant 26		Culinary custodian /Elder	Female	65–70
Participant 27		Culinary custodian/Elder	Female	55
Participant 28		Indigenous-food vendor	Female	25
Participant 29		Culinary custodian /Elder	Female	48
Participant 30	Cultural Village in Lilongwe	Chingalire culinary custodian/Elder	Male	50–55

3.4.1 Findings and discussions

This study aims to investigate how traditional Indigenous food knowledge contributes to modern wellbeing, specifically using the PERMA model. This model focuses on Positive Emotions, Engagement, Relationships, Meaning, and Accomplishment. The data were analyzed

Table 3.2 Semi-structured interview guide (main and follow-up questions)

	Interview guide for culinary custodians, Indigenous ingredients vendors, herbalists	Interview guide for restaurant owners, chefs and Indigenous-food restaurant owners, Indigenous-food street vendors, and traditional medicine and food vendors	Interview guide Cultural Village
Introductory remark	• Explain the Indigenous cuisines of your area.		
Question 1	• How has your personal experience with Indigenous cuisine (preparation, cooking, and serving) influenced your overall wellbeing?		
Question 2	• What are some of the modern wellbeing practices being influenced by Indigenous cuisine knowledge?		
Question 3	• What role are you playing in the promotion of Indigenous cuisine knowledge? • Do you promote the use of Indigenous cuisine within your community?	• What role does your restaurant play in promoting Indigenous cuisine knowledge? • How often do you serve Indigenous cuisine on your menus? Do you share the recipes with your guests?	• What role does the Cultural Village play in promoting Indigenous cuisine knowledge? • Do you serve Indigenous cuisine only to your visitors?
Question 4	• Do you think Indigenous cuisine plays a role in creating a sense of accomplishment, meaning, and relationships in this community? Mention particular dishes or ingredients.		
Question 5	• Do you share knowledge of Indigenous cuisines as a community? And how do you share it and with whom? • Do you sometimes conduct cooking classes and what benefit does it benefit you or the community? • What is your main goal in sharing Indigenous cuisine knowledge with the community? • Are there any food rituals or taboos associated with food?		
Question 6	• What are the modern wellbeing practices that you think are being influenced by your knowledge of Indigenous cuisine? • Do you think Indigenous cuisine knowledge facilitates social connections and strengthens relationships within this community?		
Question 7	• In what ways do you think integrating all the mentioned Indigenous cuisine knowledge into modern wellbeing practices enhances positive emotion, personal meaning, accomplishment and relationships?		

using content analysis with a focus on the aspects of the previously mentioned PERMA model. Five themes emerged.

3.4.1.1 Theme 1: Modern wellbeing practices influenced by Ingenious cuisines

Integrating Indigenous cuisine knowledge into modern wellbeing practices has seen some Indigenous menus being learned from Elders, as they offer health benefits. Malawi's cuisine is influenced by immigration, and it is almost similar to most southern African countries. Before independence, Nkhoma (2020) noted that Lomwe immigrants, who came to southern Malawi from Mozambique, introduced cassava, which shortly became the main staple for people in lake-shore areas, where the soil was unsuitable for maize production. Cassava is eaten both as a tuber and can be pounded and dried to produce a powder that will be used to prepare *Kondowole* (a traditional Malawian dish made from cassava flour and hot water). Before independence, the local people were used to eating *Nsima* (a thick, dough-like porridge made from maize (corn) flour and water) with various relishes (legumes, meat and fish) (Nkhoma, 2020). The research revealed that starches such as *Nsima* are an important food in the everyday lives of the local Indigenous people and are valued in almost all functions. *Nsima* was mentioned as one of the key starches. As one participant (P30) mentioned:

> *Nsima* is maize meal porridge and a staple food made from maize flour, it represents unity and it is central to social gatherings and family meals. *Nsima* is mostly prepared in almost all of the cultural gatherings in the villages… .

Evidence of *Nsima* being eaten in the modern day shows that it has evolved without being distorted and that the preparation remains the same, and it shows further how traditional cuisine knowledge in modern culinary practices results in a sense of achievement as it has stood the test of time. One participant (P15) mentioned:

> *Kudya kwaine nsima ndimoyo ndipo nditha kudya china chili chonse koma ngati palibepo nsima nde sindikutha. Ana anga katakana zaka 8 ndimayamba kuwapunzisa kupika nsima chifukwa chuzindikilo changa ndinsima. sindine munthu popanda nsima* [Eating of *Nsima* is life and I can eat all other foods but if I haven't eaten *Nsima* I will not be full. With my children, the moment they reach 8 years I start teaching them how to prepare *Nsima* because this is my identity I am nothing without *Nsima*.]

3.4.1.2 Theme 2: Indigenous cuisine that fosters engagement and meaning

Nsima and *Kondowole* are two popular starches eaten by Malawians, including plantains. These foods are eaten to nourish the body but, at the same time, but, at the same time, they bring a sense of cultural pride as Malawians have managed to preserve the cultural preparation of the dishes. Communities are involved in the processing stages, especially of the cassava flour used in the preparation of *Kondowole*, so that there is no distortion in the preparation processes. It was observed that during the preparation and cooking stages there is deep focus and absorption in the task, which shows that the community gets so engaged in the preparation stages to the extent that at times they lose track of time.

These starches are still preferred even after modernization, which shows that the communities have a special attachment to them. Besides their health benefit in modern-day wellbeing, they also bring a sense of identity to the people of Malawi, especially those from the northern region. Analyzing the present-day cuisine, it may be noted that these dishes are still being served in households and most of the eateries around the country. In Nkhata Bay, *Kondowole* is a symbol of cultural identity for the people of the northern part of Malawi. In most cases, that is what differentiates them from the other areas of Malawi. Some participants (P27) said that, at times, they eat it not because they are hungry but because it draws them closer to home, even if they are away from home:

> *Kondowole* is *Nsima* made from cassava flour, which goes through many processes before being pounded. Sharing traditional meals fosters a sense of belonging and connection to ancestral heritage. When people gather around food, they share stories, rituals and knowledge, thereby strengthening their cultural bonds... .

In the PERMA Model of wellbeing, serving traditional dishes provides a sense of meaning among societies because serving traditional dishes in eateries and households symbolizes cultural pride, which contributes to promoting and preserving cultural identity (Tiwari, 2021).

3.4.1.3 Theme 3 - Healthy eating in Indigenous cuisines and modern wellbeing practices

Healthy eating is essential to wellness; not only does it impact the ability to think clearly but it also affects someone's mood and energy levels. These days, people prefer to eat healthily, and it has been observed that some people are now very conscious of what they eat (Macdiarmid *et al.*, 2016). Most people in Malawi prefer eating their Indigenous relishes that are prepared the traditional way. In the Karonga area, in the northern Region of Malawi, there are some relishes, like boiled chicken flavored with ginger or Mondia whatei (*Gondolosi*), that are eaten with roasted plantains. Different views were given on using some of the ingredients in cooking. For example:

> Some ingredients are used to feel good and provide strength, especially among us men. (P11, P17)

Leafy vegetables like blackjack are used as relish at the same time, and are believed to have medicinal benefits (Otang-Mbeng & Mashabela, 2020). Demi (2014) states that, in addition to these cultural values, African Indigenous foods are also medicinal, which requires Africans to preserve them for posterity. Participants P3, P7, and P17 pointed out that the inclusion of Mondia Whitei in the preparation is also believed to cure some ailments. Smoky (2024) states that the medicinal value of Mondia Whitei is slowly being acknowledged, thereby unlocking its full potential, and adds that revealing its secrets could revolutionize our approach to health and overall wellbeing. Integrating the healthy eating practices of traditional cuisines into society supports diets that align with the PERMA model, by promoting physical wellbeing through nutritious food choices, enhancing positive emotions, engaging individuals in cultural practices, and reinforcing cultural meaning and identity.

In the Mzuzu area (Mzuzu is the capital of Malawi's Northern Region), participant P5 highlighted that although Zingwangwa market is a marketplace for farm produce it is more than just a place to buy fresh farm produce: it is a cultural landmark and economic centre that reflects the vibrancy and diversity of Malawian society. Most of the fresh farm produce is available all year round because people make use of traditional irrigation and diets are based on locally available ingredients from the market or their local fields. As cited by Mkwambisi *et al.* (2023), production is largely subsistence-based and smallholder farmers remain the main producers and suppliers of food and approximately 90% of Malawi's food comes directly from domestic harvests and household food availability is determined primarily by own production. Modern food preparation adapts to traditional food preparation, which is informed by Indigenous knowledge passed on from generation to generation. It is noted (Jones, 2015). that some cooking methods are influenced by low-income levels – members are unable to purchase fancy ingredients as their source of income is agriculture.

The Zingwangwa market sells fresh produce from local farmers and has a section that also sells traditional medicines believed to treat certain diseases:

> These traditional medicines can be mixed with the traditional foods in the preparation stages or can be eaten raw. (P5)

Data collected in the Mzuzu community highlight that besides taking these herbal medicines as medicines, some cultural practices among societies are known to treat some ailments through taking traditional meals. Participant P7, who is also well-versed in traditional medicines, highlighted that:

> if one feels constipated, they are encouraged to drink sauce from boiled sweet potato leaves. This relish treats constipation and it's knowledge that has been passed on through generations.

As Moyo *et al.* (2016) observed, the preparation process is crucial in making a cuisine uniquely identifiable with a particular group.

3.4.1.4 Theme 4: Modern wellbeing practices through Indigenous cooking classes

It was observed that, among the Malawian societies, there are some cultural villages that promote culture through Indigenous cuisines, such as Chingalire Cultural Village in Lilongwe, which offers a unique and vibrant culinary heritage. The village offers visitors an experience of traditional Malawian life and a living museum where visitors can learn about Malawian culture, traditions, and Indigenous knowledge. Chingalire Cultural Village is one of the few cultural villages in the country that is spearheading the marketing of Indigenous cuisines by offering cooking lessons to visitors, showcasing a vibrant culture in culinary:

> Yes, we do conduct cookery classes conducted by our kitchen staff and some local women from villages around Chingalire who we have trained to help prepare traditional meals for tourists. These women have the traditional knowledge of traditional cuisines gained from their parents and ancestors. Chingalire makes sure that these traditional foods are prepared in such a way that they are accepted by healthy standards and care.... (P 30)

These lessons bring a sense of engagement between the community and the people who will be taught how to prepare the meals. Food serves as a tangible expression of cultural heritage and collective memory (Lee, 2023). The eating culture of communities carries a large history in the wellness and wellbeing of societies. The village does a number of cooking demonstrations for visitors and visitors can learn how to prepare traditional Malawian dishes using local ingredients. Farmer and Cotter (2021) suggest that the current modern American lifestyle, which consists of displacing human energy with mechanical energy and displacing household food production with industrial food production, may contribute negatively to our psychosocial health. The sharing of knowledge and demonstrations contributes to the overall wellbeing of the societies (Dillette *et al.*, 2021), illustrated by the fact that the majority of wellness tourists place value on food that is fresh, local, nutrient-rich, energizing and well-prepared.

Malawi traditional cuisine is not complicated and the cooking methods involve boiling, barbequing and sometimes frying. Participants P24 commented:

> when boiling, especially foods like pumpkins and maize, we use methods that make sure that the food doesn't lose nutrients in water. It is only now after attending school that we are now relating our African cooking methods and what we read in culinary books, that we apply science in our Indigenous cooking.

The cuisine differs in the way it is cooked and what is used to cook, depending on how the Indigenous knowledge has been preserved and is being used among the community. The rapid pace of modernization and urbanization poses significant challenges to the preservation of Indigenous knowledge systems in urban areas. It has been noted that most communities prefer their local foods as they believe they save them from diseases as well as keeping them fit. As stated by Lock *et al.* (2005), moving from traditional foods to more refined Western diets globally has

Figure 3.2 Vegetable market
Source: Mkwambisi *et al.*, 2023.

been linked to increases in the prevalence of chronic non-communicable diseases. Over the years, more people have migrated to urban areas, and some traditional practices are often abandoned in favor of more convenient but less nutritious dietary options. As cited by Fieldhouse (2013), modern societies seem to be converging to a pattern of a diet high in saturated fat, sugar, and refined foods, and low in fiber, which is often termed the Western diet. However, in the face of modernization, local food has remained one of the key foods consumed by societies in Malawi. Indigenous food practices often emphasize a universal approach to wellbeing, integrating physical, mental, and spiritual health. This aligns with the PERMA model's goal of promoting comprehensive wellbeing, because societies are still valuing their traditional foods even in the face of modernization.

The vegetable vendor is smiling (Figure 3.2) and is happy with what he is doing, and it shows some sense of meaning as the vendor provides fresh, healthy food to the community.

3.4.1.5 Theme 5: Modern wellbeing practices through food rituals

Promoting cultural resilience through food rituals brings accomplishments to Malawi societies. Traditionally, there were some cultural practices in the food consumed and the preparation methods that were identified to nurture the body and the wellbeing of people, and this knowledge has been passed through generations. Kuhnlein and Chotiboriboon (2022) highlight that the knowledge systems of Indigenous peoples embrace: the use of food resources known and used in the culture, intergenerational wellbeing, traditional knowledge, and preferences to create food security and food sovereignty. As participant P6 related:

> Some foods are known to be used on certain parameters for the wellbeing of people and eaten according to gender. There are some foods which pregnant women are encouraged to eat because it helps to support both the expecting mother and the unborn child....

De Diego-Cordero *et al.* (2021) postulate that the cultural eating practices carried out during pregnancy and lactation aim to ensure a successful pregnancy and a timely delivery. There are also restrictions on the food that expectant mothers can eat: these restrictions are recommendations from mothers, mothers-in-law, grandmothers and senior female members of the community. Kang *et al.* (2019) state that appropriate nutrition during pregnancy and lactation is essential – given the increased nutritional requirements during these periods – to promoting both maternal and newborn growth and wellbeing.

Because of traditional practices, women are discouraged from eating certain foods because of the belief that these foods may hurt the mother as well as the unborn baby. In a study undertaken by Walters *et al.* (2019), there was evidence that pregnant adolescents in Malawi avoid several nutritious foods during pregnancy, revealing a need to address food taboos during antenatal care. Chakona and Shackleton (2019) say that the reasons for not consuming taboo foods range from issues that may affect the mother during delivery to health issues primarily affecting the child. Women are discouraged from eating food such as eggs, cabbage, okra, pork, mice, bananas, sugarcane, and groundnuts. Traditionally, these foods are said to harm the unborn baby as well as cause difficulties when giving birth. Mapara (2009) pointed out that Indigenous knowledge is mainly stored in people's minds and passed on through generations by word of mouth rather than in written form.

3.5 Conclusion

The integration of Indigenous cuisines into modern wellbeing practices in Malawi's communities is a testament to the enduring richness of the society's culinary culture. Modern wellbeing practices are designed to enhance various aspects of life and to contribute to overall health and happiness. Incorporating a combination of these practices can help create a balanced and fulfilling lifestyle among societies.

Theoretically, this chapter contributes to the literature on how knowledge of Indigenous cuisines impacts the wellbeing of modern communities, using the PERMA model. Knowledge of Indigenous cuisines in societies strengthens the bonds among societies, which are to be protected as they promote identity and community overall wellbeing. The study highlights the importance of Indigenous cuisines as an important part of cultural identity in societies, emphasizing how knowledge of Indigenous cuisines enhances individual and community wellbeing. Indigenous cuisines reflect a rich food culture, bring a sense of meaning, purpose, and relationships that are bonded together. The Malawian Indigenous food culture follows certain taboos and these taboos also represent values, beliefs, and traditions that contribute to a sense of identity and meaning. Adherence to these taboos offers individuals a sense of purpose and connection to their cultural heritage. Taboos associated with Indigenous cuisine in a society reflect aspects of the PERMA model by contributing to cultural identity, evoking positive emotions, encouraging engagement in cultural practices, strengthening social relationships among societies, and promoting a sense of accomplishment and meaning within the Elders of the community.

This study is not without limitations. Firstly, the sample size was limited to a few societies and more societies could have been included because Indigenous cultures are different and what works for one community may not apply to another community. This variability can limit the generalizability of findings. Secondly, the study gathered more data from the elderly (custodians) of the societies: different views may come out from the GenZ and may bring a different perspective on issues of food and culture due to their exposure to technology and diverse food. In order to support wellness among societies in the wake of modern technology and contemporary lifestyles, future studies could explore how other communities – including the marginalized ones – and the younger generation view Indigenous cuisine practices as sustainable culinary practices. Such a study may leverage the PERMA framework and use a mixed research methodology.

In conclusion, the study reveals that integrating Indigenous cuisines into modern wellbeing practices in Malawi societies evokes Positive Emotions, Engagement, Relationships, Meaning, and Accomplishment, which are key quadrants in modern wellbeing practices as stated by the PERMA model of wellness. The use of Indigenous ingredients and respect for food rituals are some of the key aspects that Malawi Indigenous people still hold to and that give them meaning and connections.

References

Bisai, S., Dutta, S. and Das Mohapatra, P.K. (2023) Traditional food consumption pattern and nutritional status of Oraons: An Asian Indian Indigenous community. *Frontiers in Sustainable Food Systems* 7, 969264.

Björk, P. and Kauppinen-Räisänen, H. (2016) Local food: A source for destination attraction. *International Journal of Contemporary Hospitality Management* 28 (1), 177–194.

Blumenkrantz, D.G. (2016) *Coming of Age the Rite Way: Youth and Community Development through Rites of Passage*. Oxford University Press.

Chakona, G. and Shackleton, C. (2019) Food taboos and cultural beliefs influence food choice and dietary preferences among pregnant women in the Eastern Cape, South Africa. *Nutrients* 11 (11), 2668.

Coté, C. (2016) 'Indigenizing' food sovereignty. Revitalizing Indigenous food practices and ecological knowledges in Canada and the United States. *Humanities* 5 (3), 57.

de Diego-Cordero, R., Rivilla-Garcia, E., Diaz-Jimenez, D., Lucchetti, G. and Badanta, B. (2021) The role of cultural beliefs on eating patterns and food practices among pregnant women: A systematic review. *Nutrition Reviews* 79 (9), 945–963.

Demi, S.M. (2014) African Indigenous food crops: Their roles in combatting chronic diseases in Ghana. MA thesis, University of Toronto.

Demientieff, L.X., Rasmus, S., Black, J.C., Presley, J., Jauregui-Dusseau, A., Clyma, K.R. and Jernigan, V.B.B. (2023) Supporting traditional foodways knowledge and practices in Alaska Native communities: The Elders Mentoring Elders camp. *Health Promotion Practice* 24 (6), 1101–1104.

Dillette, A.K., Douglas, A.C. and Andrzejewski, C. (2021) Dimensions of holistic wellness as a result of international wellness tourism experiences. *Current Issues in Tourism* 24 (6), 794–810.

Farmer, N. and Cotter, E.W. (2021) Wellbeing and cooking behaviour: Using the positive emotion, engagement, relationships, meaning, and accomplishment (PERMA) model as a theoretical framework. *Frontiers in Psychology* 12, 560578.

Fieldhouse, P. (2013) *Food and Nutrition: Customs and Culture*. Springer.

Gewa, C.A., Stabile, B., Thomas, P., Onyango, A.C. and Angano, F.O. (2023) Agricultural production, traditional foods and household food insecurity in Rural Kenya: Practice, perception and predictors. *Journal of Hunger & Environmental Nutrition* 18 (4), 540–563.

Goodman, F.R., Disabato, D.J., Kashdan, T.B. and Kauffman, S.B. (2018) Measuring wellbeing: A comparison of subjective wellbeing and PERMA. *The Journal of Positive Psychology* 13 (4), 321–332.

Jernigan, V.B.B., Taniguchi, T., Nguyen, C.J., London, S.M., Henderson, A., Maudrie, T.L., Blair, S., Clyma, K.R., Lopez, S.V. and Jacob, T. (2023) Food systems, food sovereignty, and health: Conference shares linkages to support Indigenous community health. *Health Promotion Practice* 24 (6), 1109–1116.

Jones, A.D. (2015) Household food insecurity is associated with heterogeneous patterns of diet quality across urban and rural regions of Malawi. *World Medical & Health Policy* 7 (3), 234–254.

Joseph, L. and Turner, N.J. (2020) 'The old foods are the new foods!': Erosion and revitalization of Indigenous food systems in northwestern North America. *Frontiers in Sustainable Food Systems* 4, 596237.

Kang, Y., Hurley, K.M., Ruel-Bergeron, J., Monclus, A.B., Oemcke, R., Wu, L.S.F., Mitra, M., Phuka, J., Klemm, R. and West, K.P. (2019) Household food insecurity is associated with low dietary diversity among pregnant and lactating women in rural Malawi. *Public Health Nutrition* 22 (4), 697–705.

Kasimba, S., Covic, N., Motswagole, B., Laubscher, R. and Claasen, N. (2019) Consumption of traditional and Indigenous foods and their contribution to nutrient intake among children and women in Botswana. *Ecology of Food and Nutrition* 58 (3), 281–298.

Keating, L.A. and Heslin, P.A. (2015) The potential role of mindsets in unleashing employee engagement. *Human Resource Management Review* 25 (4), 329–341.

Kesa, H., Tchuenchieu Kamgain, A.D., Kwazi Zuma, M. and Mbhenyane, X. (2023) Knowledge, perception and consumption of Indigenous foods in Gauteng region, South Africa. *International Journal of Environmental Research and Public Health* 20 (20), 6961.

Kuhnlein, H.V. (2015) Food system sustainability for health and wellbeing of Indigenous Peoples. *Public Health Nutrition* 18 (13), 2415–2424.

Kuhnlein, H.V. and Chotiboriboon, S. (2022) Why and how to strengthen Indigenous peoples' food systems with examples from two unique Indigenous communities. *Frontiers in Sustainable Food Systems* 6, 808670.

Kumar, S. and Lakshminarayana, M.B. (eds) (2024) *Indigenous People-Traditional Practices and Modern Development*. InTech Books.

Lee, K.S. (2023) Cooking up food memories: A taste of intangible cultural heritage. *Journal of Hospitality and Tourism Management* 54, 1–9.

Lock, K., Pomerleau, J., Causer, L., Altmann, D.R. and McKee, M. (2005) The global burden of disease attributable to low consumption of fruit and vegetables: Implications for the global strategy on diet. *Bulletin of the World Health Organization* 83 (2), 100–108.

Lopes, C.V.A., Mihrshahi, S., Hunter, J., Ronto, R. and Cawthorne, R. (2024) Co-designing research for sustainable food systems and diets with Aboriginal communities: A study protocol. *International Journal of Environmental Research and Public Health* 21 (3), 298.

Mac Con Iomaire, M. and Nic Philibín, C. (2022) Exploring the food-related intangible cultural heritage of Bealtaine (May Day) within the Irish Folklore Commission's Schools' Collection Digital Archive. *Études irlandaises* 47 (1), 15–32.

Macdiarmid, J.I., Douglas, F. and Campbell, J. (2016) Eating like there's no tomorrow: Public awareness of the environmental impact of food and reluctance to eat less meat as part of a sustainable diet. *Appetite* 96, 487–493.

Manyozo, L. (2018) The context is the message: Theory of Indigenous knowledge communication systems. *Javnost-The Public* 25 (4), 393–409.

Mapara, J. (2009) Indigenous knowledge systems in Zimbabwe: Juxtaposing postcolonial theory. *The Journal of Pan African Studies* 3, 139–155.

Marovelli, B. (2019) Cooking and eating together in London: Food-sharing initiatives as collective spaces of encounter. *Geoforum* 99, 190–201.

Martela, F. and Pessi, A.B. (2018) Significant work is about self-realization and broader purpose: Defining the key dimensions of meaningful work. *Frontiers in Psychology* 9, 363.

Masuku, M.M. and Bhengu, A.S. (2021) The value of Indigenous foods in improving food security in Emaphephetheni rural setting. *Indilinga African Journal of Indigenous Knowledge Systems* 20 (1), 13–23.

Maudrie, T.L., Colón-Ramos, U., Harper, K.M., Jock, B.W. and Gittelsohn, J. (2021) A scoping review of the use of Indigenous food sovereignty principles for intervention and future directions. *Current Developments in Nutrition* 5 (7), nzab093.

Mbhenyane, X.G. (2017) Indigenous foods and their contribution to nutrient requirements. *South African Journal of Clinical Nutrition* 30 (4), 5–7.

Mkwambisi, D., Nkhono-Mvula, T., Kankwamba, H., Gurkan, C., Hobeika, A., Abera, D., Herlant, P., Orbell, C., Khosla, P. and Quiroz Gonzalez, C. (2023) *Food Systems Profile – Malawi. Catalysing the Sustainable and Inclusive Transformation of Food Systems.* European Union and CIRAD. https://doi.org/10.4060/cc4237en.

Moyo, C., Ngulube, P. and Kazembe, C. (2016) Preserving knowledge about Indigenous cuisine for posterity in Zimbabwe. *Indilinga African Journal of Indigenous Knowledge Systems* 15 (1), 136–152.

Nkhoma, B.G. (2020) 'We are what we eat': Nutrition, African diets and the state in colonial Malawi, 1920s–1960. *Journal of Southern African Studies* 46 (6), 1219–1235.

Okoye, J. and Oni, K. (2017) Promotion of Indigenous food preservation and processing knowledge and the challenge of food security in Africa. *Journal of Food Security* 5 (3), 75–87.

Oloko, M., Robson, J.P. and Reed, M.G. (2024) The opportunities and values of procuring and preserving food within co-existing Indigenous and local food systems: Insights from Canada's West Coast. *Food Ethics* 9 (2), 1–22.

Otang-Mbeng, W. and Mashabela, M.N. (2020) A review of beneficial phytochemicals and postharvest studies on some Indigenous leafy vegetables from the Mpumalanga Province of South Africa. *Medicinal Plants – International Journal of Phytomedicines and Related Industries* 12 (4), 533–544.

Penafiel, D., Cevallos-Valdiviezo, H., Espinel, R. and Van Damme, P. (2019) Local traditional foods contribute to the diversity and species richness of rural women's diet in Ecuador. *Public Health Nutrition* 22 (16), 2962–2971.

Peng, J., Yang, X., Fu, S. and Huan, T.C.T. (2023) Exploring the influence of tourists' happiness on revisit intention in the context of traditional Chinese medicine cultural tourism. *Tourism Management* 94, 104647.

Ramos-Molina, B., Queipo-Ortuño, M.I., Lambertos, A., Tinahones, F.J. and Peñafiel, R. (2019) Dietary and gut microbiota polyamines in obesity- and age-related diseases. *Frontiers in Nutrition* 6, 24.

Seligman, M.E.P. (2011) *Flourish: A Visionary New Understanding of Happiness and Wellbeing*. Simon & Schuster.

Seligman, M. (2018) PERMA and the building blocks of wellbeing. *The Journal of Positive Psychology* 13 (4), 333–335.

Smoky, H. (2024) Enchanting roots: The culinary and medicinal wonders of Mondia Whitei [online]. *Medium*, 12 January. Available at https://medium.com/@smokyhazel/enchanting-roots-the-culinary-and-medicinal-wonders-of-mondia-whitei-3deebc943a99.

Sultana, R., Muhammad, N. and Zakaria, A.K.M. (2018) Role of Indigenous knowledge in sustainable development. *International Journal of Development Research* 8 (2), 18902–18906.

Takaidza, S. (2023) Indigenous South African food: Nutrition and health benefits. In M. Soto-Hernández, E. Aguirre-Hernández and M. Palma-Tenango (eds) (2024) *Phytochemicals in Agriculture and Food* (Ch. 6). IntechOpen.

Tiwari, R. (2021) Residents' perception of the role of local cuisine as a tourism product in destination marketing. *Journal of Hospitality Application & Research* 16 (2), 45–62.

Walters, C., Bendulo, P. and Stoecker, B.J. (2019) Assessment of dietary diversity, antenatal care, food taboos, meal frequency, and nutritional status of pregnant adolescents in rural Malawi: A cross-sectional study. *African Journal of Food, Agriculture, Nutrition and Development* 19 (3), 14555–14570.

Wijaya, S. (2019) Indonesian food culture mapping: A starter contribution to promote Indonesian culinary tourism. *Journal of Ethnic Foods* 6 (1), 1–10.

4 Balancing Minds and Lives: Student Awareness and Wellbeing through Wellness Programmes in Private Higher Education

Willy Hannes Engelbrecht and Susanna Cornelia (Corné) Engelbrecht

4.1 Introduction

The South African higher education (HE) sector plays an instrumental role in promoting the importance of students being active independent contributors to the local economy, while promoting individual and community wellbeing (Eloff & Graham, 2020; Henrico, 2022). However, Eloff and Graham (2020) note that the demand for treatment to improve student wellbeing and health far exceeds the resources available at higher education institutions (HEIs). Nevertheless, wellness models play an important part in establishing awareness and driving conversation among students to take control of their health by carefully reviewing their lifestyle decisions (Goss & Cuddihy, 2010; Majeed & Kim, 2022; Oliver *et al.*, 2018). Simple changes like exercise, mental exercises, and social engagements with like-minded individuals can advance wellness.

The Higher Health non-profit organisation, established by the Department of Higher Education and Training (DHET), enables South African public tertiary education institutions to develop youth health services and to implement them to students (Higher Health, 2024). The programmes implemented by Higher Health promote a healthy lifestyle and require students to actively participate in activities that promote healthy living and wellness. Private higher education institutions (PHEIs) in South Africa are excluded from this initiative, and have to self-fund, develop, and implement health training and support programmes for their students, emphasising the extent to which PHEIs are excluded from such government-funded initiatives. There is a lack of studies exploring the importance and relevance of student wellness in the South African private HE sector. Although the government-funded Higher Health programme exists, its focus is on providing wellness and health support for all government-funded institutions not just the private HEI. The increased pressure by HEIs on students having to successfully and in minimum time complete their qualifications, while having to navigate various socioeconomic, sociocultural and other personal challenges, places unnecessary pressure on students, which increases the need for adequate wellness support programmes whilst they are studying, yet this was not needed prior to the commencement of their studies (Eloff *et al.*, 2022; Henrico, 2022). With the continued growth within the private HE sector in South Africa, it is critical that the PHEI learn from the public sector's experiences and promote the implementation of adequate wellness programmes that detect student wellness concerns early on in their tertiary journey, so as to adequately support students with navigating the socioeconomic challenges they face during this time (Eloff & Graham, 2020; Govender *et al.*, 2019; Henrico, 2022; Nelson *et al.*, 2020). To date, the private HE sector serves approximately 200,000 students across 135 institutions of higher learning (Council on Higher Education (CHE), 2024). The socioeconomic challenges that students face in the private HE sector is the same, if not more challenging, than in the public funded HE sector and therefore institutions of higher learning in the private HE sector must ensure sufficient wellness programmes are developed and implemented to promote student success. The primary objective of this study is to explore the relationship that exists between the six dimensions of wellness and their relevance towards students studying towards a hospitality programme at a PHEI in South Africa. The secondary aim of this study is to determine student awareness of and participation in student wellness programmes at the selected PHEI.

4.2 Literature Review

The academic success of students studying at HEIs depends on various factors, including student wellness (Thomas & Maree, 2022). The United Nations (UN) Sustainable Goal 3 emphasises the importance of good health and wellbeing for all citizens. Unquestionably, HEIs must develop and implement student wellness programmes that promote a healthy lifestyle among students (Eloff & Graham, 2020). Mullen (1986) defined wellness as the attitudes of students participating in activities aimed towards improving their quality of life while enabling them to foster a higher level of functioning compared to their counterparts. The UN World Health Organization (WHO, 2023), notes that an individual's health is determined by their physical, mental, and social wellbeing (Hashimoto *et al.*, 2015; Owen, 2002). Govender *et al.* (2019) noted that, from a South African perspective, wellness is defined in relation to the psychological or physiological wellbeing of an individual.

The multidimensional and holistic concept of wellness has received considerable attention (Avci & Güngör, 2023). Available wellness models emphasise the complexity of wellness and the various interrelated components that support health holistically (Goss & Cuddihy, 2010; Govender *et al.*, 2019; Oliver *et al.*, 2018; Seligman & Csikszentimihalyi, 2000). Although health is a critical component of wellness, this study applies the concept of wellness from the view of Hettler (2005) and the National Wellness Institute (2023). Hettler and the National Wellness Institute agree that the fundamental concept of wellness is positioned in an individual's awareness of their being and their active pursuit of a more meaningful existence. Hettler's holistic wellness model exposes six dimensions of wellness, namely 'physical, spiritual, intellectual, social, emotional, and occupational' (see Figure 4.1). Wellness is viewed by Hettler (2005) and by Avci and Güngör (2023) as an individual's ability to expand their intellectual, interpersonal and cultural context through engagements with others that develop and grow their intellectual abilities to obtain self-actualisation, the highest form of psychological state of position that individuals want to achieve. The latter is supported by Baldwin *et al.* (2017), Botha and Brand (2009) and Owen (2002) adding that individuals must take responsibility for promoting a healthier lifestyle in order to experience wellness.

The six-dimensions-of-wellness model has been applied in various HE contexts, such as the assessment of a psychometric questionnaire

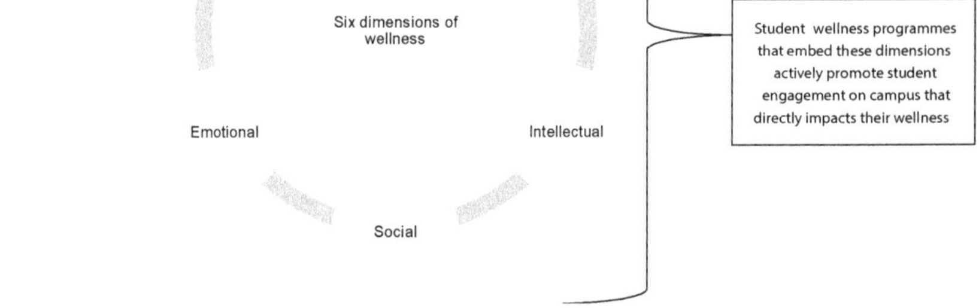

Figure 4.1 The six dimensions of student wellness (adapted from Hettler, 2005)

(Gradidge & De Jager, 2011), wellness models for managers in tertiary institutions (Botha & Brand, 2009), and student wellness (Botha & Cilliers, 2012; Van Lingen *et al.*, 2011). Additionally, most studies focus on the wellness of academics (Barkhuizen, 2005; Coetzee, 2004; Viljoen, 2006). This highlights the limited research on student wellness using the six-dimensions-of-wellness model (Hettler, 1984). Therefore, it is both relevant and critical to apply the six dimensions of wellness from a student's perspective at a South African private HEI, with particular emphasis on students studying hospitality programmes. HEIs need to embed the six dimensions from Hettler's Holistic Wellness Model to ensure that students are adequately supported, developed and prepared to manage their wellness professionally and personally (Baldwin *et al.*, 2017; Dillette *et al.*, 2020; Henrico, 2022; Oliver *et al.*, 2018).

Physical wellness requires students to follow a healthy diet and make lifestyle choices that positively contribute to their physical health (Baldwin *et al.*, 2017; Botha & Barnd, 2009; Oliver *et al.*, 2018). Individuals focused on achieving their psychological needs experience reduced levels of stress and anxiety whilst performing better with professional or academic tasks (Avci & Güngör, 2023). Furthermore, positive lifestyle choices include exercising regularly and avoiding harmful activities like smoking and consuming alcohol. Spiritual wellness relates to the extent to which students have a sense of purpose and balance their personal needs with external societal demands (Baldwin *et al.*, 2017; Botha & Brand, 2009; Oliver *et al.*, 2018). Intellectual wellness focuses on a student's willingness to undertake new learning (with an open mind to environmental changes) and accept or reject new knowledge based on evidence (Baldwin *et al.*, 2017; Botha & Brand, 2009; Oliver *et al.*, 2018).

Social wellness focuses on the student's ability to participate harmoniously and perform effectively in society, promoting social justice by correcting past injustices (Baldwin *et al.*, 2017; Botha & Brand, 2009; Nelson *et al.*, 2020; Oliver *et al.*, 2018). Emotional wellness concerns a student's ability to reflect critically on the daily challenges of society and finding the right mechanism to manage their bias (Baldwin *et al.*, 2017; Botha & Brand, 2009; Oliver *et al.*, 2018; Thomas & Maree, 2022). Occupational wellness is the ability of the student to understand the world of work and actively contribute towards building a better society through daily professional activities (Baldwin *et al.*, 2017; Botha & Brand, 2009; Oliver *et al.*, 2018).

4.2.1 Student wellness programmes

The lack of student wellness programmes has dire consequences once students move into the world of work, with employers having to manage employee wellness for people who have not had this experience or who might have pre-existing wellness problems (Eloff & Graham, 2020). Henrico (2022) asserts that meaningful and sincere student wellness programmes should be implemented at HEIs due to the extremely fast pace at which the world is moving. Student wellness programmes are expensive, time intensive, and require experienced well-trained professionals. Although student wellness programmes are sometimes available at HEIs, they often lack implementation, monitoring and evaluation to ensure that they are relevant, as the socioeconomic, sociocultural, financial, and environmental challenges differ between geographical locations (Eloff & Graham, 2020; Henrico, 2022). Wellness programmes must therefore be uniquely-designed intervention strategies with the intention to support students in managing their emotions during their studies (Sieberhagen *et al.*, 2011). The implementation and monitoring of wellness programmes by HEIs will enable institutions to better gauge student wellness and understand the challenges they face (Goss & Cuddihy, 2010). HEIs need to understand the importance of student wellness programmes and to communicate effectively the opportunities these programmes offer to students (Goss & Cuddihy, 2010).

4.2.2 Promotion and participation in wellness programmes

HEIs need to utilise wellness programmes and promote them as a supporting mechanism that makes the transition between school and HE easier for students. Varga *et al.* (2021) note that the wellness of hospitality employees is critical, as this demanding sector has a high rate of alcohol abuse and suicide. Student wellness programmes can be embedded in the curriculum to ensure students are aware of and participate in them (Henrico, 2022; Sun & Davison, 2023). It is critical that HEIs pay special attention to wellness assistance for students studying towards a hospitality-related programme. Inclusion of wellness programmes in the curriculum will enable students to gain a better understanding of how to manage emotions and challenges from a professional and personal perspective (Goss & Cuddihy, 2010; Horton & Snyder, 2009). Hospitality students must be adequately prepared for the hospitality profession, as it comes with unique challenges associated with managing guest expectations and experiences (Varga *et al.*, 2021). This will contribute to their wellbeing, as they will have a better idea of what to expect from the sector. Participation in wellness programmes will better prepare students for the world of work. HEIs should also engage with employers who take on students during work placement learning, to ensure that wellness programmes are available for students (Varga *et al.*, 2021). Varga *et al.* (2021) found that employees who participated in wellness programmes reported that their overall wellbeing is good. This highlights the importance of HEIs promoting the usefulness and advantages of wellness programmes to students and making such programmes available. Wellness programmes improve morale, improve physical and mental health, motivate students to continue with their studies, and enable students to improve their academic performance, to name but a few their merits (Okereke & Adinma, 2022). Although most research conducted on student wellness falls within the health sciences, HEIs must focus on the importance of wellness programmes for students across all professional qualifications offered at HEI.

4.3 Research Design

Following an interpretivist philosophical framework, this qualitative study was supported by an inductive approach that informed the research objective. The research design enabled the researchers to gather in-depth data on student understanding and awareness of wellness programmes at their PHEI. The study population consisted of students enrolled in a hospitality programme at a PHEI with campuses in South Africa's Gauteng province. Given that there was no complete database of these students available (Engelbrecht *et al.*, 2023), a sample that represents the population was selected. The interviews focused on exploring student understanding of wellness, the extent to which they might be practising any of the wellness dimensions, and their awareness of the available wellness programmes at the PHEI where they are enrolled. Furthermore, the interviews asked students to identify wellness programmes they would like to see more of at the institution. Convenience sampling was applied, which involved a campus representative informing students of the interviews that would be conducted on a predetermined date and time at the campus. Only students who were willing to participate were interviewed.

Sixteen students across three of the PHEIs' campuses in the Gauteng Province of South Africa participated in the in-depth semi-structured interviews, which were held in November 2023. The interviews were scheduled on campus for 45–60 minutes in a meeting room and were recorded, with the consent of the participants, for further data analysis. The academic heads of the respective campuses informed students in advance of the research and the day on which the semi-structured in-depth interviews would take place. A reminder of the interviews for the research project was shared with students on the day of data collection and the voluntary nature of their participation was clearly articulated in all communications.

Following the data collection, content analysis was used to analyse the data gathered from the semi-structured in-depth interviews to identify themes related to students' understanding of their level of participation in, and awareness of, wellness programmes at the specific PHEI. The interviews were all transcribed and coded whereafter key themes were identified from the transcribed recordings. The six themes that were identified provide a student's perspective on the extent to which student wellness is understood, which enables PHEIs to actively implement mechanisms to create awareness of and promote student wellness programmes. The repetition of student responses during the interviews confirmed that theoretical saturation was achieved (Engelbrecht *et al.*, 2023; Onwuegbuzie *et al.*, 2009).

Ethical clearance was obtained from the particular PHEI where the research was conducted. All participants were adequately informed of the study's purpose, how their personal information would be protected, their right to cancel the interview at any point, and their right to request a report from the researchers on the findings (if interested). Informed consent was obtained from all participants before each interview commenced. Recommendations are based on the themes and student remarks on their participation in wellness programmes at their PHEI and awareness of the various wellness types.

4.4 Presentation and Discussion of Findings

The primary aim of this study was to determine if the six dimensions of wellness are relevant to hospitality students within a PHEI in South Africa. The secondary aim is to determine if students are aware of and participate in the student wellness programmes offered by the respective PHEI. The six dimensions loaded in a unique order, emphasising what students at a PHEI seek when it comes to wellbeing. Physical wellbeing was listed as the most important theme, obtaining a 26% frequency rating, followed by emotional wellbeing at 20%. Social wellness (17%) was the third most important theme, followed by spiritual wellness (14%) and occupational wellness (13%). The least important theme was intellectual wellness (10%). As this study was conducted in an educational setting one would have expected intellectual wellness to have obtained a higher ranking. However, this was not the case.

After careful consideration of each campus, it is evident that Campus 2 and Campus 3 align in terms of physical wellness (20% each) and emotional wellness (16% and 17% respectively), while Campus 1 rates physical wellness at 30% and emotional wellness at 23%. Social wellness, spiritual wellness and occupational wellness were similar at Campus 1 (13%, 14%, 13%) and Campus 3 (17%, 13%, 17%). Campus 2's rankings for social wellness (30%), spiritual wellness (18%) and occupational wellness (7%), were quite different from those of Campus 1 and Campus 3. Intellectual wellness ranked 7% (Campus 1), 9% (Campus 2) and 16% (Campus 3). Table 4.1 summarises the frequency difference for the three campuses.

Theme 1, physical wellbeing, requires students to make healthy lifestyle choices, including following a healthy diet and exercising regularly. These two aspects of physical wellbeing contribute positively

Table 4.1 Thematic analysis frequency per campus

	Campus 1	Campus 2	Campus 3	Cumulative Totals
Theme 1: Physical	30%	20%	20%	26%
Theme 2: Emotional	23%	16%	17%	20%
Theme 3: Social	13%	30%	17%	17%
Theme 4: Spiritual	14%	18%	13%	14%
Theme 5: Occupational	13%	7%	17%	13%
Theme 6: Intellectual	7%	9%	16%	10%

to student physical health (Baldwin *et al.*, 2017; Botha & Brand, 2009; Oliver *et al.*, 2018). The respondents acknowledged that physical activity and healthy eating are key to physical wellbeing; however, they tend to neglect these aspects during times of high stress, like assignment submissions, closed-book assessments, or preparing a meal within a specific timeframe in the kitchen. Given the packed academic programme, with restricted academic time (campus-based learning) before entering the workplace, respondents noted that they sleep between 6 and 8 hours a night, with some sleeping less than 3 hours a night, and others sleeping more than 8 hours a night. Respondents noted that physical wellness includes participation in a hobby of some sort, like playing sports, reading, or exercising to relax and unwind.

Emotional wellness ranked the second most important theme among participants. The participants noted that regular reflection on the daily challenges faced by themselves and society ensures that they stay in touch with what is happening in the world. The key aspects of emotional wellness include stress and the management thereof. Given the ever-changing hospitality environment, emotional wellness can be difficult to maintain. Participants noted that asking for assistance and remaining focused on the end goal enabled them to focus on achieving success and maintaining good levels of emotional wellness. Furthermore, participants expressed the importance of extracurricular activities or hobbies that support emotional wellness.

Theme 3, social wellness, is a student's ability to participate harmoniously and perform effectively in society (Baldwin *et al.*, 2017; Botha & Brand, 2009; Oliver *et al.*, 2018). Participants noted that having a good social support structure in place and relying on family and friends makes it easier to adapt to HEI life. Together with a good social support structure is knowing that there are enough social and support events hosted on campus that promote social wellness among students.

The fourth most important theme, spiritual wellness, focuses on the student's ability to know their purpose in life and to use it to balance their personal needs with societal demands (Baldwin *et al.*, 2017; Botha & Brand, 2009; Oliver *et al.*, 2018). The participants showed a high level of maturity in acknowledging that the responsibility for their wellness sits with them. They noted that, while external forces like campus life and finances impact their wellbeing, they would participate in initiatives that promote and support their wellness if available. Lastly, faith was listed as another key aspect of spiritual wellness that contributes to overall wellbeing.

Occupational wellness was ranked the fifth most important theme among the hospitality students. It is evident that students are mature and therefore understand the world of work based on curriculum's placement opportunities. Work placement has taught students the importance of effective time management and a conducive work environment that ensures stable and positive occupational wellness experiences. The participants noted that a lack of communication and poor communication strategies often negatively impact wellness, as they can create additional stress.

Intellectual wellness was ranked the least important theme based on participant feedback during the in-depth interviews. This theme focuses on the student's willingness to learn new skills and competencies in a changing environment. Participants noted that most setbacks are perceived as learning opportunities, and having the ability to improve intellectual wellness has a positive impact on improving overall wellness. The participants acknowledge that they often feel invisible for the duration of their studies, which directly affects their productivity and mental wellbeing.

This study provides a clear perspective on the types of wellness that affect students at the PHEI in question, which offers hospitality-related programmes. The theme rankings emphasise the importance of wellness categories for students at a hospitality establishment. The PHEI in question needs to consider a critical review of its student wellness programme offerings and services.

4.5 Recommendations

This study makes the following practical recommendations for HEIs and the hospitality industry on promoting the importance of student wellness and ensuring students, graduates and employees participate in wellness programmes.

First, the PHEI in question needs to ensure that physical exercise facilities are available on campus, and that students are motivated to exercise. In addition, the PHEI must request the campus canteen to shift its focus to more healthy food options for students. This messaging will inspire students to make good lifestyle choices and join the world of work as healthy and active citizens.

Second, students understand the importance of taking responsibility for their wellness by surrounding themselves with supportive family, friends, and colleagues. For students to take responsibility for their wellness, the PHEI needs to make adequate support and training available to them.

Third, students move between campus and industry placements during their studies. This emphasises the additional social interactions and campus engagements that are needed to establish a solid bond among students and alumni, while enabling peer-to-peer learning.

Fourth, students should start a hobby or participate in sport and cultural events on campus, as this is the easiest way to establish relationships and promote mental wellness. The PHEI can encourage students to participate in sporting or cultural events by establishing clubs of interest that students can engage with. This is a unique way of promoting emotional wellness among students.

Finally, the PHEI and its industry partners need to collaborate on developing employee and internship wellness programmes, which focus on physical wellness, emotional wellness and the other types of wellness. The PHEI can ensure that students are adequately prepared for industry placement by promoting the completion of a wellness course, emphasising the key types of wellness and how they manifest in the industry.

4.6 Conclusions

This study explored hospitality students' awareness of the six wellness categories and whether they participate in any wellness programmes offered at the PHEI. The study was informed by an interpretivist philosophy and applied a qualitative research method to collect data on student awareness of and participation in wellness programmes at a PHEI in Gauteng. Participants were based at Gauteng campuses, and through content analysis, six themes were identified that ranked the various wellness categories according to importance.

The PHEI in question needs to consider reviewing the student wellness programmes on offer to ensure that students are well prepared for industry engagement during and after the completion of their studies. In addition, collaboration between the PHEI and its industry partners can bring change throughout the hospitality industry by promoting the importance of student and employee wellness. This will create greater awareness of the importance of wellness while studying and working in the hospitality industry.

This study makes significant contributions to the field by highlighting the importance of developing, implementing and promoting student wellness programmes across all PHEIs in South Africa and not just the institution under study. Lastly, it is recommended that student awareness of and participation in wellness programmes be expanded across PHEIs to understand if the broader student population are aware of and use the wellness programmes available at their institution.

The limitation of this study is that a single PHEI in Gauteng offering hospitality specific programmes was used for data collection, instead of engaging with multiple PHEIs offering hospitality programmes not just in Gauteng but the rest of South Africa. Such a single-provider, single-programme and single-province approach restricts the researchers in generalising the findings of this project across any of the other campuses of the specific PHEI, and that of other providers both in Gauteng and the rest of South Africa, offering hospitality, tourism and other programmes. This limitation can be resolved with a follow-up research study in which multi-site PHEI in South Africa participate in a quantitative online survey focused on student awareness and participation in wellness programmes at their respective institutions. This will ensure that the student sample population sharing its views and opinions on student wellness programmes at PHEI in South Africa is more diverse.

References

Avci, M. and Güngör, A. (2023) Examining the relationships between basic psychological needs and wellness in college students: The mediating role of stress coping styles. *International Journal of Psychology and Educational Studies* 10 (1), 113–126.

Baldwin, D.R., Towler, K., Oliver, M.D. and Datta, S. (2017) An examination of college student wellness: A research and liberal arts perspective. *Health Psychology Open* 4 (2), 1–9.

Barkhuizen, E.N. (2005) Work wellness of academic staff in South African higher education institutions. Doctoral dissertation, North-West University. https://dspace.nwu.ac.za/handle/10394/713.

Botha, L. and Cilliers, C. (2012) 'Adolescent' South Africa (18 years since democratization): Challenges for universities to optimize wellness as a prerequisite for cognitive development and learning in a diverse society. *Journal of Cognitive Education & Psychology* 11 (3), 241–255.

Botha, P.A. and Brand, H. (2009) Development of a holistic wellness model for managers in tertiary institutions. *SA Journal of Human Resource Management* 7 (1), 1–10.

Coetzee, S.E. (2004) Work wellness at a higher education institution in South Africa. Doctoral dissertation, North-West University. https://repository.nwu.ac.za/bitstream/handle/10394/384/coetzee_se.pdf?sequence=1&isAllowed=y.

Council on Higher Education (CHE) (2024) Vital Stats: Public and private higher education data for 2021. https://www.che.ac.za/sites/default/files/publications/PUB_VitalStats%202021_Public%20and%20Private%20Higher%20Education%20Data_2023%5B66%5D.pdf.

Dillette, A.K., Douglas, A.C. and Andrzejewski, C. (2020) Dimensions of holistic wellness as a result of international wellness tourism experiences. *Current Issues in Tourism* 24 (6), 794–810.

Eloff, I. and Graham, M. (2020) Measuring mental health and wellbeing of South African undergraduate students. *Global Mental Health* 7 (34), 1–10.

Eloff, I., O'Neil, S. and Kanengoni, H. (2022) Factors contributing to student wellbeing: Student perspective. In L. Schutte, T. Guse and M.P. Wissing (eds) *Embracing Wellbeing in Diverse African Contexts: Research Perspectives* (pp. 219–246). Springer Nature. https://doi.org/10.1007/978-3-030-85924-4_10.

Engelbrecht, W.H., Van Greunen, C. and Ramgovind, P. (2023) Factors that influence student choice to study at a Private Higher Education Institution in South Africa.

In S. Adendorff, C. Terblanche and K. Brits (eds) *Conference Proceedings: SAIMS (Southern African Institute for Management Scientist) 34th Annual Conference* (pp. 106–117). Centurion.

Goss, H. and Cuddihy, T.F. (2010) Wellness in higher education: A transformative framework for health-related disciplines. *Asia-Pacific Journal of Health, Sport and Physical Education* 1 (2), 29–36.

Govender, K., Bhana, A., McMurry, K., Kelly, J., Theron, L., Meyer-Weitz, A., Ward, C.L. and Tomlinson, M. (2019) A systematic review of the South African work on the wellbeing of young people (2000–2016). *South African Journal of Psychology* 49 (1), 52–69.

Gradidge, D.H. and De Jager, A.C. (2011) Psychometric properties of the wellness questionnaire for higher education. *South African Journal of Psychology* 41 (4), 517–527.

Hashimoto, J., Tsutsumi, A. and Iztusu, T. (2015) Fundamental power in life: mental health and wellbeing as a global priority [online]. Our World (United Nations University). https://ourworld.unu.edu/en/fundamental-power-in-life-mental-health-and-wellbeing-as-a-global-priority#:~:text=The%20World%20Health%20Organization's%20(WHO,of%20everyone%20to%20enjoy%20the.

Henrico, K. (2022) Sustaining student wellness in higher educational institutions: Possible design principles and implementations strategies. *Journal for Transdisciplinary Research in Southern Africa* 18 (1), a1114.

Hettler, B. (2005) Think peace, act peace [online]. Accessed 14 November 2023, http://www.hettler.com.

Hettler, W. (1984) Wellness: Encouraging a lifetime pursuit of excellence. *Health Values* 8 (4), 13– 17.

Higher Health (2024) *Annual Report 2022/2023*. Higher Health. https://higherhealth.ac.za/wp-content/uploads/2024/05/HigherHealth-Annual-Report-202223_V7_LV.pdf.

Horton, B.W. and Snyder, C.S. (2009) Wellness: Its impact on student grades and implications for business. *Journal of Human Resources in Hospitality & Tourism* 8, 215–233.

Majeed, S. and Kim, W.G. (2022) Emerging trends in wellness tourism: A scoping review. *Journal of Hospitality and Tourism Insights* 6 (2), 853–873.

Mullen, K. (1986) Wellness: The missing concept in health promotion programming for adults. *Health Values: The Journal of Health Behavior, Education & Promotion* 10 (3), 34–37.

National Wellness Institute (2023) About wellness. Accessed 31 October 2024, https://www.nationalwellness.org/page/AboutWellness.

Nelson, R.B., Asamsama, O.H., Jimerson, S.R. and Lam, S. (2020) The association between student wellness and student engagement in school. *Journal of Educational Research and Innovation* 8 (1), 1–26.

Okereke, B.C. and Adinma, E.D. (2022) Participating in wellness programmes in the workplace: Exploring perspective of perceived barriers and incentives among employees of federal university of technology, Owerri. *International Journal of Advanced Academic Research* 8 (12), 10–26.

Oliver, M.D., Baldwin, D.R. and Datta, S. (2018) Health to wellness: A review of wellness models and transitioning back to health. *The International Journal of Health, Wellness and Society* 9 (1), 41–55.

Onwuegbuzie, A.J., Dickinson, W.B., Leech, N.L. and Zoran, A.G. (2009) A qualitative framework for collecting and analysing data in focus group research. *International Journal of Qualitative Methods* 8 (3), 1–21.

Owen, T.R. (2002) *Student and Employee Wellness in Higher Education: A Literature Review.* Education Resource Information Center Document Reproduction Service, ED46205 1.

Seligman, M.E.P. and Csikszentmihalyi, M. (2000) Positive psychology: An introduction. *American Psychologist* 55 (1), 5–14. https://doi.org/10.1037/0003-066X.55.1.5.

Sieberhagen, C., Pienaar, J. and Els, C. (2011) Management of employee wellness in South Africa: Employer service provider and union perspectives. *South African Journal of Human Resource Management* 9 (1), 1–14.

Sun, S. and Davison, C. (2023) University preparation programs in Australia: International student perspectives. *Sage Open* 13 (2), 1–16.

Thomas, T.A. and Maree, D. (2022) Student factors affecting academic success among undergraduate students at two South African higher education institutions. *South African Journal of Psychology* 52 (1), 99–111.

Van Lingen, J.M., Van Douman, D.L. and Van Wannenburg, I. (2011) A cross-sectional exploration of the relationship between undergraduate nursing student wellness and academic outcomes at a South African higher education institution. *South African Journal of Psychology* 41 (3), 396–408.

Varga, S., Mistry, T.G., Ali, F. and Cobanoglu, C. (2021) Employee perceptions of wellness programs in the hospitality industry. *International Journal of Contemporary Hospitality Management* 33 (10), 3331–3351.

Viljoen, J.P. (2006) Work wellness in a University of Technology in South Africa. Doctoral dissertation, North-West University. https://dspace.nwu.ac.za/handle/10394/1273?show=full.

World Health Organization (2023) Health and wellbeing. https://www.who.int/data/gho/data/major-themes/health-and-wellbeing.

5 Wellness Tourism and Pastoral Culture: Exploring their Symbiotic Relationship

Aditi Choudhary and Mahima Gopalkrishna

5.1 Introduction

Wellness tourism is commonly understood as travel to preserve or improve an individual's health and wellbeing (Global Wellness Institute, 2024). In 2022, the global wellness tourism sector was valued at approximately USD 814.6 billion and has been projected to grow at a compound annual rate of 12.42% between 2023 and 2030 (Grand View Research, 2024). As the wellness tourism industry expands and destinations across the world receive increasing exposure for their unique wellness offerings, there is a rising trend towards 'Indigenous wellness,' for its potential to offer authentic experiences to tourists (Trendium, 2023).

Indigenous people – custodians of unique cultures and of distinct interactions with their environment – encompass diverse languages, beliefs, and social, economic, and political systems (United Nations, 2024). Globally, approximately 476 million Indigenous individuals inhabit about a quarter of the Earth's surface (World Bank, 2023). Within this population, mobile Indigenous groups – such as nomadic pastoralists, sea nomads, shifting agriculturalists, and hunter-gatherers – rely on mobility to access common natural resources, thereby shaping a unique cultural identity (IUCN, 2024). Their dynamic lifestyles and profound connection to nature make these mobile Indigenous communities especially well suited for wellness tourism, providing authentic and enriching experiences for contemporary wellness seekers. This being so, this chapter explores the development of pastoral-based wellness tourism, particularly within the Indian context, which hosts a mobile Indigenous population of approximately 13 million (Köhler-Rollefson & Kishore, 2021).

Building on the concept of 'high-level wellness' pioneered by Dunn (1959) and its relationship with the environment, this study explores how the distinctive lifestyles and traditional knowledge systems of pastoralist communities can be integrated into wellness tourism, aligning with its core principles of holistic wellbeing: the harmony of body, mind, and spirit, and environmental awareness. It examines how pastoral wellness tourism can enhance tourist satisfaction and wellbeing while supporting pastoralists' livelihoods by ensuring fair prices for their products. It also aims to diversify the wellness tourism sector by offering unique experiences and fostering interactions that elevate the social standing of pastoral communities.

5.2 The Intersection of Pastoral Lifestyle and Wellness Tourism

5.2.1 Pastoralists and their distinctive livelihood

The lifestyle of pastoralists is distinctive, defined by their nomadic way of life. These communities boast significant cultural diversity and a wealth of Indigenous knowledge, particularly in Indigenous medicine and sustainable practices vital for their wellbeing and that of their livestock (Secretariat of the Convention on Biological Diversity, 2010). Approximately 500 million pastoralists globally manage about one million livestock (Rowe, 2023). In India, 10–13 million pastoralists raise 40% of the nation's domesticated breeds (Centre for Pastoralism, 2024). Due to their adaptable lifestyle, pastoralists are known for their minimalistic needs, including their diet, which supports their physically demanding work.

Pastoralists contribute significantly to India's milk production, accounting for approximately 53% of the country's total (Rahman, 2023). Particularly in Asia and Africa, non-bovine milk supports food security and family income for approximately 150 million producers (Tsakalidou & Papadimitriou, 2016). Non-bovine milk, i.e. milk derived from numerous non-bovine species such as goats, sheep, and camels, also forms a key aspect of their diet. Its consumption has existed for centuries among Indigenous populations and is an integral part of their ancient and folk-medicine systems (Siddiqui *et al.*, 2023). Although stereotypes questioning the hygiene and health benefits of non-bovine milk have contributed to its marginalization (Park & Haenlein, 2006), recent studies show that non-bovine milk contains natural compounds that can help fight infections, reduce blood pressure, boost the immune system, and protect the body from damage, making it useful for both health and nutrition (Vadher *et al.*, 2025: 2). For instance, camel milk, notable for its high vitamin C content and low lactose levels, is especially beneficial for lactose-intolerant individuals and has demonstrated various therapeutic effects, including diabetes prevention (Gammoh *et al.*, 2020).

Sheep milk is increasingly used in dairy products like cheese and yoghurt due to its high nutritional value (Balthazar *et al.*, 2017), whereas goat milk is celebrated for its digestibility, aiding in managing conditions such as low bone density and anaemia (Nayik *et al.*, 2021). Despite the medical importance of non-bovine milk, its production faces several challenges, including loss of access to pastures, livestock health issues, market access difficulties, and the changing aspirations of pastoral youth who are moving away from traditional livelihoods (Singh, 2023).

Particularly in the Indian state of Rajasthan, there exists rich livestock diversity and a variety of pastoral nomadic communities, such as Raika/Rabari, Gujjar, Charan, Rajput, Meghwal and Sindhi Muslim (Sharma *et al.*, 2003). With the state having 84% of India's camel population, camels have been declared the state animal. However, recent times have witnessed a reduction in the number of camels, which has become a major concern for the state and its pastoral communities, which depend on camels for their livelihood (Sultana, 2022). In such circumstances, pastoralists, seeking alternative livelihood options, are turning towards tourism. This shift has the potential to generate backward linkages that enable pastoralists to preserve their traditional livelihoods while also contributing to the conservation of their camel populations.

5.2.2 Rising tourism experiences with pastoralists

The development of tourism experiences centered on pastoralist communities is gaining momentum globally. For example, the Sami Indigenous population has embraced tourism, created additional income streams, while preserving their cultural heritage (Visit Norway, 2024). Similarly, Tibetan herding communities in Tashigang have adapted to tourism by converting their homes into guesthouses, benefiting from increased tourist footfall (Mansingka, 2016). Mongolia, with its vast grazing lands, has leveraged cultural and nature-based tourism to improve pastoral livelihoods while conserving its natural resources (Reading *et al.*, 2010). In India, the Gaddi pastoralist community of Bhaloli village in Himachal Pradesh has pioneered tourism-based initiatives that not only boost local economies but also promote cultural preservation and sustainable practices (*The Tribune*, 2024).

Rajasthan has already made substantial progress in promoting eco-tourism experiences around non-bovine animals (Patel, 2023). These initiatives often focus on immersive eco-tourism experiences that provide insights into the semi-nomadic lives of the Raika tribe, who are renowned for their deep bond with camels, their knowledge of medicinal herbs, ethno-veterinarian practices, and culinary specialties (Dale, 2021). These tourism experiences – featuring spending a day with traditional Raika camel breeders, the preparation of camel milk chai and other milk-based food and stories of semi-nomadic life – have considerably attracted tourists (Chaiwallah, 2013; Köhler-Rollefson, 2024).

These interactions with the pastoral communities have made room for tourists to learn about camel milk (Jafa, 2021), incorporating the potential to raise awareness of its nutritional benefits and fostering a deeper appreciation for the traditional wellness in the pastoral lifestyle. A growing number of tourists view the experience as getting close to nature, spending stress-free time, and learning and appreciating the pastoral culture, thereby enhancing their wellbeing (Memsahib in India, 2021).

5.2.3 Evolving interests and motivations of wellness tourists

Many studies have explored tourist motivations for wellness-based experiences (Gan *et al.*, 2023; He *et al.*, 2023; Kessler *et al.*, 2020), with some segmenting tourists by purpose (Lim *et al.*, 2015). Bočkus *et al.* (2023) classified wellness tourism motivations based on needs, such as relaxation (stimulus avoidance), physical enhancement (health rehabilitation and beautification), emotional fulfillment, connection with nature, social interaction, and intellectual growth. These motivations are broadly categorized into physical, emotional, occupational, spiritual, social, and intellectual dimensions (Smith & Puczkó, 2015). The COVID-19 pandemic reshaped wellness tourist motivations, with a stronger focus on safety, stress relief, and new wellness experiences, particularly among Millennials (Tran, 2021). This shift has opened opportunities for innovative wellness tourism products.

In line with changing tourist interests, food wellness experiences have emerged as a crucial component of gastronomic wellness and are increasingly seen as a strategic lever for enhancing tourist wellbeing. (Forlani *et al.*, 2022: 522). Dairy farm tours, often set in scenic rural areas with animals like goats and cows, offer visitors a chance to learn about local dairy production while enjoying unique stays in farmhouses or cabins. These tours often include visits to livestock areas and processing units, along with food-tasting experiences like cheese sampling, making them a popular agritourism activity (Acorn Tourism Consulting Limited, 2024).

Aligned with this global trend, it can be observed that India's value-added dairy market is growing at more than 20% annually (Centre for Pastoralism, 2024), thus creating a substantial opportunity to develop tourism around non-bovine milk both as a unique experience for tourists as well as a viable livelihood option for producers (Tengli *et al.*, 2019). Along with this, for a country such as India with its rich cultural heritage, the overall pastoral experience can be a value addition to non-bovine milk/dairy-based tourism. The rising initiatives of pastoral tourism along with the growing interests of the wellness tourist population demonstrate a potential link between the pastoralist lifestyle and wellness tourism, creating an intersection for research (Figure 5.1).

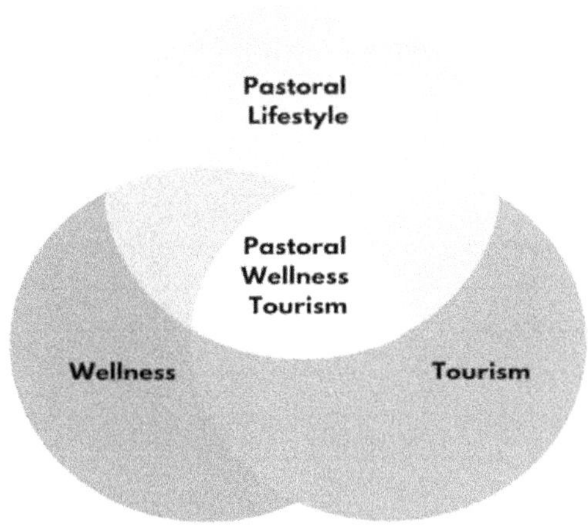

Figure 5.1 Visual representation of the intersections of pastoral wellness tourism
Source: Author illustration.

5.3 Research Methodology

5.3.1 Data collection

To explore the potential intersections between the lives of Rajasthan's pastoral communities and wellness tourism, data were gathered directly from community members. Given their marginalization and lack of formal education due to isolation, conversational interviews were employed to ensure that both the questions and answers were comprehended as intended (Conrad & Schober, 1999). A semi-structured questionnaire (Table 5.1) was used to conduct 12 in-depth interviews (IDIs) with members of pastoral communities, including the Raika (also

Table 5.1 Questionnaire used in the IDI to collect data from the members of pastoral communities of Rajasthan

Describe your occupation and main source of income. (Sharma *et al.*, 2003)
Describe your daily lifestyle as a pastoralist. (Dyson-Hudson & Dyson-Hudson, 1980)
What are the biggest challenges that you face? (Dimelu *et al.*, 2017)
What are the dietary habits and typical foods consumed in your community? (Li *et al.*, 2023)
Why is non-bovine milk consumed by the community members? (Degen, 2007)
How do traditional knowledge systems contribute to your overall wellbeing? (Sharifian *et al.*, 2022)
What are the advantages of living with nature as a part of your lifestyle? (Secretariat of the Convention on Biological Diversity, 2010)
How do the spiritual practices that you follow impact your sense of inner peace? (Siripurapu & Iyengar, 2022)
What is special about the pastoral-based communities that would attract an outsider?
Which parts of your lifestyle or traditions do you think would benefit the wellbeing of tourists if shared with them?

Table 5.2 Demographic profile of the 12 interview respondents

Respondent No.	Respondent name	Age	Gender	Community
R1	Ambalal	50	Male	Bhil
R2	Meena Garasia	35	Female	Garasia
R3	Suresh	30	Male	Meena
R4	Bhurmal Singh	70	Male	Raika
R5	Gamna Ram	30	Male	Raika
R6	Madhavram Dewasi	55	Male	Raika
R7	Papu Ram Devasi	47	Male	Raika
R8	Udai Singh	68	Male	Meghwal
R9	Sumer Singh	60	Male	Rajput
R10	Jagmal Singh	54	Male	Raika
R11	Jai Sangh	73	Male	Raika
R12	Kamla Gabru	33	Female	Raika

known as Rabari or Devasi), Rajput, Meena, Garasia, Meghwal, and Bhil tribal communities (Table 5.2). Respondent names referenced in this study are real and included with their permission. The interviews were conducted in the Hindi language.

The interviewer, a tourism expert with experience of working with mobile Indigenous populations in rural areas, was well acquainted with the region and its pastoral communities. To include the views of both migratory and settled pastoralists, the areas where pastoralists were commonly found were identified through preliminary research, and visits were made to these locations between August 2023 and January 2024 to align with seasonal pastoral movements. July–September marks the start of monsoon migration, while October to January offers better accessibility as pastoralists descend from the mountains due to winter. Using a convenience sampling approach, pastoralists who were available from their pastoral activities during daytime hours were interviewed for approximately 90 minutes, covering topics such as the pastoralists' way of life, their food practices (particularly the use of non-bovine milk), and their traditional knowledge systems.

5.3.2 Data analysis

The data collected from the interviews were transcribed and translated from Hindi to English. To systematically analyse the data, the transcripts were coded using Taguette, a web-based tagging tool. The process of tagging involved identifying recurring themes and patterns within the responses. For instance, any mention of medicinal practices or treatments was tagged as '*Traditional Healing*'. Similarly, references to diet and food practices were labeled as '*Traditional Food*' or '*Nutrition,*' depending on the context. Mentions of practices or knowledge passed down through generations were tagged as '*Indigenous Knowledge.*' Discussions about remedies derived from natural sources were coded as '*Natural Remedies.*'

When interviewees talked about their lifestyle in terms of low stress and harmony with their surroundings, these were tagged as '*Stress-free Living*' or '*Environmental Harmony.*' Statements reflecting mindfulness, or a conscious connection with their daily activities, were tagged as '*Mindfulness.*' Descriptions of their nomadic lifestyle and the benefits associated with it were labeled '*Nomadic Living.*' Expressions of community bonding, spirituality, and collective healing practices were tagged as '*Spiritual Unity and Healing.*' This structured approach to coding allowed for a comprehensive analysis of the data, ensuring that the major themes relevant to wellness tourism and the pastoral lifestyle were thoroughly explored and documented.

5.4 Findings and Discussion

5.4.1 Exploring the potential of pastoral wellness tourism in Rajasthan

The background context of the study derives from Dunn's concept of 'high-level wellness' (1959), which introduced wellness as an integrated and active process that maximizes an individual's potential within their environment. The health grid proposed by Dunn differentiates between poor and high-level wellness in favorable and unfavorable environments, highlighting the critical role that environmental factors play in a person's overall wellbeing. Dunn's model emphasizes that wellness is not simply the absence of illness but a dynamic balance between an individual's internal state and their external surroundings.

Building further on Dunn's framework, Dillette *et al.* (2020) focused on wellness by categorizing its understanding into four key dimensions: body, mind, spirit, and the natural environment. These dimensions reflect the holistic nature of wellness, integrating physical health, mental wellbeing, spiritual fulfillment, and a strong connection with the environment. Thus, this study adopts the framework of Dillette *et al.* (2020) to explore the relationship between pastoral-based wellness and wellness tourism. By framing pastoral-based wellness tourism as a holistic experience, this study connects the pastoralists' lifestyle, deeply tied to their body, mind, spirit, and natural environment, with the wellness tourism experience.

5.4.2 Dimension 1: Body/physical health

Physical wellbeing, in terms of better health, is one of the core objectives of wellness tourism. The dimension of body-related wellness concerning pastoral lifestyle can be divided into two sub-dimensions: (1) Organic food and physical fitness and (2) Traditional healing.

5.4.2.1 Sub-dimension 1: Organic food and physical fitness

Pastoral communities' unique lifestyles have stayed consistent over the years with chemical-free production, i.e. organic living. The statements of the pastoral community members related to organic food consumption are presented in Table 5.3, corresponding to the tags identified.

Pastoralists have reduced exposure to harmful substances, likely due to their reliance on natural resources, traditional knowledge, limited income, and minimal use of processed products. The traditional diets of pastoral communities are rich in essential nutrients, including healthy fats, fibre, and natural vitamins and minerals (R1, R10). Using

Table 5.3 Extracts from transcripts tagged 'Organic food and physical fitness'

Tags	References
Organic, Natural and Healthy Living	'**Organic living** is becoming popular now, but we have been practicing it naturally for many years. This lifestyle supports our health by avoiding chemicals.' (R3) 'We practice **organic farming**, specifically cultivating crops without the use of pesticides to retain its natural nutrients.' (R10)
Healthy, Non-bovine Milk, Nutrition	'We use the milk from our livestock to prepare ghee, which is a staple in our diet and very healthy for our children. Ghee made from non-bovine milk is rich in **essential fats for the body**.' (R1) 'Camel milk has medical advantages. It can be converted into powder and sold. This is already done in the UAE. Camel milk is known for its beneficial properties, helping in the **management of diabetes**.' (R4) 'The Raika community drinks homemade milk, including goat and buffalo milk, which we believe contributes to our good health due to its **natural properties**.' (R6) 'Our simple food often involves roasted bread from the dam, eaten with onions or goat's milk. This diet is nutritious and **easy to digest**.' (R8) 'Goat's milk is a common ingredient here, and its taste is distinct and beneficial. Our traditional tea made with goat's milk is appreciated for its **natural taste and is said to cure multiple diseases**.' (R7)
Healthy, Traditional, Nutrition, Organic	'Our daily food includes roti and vegetables, often made with bajra. Special festival foods include churma, lentils, and lapsi, which are **nutritious and provide balanced energy**.' (R5)
Living, Preventative Health	'We enjoy **traditional foods** such as khadi and a special dish called lapsi during festivals, made from wheat grain, sugar, and ghee. Kadhi dal is also preferred. These dishes are **wholesome and provide essential nutrients**.' (R7) 'Our traditional diet includes dal, khadi, roti, and vegetables. Pulses such as moth, moong, and gram lentils are common, while bajra (millet) is a staple in winter, often made into soft, ghee-coated roti. Almonds are also part of our fiber- and healthy fat-rich diet.' (R10)
Physical Health, Longevity, Active Lifestyle	'Regular **physical activity** in the form of movement with livestock is key to our good health, allowing us to work easily even at an old age. Some of our community members live up to a hundred years while maintaining an **active lifestyle**. This shows the importance of staying active for longevity.' (R6)
Traditional Practices	'Our traditional cooking involves using clay utensils, which is believed to **preserve the nutrients** in the food and contribute to better health.' (R6) 'We have unique cultural practices, such as searching for edible berries and making tea from leaves in the jungle. These practices **connect us to nature**.' (R8)

traditional cooking methods and utensils, such as clay pots, helps preserve the nutritional value of food, ensuring that meals are both healthy and flavorful (R6). Non-bovine milk, such as goat and camel milk, is noted for its health benefits (R6, R8, R7, R9), including better digestion and the prevention and management of diseases like diabetes (R8). For some, continuing their diet's tradition is linked with their belief and pride in their generational inheritance (Singh & Tiwari, 2014). In contrast, others believe that this diet sources them what is required to carry out their labor-intensive profession of rearing livestock.

For wellness tourism, this pastoral wellness experience can offer tourists a detoxifying effect, introducing them to healthier ways of living during their vacation, especially considering the increase in adulterated food and unhealthy lifestyles (Farhud, 2015). Consuming these traditional foods can provide a nutrient-dense diet that supports overall health while at the same time understanding the tradition, thereby fostering a connection. This exposure to traditional diets during vacation can trigger exposure and adoption of better living practices that prevent health complications.

In addition to a healthy diet, physical activity is a cornerstone of the pastoral lifestyle, contributing significantly to the health and longevity of community members (R6). Daily activities such as herding livestock provide consistent, moderate exercise that improves physical fitness. It also provides a sense of accomplishment and connection to nature, commonly appreciated by tourists who prefer wellness experiences (Liu *et al.*, 2023).

5.4.2.2 Sub-dimension 2: Traditional healing

While one sub-dimension focuses on cultivating a healthier lifestyle through food intake and creating healthier living scenarios proactively, the second sub-dimension related to the body concerns treating illness through traditional healing practices followed by pastoral community members. Table 5.4 captures the extracts from transcripts tagged 'Traditional Healing'.

It includes a unique skillset centered on knowledge of the human body and nature's medicinal properties. Although this is closely linked with medical tourism, due to its deep cultural heritage, it has the potential to be integrated into natural approaches to the wellness category. The effectiveness of such techniques is evident in the community's firm reliance on natural healing and minimal limited dependency on hospitals (R9). The traditional practices of using medicinal plants for preparing teas and drinks positively impact the body's immune system (R7, R11). Making herbal tea is rich in beneficial compounds and may provide nutrients and bioactive chemicals that help offset poor-quality diets (Poswal *et al.*, 2019). These remedies can help alleviate common ailments, boost immunity, and be a natural alternative to chemical-based treatments. Using locally sourced ingredients like turmeric for wounds,

Table 5.4 Extracts from transcripts tagged 'Traditional healing'

Tags	References
Herbal Medicine	'The Dewasi community has a unique tea-drinking tradition using leaves and herbs, which we claim have health benefits. These herbs are known for their **medicinal properties**.' (R7)
Traditional Healing, Indigenous	'A knowledgeable old doctor treats animals using a traditional approach that involves heating and cooling to cure diseases. **Home-made medicine**, passed down through generations, such as heating oil, is used for various ailments. This method reflects our deep understanding of natural healing.' (R1)
Knowledge, Natural Remedies	'We treat sick animals with Indigenous medicines and specific rituals using the neem tree. Neem's **natural properties** help us stay healthy and repel diseases.' (R5)
	'For problems like diseases from mosquitoes, we use neem leaves to make smoke that repels mosquitoes, offering a **natural and effective solution**.' (R6)
	'Our traditional healing methods are so strong that we usually **do not go to hospitals** in case of illness or injuries. The Raika community is known for its **reliance on natural healing**.' (R2)
	'We treat injuries and wounds using various methods, such as inserting needles for internal wounds, using antibiotics, and applying **homemade remedies** like turmeric for external injuries. These practices showcase our comprehensive knowledge of traditional healing.' (R7)
	'We use home remedies, such as splinting for broken bones and using **soil to stop bleeding**. Our community knows more than eighteen soil gradients that interact with the body, highlighting our **deep connection with nature**.' (R5)
	'We place importance on natural healing, **using turmeric and the leaves of English Bawaliya to treat wounds.** We believe in the power of **saliva for skin diseases, as seen in animals licking their injuries**, which reflects our understanding of natural processes.' (R6)
	'The Raika community relies on **ayurveda for health treatments** and has limited dependency on hospitals. We possess in-depth knowledge of traditional healing methods, ensuring our health through natural means.' (R9)
	'We still use Indigenous medicine, especially for animals. **Nettle leaves and burned kernel coal** are used for their medicinal purposes, showcasing our reliance on natural resources.' (R3)
	'For winter colds, we prepare a **drink from the leaves** of a specific plant found in the jungle. This **natural remedy** helps us stay healthy during the cold season.' (R11)
	'Indigenous practices, such as **using sand for breathing difficulties**, were common. These practices highlight our innovative use of natural resources for health.' (R4)

soil for bleeding, and neem for medicinal purposes showcases time-tested healing techniques rooted in a deep understanding of the ecosystem. Engaging with these practices not only enlightens tourists about the healing power of nature but also allows them to experience the benefits of natural ingredients while emphasizing the body's ability to recover with minimal external intervention.

5.4.3 Dimension 2: Mind

Mind-related wellness is an essential aspect of overall wellbeing. Travelling is generally known to enhance mental health (WTTC, 2020), but travelling specifically for wellness is a powerful method to improve

Table 5.5 Extracts from transcripts tagged 'Mind'

Tags	References
Adaptability, Emotional Wellbeing, Simplicity, Nature's Impact,	'We set up temporary camps during migration, with families living together in tents. The camps change locations regularly, teaching us to **adapt to the changing environment**. This has taught us many important life lessons, the biggest of all being that nature is the mightiest.' (R5) 'Our migration is flexible, and we adapt to the conditions of the land. If we find grass and water in a particular area, we stay there; if not, we move on. This flexibility keeps us **mentally resilient** and connected to nature.' (R11) 'Due to our movement, we are not attached to material things. Living with nature keeps us **emotionally burden-free**. Our surroundings cheer us up and make us **feel good**.' (R10)
Stress-free Living, Environmental Harmony, Mindfulness	'We lead stress-free and environmentally friendly lives. **Living close to nature** brings a **sense of peace** and simplicity.' (R8)
Stress Relief, Escape from Urban Life, Escape from Noise, Peaceful Environment	'Tourists often say they are tired of the stress of living in high-rise buildings in urban areas and miss contact with nature. They come to visit our areas and camp around because they **want to be with nature**.' (R12) 'Our camps are far from the city, **away from traffic, and hence very quiet**. This tranquility provides a **mental escape** from the noise and stress of city life.' (R2)

various aspects of a tourist's life. This includes mental and physical health and a sense of purpose and happiness (Li *et al.*, 2022). Wellness tourism can contribute to mental restoration by fostering a sense of peace, enhancing mental control, and promoting emotional balance (Liao *et al.*, 2023), alongside building mental resilience. Table 5.5 summarizes the extracts from transcripts tagged 'Mind'. In a society grappling with unhealthy lifestyles, declining birth rates, increasing mental health issues, and early-life health crises (Agrodimou, 2019), the pastoral lifestyle, characterized by its simplicity and close connection to nature, presents an ideal solution.

Tourists immersing themselves in nomadic lifestyles can build mental strength and resilience by adapting to new situations, learning to live with minimal resources, and appreciating the power of nature. The lack of attachment to material possessions and the simplicity of living close to nature contribute to emotional freedom and wellbeing (R8). This minimalist lifestyle can significantly reduce emotional burdens and foster a deep sense of peace and contentment, reducing stress and anxiety.

Additionally, the tranquility and peace found in pastoral camps (R2), far removed from the noise and stress of urban environments, provide a valuable mental escape and rejuvenation (R12), which aligns with the motivations of tourists on wellness vacations (Tiwari & Hashmi, 2022). Such experiences offer a break from the constant stimulation and demands of busy life, promoting mental health through restorative experiences. Tourists benefit from the serene environment and the slower pace of life, allowing for mental relaxation and ultimately supporting overall mental wellness.

5.4.4 Dimension 3: Spiritual health

Spirit-related wellness encompasses the development of a strong sense of self, enhancing relationships with others and the environment to improve one's sense of identity, self-satisfaction, love, respect, comfort, and inner balance (Bahmani *et al.*, 2021, as cited in Shahrabi & Ramezanloo, 2023). Indeed, spiritual wellbeing is a crucial factor contributing to positive health outcomes and overall quality of life (Bai & Lazenby, 2015).

The pastoral lifestyle, rich in traditions, spiritual practices, and a strong sense of community, plays a crucial role in spiritual wellness (Table 5.6: R5, R7). Celebrating festivals together fosters deep community bonds, creating a sense of belonging, and promoting cooperation, mutual support, and a collective spirit, all of which are essential for spiritual wellbeing. The various spiritual practices and rituals of pastoral communities emphasize a profound connection to the divine and the natural world. These rituals include seeking blessings for animals, using medicinal herbs in worship, and performing ceremonies to remove negative energy (R8), all integral to the community's spiritual life. Such practices underscore the community's belief in the power of spirituality to maintain health.

Additionally, these rituals connect individuals to their cultural heritage, fostering a sense of continuity with age-old traditions (R3). They provide space for reflection, healing, and spiritual growth, contributing to a profound inner peace. For tourists, participating in these rituals can offer a unique and enriching experience that enhances emotional health and belief

Table 5.6 Extracts from transcripts tagged 'Spiritual health'

Tags	References
Spiritual Unity and Oneness	'Our unique traditions, like the requirement of owning a camel for marriage and specific festivals like Diwali, **bring us together** and strengthen our community bonds.' (R5)
	'We gather and perform rituals to **seek blessings for our animals**, especially camels, fostering a deep spiritual connection.' (R5)
	'Our rituals involve walking to the river and taking care of animals. We celebrate our beliefs together with all family and community members, fostering a strong **spirit of oneness**.' (R2)
	'Despite not using money for services, we have a strong sense of **community bond and cooperation**, supporting each other and engaging in voluntary activities.' (R7)
Spiritual Healing, Herbal Worship, Negative Energy Removal, Mantra Recitation	'Our worship practices involve coconuts and specific leaves, especially for deities like Shiva, integrating **medicinal herbs** that are unique to our region.' (R6)
	'We perform rituals to remove negative energy, recite mantras, and use **turmeric and saliva for healing**, believing in the power of our spiritual practices.' (R8)
	'Our unique rituals include monthly gatherings and a two-day event during Poonam at a temple, where we **believe in a Baba** who understands **the soul of the Goddess and acts as a healer**.' (R8)
	'We seek healing from Bhopa; they perform **rituals to cure the sick and restore health**. This practice underscores our spiritual connection to health and wellbeing.' (R3)

systems and enriches their cultural understanding, thus adding depth to their wellness journey. For example, the birth of a camel is a joyful event for the Raika family. They use the first milk from the camel to prepare a local dessert called *Kheer*, which is sweet rice cooked in milk. This dish is initially offered to their gods and then consumed by the family – a tradition believed to impart the strength and vitality needed to care for their animals (Tripathi & Rajput, 2006).

5.4.5 Dimension 4: Environment

Environmental inspiration for tourists is multifaceted and influenced by various factors (Zheng *et al.*, 2022), thus making environment-related wellness equally complex. This dimension can provide tourists with experiences that bring them closer to nature, fostering a sense of appreciation for the natural world. When tourists engage with new environments, they often discover exciting options and experiences they were previously unaware of (Teng, 2021). This is particularly true for pastoral Indigenous communities. Table 5.7 captures that in extracts from transcripts tagged 'environment'.

As previously stated, the pastoral lifestyle is deeply intertwined with nature, as community members spend considerable time working in fields, migrating with livestock, and finding natural shelter (R3). For these communities, the connection to the environment is evident in every aspect of their lives. From constructing shelters using locally-sourced natural materials to fulfilling basic needs such as protection, a sense of belonging, and entertainment, their lifestyle is intricately linked to their natural surroundings.

Table 5.7 Extracts from transcripts tagged 'Environment'

Tags	References
Sustainable Construction, Eco-friendly Homes	'Our houses are constructed using **local materials** like grass and thatch for cooling in summer and warmth in winter. We use cow dung for the bottom fence.' (R7)
Nomadic Living, Resilience	'We **live in the jungle**, face **extreme weather conditions**, and make a living by lighting fires. Our nomadic lifestyle involves moving to areas with good grass.' (R9)
	'We work in the fields, **migrate for our livestock**, and walk long distances. We **stay in nature** whenever we find appropriate **natural shelter** and eat whatever is found around us, keeping us close to nature.' (R3)
Animal–Human Bond, Connection	'Families go together, led by elders, maintaining a **connection with their animals**.' (R10)
Fresh Environment, Open-Sky Living, Green Hills	'Tourists can live with us among our green hills and small huts. Our environment makes us **feel fresh every day**, especially in the monsoon when this place becomes completely green and heavenly.' (R2)
	'During migration, we camp in areas with minimal wind and good conditions. We tie camels, make bread, and **sleep under the open sky**, finding suitable places each day.' (R10)

Their knowledge of the properties and benefits of naturally-sourced materials, along with their sustainable utilization methods, is remarkable. For example, the use of grass and thatch in construction provides natural insulation, keeping homes cool in the summer and warm in the winter. Additionally, cow dung is used for fencing (R7), a practice generally adopted in rural parts of the country.

5.5 Conclusion

This study examines the opportunity to develop pastoral-based wellness tourism in India. It also focuses on integrating pastoralists' distinctive lifestyles and traditional knowledge systems, which are essential for developing wellness tourism. The research also evaluates the potential of this unique offering to enhance the wellness tourism experience, thereby improving tourists' overall satisfaction and wellbeing.

Breaking down the aspects of pastoral life into the dimensions identified by Dillette *et al.* (2020), the study reveals clear linkages between pastoral life and wellness tourism, making it an auspicious wellness offering. Pastoral wellness tourism offers a unique opportunity to promote physical health through organic living and traditional diets. The pastoral communities' reliance on chemical-free food production, nutrient-rich diets, and the consumption of non-bovine milk, which has noted health benefits, provides tourists with alternative, healthy dietary options. Additionally, the active lifestyle of pastoralists offers tourists a chance to engage in physical fitness in a natural setting. Pastoral communities' traditional healing practices enhance physical health and offer a cultural and educational experience, enriching the tourists' understanding of natural healing. Tourists can experience a peaceful escape from the urban hustle, promoting mental relaxation and stress relief. Confirming the findings of Sheldon (2020), this study points out that participating in community rituals and spiritual practices offers tourists a profound sense of connection and inner peace. Also, pastoral communities' sustainable living practices and eco-friendly construction methods offer tourists a model of harmony with nature (Belliggiano *et al.*, 2021). Due to the reduction in pasture lands, many previously nomadic communities have transitioned to semi-nomadic and transhumance lifestyles. Tourism can be leveraged as a developmental tool to support the livelihoods of these transitioning communities, particularly by creating wellness tourism experiences centered around their way of life.

These wellness tourism experiences immerse visitors in pristine environments with minimal pollution, offer access to natural water sources and to sustainable agricultural practices, reducing exposure to harmful chemicals and occupational hazards. This connection to nature promotes physical wellbeing through the consumption of organic foods and participation in the physical activities inherent to the pastoral lifestyle, fostering a holistic approach to wellness.

Additionally, the findings of the study stress that the social environment in pastoral communities, characterized by strong family bonds and communal support, positively influences lifestyle choices, promoting active living (Nnko *et al.*, 2021). Thus, pastoral wellness offers a holistic approach that encompasses both health and a favorable environment. It provides tourists with an authentic, health-enhancing experience that aligns with high-level wellness principles, creating a balanced environment conducive to overall wellbeing. More importantly, developing pastoral-related wellness tourism can diversify and democratize the wellness sector, shifting from a luxury-oriented activity to a nature-centric experience accessible to all segments of tourists.

Beyond the value of pastoral wellness to wellness tourism, it increases awareness and appreciation of the pastoral lifestyle and its products, such as non-bovine milk and artisanal byproducts. This can drive higher market demand and better prices, helping mitigate one of the biggest challenges that pastoralists face. However, achieving this synergy requires government support, particularly in positioning pastoral wellness tourism as a community empowerment strategy. The tourism industry must also adopt an approach to pastoral wellness tourism that enhances tourists' wellbeing, supports the pastoralists' wellbeing, and preserves the destination environment. This will prevent potential negative impacts on the community and the environment.

This study reveals that pastoral wellness tourism offers a holistic approach to wellbeing, encompassing physical, mental, spiritual, and environmental health. The traditional practices, organic diets, natural healing methods, and serene environments of pastoral communities provide an authentic and enriching wellness experience that meets the contemporary demands of tourists seeking holistic health and rejuvenation. These findings suggest significant opportunities for developing and promoting pastoral wellness tourism by highlighting the unique attributes and benefits of pastoral wellness as a distinct and valuable segment of the wellness tourism industry. Further research could explore the potential of 'nutraceutical tourism' in India, explicitly leveraging the nutritional aspects of non-bovine milk and tourism for the sustainable advancement of local communities.

Funding Statement

The study was conducted based upon data collected for a Research Project funded by the Ministry of Tourism, Government of India.

References

Acorn Tourism Consulting Limited (2024, November 13) The European market potential for agritourism. [Acorn Tourism Consulting Limited on behalf of the CBI; cbi.eu.] https://www.cbi.eu/market-information/tourism/agritourism/market-potential.

Agrodimou, A. (2019) Wellness tourism: Through the lens of millennials' attitude: An exploratory qualitative study. Master's thesis, Jonkoping University.

Bahmani, A., Motaghi, S. and Aslani, F. (2021) Investigating the role of spiritual orientation on tourists' morale with the mediating role of spiritual wellbeing. *International Journal of Tourism, Culture & Spirituality* 5 (1), 37–57. https://doi.org/10.22133/ijts.2021.297371.1071.

Bai, M. and Lazenby, M. (2015) A systematic review of associations between spiritual wellbeing and quality of life at the scale and factor levels in studies among patients with cancer. *Journal of Palliative Medicine* 18 (3), 286–298. https://doi.org/10.1089/jpm.2014.0189.

Balthazar, C.F., Pimentel, T.C., Ferrão, L.L., Almada, C.N., Santillo, A., Albenzio, M., Mollakhalili, N., Mortazavian, A.M., Nascimento, J.S., Silva, M.C., Freitas, M.Q., Sant'Ana, A.S., Granato, D. and Cruz, A.G. (2017) Sheep milk: Physicochemical characteristics and relevance for functional food development. *Comprehensive Reviews in Food Science and Food Safety* 16 (2), 247–262. https://doi.org/10.1111/1541-4337.12250.

Belliggiano, A., Bindi, L. and Ievoli, C. (2021) Walking along the sheeptrack… rural tourism, ecomuseums, and bio-cultural heritage. *Sustainability* 13 (16), 8870.

Bo kus, D., Vento, E., Tammi, T., Komppula, R. and Kolesnikova, N. (2023) Comparing the motivations behind wellness tourism in three source markets. *European Journal of Tourism Research* 33, 3303. https://doi.org/10.54055/ejtr.v33i.2786.

Center for Pastoralism (2024) Milk matters: Enhancing returns from pastoral milk. Center for Pastoralism. https://centreforpastoralism.org/milk-matters-enhancing-returns-from-pastoral-milk/.

Chaiwallah (2013) Camel milk chai: A desert delight. *Chai Wallahs of India*, 17 November. http://chaiwallahsofindia.com/2013/11/camel-milk-chai-desert-delight/.

Conrad, F.G. and Schober, M.F. (1999) Conversational interviewing and data quality. *Federal Committee on Statistical Methodology Conference*. https://nces.ed.gov/FCSM/pdf/V_B_Conrad2_FCSM1999.pdf.

Dale, C.-L. (2021) Rajasthan – The land of camels and eco-tourism dreams. *Aspect County*, 12 April. https://www.aspect-county.co.uk/articles/leisure-travel/rajasthan-the-land-of-camels-and- eco-tourism-dreams.

Degen A.A. (2007) Sheep and goat milk in pastoral societies. *Small Ruminant Research* 68 (1–2), 7–19. https://doi.org/10.1016/j.smallrumres.2006.09.020.

Dillette, A.K., Douglas, A.C. and A., Carey (2020) Dimensions of holistic wellness as a result of international wellness tourism experiences. *Current Issues in Tourism*. https://doi.org/10.1080/13683500.2020.1746247.

Dimelu, M.U., Salifu, D.E., Enwelu, A.I. and Igbokwe, E.M. (2017) Challenges of herdsmen–farmers conflict in livestock production in Nigeria: Experience of pastoralists in Kogi State, Nigeria. *African Journal of Agricultural Research* 12 (8), 642–650.

Dunn, H.L. (1959) What high-level wellness means. *Canadian Journal of Public Health/Revue Canadienne de Santé Publique* 50 (11), 447–457. http://www.jstor.org/stable/41981469.

Dyson-Hudson, R. and Dyson-Hudson, N. (1980) Nomadic pastoralism. *Annual Review of Anthropology* 9, 15–61. http://www.jstor.org/stable/2155728.

Farhud D.D. (2015) Impact of lifestyle on health. *Iranian Journal of Public Health* 44 (11), 1442–1444.

Forlani, F., Dini, M. and Pencarelli, T. (2022) The importance of food and beverages in wellness experiences: A cross-continental analysis of tourists' perceptions. *British Food Journal* 124 (13), 520–540.

Gammoh, S., Alu'datt, M.H., Tranchant, C.C., Al-U'datt, D.G., Alhamad, M.N., Rababah, T., Kubow, S., Haddadin, M.S.Y., Ammari, Z., Maghaydah, S. and Banat, H. (2020, July). Modification of the functional and bioactive properties of camel milk casein and whey proteins by ultrasonication and fermentation with Lactobacillus delbrueckii subsp. lactis. *LWT*, 129. https://doi.org/10.1016/j.lwt.2020.109501.

Gan, T., Zheng, J., Li, W., Li, J. and Shen, J. (2023) Health and wellness tourists' motivation and behavior intention: The role of perceived value. *International Journal of Environmental Research and Public Health* 20 (5), 4339.

Global Wellness Institute (2024) What is Wellness? Wellness Tourism. *Global Wellness Institute*. https://globalwellnessinstitute.org/what-is-wellness/what-is-wellness-tourism/.

Grand View Research (2024) *Wellness Tourism Market Size & Trends Analysis Report, 2030*. Grand View Research. https://www.grandviewresearch.com/industry-analysis/wellness-tourism-market.

He, M., Liu, B. and Li, Y. (2023) Tourist inspiration: How the wellness tourism experience inspires tourist engagement. *Journal of Hospitality & Tourism Research* 47 (7), 1115–1135.

IUCN (2024) Mobile Indigenous peoples and biodiversity conservation [online]. International Union for Conservation of Nature. https://portals.iucn.org/library/sites/library/files/resrecfiles/WCC_2008_RES_53_EN.pdf.

Jafa, N. (2021, November 29) Camel tourism in recreated heritage homestay DevShree Deograh – Rajasthan [online]. https://navinajafa.wordpress.com/2021/11/29/camel-tourism-in-recreated-herit age-homestay-devshree-deograh-rajasthan/.

Kessler, D., Lee, J.H. and Whittingham, N. (2020) The wellness tourist motivation scale: A new statistical tool for measuring wellness tourist motivation. *International Journal of Spa and Wellness* 3 (1), 24–39.

Köhler-Rollefson, I. (2024) More cheese please. https://www.canva.com/design/DAEFHWYSkiU/w4Po9XCKCLvNXgme0EtTrg/view?website#2:more-cheese-please.

Köhler-Rollefson, I. and Kishore, K . (2021, September 7) *Pastoralism in India: Rangeland, Not Wasteland*. Heinrich Böll Stiftung. https://eu.boell.org/en/2021/09/07/pastoralism-india-rangeland-not-wasteland.

Li, S., Li, Y., Wang, W., Jiao, J., Degen, A.A., Zhang, T., Bai, Y., Zhao, J., Kreuzer, M. and Shang, Z. (2023) Dietary habits of pastoralists on the Tibetan plateau are influenced by remoteness and economic status. *Food Research International* 174, 113627.

Liao, C., Zuo, Y., Xu, S., Law, R. and Zhang, M. (2023) Dimensions of the health benefits of wellness tourism: A review. *Frontiers in Psychology* 13, 1071578.

Lim, Y.J., Kim, H.K. and Lee, T.J. (2015) Visitor motivational factors and level of satisfaction in wellness tourism: Comparison between first-time visitors and repeat visitors. *Asia Pacific Journal of Tourism Research* 21 (2), 137–156. https://doi.org/10.1080/10941665.2015.1029952.

Liu, L., Zhou, Y., and Sun, X. (2023) The impact of the wellness tourism experience on tourist wellbeing: The mediating role of tourist satisfaction. *Sustainability* 15 (3), 1872.

Mansingka, S. (2016) Stay at Tashigang, a village in the clouds. *Times of India*, 13 July. https://timesofindia.indiatimes.com/travel/things-to-do/stay-at-tashigang-a-village-in-the-clouds/articleshow/53192610.cms.

Memsahib in India (2021) The Raika journey – Immersive tourism supporting the camel herders of Rajasthan. *Memsahib in India*, 14 November. https://memsahibinindia.com/2021/11/14/the-raika-journey-immersive-tourism-supportin g-the-camel-herders-of-rajasthan/.

Nayik, G.A., Jagdale, Y.D., Gaikwad, S.A., Devkatte, A.N., Dar, A.H., Dezmirean, D.S., Bobis, O., Ranjha, M.M.A.N., Ansari, M.J., Hemeg, H.A. and Alotaibi, S.S. (2021) Recent insights into processing approaches and potential health benefits of goat milk and its products: A review. *Frontiers in Nutrition* 8, 789117. https://doi.org/10.3389/fnut.2021.789117.

Nnko, H.J., Gwakisa, P.S., Ngonyoka, A. and Estes, A. (2021) Climate change and variability perceptions and adaptations of pastoralists' communities in the Maasai Steppe, Tanzania. *Journal of Arid Environments* 185, 104337.

Park, Y.W. and Haenlein, G.F.W. (eds) (2006) *Handbook of Milk of Non-Bovine Mammals*. Wiley.

Patel, C. (2023) Getting up close and personal with India's camel-herding Raika people of Rajasthan. *The National*, 9 March. https://www.thenationalnews.com/travel/2023/03/09/getting-up-close-and-personal-with-indias-camel-herding-raika-people-of-rajasthan/.

Poswal, F.S., Russell, G., Mackonochie, M., MacLennan, E., Adukwu, E.C. and Rolfe, V. (2019) Herbal teas and their health benefits: A scoping review. *Plant Foods for Human Nutrition* 74, 266–276.

Rahman, P. (2023) Rajasthan: India counts its livestock, but not the people who herd them. *Indiaspend*, 20 February. Retrieved July 7, 2024, from https://www.indiaspend.com/data-gaps/rajasthan-india-counts-its-livestock-but-not-the-pe ople-who-herd-them-853578.

Reading, R.P., Bedunah, D. and Amgalanbaatar, S. (2010) Conserving Mongolia's grasslands, with challenges, opportunities, and lessons for North America's Great Plains. *Great Plains Research: A Journal of Natural and Social Sciences* 20 (Spring), 85–107.

Rowe, M. (2023) Pastoralism under threat. *Geographica* (3 January 2023). https://geographical.co.uk/wildlife/pastoralism-under-threat.

Secretariat of the Convention on Biological Diversity (2010) *Pastoralism, Nature Conservation and Development: A Good Practice Guide.* CBD. https://www.cbd.int/development/doc/cbd-good-practice-guide-pastoralism-booklet-web-en.pdf.

Shahrabi Farahani, M. and Ramezanloo, M. (2023) The role of wellness tourism in tourist's spiritual health (case study: Baghestan Recreation and Tourism Village). *International Journal of Tourism, Culture and Spirituality* 6 (2), 97–122.

Sharifian, A., Fernández-Llamazares, Á., Wario, H.T., Molnár, Z. and Cabeza, M. (2022) Dynamics of pastoral traditional ecological knowledge: A global state-of-the-art review. *Ecology and Society* 27 (1), article 14.

Sharma, V.P., Köhler-Rollefson, I. and Morton, J. (2003) *Scoping Study on Pastoralism in India.* Centre for Management in Agriculture, Indian Institute of Management and League of Pastoral Peoples.

Sheldon, P.J. (2020) Designing tourism experiences for inner transformation. *Annals of Tourism Research* 83, 102935.

Siddiqui, S.A., Salman, S.H.M., Redha, A.A., Zannou, O., Chabi, I.B., Oussou, K.F., Bhowmik, S., Nirmal, N.P. and Maqsood, S. (2023) Physicochemical and nutritional properties of different non-bovine milk and dairy products: A review. *International Dairy Journal* 148, 105790.

Singh, A. and Tiwari, R. (2014) Sustainable rural development through tourism practices: A case study of Ranakpur, Rajasthan. *Pacific Business Review International* 7 (5), 30–35.

Singh, R. (2023, February 3) Waves of change: Emerging pastoral advocacy and representation in India. *PASTRES*, 3 February. https://pastres.org/2023/02/03/waves-of-change-emerging-pastoral-advocacy-and-represe ntation-in-india/.

Siripurapu, K.K. and Iyengar, S. (2022) *Biocultural Diversity and Culture Animals of Mobile Pastoralism.* WASSAN Publication https://www.wassan.org/wp-content/uploads/2022/03/WASSANPublication_KannaSiripurapuandSushmaIyengar_25022022.pdf.

Smith, M. and Puczkó, L. (2015) More than a special interest: Defining and determining the demand for health tourism. *Tourism Recreation Research* 40 (2), 205–219.

Sultana, K.S. (2022) *India's Biggest Rural Media Platform.* Gaon Connection. https://en.gaonconnection.com/our-environment/camels-rajasthan-crisis-tourism-jaisalmer-desert-sodhan-village-bikaner-border-security-force-safari-livelihood-ustra-vikas-yojana/.

Teng, H.Y. (2021) Can film tourism experience enhance tourist behavioural intentions? The role of tourist's environmental engagement. *Current Issues in Tourism* 24 (18), 2588–2601.

Tengli, M.B., Meena, B.S., Paul, P. and Onte, S. (2019) Dairy tourism, a new facet of dairy entrepreneurship: Visitor perception. *Indian Journal of Dairy Science* 72 (3), 347–351.

The Tribune (2024) 'Mystic Village', run by Gaddi community in Chamba, gets Responsible Tourism award. *The Tribune*, 25 February (India). https://www.tribuneindia.com/news/himachal/mystic-village-run-by-gaddi-community-in-chamba-gets-responsible-tourism-award-594703.

Tiwari, R. and Hashmi, H. (2022) Integrating concepts of destination image, travel motivations, expectation, and future behavior to create a model of wellness travel intentions. *International Journal of Spa and Wellness* 5 (2), 185–206. https://doi.org/10.1080/24721735.2022.2057714.

Tran, Q. (2021) Wellness travel motivation post COVID-19 case: Vietnam. Bachelor's thesis, Lapland University of Applied Sciences.

Trendium (2023) Wellness tourism's next wave: Indigenous travel. *Global Wellness Summit*, 11 April. https://www.globalwellnesssummit.com/blog/wellness-tourisms-next-wave-Indigenous-travel/.

Tripathi, H. and Rajput, D.S. (2006) Customs and beliefs of Raika pastoralists of Rajasthan associated with camel husbandry. *Indian Journal of Traditional Knowledge* 5 (2), 284–286. https://nopr.niscpr.res.in/handle/123456789/6854.

Tsakalidou, E. and Papadimitriou, K. (eds) (2016) *Non-Bovine Milk and Milk Products*. Elsevier Science.

United Nations (2024) *Indigenous Peoples, Indigenous Voices: Fact Sheet. Who Are Indigenous Peoples?* United Nations. https://www.un.org/esa/socdev/unpfii/documents/5session_factsheet1.pdf.

Vadher, R., Gawai, K.M., Singh, B.P., Sarkar, P. and Hati, S. (2025) Production, characterization and biofunctionalities of bioactive peptides from non-bovine species of milk: A review. *Indian Journal of Animal Health* 64 (1), 1–20. https://doi.org/10.36062/ijah.2024.04024.

Visit Norway (2024) Experience the Sami culture in Norway. Visit Norway. https://www.visitnorway.com/typically-norwegian/sami-people/.

World Bank (2023) Indigenous peoples overview [online]. https://www.worldbank.org/en/topic/Indigenouspeoples.

WTTC (2020) 9 reasons travel is good for your mental health. *World Travel & Tourism Council hub,* 2 November. https://travelhub.wttc.org/blog/9-reasons-travel-is-good-for-your-mental-health

Zheng, K., Kumar, J., Kunasekaran, P. and Valeri, M. (2022) Role of smart technology use behaviour in enhancing tourist revisit intention: The theory of planned behaviour perspective. *European Journal of Innovation Management* 27 (3), 872–893.

6 Exploring New Trends in Health Diets in Wellness Tourism: An Investigation of the Key Attributes of the Chinese Wellness Tourist

Yuchen Ti, Timothy J. Lee and Jing Zhuo

6.1 Introduction

Global wellness tourism market size grew 8% annually from 2017 to 2019 reaching $720 billion. However, it then took a major hit with the market shrinking by 39.5% to $436 billion. Subsequent to the Covid-19 epidemic, the sector is forecast to reach $1.2 trillion by 2027 (Global Wellness Institute, 2021). The annual growth rate projected for wellness tourism through 2025 is an impressive 21%, reflecting new traveler values relating to nature, sustainability and mental health, as well as a period of rapid recovery from pent-up demand during 2021 and 2022. With travelers seeking destinations, wellness tourism offers experiences promoting physical, mental and spiritual wellbeing. Against the background of a rapidly transforming global tourism industry, wellness tourism in China has emerged as a vibrant sector.

In the Chinese market, one important aspect of wellness tourism is the emphasis on health diets and food treatment associated with Chinese medical tourism, as nutrition plays a vital role in maintaining overall health based on the history of Chinese cuisine, healthy cooking methods, and the ingredients in Chinese medicine. This chapter emphasizes the integration of traditional Chinese medicine diets, Traditional Chinese Medicine (TCM) tourism and contemporary wellness practices. In China, medical tourism is noted in several cities, often in combination with dietary trends and demographic shifts (Zhang *et al.*, 2020). Also, the chapter introduces new products in the food business and shows how emerging trends in healthy diets foster the city destination of wellness tourism. Beyond food tasting, tourists also perceive new innovative wellness tourism products to be a means of getting closer to a destination's identity. Understanding the key attributes of wellness tourists – specifically their preferences for health diets – can therefore help destination marketers and wellness retreat operators design tailored experiences that cater to tourists' needs (Ding *et al.*, 2024).

6.2 The Demographic Issue of China's Aging Population

According to reports by the Chinese Government (*Government Work Report*, 2022), the statistics show that China's population aged 65 and above increased from 26.32 million to 200 million between 1953 and 2021, an increase from 4.4% to 14.2%. Historically, the degree of aging increased by 0.15% annually between 1990 and 2000, 0.18% between 2000 and 2010, and 0.46% between 2010 and 2020, indicating that the new pattern is a significant acceleration of aging. According to World Health Organization statistics, China currently has the largest elderly population in the world, projected to reach 402 million residents aged 60 and over by 2040, accounting for 28% of the total population (World Health Organization, 2017). It is estimated that in 2035 China's elderly population aged 65 and above will reach 327 million and, by 2050, it will reach 393 million, accounting for 21.8% and 26.2% of the world's elderly population, respectively. Finally, by 2050, the total elderly population will exceed 400 million. Among them, the population aged 80 and above will reach 94.48 million, accounting for 21.78% of the elderly population. In 2051, the population aged 65 and above in China will reach its peak at 437 million, approximately twice the number of children. (Work Report of National Administration of Traditional Chinese Medicine, 2011).

By 2070, the percentage of people over 60 years old in China is predicted to exceed Japan and the United States, and China will become an aging country. The increasingly large elderly population base will bring broad market prospects for middle-aged and elderly tourism (Zhang *et al.*, 2019). With the development of China's economy and the improvement of retirement benefits, this age group has begun to pay attention to their quality of life and the richness of their life in later years. They are eager to go out and experience a different life when they have money and leisure time. Health tourism is thus showing vigorous and continuous growth: the market prospects are very bright and health tourism is ushering in major development opportunities.

In addition, with the improvement in living standards and the change in consumption concepts, tourism has become an option for more middle-aged and elderly people who wish to pursue a healthy lifestyle and meet their spiritual and social needs. Statistics show that the average annual growth rate of China's elderly cultural tourism consumption reached 23% between 2016 and 2020. At year-end 2022, there were 280.04 million people aged 60 or above, accounting for 19.8% of China's total population. As this age group`s awareness of health priority continues to increase, in order to meet people's urgent needs for high-quality and healthy lifestyles, it is expected that, by 2050, health care and leisure industry participants will include up to 350 million people, and the consumption potential of the elderly population will grow to about 106 trillion yuan (Wang & Ren, 2024).

6.3 The Rise of Wellness Tourism in China

In recent years, the growth of wellness tourism in China has been driven by a combination of historical and cultural practices. Given contemporary trends, wellness tourism is expected to meet the needs of an increasingly diverse clientele. Although wellness tourism in China is still in its nascent stages, it has the potential to create new opportunities and enhance the overall competitiveness of China's tourism industry (Heung & Kucukusta, 2013). The country's rapid economic growth has led to a notable increase in the disposable income of the middle class, which has also enabled an increasing number of individuals to engage in wellness-oriented travel. The growth of wellness tourism has been driven by an increased awareness of health and wellness globally: this heightened health awareness and the leisure demands of different groups of consumers has rendered wellness tourism an increasingly appealing investment opportunity (He *et al.*, 2022). However, health tourism in China is in its fledgling period and will only gradually become the trend of the development of China's tourism industry in the future (Yu, 2019).

In the present era, wellness tourism has expanded by combining traditional practices with healthy diets, thereby attracting a diverse demographic of participants. Concurrently, reports of the Chinese government emphasize that expanding the silver economy is an important measure to actively develop care programs and better services for elderly people and to promote high-quality development that will benefit both the present and future. Consequently, there has been a corresponding rise in demand for wellness services that are tailored to the specific needs of older adults, incorporating specialized health diets, rehabilitation programs and leisure tourism. Technological advances and modern work practices have brought in lifestyle changes coupled with drastic changes in eating habits and food items. Presently, the abundant availability of fast food and other unhealthy options has given rise to various lifestyle disorders like diabetes, hypertension, obesity, etc., among the younger generations (Pagaldiviti & Dash, 2023). It would appear that a health and diet-focused approach is becoming a necessity within the field of wellness tourism (Lee *et al.*, 2024).

Diet-focused wellness tourism in China has also been propelled by socioeconomic, demographic, and cultural transformations. Traditionally, wellness has been a pivotal element of Chinese culture, exemplified by enduring practices such as food therapy, tai chi (yin–yang imbalance), Qigong and acupuncture, which are integral to everyday life (Shen *et al.*, 2010). Additionally, TCM plays a significant role in food therapy and the treatment field (Yau *et al.*, 2023). It contains a variety of health, healing and longevity therapies that have evolved over thousands of years, forming a complex medical system. Liu *et al.* (2016) conducted a study that mentioned various kinds of bioactive peptides that have been identified from TCM and which are related to their traditional known efficacy, especially the protein-rich versions. The practice of food therapy includes TCM soups and bottled herbal drinks, which have developed in many places in China (Yau *et al.*, 2023). TCM offers accumulated wisdom and experience and inspiration for contemporary medical and pharmacological research, as well as advancing integrative healthcare for future generations (Cooper *et al.*, 2015; Marshall, 2020).

Thus, consumers can derive both therapeutic benefits and happiness of travel from TCM tourism experiences; and tourists' happiness has a positive effect on memorable tourism experience and revisit intentions (Peng *et al.*, 2023). Food, culture, and TCM knowledge can combine to give tourists an unforgettable travel experience. Some researchers have introduced destinations with TCM museums, hot-spring resorts, and National Mountain Park and Chinese medicine plant parks (Peng *et al.*, 2023; Xie *et al.*, 2022). In TCM tourism, this also reflects a cultural lifestyle and way of living with a harmonious environment (such as the relationship between spirit, emotion, energy and heaven) that can collectively lead to health issues being solved (Wen *et al.*, 2021).

The findings of Zhong *et al.* (2023) reveal that the trend in health tourism development can be industrialized, diversified, and systematic under the guidance of recent policies. Furthermore, the Chinese government's preferential policies and substantial investment supporting wellness tourism have played a pivotal role in its growth (Li *et al.*, 2024). The impact of global wellness trends has also been considerable, which has positively influenced Chinese consumer preferences and stimulated a growing interest in wellness-based tourism (Lan *et al.*, 2022). The synergies of economic progress, demographic change, government support, and global influence will continue to drive a boom in wellness tourism. As wellness tourism continues to flourish, it will likely adapt to meet the unique demands of an aging population, reinforcing TCM's role as a vital component in the pursuit of health and wellness in contemporary China.

6.3.1 Key attributes of Chinese wellness tourists

Hofstede's (1984) cultural dimensions model identified several core dimensions, which included Individualism/Collectivism, Masculinity/ Femininity, Long-term/Short-term Orientation, and Indulgence/Restraint. These dimensions could be instrumental in measuring how tourists in different age ranges demonstrate their preference in wellness tourism. It has been demonstrated that wellness tourists display considerable diversity. The current market for health and wellness tourism is primarily comprised of individuals belonging to the older age group, those with suboptimal health and those suffering from illness, as well as those seeking to enhance their quality of life (Erfurt-Cooper & Cooper, 2009; Yu, 2019).

It has been demonstrated that wellness tourists display considerable diversity in their age ranges. There is increasing participation from millennials to elderly people, which illustrates the extensive appeal of wellness tourism across generations (Yoo *et al.*, 2018). Furthermore, there is a great prevalence of female tourists participating in wellness tourism, driven by personal health aspirations and social influences (Torres *et al.*, 2014). For example, for the young generation and for children, programs focus on sightseeing and cultural experience in destinations like the herb garden or national park; for women, experience programs focus on beauty and health-care practices such as water therapy of hot springs and detoxification (Peng *et al.*, 2023).

From the economic perspective, the profile of the wellness tourist varies considerably. However, older tourists are more likely to be satisfied with entertainment experiences than younger tourists are (Liu *et al.*, 2023). Also, those people with greater financial resources are often drawn to high-end wellness retreats offering exclusive experiences, whereas the growing middle class views wellness tourism as a viable form of low-cost self-care and health management (McGroarty, 2020).

Chinese tourists who engage in wellness tourism demonstrate a pronounced commitment to health and wellbeing. They expect to seek out travel experiences that align closely with their lifestyle choices and dietary requirements. Such tourists tend to display a discerning preference regarding their travel choices. They invariably prefer destinations that offer both relaxation, cultural immersion, and tangible health benefits. The popularity of personalized wellness programs, which often blend traditional Chinese medicinal practices with modern wellness approaches, also significantly influences their travel decisions (Plog, 2001).

6.3.2 Research on wellness tourism destinations

Research on wellness tourism destinations focuses on the attitudes of local residents (Han *et al.*, 2017), and the planning of health space and the evaluation of destination suitability (Kim *et al.*, 2019). In terms of local residents' attitudes, a comprehensive perception of self-reference value, group reference value and destination development value brought by residents after the development of health tourism will affect residents' tourism participation behavior significantly and positively (Kim *et al.*, 2019). It has also been noted that previous knowledge of wellness tourism can induce a positive emotional experience of local residents, and further promote the supportive behavior of residents on the basis of value perception (Chen *et al.*, 2022). As the 'master' of tourist destination resources, community residents should be the direct beneficiaries of voluntary development and utilization (Han *et al.*, 2017). In the practice of health tourism, local residents' right to know, right to participate, right to manage and right to supervise should be protected in order to realize the sharing of tourism development results.

Wellness tourism is an activity for tourists to release pressure and undergo self-cultivation in the ecological health space. Therefore, the planning and design of health tourism destinations and landscape construction play a key role in the tourist experience. In the development and planning process of health tourism destinations, the ecological, health, recuperation and other elements are integrated into the landscape design, emphasizing functional zoning, and paying attention to diet design, to help tourists realize physical and mental recovery (Lee *et al.*, 2020). On the basis of paying attention to the design of tourists' vision and taste, tourists are encouraged to realize the experience of physical and mental recovery by guiding them to participate in farming experience, traditional food production, chatting and communication. By integrating rural culture and local conditions into health tourism activities, we can build a 'slow tourism' scene experience away from the hustle and bustle of the city and build a restorative environmental space to help tourists achieve physical and mental health.

According to the statistics, the top five Chinese medicine tourism items that respondents in the aged group chose are massage therapy (42.7%), Chinese medicinal diet therapy (39.6%), acupuncture therapy (32.7%), cupping therapy (31.5%) and Taijiquan (30.2%) (Wang *et al.*, 2021). Wellness tourism destinations in China are exemplified by a number of renowned retreats that effectively combine traditional Chinese elements with contemporary wellness practices. These retreats provide not only a tranquil environment but also a holistic approach to a healthy diet, which appeals to both domestic and international tourists (Sarah *et al.*, 2017). This chapter presents some research-based dimensions of the healthy diet in the context of Chinese culture. Figure 6.1 illustrates the research dimensions of a healthy diet.

6.3.3 Dietary trends in wellness tourism

As Chinese wellness tourists are seeking destinations that cater to their specific healthy diet preferences, the impact of dietary trends is becoming stronger. The growing interest in plant-based diets among

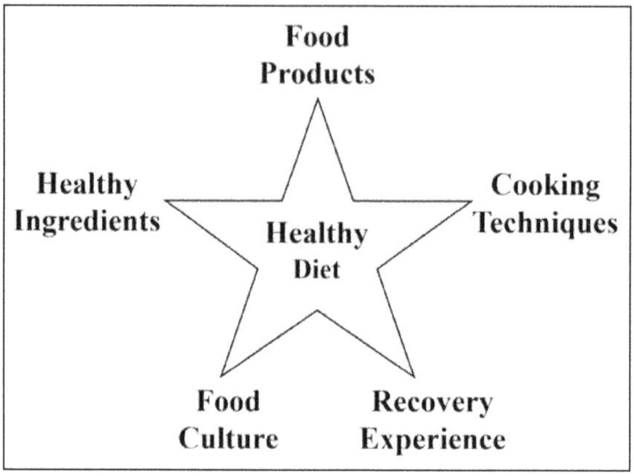

Figure 6.1 The research dimensions of a healthy diet
Source: The authors, 2024.

Chinese wellness tourists reflects a wider trend in healthy diet. More wellness retreats are incorporating vegetarian and vegan options into their health programs. A substantial body of scientific evidence indicates that individuals who adhere to a vegetarian diet are less likely to develop chronic diseases, including but not limited to obesity, cardiovascular disease, cancer and type 2 diabetes, compared to those who do not follow a vegetarian diet (Kim *et al.*, 2017). This shift meets the dietary requirements of a diverse clientele while also resonating with their ethical and health-conscious values.

Furthermore, there is an inclination towards organic and locally sourced foods, driven by concerns for food safety and environmental sustainability (Ballute & Berger, 2014). In response to these concerns, wellness retreats are emphasizing the use of fresh, organic ingredients to increase the appeal of their tapping into the desire for a clean diet. In addition, the integration of traditional Chinese foods and medicinal herbs into healthy diets is becoming more common, with those elements being valued for their health benefits and deep cultural significance (Marshall, 2020). Such practices not only enhance the quality of the wellness experience but also situate it within the broader context of Chinese culinary heritage. The integration of organic agritourism and rural tourism into organic agriculture and a non-toxic and healthy environment enables tourists to disengage from the stress and chaos of urban life, experience a peaceful and idyllic rural lifestyle, and satisfy the requirements of a healthy and tranquil existence (Xue & Shen, 2022). Moreover, there is a growing interest in *functional* foods, which are fortified with nutrients that provide additional health benefits (Weng & Chen, 1996). In response to this demand, wellness retreats are increasingly incorporating these foods into their meal offerings, with the aim of catering to health-conscious tourists who seek tangible health improvements through their dietary choices.

This growing emphasis on healthy eating has led to the development of a range of specialized wellness tourism experiences. Nowadays the concept of cleansing and rejuvenating the body system is gaining attractiveness and being spread through the press, social media, magazines, books and celebrities' stories (Khalil, 2017). Detox diets, which emphasize cleansing diets and nutritional programs, have become a popular choice among tourists seeking to reset their health and wellbeing. Furthermore, numerous wellness centers provide workshops and educational programs on nutrition, thus assisting tourists in making informed dietary choices. The provision of personalized dietary plans to address specific health requirements and personal preferences has become a standard feature of wellness tourism. The intricate interaction between dietary preferences and wellness diet service reveals a dynamic landscape for wellness tourism, where wellness and healthy diet converge seamlessly.

6.3.4 The integration of traditional Chinese medicine and healthy diet practices

The combination of traditional Chinese medicine (TCM) with contemporary healthy diet practices in wellness tourism represents a pivotal trend in China's rapidly expanding wellness tourism diet. Traditional Chinese medicine is a system of medicine that originated in ancient China and is based on the principles of achieving balance and harmony within the body, which includes a variety of practices, including acupuncture, herbal medicine and Qigong. These methods are renowned for their holistic approach to health, addressing the physical, mental and spiritual dimensions of wellbeing simultaneously (Marshall, 2020). TCM has been demonstrated to be efficacious in the rehabilitation of abnormal physical problems induced by chronic drug use. These benefits include improvements in immune function, an increase in working memory, and a reduction in the risk of developing neurological disorders (Kim & Hyun, 2024; Xiao & Tao, 2017).

In contemporary wellness contexts, the integration of TCM and healthy diet represents a significant draw for wellness destinations, attracting tourists who are keen to engage with a synthesis of traditional and modern health practices. A medicated diet is delicious food made under TCM theories, with nutritional and Chinese cooking technologies guidance, and with great color, aroma and taste (Weng & Chen, 1996). A significant number of wellness programs incorporate TCM foods and herbal treatments, offering guests the opportunity to experience traditional remedies that address contemporary health concerns. This synthesis serves to enhance the therapeutic experience, while also enriching the culture of wellness offerings.

6.3.5 Chinese medicinal diet in wellness tourism

A medicinal diet is a good way to combine medical food and nutrition. It combines Chinese medicine and Chinese food, and medicine and food treatment, which is able to not only cure diseases but also to enhance immunity. From the perspective of function, medicinal diets can be divided into health care, prevention, rehabilitation, and treatment, respectively for different market groups, among which health care and prevention are most suitable for combining local characteristics of medicinal materials and agricultural products for promotion (Wang *et al.*, 2021). For example, the tourism products surrounding the Chengde Mountain Resort (a large complex of imperial palaces) integrate elements of Chinese royal history to create unique culinary experiences (Chengde Travel Guide, 2024). With the developing and promoting the concept of seasonal Chinese medicinal diet, regional rural tourism practices the combination of seasonal TCM as the food ingredients and diet which emphasizing the different season for eating different ingredients healthily.

6.3.6 Religious meditation and retirement

In recent years, the Chinese people have begun to pay greater attention to external health influencers (environmental quality), but also to the pursuit of inner clarity and self-cultivation, and meditation culture is popular. Many destinations have built meditation houses to attract tourists. In cooperation with domestically famous religious meditation places such as Qiandao Lake, high-end living products with Taoism, Buddhism and Chinese classics as their core have been developed to meet the needs of the elderly to enhance their spiritual beliefs (Zhang *et al.*, 2019).

6.3.6.1 Case Study 1: Chengdu, Sichuan Province, China

Six Senses Qing Cheng Mountain retreat, situated in Chengdu, is an exemplary case of a healthy diet-based wellness tourism destination. This retreat is distinguished by its harmonious integration of TCM with contemporary healthy diet practices. Tourists have the opportunity to engage in treatments that incorporate acupuncture, herbal remedies and tai chi, which fulfill the objective of achieving a state of harmonious integration between body and mind. Also, the retreat is renowned for its luxurious accommodation and comprehensive wellness programs, which include traditional Chinese therapies, yoga and meditation.

The dining options of the destination are based on a farm-to-table principle, which demonstrates a focus on organic and seasonal ingredients. A diet comprising organic produce contains lower levels of pesticide residues than a diet based on conventional produce (Henderson, 2009). Consequently, consuming a diet comprising organic produce reduces human exposure to pesticides (Forman *et al.*, 2012). This approach aligns with the principles of sustainable and health-conscious dining. The restaurant on the premises offers a menu comprising a plethora of organic, locally sourced ingredients, catering to a multitude of dietary requirements, which offers a diverse guest food products experience (He *et al.*, 2019). Furthermore, a range of comprehensive treatments, including massage therapy and detox programs, is available, thereby ensuring a comprehensive wellness experience. In addition, the retreat enhances its wellness offerings with cultural experiences, including traditional Chinese tea ceremonies and cultural workshops, which allow guests to gain a deeper understanding of China's rich health culture (Rousta & Jamshidi, 2020).

With a focus on both physical and mental wellbeing, the personalized diet plans are meticulously crafted to meet individual health needs (Boniface, 2003). The cuisine at the retreat is aligned with healthy diet trends, featuring dishes that are health conscious and incorporate traditional Chinese medicinal foods (Pai *et al.*, 2024; Richards, 2021). This case study demonstrates how wellness retreats in China respond to global wellness tourism trends, combining traditional practices with healthy diet requirements and preferences.

6.3.6.2 Case study 2: Chengde, Hebei Province, China

There are 670 categories of Chinese Traditional Medicine resources in Chengde, and more than 20 other kinds of precious Chinese medicinal materials. There are 54 TCM planting demonstration parks covering more than 6400 hectares in total. There are 27 TCM production and management enterprises in the city and the total assets of these enterprises are 900 million Chinese yuan ($126 million). At this stage, the development of the TCM industry in Chengde is based on the cultivation of Chinese medicinal materials and a secondary industry based on the production of proprietary Chinese medicine. The wellness tourism industry based on TCM is still in the initial stage of 'flower tour' and 'ticket tour' but is expected to diversify in the future (CRI Online, 2023). Chengde integrates TCM elements into tour packages such as medicinal bath, aromatherapy, scraping and massage, as the vanguard of TCM tourism in Chengde (Yan, 2021).

Taking the medicinal bath as an example of adding Chinese medicine ingredients into hot springs, using the spring to promote blood circulation and metabolism, the volatile oil, alkaloids, glycosides and other substances in Chinese medicine directly act on the human body and improve the curative effect. In response to the common modern diseases, the development of several general-purpose medicine bath kits, suitable for different groups of people (Gong *et al.*, 2020) is being pursued. Chinese dehumidifying drugs, such as *kudzu* powder, parsnips and so forth, are selected for rheumatism and arthralgia (Yan, 2021). Cold dampness can be added to warm heat to dispel cold medications. Thus, depending on the needs of the consumer and its chemical composition, a spring can provide different treatments and services to the tourists.

At present, the traditional Chinese medicines planted on a large scale in Chengde mainly include *Scutellaria* and *Bai shu* (*Atractylodes macrocephala*), and the wellness benefit mainly relies on the existing TCM plantations as sightseeing. This fully develops and utilizes the added value of existing TCM to different products of tourism.

Utilizing the concepts of spring flower viewing, summer heat, autumn picking, winter health, combined with Chengde authentic medicinal materials, health tourism in the Chinese solar calendar reflects Chinese culture. For example, the experience of picking plants for Chinese herbal medicine, and healthy cooking using herbal medicine processing procedures, produces activities designed to meet the consumers' desire to return to the countryside. In plantation tourism, popular pastoral elements are introduced to form a Chinese herbal medicine industrial park integrating sightseeing, popular science experience and sales. For example, Scutellaria makes medicinal tea, and deer antlers can make Chinese medicinal wine. The wellness industry can also make peripheral products such as perfume bags with a disease prevention effect, according to the season, and promote them for different groups of customers (Yan, 2021).

6.4 New Practices of Chinese Medicine in Bakery and Beverage

A rising trend across China is for new baking products that incorporate ingredients from Chinese medicine. This is favored by many young people as well as by elder age groups. A bakery shop selling TCM health toast in Beijing named SENSE TOAST (Figure 6.2) adds a number of health ingredients from Chinese medicine, such as ginseng and lily, which taste good and are suitable for summer consumption.

Zhongjing Life, a brand of Zhang Zhongjing Pharmacy in Zhengzhou, was established in 2021 and has successively launched a series

Figure 6.2 Toast bread from SENSE TOAST bakery

Source: SENSE TOAST official website (2024).

of health products, including pastries, snacks, milk tea, cakes, drinks, bread and so on. Since 2023, it has gradually focused on the model of health bread with health tea, and its products such as wormwood sausage bread have also become popular on social media. This shop also innovates with the new trends in bakery with vegan, low-fat, high-protein and zero-sugar products, such as wolfberry soymilk taro bread, Chia seed cheese bread, barley zero-sugar bread, and black wolfberry chestnut bread. Zhongjing Life has also launched a cost-effective breakfast set, a fiber meat floss mushroom bread, and a yam oatmeal milkshake, at only 9.9 Chinese yuan ($1.4) to promote their products. At present, this brand has opened eight stores in Zhengzhou and Nanyang. Beijing Tongrentang (Figure 6.3) has also launched a batch of traditional Chinese medicine bread and herbal beverages, such as wolfberry pulp croissants, Tangerine peel cinnamon apple crisp, among other products, also selling wolfberry latte, monk fruit American cafe, tangerine peel latte and other herbal coffees.

The first affiliated hospital of Tianjin University of Chinese Medicine has also opened a Chinese medicine and food workshop focusing on European health buns. The main products are wheat moistened toast, *ejiao* soft European bun, Astragalus health package, lotus leaf heat relief package, Angelica monk fruit toast as well as other health food series. Hangzhou Fang Huichun Hall store, on the other hand, has a 'four Qi five taste, medicine and food boundless inspiration bakery'. Unlike the above two stores that have significant connections to TCM hospitals and pharmacies, this store opened in a scenic spot. And Muly Coffee shop is

Figure 6.3 Beijing Tongrentang bakery and coffee shop
Source: Author photograph, 2024.

Figure 6.4 Muly Coffee shop

Source: Muly Coffee official website, reproduced with the permission of the store owner.

in the tourist area of Tianjin Five Avenues (Figure 6.4). It has collaborated with the Tianjin TCM brand 'Darentang' to launch TCM coffee, attracting many tourists to the shop to enjoy the Chinese medical coffee beverage.

6.5 Conclusion

The growth of wellness tourism in China reflects a global phenomenon that shows how the importance of health is becoming increasingly evident. The growth and positioning of wellness tourism in China is nowadays indicative of a complex interplay between cultural heritage, economic growth and health awareness. China is positioned to assume a prominent role in the global wellness tourism market. In this context, dietary choices in wellness tourism are significant in the development of wellness tourism.

As Chinese tourists become increasingly health conscious, they are seeking experiences that align with their dietary preferences and wellness objectives. The incorporation of traditional Chinese medicine into contemporary healthy diet practices serves to enhance the wellness tourism experience, offering a distinctive combination of ancient wisdom and modern health trends. Moreover, the incorporation of dietary innovations and personalized health regimens reflects the evolving preferences of Chinese and international tourists alike. An awareness of these trends and characteristics will enable those responsible for the management of wellness tourism destinations, government officials, and restaurateurs to better cater to the evolving needs and preferences of Chinese wellness tourists. By prioritizing aspects such as value, food quality and service, stakeholders can enhance the appeal and efficacy of wellness tourism in China and beyond. As the aging process in China becomes an increasing issue, so people's demands for a better life are increasing, and they are looking to tourism activities to meet their physical and psychological needs. Driven by both tourism and health, the health tourism market has been developing rapidly in recent the years after COVID-19, and health tourism is playing an increasingly important role.

This study has identified a number of important points for health tourism. Firstly, there is a need to enrich the research scope of health tourism. Health tourism has expanded from initial niche markets such as hot-spring tourism and forest tourism to incorporate TCM tourism and medical tourism, and the research scope of wellness tourism is constantly expanding. Follow-up studies should expand the research boundaries of health tourism and enrich the research content of wellness tourism, which has extremely important significance for wellness tourism research.

Secondly, research should focus on the integration of wellness tourism with other industries. Tourism has a natural coupling with many other industries, and it is more necessary to promote the integration and development of wellness tourism and other industries in the future, so that wellness tourism can penetrate various industries and consumer fields. At the same time, the empowerment of science and technology and culture has an important impact on the subject, object, and media of tourism. Through a rich wealth of evidence, health tourism is displayed in various forms, providing impetus for the development of health tourism. Similarly, when solving problems in other industries, wellness tourism can provide ideas from the perspective of tourism and inject tourism ideas and wisdom into it to better provide solutions to practical problems (Pai *et al.*, 2024).

Thirdly, further research on TCM tourism and medical tourism should be undertaken. The unique and strong culture of TCM gives China unique advantages. Scholars of medicine, tourism and other fields can conduct comprehensive research on TCM health tourism from different perspectives to promote the city through tourism. The theoretical basis, research perspectives, policies, laws and regulations relating to medical tourism need to be further improved. In the future, researchers should focus on how to effectively resolve the contradictions among tourists, destinations, and Indigenous peoples, to promote the reasonable allocation and sustainable and healthy development of destination wellness tourism resources and to create more high-quality and healthy tourism products.

References

Ballute, A.K. and Berger, P.D. (2014) The perceptions of and motivations for purchase of organic and local foods. *Journal of Contemporary Issues in Business Research* 3 (1), 1–18.

Boniface, P. (2003) *Tasting Tourism: Travelling for Food and Drink*. Ashgate Publishing Limited: Aldershot.

Chen, H.L., Zhang, M., Dong, F.Y. and Lai, S.C. (2022) Health tourism research in multiple perspectives: A review and perspectives. *Resource Development & Market* 38 (7). https://doi.org/10.3969/j.issn.1005-8141.2022.07.012.

Chengde Travel Guide (2024) Adventure & Tour China. Available online at https://www.adventuretourchina.com/destination/chengde/ (accessed on 16 July 2025).

Cooper, M., Vafadari, K. and Hieda, M. (2015) *Current Trends and Emerging Issues in Medical Tourism*. IGI Press.

Ding, X., Ma, X.X., Meng, P.F., Yue, J.Y., Li, L.P. and Xu, L.R. (2024) Potential effects of Traditional Chinese Medicine in anti-aging and aging-related diseases: Current evidence and perspectives. *Clinical Interventions in Aging* 19, 681–693

Erfurt-Cooper, P. and Cooper, M. (2009) *Health and Wellness Tourism: Spas and Hot Springs*. Channel View Press.

Forman, J., Silverstein, J., Committee on Nutrition, Council on Environmental Health, American Academy of Pediatrics (2012) Organic foods: Health and environmental advantages and disadvantages. *Pediatrics* 130 (5), e1406–e1415.

Global Wellness Institute (2021) The global wellness economy: Looking beyond COVID – individual sectors. https://www.globalwellnessinstitute.org.

Gong, X., Chen, N.H., Ren, K., Jia, J.Y., Wei, K.H. and Li, M.H. (2020) The fruits of *Siraitia grosvenorii*: A review of a Chinese food-medicine. *Frontiers in Pharmacology* 10, 1400.

Government Work Report (2022) Available online at http://www.gov.cn/zhuanti/2022lhzfgzbg/index.htm (accessed on 9 November 2024).

Han, J., Lee, T.J. and Ryu, K. (2017) The promotion of health tourism products for domestic tourists. *International Journal of Tourism Research* 20 (2), 137–146. https://doi.org/10.1002/jtr.2161.

He, M., Liu, B. and Li, Y. (2022) Recovery experience of wellness tourism and place attachment: Insights from feelings-as-information theory. *International Journal of Contemporary Hospitality Management* 34 (8), 2934–2952.

He, S.M., Li, J., Hu, J.Y., Chen, Q.L. and Shu, W.Q. (2015) Effectiveness of Traditional Chinese Medicine (TCM) treatments on the cognitive functioning of elderly persons with mild cognitive impairment associated with white matter lesions. *Shanghai Archives of Psychiatry* 27 (5), 289.

Henderson, J.C. (2009) Food tourism reviewed. *British Food Journal* 111 (4), 317–326. https://doi.org/10.1108/00070700910951470.

Heung, V.C. and Kucukusta, D. (2013) Wellness tourism in China: Resources, development and marketing. *International Journal of Tourism Research* 15 (4), 346–359.

Hofstede, G. (1984) *Culture's Consequences: International Differences in Work-Related Values*. Sage.

Khalil, M.T. (2017) Impact of a detox diet paradigm in weight management. *Izzivi Prihodnosti* 2, 237–55.

Kim, H.L. and Hyun, S.S. (2024) Paradoxical effects of tourism ethnocentrism on domestic tourism: The moderating effect of pandemic anxiety travel. *International Journal of Tourism Research* 26(1), e2628. https://doi.org/10.1002/jtr.2628.
Kim, K., Lee, T.J. And Ryu, K. (2017) Alternative healthy food choice for tourists: Developing Buddhist temple cuisine. *International Journal of Tourism Research* 20 (3), 267–276. https://doi.org/10.1002/jtr.2162.
Kim, S., Um, S. and Lee, T.J. (2019) Healing effects from the on-site experiences of tourists. *International Journal of Tourism Research* 22 (2), 192–201. https://doi.org/10.1002/jtr.2328.
Lan, D.Z., Li, L.D., Wei, H.B. and Zhou, S.K. (2022) A qualitative study on the demand of traditional Chinese medicine health tourism and its influencing factors for the elderly in northeast Sanya City. *Guangxi Medical Journal* 44, 15.
Lee, S., Lee, N., Lee, T.J. and Hyun, S.S. (2024) The influence of social support from intermediary organizations on innovativeness and subjective happiness in community-based tourism. *Journal of Sustainable Tourism* 32 (4), 795–817. https://doi.org/10.1080/09669582.2023.2175836.
Lee, T.J., Han, J.S. and Ko, T.G. (2020) Health-oriented tourists and sustainable domestic tourism. *Sustainability* 12 (12), 4988. https://doi.org/10.3390/su12124988.
Li, X., Hyun, S.S. and Kim, H. (2024) Perception of medical practitioners on the importance of medical tourism services. *International Journal of Tourism Research* 26 (1), e2617. https://doi.org/10.1002/jtr.2617.
Liu, L., Zhou, Y. and Sun, X. (2023) The impact of the wellness tourism experience on tourist wellbeing: The mediating role of tourist satisfaction. *Sustainability* 15 (3), 1872.
Liu, M., Wang, Y.P., Liu, Y.H. and Ruan, R. (2016) Bioactive peptides derived from traditional Chinese medicine and traditional Chinese food: A review. *Food Research International* 89 (Pt 1), 63–73.
Marshall, A.C. (2020) Traditional Chinese Medicine and clinical pharmacology. In F.J. Hock and M.R. Gralinski (eds) *Drug Discovery and Evaluation: Methods in Clinical Pharmacology* (2nd edn, pp. 455–482). Springer International.
McGroarty, B. (2020) *Resetting the World with Wellness: Human Connection in a Time of Physical Distancing*. Global Wellness Institute. https://globalwellnessinstitute.org/industry-research/resetting-the-world-with-wellness/.
Pagaldiviti, S.R. and Dash, A. (2023) Wellness tourism: Reviving healthy food and lifestyle. *International Journal of Positivity & Wellbeing* 1 (1), 53–61.
Pai, C.K., Chen, H., Lee, T.J., Hyun, S.S., Liu, Y. and Zheng, Y. (2024) The impacts of under-tourism and place attachment on residents' life satisfaction. *Journal of Vacation Marketing* 30 (4), 694–712. https://doi.org/10.1177/13567667231164807.
Peng, J.M., Yang, X.Y., Fu, S.H. and Huan, T.C. (2023) Exploring the influence of tourists' happiness on revisit intention in the context of Traditional Chinese Medicine cultural tourism. *Tourism Management* 94, 104647.
Plog, S. (2001) Why destination areas rise and fall in popularity: An update of a Cornell Quarterly Classic. *Cornell Hotel and Restaurant Administration Quarterly* 42 (3), 13–24.
Ren, Z.P. (2023) China Aging Research Report 2022. https://mp.weixin.qq.com/s/GMa3hOF66Ucaw9RteEdq3g.
Richards, G. (2021) Evolving research perspectives on food and gastronomic experiences in tourism. *International Journal of Contemporary Hospitality Management* 33 (3), 1037–1058.
Rousta, A. and Jamshidi, D. (2020) Food tourism value: Investigating the factors that influence tourists to revisit. *Journal of Vacation Marketing* 26 (1), 73–95.
Sarah, R., Labensky, H., Alan, M., Martel, P.A., Malley, F., Bevan, A. and Sicoli, S. (2017) *On Cooking: A Textbook of Culinary Fundamentals* (7th Canadian edn). Pearson Education.
Shen, C.Z., Pang, S.M.-C., Kwong, E.W.-Y. and Cheng, Z.Q. (2010) The effect of Chinese food therapy on community dwelling Chinese hypertensive patients with Yin-deficiency. *Journal of Clinical Nursing* 19 (7–8), 1008–1020.

Torres, E.N., Fu, X. and Lehto, X. (2014) Are there gender differences in what drives customer delight? *Tourism Review* 69 (4), 297–309.

Wang, Y. and Ren, G.Z. (2024) The latest trends and policy recommendations for my country's smart elderly care industry. *The International Institute of Green Finance of Central University of Finance and Economics*. https://iigf.cufe.edu.cn/info/1012/8709.htm.

Wang, Y.Q., Lv, D.K., Liu, Y. and Zhang, G.H. (2021) Research on the development mode and path of northeast and Beijing-Tianjin-Hebei residential health tourism under the background of global tourism. *Modern Management* 11 (1), 1–8. https://doi.org/10.12677/mm.2021.111001.

Wen, J., Wang, C.F. and Kozak, M.A. (2021) Post-COVID-19 Chinese domestic tourism market recovery: Potential influence of traditional Chinese medicine on tourist behaviour. *International Journal of Tourism and Hospitality Research* 32 (1), 121–125.

Weng, W. and Chen, J. (1996) The Eastern perspective on functional foods based on traditional Chinese medicine. *Nutrition Reviews* 54 (11), S11–S16.

Work Report of National Administration of Traditional Chinese Medicine. The Trend of Population Aging in China in the 21st Century. Available online at http://www.natcm.gov.cn/renjiaosi/gongzuodongtai/2018-03-24/1768.html (accessed on 16 July 2025).

World Health Organization. Ageing and Health in China (2017) Available online at https://www.who.int/china/health-topics/ageing (accessed on 16 July 2025).

Xiao, L.J. and Tao, R. (2017) Traditional Chinese Medicine (TCM) therapy. *Substance and Non-Substance Addiction* 1010, 261–280.

Xie, L.H., Guan, X.H., He, Y.X. and Huan, T.C. (2022) Wellness tourism: Customer-perceived value on customer engagement. *Tourism Review* 77 (3), 859–876.

Xue, L.L. and Shen, C.C. (2022) The sustainable development of organic agriculture: The role of wellness tourism and environmental restorative perception. *Agriculture* 12 (2), 197.

Yan, X. (2021) Development opportunities and strategies of TCM health tourism in Chengde after the epidemic. *Tourism Today* 19 (3), 67–69.

Yau, H.Y., Yeung, W.L., Yeung, K.Y.A. and Lee, Y.P. (2023) Complementary and alternative medicine: Consumers' experience with food therapy in Traditional Chinese Medicine in Hong Kong. *Alternative Therapies in Health and Medicine* 29 (5), 178–187.

Yoo, C.-K., Yoon, D. and Park, E. (2018) Tourist motivation: An integral approach to destination choices. *Tourism Review* 73 (2), 169–185. https://doi.org/10.1108/TR-04-2017-0085.

Yu, Z.P. (2019) Health and wellness tourism in China: Concept and development. *Journal of Landscape Research* 11 (6), 148–150.

Zhang, S.Q. and Li, J.C. (2021) An introduction to traditional Chinese medicine, including acupuncture. *The Anatomical Record* 304 (11), 2359–2364.

Zhang, Y., Lee, T.J. and Xiong, Y. (2019) From comrades to Bodhidharma: A Bourdieusian analysis of the spiritual experience of Chinese seasonal tourists. *International Journal of Tourism Research* 21 (6), 801–812. https://doi.org/10.1002/jtr.2306.

Zhang, Y., Lin, Z. and Lee, T.J. (2020) Wellness-oriented seasonal tourism migration: A field relationship study in China. *International Journal of Tourism Research* 23 (4), 491–503. https://doi.org/10.1002/jtr.2420.

Zhong, L., Sun, S., Law, R., Li, X. and Deng, B. (2023) Health tourism in China: A 40-year bibliometric analysis. *Tourism Review* 78 (1), 203–217.

Theme 2
Innovation and Technology in Wellness, Wellbeing and Tourism

7 Exploring Innovations in Tourism, Wellbeing and Sustainability through the Intersection of Neurosciences and Computing

Altair Sancho-Pivoto, Carla Fraga and Patrick Moratori

7.1 Introduction

Technological advancements that enable the proliferation of a new level of wellbeing-oriented experiences within the realm of tourism are pivotal at the dawn of the 21st century – a century that has already been marked by a pandemic caused by COVID-19, the SARS epidemic, and various other health-related problems, and that is grappling with the consequences of environmental imbalances such as climate change (Mody, 2023). This requires any scientific study or marketing endeavor committed to the ethical standards of living in the 21st century to delve deeply into sustainability and wellbeing (wellness), notably the Sustainable Development Goals (SDGs) and Agenda 2030 (United Nations, 2015).

It is our contention that the interface between neurosciences and computing holds the potential to yield insights into sustainability and wellbeing, both for planners and managers and, on an epistemological level, for advancing our understanding of the phenomenon in question. Firstly, grounded in the narrative literature, we address the theoretical and conceptual aspects stemming from the convergence of neuroscience and computing. For instance, in the big data context and from the affective computing (AC) view it is possible to extract human emotions at touristic spots by facial expressions in photos georeferenced using computer vision (Kang *et al.*, 2019).

Moreover, Sikora *et al.* (2018) researched soundscapes of an archeological site in Croatia and recreated with audio the medieval period using augmented reality (AR). Therefore, the interface between neurosciences and computing can improve innovations to align tourism, wellbeing and sustainability in the 21st century. Picard (2003: 61) emphasized: '... emotions, perhaps more so than thoughts, are ultimately personal and private'. Consequently, innovation requires us to discuss its ethical aspects. In this direction, recently, Gratch (2024) addressed this problem in a guest editorial on ethics in affective computing.

Secondly, the chapter employs two distinct research methods to expand upon existing knowledge: (1) a systematic review of the literature using Rayyan software to comprehensively gather and assess relevant studies; and (2) a detailed textual analysis using Iramuteq software (2020 version), to scrutinize text-based data. By integrating these approaches, the chapter navigates beyond traditional boundaries, offering new insights that challenge the established norms within the thematic area.

Finally, the chapter provides a framework that embraces several valuable technologies and tools (eye-tracking, electroencephalogram, facial coding, among others) for the development of studies concerning this subject matter, whether they be of a marketing or academic nature.

The chapter highlights that wellbeing is not merely a trend but a foundational lens through which the tourism of the 21st century must be envisioned. With interdisciplinary collaboration and ethical awareness, tourism can evolve into a platform for regenerative experiences that uplift individuals, communities, and ecosystems alike.

7.2 The Role of Neuroscience and Computing in Planning and Management Tourism

In the 21st century, the relationship between neurosciences and computing science has provided a new path to understanding the planning and management of tourism, including debates about wellbeing and development originating in sustainability statements such as the 17 sustainable development goals (SDGs; 'Transforming our world: The 2030 Agenda for Sustainable Development'; see United Nations, 2015). This is so with regard to ontological and epistemological perspectives, but it also happens *pari passu* as a result of demand from the tourism market. For instance, Scott (2020) explained that the new frontier of knowledge in tourism is the alliance of the social sciences and neurosciences. Hence, the joining of technologies and human dimensions has been a new paradigmatic step in the direction of transdisciplinary understanding. If the cognitive revolution was the condition that allowed homo sapiens to reach the present day (Harari, 2012), the new technologies involving neurosciences and computing look like a possible next level on humanity's timeline.

Before its recognition as a modern science in the early 20th century, our understanding of the brain's features was primarily derived from physics, biology and other related disciplines, as noted by Rooney (2018). Consequently, authorities such as Bear *et al.* (2017) advocate that neuroscience is inherently interdisciplinary. They categorize the field of neuroscience into five analytical dimensions: molecular, cellular, systemic, behavioral, and cognitive. Given this framework, addressing theoretical and practical challenges at the intersection of tourism and wellbeing, especially those compounded by sustainability issues, necessitates an in-depth exploration of both the behavioral and cognitive aspects.

Al-Nafjan *et al.* (2023: 3) show that the most widely employed modalities in neuromarketing are electroencephalography (EEG), eye-tracking (ET), galvanic skin response (GSR), facial electromyography (EMG), facial action coding (FAC) and heart rate (HR). Cardoso *et al.* (2024), when trying to demystify neurotourism (neurosciences and tourism) based on these, highlighted:

> an incongruity. On one hand, it arises from the fact that artificial intelligence does not qualify as a neuroscientific method, and on the other hand, the omission of neuroscience and neuromarketing prevents the holistic interdisciplinary nature of the neurotourism concept from emerging. (Cardoso *et al.*, 2024: 5)

While artificial intelligence (from the computing research field) is not part of neuroscientific methods *per se*, knowing more about computing and more about the connections among affective computing and the neurosciences, about the relationship between artificial and human intelligence, the role of virtual or/and augmented realities, and advances in robotics (among other perspectives) could be significant to advances in what can be studied in tourism, wellbeing and sustainability by each neuroscientific method. Table 7.1 shows the relationship between the neurosciences and computing technologies. The resolution (spatial and temporal) of each method provides a scenario that requires decisions on what can be studied. If the proposal is to understand the construct of 'emotion' by spatial resolution, fMRI (functional magnetic resonance imaging) is more useful than EEG. In contrast, if the goal is to study by temporal resolution, EEG would be recommended rather than fMRI. From an experimental approach, Moratori *et al.* have commented:

> create a ground-truth dataset for affective computing to facilitate in particular the application and development of computational intelligence and other automated reasoning techniques. Following a multi-disciplinary approach, we highlight the need for but also the challenge of creating such a dataset that provides validated mappings of physiological data to a series of affective states ['happy', 'neutral' and 'sad' in our case]. (Moratori, 2013: 128)

Table 7.1 Methods: Resolutions and constructs

Method	**Resolution**		**Construct**				
	Spatial	Temporal	Emotion	Attention	Memory	Arousal	Engagement
EEG (>32 channels)	Low	High	Yes	Yes	Yes	No	Yes
EEG (few channels)	Low	High	Yes	No	No	No	Yes
fMRI[(a)]	High	Low	Yes	Yes	Yes	No	Yes
TMS[(b)]	Low	High	Yes	No	No	No	No
Eye-tracking[(c)]	Low	High	No	Yes	No	Yes	Yes
Facial coding	Low	Low	Yes	No	No	No	No
Skin conductance	Low	Low	No	No	No	Yes	No
Wearable devices [(d)]	Low	Low	Yes	No	No	No	No
Electrophysiology[(e)]	High	High	Yes	Yes	Yes	No	Yes

Note: The method allows for the study of: (a) pricing, reward and pain; (b) cognition and executive functions; (c) response time, recognition and salient features; (d) location and movement; (e) pain, reward, willingness to pay, associative decision-making and unconscious processes. Adapted from Cerf (2017).

These researchers utilized neuro-methodologies such as GSR and HR to illustrate the complexity of conducting 'laboratory-style' experiments aimed at capturing emotional responses. In summary, effective planning and management of tourism in the 21st century using neuroscience methodologies requires a nuanced understanding of four critical aspects: (1) each neuroscience method yields distinct results; (2) the spatial and temporal resolutions of each method are tailored to specific research needs; (3) various phenomena, including emotions, attention, and engagement, can be analyzed using multiple methods (for example, comparing EEG and fMRI in measuring emotional responses); and (4) the selection of the experimental setting – whether within a controlled laboratory environment or in natural settings – significantly influences the control of variables and the outcomes of the research.

While tourism is traditionally viewed through the lens of consumer studies, the methodologies outlined in Table 7.1 extend beyond analyzing touristic consumer behavior to encompass a broader range of research objectives. The forthcoming section delves into how innovations in tourism and wellbeing, particularly those rooted in sustainable practices, are being shaped by neuroscientific approaches. Notably, the integration of neuroscience with computational fields such as affective computing is proving instrumental in forging paths toward innovation, as evidenced by seminal works like those of Cerf (2017), Picard (2003), Sikora *et al.* (2018), and Kang *et al.* (2019).

7.3 Looking for Innovation on Tourism and Wellbeing from Sustainable Perspectives

This chapter focuses on elucidating the interrelationships between the constructs 'tourism and wellbeing' and 'sustainability'. This analysis aims to unpack their theoretical and conceptual dynamics (see subsection 7.3.1). Additionally, the chapter utilizes the state-of-the-art methodology of factorial analysis of correspondence (FAC) to probe these themes. By employing a Cartesian plane and the hypergeometric law (Salviati, 2017), this analytical approach enables the identification of predominant research emphases within the field. Simultaneously, it highlights outlier studies that deviate from the norm, thereby challenging the existing status quo and expanding the field's boundaries.

7.3.1 Constructs

The form of tourism concerned with health, wellness and wellbeing is a broad concept and includes ideas around both curing ills and maintaining health (Erfurt-Cooper & Cooper, 2009). For example, health-related travel can include activities as diverse as spas, seawater treatments and pilgrimages to sacred sites for physical healing and spiritual cleaning as well as travel for medical or surgical interventions. The literature detailing the plethora of research studies undertaken in these areas has grown in importance in the tourism discourse over the last decade and, during this period, more holistic notions of wellbeing which emphasize emotional and psychological aspects would seem to be emerging as significant (Cooper *et al.*, 2015; Hartwell *et al.*, 2018).

Tourism has the potential to rejuvenate both the mind and the body, provide opportunities to acquire skills, improve self-esteem, and to increase awareness of nature, personal development, and identity formation. Therefore, tourist experiences capable of encompassing the perspective of health prevention/improvement and improving the quality of life have become central. The debate around this aspect has been amplified due to the COVID-19 pandemic. Some studies already point to emerging trends in the travel and tourism sector, such as the change in people's behavior regarding their preference for less crowded destinations, greater commitment to sustainability principles, and the capability of providing experiences more linked to wellbeing and health (Andreu *et al.*, 2021; Ximenes *et al.*, 2020). According to Andreu *et al.*:

> Wellness is related to health practices and can help recover traditional wellness methods and reduce the mental health epidemic. Wellness also plays a role in protecting natural and cultural assets, supporting environmental protection and promoting sustainable tourism. (Andreu *et al.*, 2021: 4)

A recent study conducted by Zhang *et al.* (2023) in China's Buddhist mountains, for example, identified spiritual values as transcendence, general connectedness, inner balance, positive life direction, and special religious feelings. They also explored the impact of these spiritual values on tourists' psychological wellbeing, and the results revealed that the more easily attained spiritual values (general connectedness, positive life direction and special religious feelings) had a greater influence on psychological wellbeing than the less easily attained spiritual values (transcendence and inner balance). Positive emotion and meaning, as components of psychological wellbeing, were strongly influenced by the three spiritual values (general connectedness, positive life direction, and special religious feelings), whereas engagement, accomplishment and relationships were influenced by fewer spiritual values.

Other studies have focused attention on the wellbeing perceived by local communities that host tourists. Ke *et al.* (2022) led a study that aimed to assess the benefits of mangrove forests in Malaysia and Indonesia and their impact on the subjective and psychological wellbeing of coastal communities, and also to understand the challenges that coastal communities face that limit sustainable wellbeing. Among the main benefits perceived are: (1) an emphasis on the advantages of living in natural countryside; (2) natural resources supporting employment, income and family security; and (3) an increase in subjective and psychological wellbeing. According to the authors, overall, the respondents felt happy because the combination of job security and leisure activities helps them feel content and satisfied. The analysis also suggests that the combination of exposure to coastal environments and stress reduction promotes good mental health. Consequently, the findings from this study imply that coastal mangrove forest management plays an important role in the living conditions of coastal communities and their subjective and psychological wellbeing.

In addition to being an innovative and challenging research theme, the relationship between tourism, wellbeing, and health has also influenced the positioning of destinations in the tourism market, which tends to invest in products and services linked to the promotion of health and wellbeing in a broad sense, focusing on psychological/mental health and the development of spirituality and self-awareness, through more holistic and transformative experiences (Guerra *et al.*, 2022) – for example, the Caldas da Cavaca thermal spa resort in Portugal. In this study, Guerra *et al.* highlight innovative practices within health and wellness tourism destinations that prioritize enhancing human wellbeing. The study advocates that the Caldas da Cavaca thermal spa resort distinguish itself as a pioneering wellness destination. It suggests that the resort could promote a healthy lifestyle through serene, nature-infused experiences that offer both relaxation and rejuvenation in a tranquil setting.

At the same time, studies like Wiltshier (2020) emphasize that, in addition to measuring the economic significance of this new segment in the tourism market, there is also the challenge of a better understanding of its implications in destination planning and organization, which includes minimizing generated impacts and promoting improvement in the quality of life and wellbeing of host communities, thus incorporating a multidimensional perspective of analysis.

7.3.2 State of the art

Advancing our understanding of how neuroscience and computing intersect with tourism and wellbeing is thus essential for grasping the potential for innovation in this field. Initial research, as documented in the Web of Science database for the year 2024, suggests that neuroscience is not yet a predominant topic within the broader research landscape (Table 7.2). However, with the rising recognition of emotional, cognitive and behavioral factors as critical elements in tourism studies – emphasized by Moyle *et al.* (2019) and Bastiaansen *et al.* (2019) – there is an evident need to explore this nexus further. Scott (2020) also underscores the importance of these aspects for advancing 21st-century tourism research. Subsequently, our investigation shifted to more

Table 7.2 Strings of research on the Web of Science database.

Web of Science (2024)	String	Result
First	'touris*' (topic) AND 'sustainable*' (topic) AND 'wellbeing* OR wellness* OR welfare*' (topic) AND 'neuro*' (topic).	$n = 0$
Second	'touris*' (topic) AND 'sustainable*' (topic) AND 'wellbeing* OR wellness* OR welfare*' (topic).	$n = 456$

Source: Prepared by authors from the Web of Science database (2024) on 20 March, 2024.

thoroughly defining the state-of-the-art, assessing how the integration of neuroscience and computing might drive innovative developments within the industry. Table 7.2 presents the outcomes of these research inquiries.

Following the initial results, filters for 'Article' and 'English language' were applied within the Web of Science (2024) database, narrowing the results to 347 abstracts. The authors then employed the artificial intelligence tool Rayyan (2024) for a systematic review, reading each abstract in a blinded review mode. This process led to disagreements in 174 cases. The discrepancies were meticulously analyzed and resolved based on specific inclusion and exclusion criteria that align with the constructs and objectives of the research. These criteria, and how they influenced the selection of abstracts, are detailed in Table 7.3.

As seen in Table 7.3, the second round of reviews achieved ($n = 96$) abstracts compatible with the thematic discourse. In this process, 251 abstracts were excluded. Thus, the textual corpus was formed by ($n = 96$)

Table 7.3 Criteria of inclusion and exclusion

Inclusion/Exclusion (*n*)	Criteria
Inclusion ($n = 96$)	(a) Relationship between tourism and wellbeing from the visitor's perspective: motivation for travel, perceptions, and outcomes of tourism experiences (b) Relationship between tourism and wellbeing from the perspective of host communities: perceptions and studies on the effects of tourism on local populations/communities
Exclusion ($n = 251$)	(a) Animal welfare; impacts of tourism in natural areas, focusing on wildlife habitats (b) Sustainability policies in various areas (health, agriculture, cities, among others) unrelated to the tourism phenomenon (c) Wellbeing in work environments, unrelated to tourism (d) Wellbeing as a result of various activities/practices, including tourism, without focusing on understanding the meanings/dimensions of wellbeing for local communities (e) Ecotourism, unrelated to the wellbeing of visitors or local communities (f) Studies focused on tourism impacts, destination management based on sustainability assumptions, where wellbeing is more of a broad and generic outcome of adopting sustainability principles than an actual research topic (g) Generic studies on sustainability, sustainable policies in destinations, SDGs, unrelated to wellbeing (h) Post-COVID studies, but unrelated to tourism and wellbeing (i) Sustainable certification of tourist destinations, eco-efficiency of destinations, climate effects and tourism (j) Ecosystem services unrelated to wellbeing

Source: The author (2024).

abstracts and has been corrected according to the instructions of Salviati (2017) and Iramuteq (2020), on how to use Iramuteq version 0.7 Alpha 2 software. Two main outputs are produced: (1) a factorial correspondence analysis (FCA), using the hypergeometric law (minimum frequency 10); (2) a similitude analysis, using graph theory, with adjustment of the minimum frequency of 20. Consideration of Figure 7.1 is an important step towards understanding the state-of-the-art thematic analysis.

Figure 7.1 shows the concentration of studies in all quarters. It proves that the relationships among these constructs (such as tourism, wellbeing, and sustainability) co-exist in the scientific literature and it comprises knowledge relevant to the planning and management of tourism challenges in the 21st century. However, some abstracts reveal a different perspective. Table 7.4 brings new scientific evidence to understanding the state-of-the-art of this theme from these different perspectives.

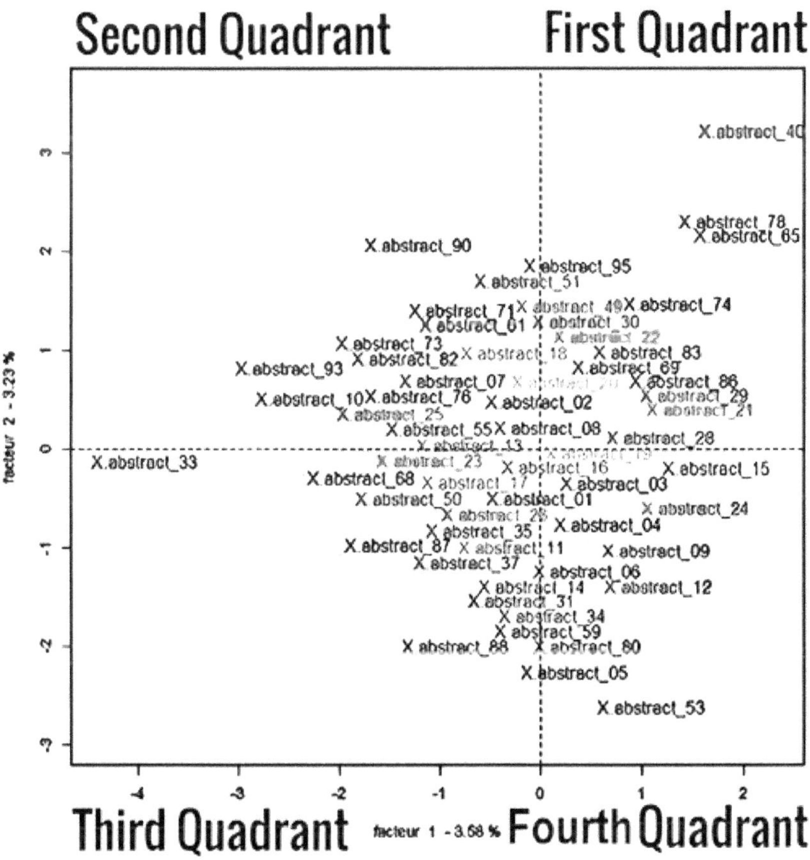

Figure 7.1 Factorial correspondence analysis (FCA)

Source: Prepared by the author (2024) using Iramuteq (2020) software.

Table 7.4 Breaking of the status quo

Quadrant	Abstracts	Breaking of the status quo
First	40, 65, 78	The relationship among adventure tourism, wellbeing and sustainability
Second	10, 90, 93	Wellbeing from an economic perspective
Third	33	Wellbeing and cultural tourism
Fourth	05 and 53	Factors affect the competitiveness of destination and their relations with satisfaction on tourism and behavior intent

Source: The author (2024).

The three studies in quadrant 1 (abstract_40, abstract_65, and abstract_78) address the theme of adventure tourism and its relationship with sustainability and wellbeing. The studies conducted by Valdivielso and Houge (2022) (abstract_40) and Farkić *et al.* (2020) (abstract_78) appear to stand out from the other studies in quadrant 1 by focusing on tourism service providers – in these cases, adventure tour guides. Valdivielso and Houge's (2022) research seeks to understand how climate change may have significant impacts on the wellbeing of guides. Meanwhile, Farkić *et al.*'s (2020) study aimed to investigate the role of adventure tour guides in facilitating the psychological wellbeing of tourists engaging in slow adventure experiences, such as kayaking and stargazing. These studies thus present an innovative proposal by suggesting a focus on the professionals responsible for providing tourism services, whose actions directly impact the quality of the experience and, consequently, promote visitors' feelings of wellbeing.

Conversely, the study by Hanna *et al.* (2019) explores whether outdoor adventure tourism can enhance one's connection with nature, potentially influencing wellbeing and fostering pro-environmental attitudes and behaviors. Through interviews with adventure tourism practitioners, this research demonstrates that activities aligned with sustainable tourism principles can significantly contribute to a deeper understanding of and engagement with sustainability; they also offer benefits for mental health and overall wellbeing. This study marks a shift from traditional approaches that focus primarily on the safety and motivations associated with adventure tourism: it acknowledges the broader impact of adventure tourism activities in cultivating wellbeing and fostering a more environmentally aware and responsible mindset among the participants.

In quadrant 2, the investigation led by Wang *et al.* (2023) (abstract_10) targets a rural area in China, examining the intersection of ecological wellbeing and the performance of rural recreation and tourism. While this study aligns with our research objectives, its data collection efforts veered slightly to explore the interplay between tourism, sustainability and wellbeing. Specifically, it assesses how economic factors like investment growth, industrial structure, and social development levels contribute to the synergy between and efficiency of ecological wellbeing and rural tourism. These factors are found to positively influence the overall effectiveness of the region's tourism and recreational activities.

Another study, conducted by Richardson *et al.* (2012) (abstract_90), deals with the impacts of wildlife conservation policies in Zambia on the wellbeing of families in game management areas (GMAs), which are the buffer zones around national parks. However, the focus of the research revolves around the economic gains of this activity, disregarding other dimensions of wellbeing. In the same vein, the work of Xie *et al.* (2010) (abstract_93) emphasizes the economic perspective, but focuses on measuring the economic values of forest ecosystem services in Beijing; therefore, it has a theme that diverges from the relationship between tourism, sustainability and wellbeing, i.e. the focus of the present investigation.

In quadrant 3, the study by Pu *et al.* (2022) (abstract_33) addresses the coupling and coordination relationship between cultural tourism (CT) and wellbeing, based on a methodology focused on constructing an index evaluation system for the levels of development of cultural tourism and wellbeing, which are divided into three stages of development – dysfunctional, transitional and coordinated – and 10 levels of coordination, including high-quality coordination.

In quadrant 4, the focus of Cha *et al.*'s (2024) work (abstract_05) was on medical tourism segments and associated motivations, which led to a proposal for market segmentation: the quality seeker, the essential services seeker and the rest seeker. Thus, the results of this study focus on strategies to reach individual markets in the medical tourism industry. On the other hand, the work of Zeng *et al.* (2021) (abstract_53) differs from the other works in the quadrant by focusing on the identification of factors affecting destination competitiveness and their relationships with tourist satisfaction and the behavioral intentions of tourists to return and recommend the location to others. Thus, the relationship between tourism, sustainability and wellbeing is not directly addressed in this study.

The analysis presents a rich but uneven landscape of research on tourism, sustainability and wellbeing. Quadrant 1 contributes the most human-centered and ethically reflective insights, while quadrants 2 and 4 illustrate the risks of economic reductionism and market-driven reasoning. Quadrant 3's attempt at measurement is valuable but needs to be balanced with contextual and interpretive approaches. Collectively, the studies affirm that wellbeing in tourism is multifaceted, encompassing providers, tourists, communities and environments. Future research should strive to integrate these dimensions more holistically, using mixed methods and intersectional frameworks that can accommodate both quantifiable metrics and nuanced narratives. There is also a clear need for ethical reflexivity, especially when dealing with emotional data, cultural practices and health-related travel.

7.3.3 The turning point: Leveraging tools from neuroscience and computing

This section outlines a strategic framework supported by neuroscience methodologies (see Table 7.1) for crafting new research initiatives, both in marketing and academia. It discusses how the factorial analysis of correspondence has illuminated frontier research areas within this field, highlighting emerging trends and gaps. To pivot effectively towards innovative breakthroughs that integrate neuroscience and computing, a deeper understanding of the existing knowledge base – the status quo of the theme – is essential. Such comprehensive insight is crucial for driving the development of pioneering studies that challenge conventional perspectives and open up new avenues of inquiry. Reflecting on the state-of-the-art findings, the second output (Figure 7.2) presents new evidence supporting the quest for innovation in tourism and wellbeing from sustainable perspectives.

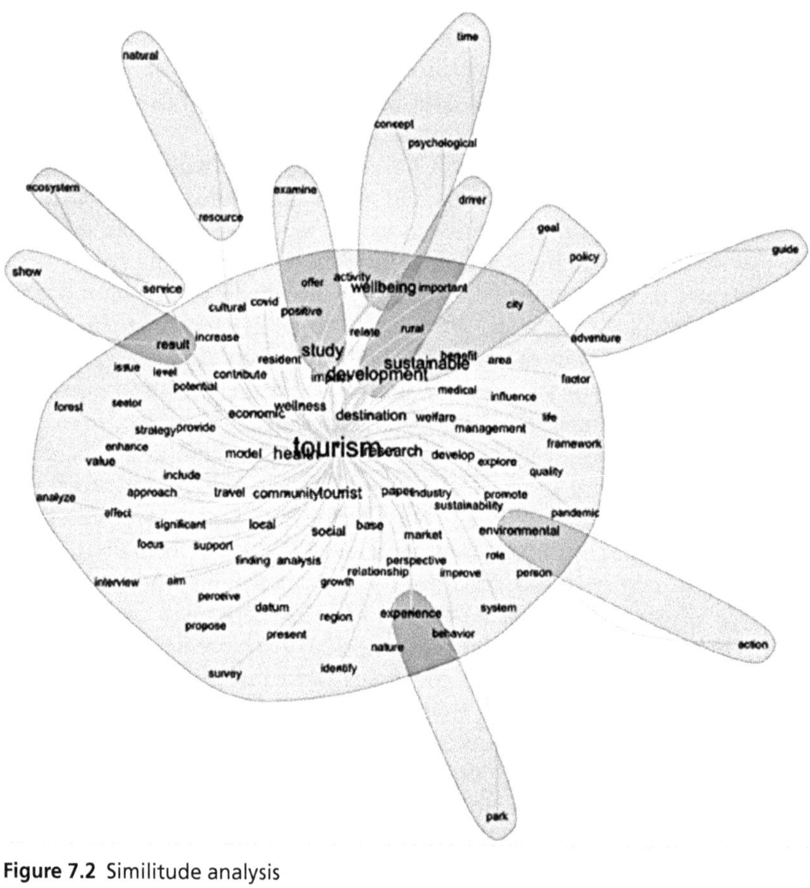

Figure 7.2 Similitude analysis

Source: Prepared by the author (2024) using Iramuteq (2020) software.

Table 7.5 Scientific evidence on the status quo of the thematic variables

Halos and sub-halos	Status quo perspectives
Central halo: Tourism	**Tourism** as a central halo provides several relationships, which include **wellness, welfare, sustainability, tourist, destination, community, model, strategy, health** among others
Sub-halo 1: Experience	The **experience** in the **park** is relevant to analysis
Sub-halo 2: Environment	The **action** at **environment** in order to achieve **sustainability** and **tourism** is a hot topic
Sub-halo 3: Adventure	**Guide and adventure** formed another dimension, including discussion as a factor
Sub-halo 4: Sustainable development	**Sustainable development** in tourism involves **benefit**, **city** and policy
Sub-halo 5: Rural	**Sustainable development** involves **the rural** dimension
Sub-halo 6: Wellbeing	The **psychological** dimension is relevant to understanding the relationship between **tourism** and **wellbeing**
Sub-halo 7: Study	The tourism **study includes offer** aspects and **positive** perspectives in the research context
Sub-halo 8: Natural resources	The **result** related to **natural resources from a** tourism perspective is an important topic. Additionally, it has a cultural aspect
Sub-halo 9: Service	The **service** relative to the **ecosystem** is another hot topic
Sub-halo 10: Results	**Tourism results** relate **to the potential** of **tourism**

Source: The author (2024).

This is achieved by showcasing the interconnectedness of key terms through graphical links (graphs) and clusters (halos). These visual representations effectively illustrate the prevailing themes and the current status quo within this field, providing a clear map for identifying areas ripe for innovative research and development. Based on graph theory (Salviati, 2017), Figure 7.2 shows the 11 word communities by halos and sub-halos (by colors), and these keywords are the substantive step to understanding the theme's status quo. Table 7.5 summarizes this discussion.

If the experience in the park is relevant to the analysis (Sub-halo 1: Experience) the scientific literature of sustainability delivered a study using EEG headbands to understand the emotional wellbeing of people in the urban wilderness. Herman *et al.* (2021) analyzed the assessing states of calmness and alertness considering the informal green spaces. The same analysis could be undertaken for formal green areas such as parks or gardens. Sub-halo 2 (Environment) highlights the action in the environment for sustainability and tourism. In this path, the mobile method is more appropriate to the research, because it allows us to investigate the 'action' from a body movement perspective. For instance, according to Cerf (2017: 77), wearable technologies can provide 'Location, movements as proxies for some emotions, which are ultimately non-neural'. An example would be research using smart watches.

Regarding Sub-halo 3 (Adventure), Figure 7.1 showed us that abstracts 40, 65, and 78 focused on the relationships between adventure tourism, wellbeing and sustainability. By contrast, in Figure 7.2 Sub-halo 3 demonstrated that the status quo of this field has a blurred zone, namely Adventure Tourism. The topic of sustainable development in tourism encompasses both urban benefits and policies (Sub-halo 4: Sustainable development), as well as rural dynamics (Sub-halo 5: Rural). Mobile methodologies such as EEG and eye-tracking, illustrated in Table 7.1, are crucial for studying tourism directly within its operational context.

Sub-halo 6 (Wellbeing) connects this field of study to innovative proposals at the intersection of neuroscience and computing. This sub-halo emphasizes the psychological dimensions crucial to understanding the nexus between tourism and wellbeing, demonstrating how neuroscientific methods can measure critical psychological constructs like emotions, attention and memory. Sub-halo 7 (Study) pertains to the analysis of offerings and their reception. Insights derived from neuroscience could revolutionize research into the decision-making processes in tourism, particularly from a sustainability standpoint. As global sustainability challenges such as Agenda 2030 and the SDGs highlight the scarcity of natural resources, so Sub-halo 8 (Natural resources) brings cultural considerations into the discourse on tourism and wellbeing. This segment underscores the potential of neuroscientific approaches to enhance our understanding of behavioral and cognitive aspects, which are pivotal in advancing 21st-century sustainability efforts. Finally, Sub-halo 9 focuses on the service aspect within the tourism and wellbeing sectors, and faces ecosystem challenges. Thus, neuroscience methods provide novel insights into consumer behavior, enriching our understanding of emotional, attentional and engagement patterns, as detailed in Table 7.1.

7.4 Discussions and Implications

The identification of wellbeing as a distinct sub-halo in the thematic analysis confirms its growing importance in tourism discourse. The framework posits that emotional and cognitive states – such as calmness, alertness, attention and memory – are integral to assessing tourist experiences. Neuroscientific tools like EEG, facial coding, and eye-tracking offer evidence-based approaches to measuring these psychological constructs in real-time, making wellbeing quantifiable in ways that traditional surveys may overlook. Furthermore, rather than restricting wellness to spa retreats or yoga holidays, the analysis extends wellbeing to urban wilderness experiences, rural tourism and adventure tourism. For instance, EEG studies in informal green spaces show how urban parks and nature-based experiences can induce calmness and restore mental energy – broadening the scope of wellness in tourism research and practice.

The analysis shows that tourism experiences can now be scientifically designed and evaluated through affective computing and wearable technology. The example of using EEG headbands in green spaces indicates the feasibility of assessing emotional wellbeing through physiological signals. This holds powerful implications for designing tourism offerings that truly enhance wellbeing, moving beyond assumptions to data-driven experience innovation. Moreover, the environment and natural resources sub-halos reveal a strong link between ecological engagement and emotional restoration. The body-movement perspective, enabled through mobile methods (e.g. smart watches, GPS tracking), allows researchers to capture how people interact physically and emotionally with nature. This is crucial for understanding eco-wellbeing, especially in post-pandemic travel patterns prioritizing regenerative, nature-based experiences.

Adventure emerges as a blurred yet promising zone in wellbeing research. Abstracts 40, 65, and 78 suggest that adventure guides, as well as slow adventure formats like kayaking and stargazing, promote psychological resilience and meaning-making. Yet the field lacks clarity, indicating an urgent need for standardized wellbeing measures in adventure tourism studies. The analysis also indicates that the integration of neuroscience and computing into wellness tourism raises ethical considerations, especially around privacy and emotional data. Tools that capture brainwaves or facial expressions must be used with informed consent and cultural sensitivity. Moreover, there's a potential to design inclusive wellness offerings – for example, for neurodiverse tourists or those with mental health needs – through a better understanding of how different brains respond to various tourism stimuli.

Sub-halos on sustainable development (urban and rural) and services highlight the policy implications of wellbeing research. With tools that measure wellbeing outcomes at individual, community and destination levels, planners and governments can align tourism policies with SDGs and Agenda 2030, ensuring that wellbeing is not just a personal gain but a collective, long-term societal objective. Further, in academia, these tools open avenues for interdisciplinary research that connects behavioral science, marketing and sustainability. In industry, measuring how a tourist *feels* in real-time can inform precision marketing, improved satisfaction, and experience personalization, ensuring that wellness is embedded across the customer journey – not just in post-visit feedback.

7.5 Conclusion

The main goals of the chapter were achieved: we integrated methodological approaches, and identified new insights that challenge the established norms, in order to explore innovations in tourism, wellbeing and sustainability through the intersection of neurosciences and computing. Thus, we provided a new framework encompassing several technologies and tools (eye-tracking, electroencephalogram, facial coding, among others) for the development of studies from neuroscience perspectives. We identified the presence of numerous interdisciplinary challenges, with ethical considerations ranking among the most relevant.

Thus, this chapter delineates the disruption of the status quo and the blurred boundaries within it from an epistemological perspective as revealed by state-of-the-art content analysis using Iramuteq software. Additionally, it discusses advances in methodology through factorial analysis of correspondence and similitude analysis for studies of this type. And, being grounded in narrative literature, the chapter explores the theoretical and conceptual dimensions arising from the integration of neuroscience and computing (Cerf, 2017). This discussion highlights two key themes: 'tourism and wellbeing' and 'sustainability', aiming to elucidate their interrelationships. The synergy between neuroscience and computing holds significant value for those managing and planning in the domains of tourism and wellbeing, particularly from a sustainability standpoint.

The insights into these constructs and the current state-of-the-art provide a robust framework for developing new research, applicable in both marketing and academic contexts. This framework addresses the existing paradigm, the areas lacking clarity, and the challenges to the status quo within this thematic area. The convergence of neuroscience, computing and tourism marks a turning point for wellness and wellbeing studies: no longer abstract ideals, they are now measurable, designable, and ethically actionable components of the tourism experience. Future directions must ensure that such approaches are inclusive, culturally sensitive and sustainability-aligned, truly redefining what it means to 'feel well' in travel.

References

Al-Nafjan, A., Aldayel, M. and Kharrat, A. (2023) Systematic review and future direction of neuro-tourism research. *Brain Science* 13, 682. https://doi.org/10.3390/brainsci13040682.

Andreu, M., Font-Barnet, A. and Roca, M. (2021) Wellness tourism – New challenges and opportunities for tourism in Salou. *Sustainability* 13, 8246. https://doi.org/10.3390/su13158246.

Bastiaansen, M., Luba, X.D., Mitas, O., Jung, T.H., Ascenção, M.P., Han, D.-I., Moilanen, T., Smit, B. and Strijbosch, W. (2019) Emotions as core building blocks of an experience. *International Journal of Contemporary Hospitality Management* 31 (2), 651–668. https://doi.org/10.1108/IJCHM-11-2017-0761.

Bear, M.F., Connors, B.W. and Paradiso, M.A. (2017) *Neurociências: Desvendando o sistema nervoso*. Artemed.

Cardoso, L., Araújo, A.F., Silva, R., Almeida, G.G., Campos, F. and Santos, L.L. (2024) Demystifying neurotourism: An interdisciplinary approach and research agenda. *European Journal of Tourism Research* 36, 3618. https://doi.org/10.54055/ejtr.v36i.3183.

Cerf, M. (2017) Methods. In M. Cerf and M. Garcia-Garcia (eds) *Consumer Neuroscience* (pp. 63–102). MIT Press.

Cha, J., Jo, M., Lee, T.J. and Hyun, S.S. (2024) Characteristics of market segmentation for sustainable medical tourism. *International Journal of Tourism Research* 26 (1), e2626.

Cooper, M., Vafadari, K. and Hieda, M. (2015) *Current and Emerging Issues in Medical Tourism*. IGI Press.

Erfurt-Cooper, P. and Cooper, M. (2009) *Health and Wellness Tourism: Spas and Hot Springs*. Channel View Publications.

Farkić, J., Filep, S. and Taylor, S. (2020) Shaping tourists' wellbeing through guided slow adventures. *Journal of Sustainable Tourism* 28 (12), 2064–2080.

Gratch, J. (2024) Guest editorial: Ethics in affective computing. *IEEE Transactions on Affective Computing* 15 (1), 1–3. https://doi.org/10.1109/TAFFC.2023.3322918.

Guerra, R., Trentin, F. and Vila-Chã, C. (2022) New sustainable practices in health and wellness tourism destinations focused on the quality of life and wellbeing. *Pasos Revista de Turismo y Patrimonio Cultural* 20 (4), 871–883. https://doi.org/10.25145/j.pasos.2022.20.058.

Hanna, P., Wijesinghe, S., Paliatsos, I., Walker, C., Adams, M. and Kimbu, A. (2019) Active engagement with nature: Outdoor adventure tourism, sustainability and wellbeing. *Journal of Sustainable Tourism* 27 (9), 1355–1373. https://doi.org/10.1080/09669582.2019.1621883.

Harari, Y.N. (2012) *Sapiens: Uma breve história da humanidade*. L & PM.

Hartwell, H., Fyall, A., Willis, C., Page, S., Ladkin, A. and Hemingway, A. (2018) Progress in tourism and destination wellbeing research. *Current issues in Tourism* 21 (16), 1830–1892.

Herman, K., Ciechanowski, L. and Przegalińska, A. (2021) Emotional wellbeing in urban wilderness: Assessing states of calmness and alertness in informal green spaces (IGSs) with Muse – Portable EEG headband. *Sustainability* 13 (4), 2212. https://doi.org/10.3390/su13042212.

Iramuteq (2020) Available at http://www.iramuteq.org/ (accessed 11 November, 2024).

Kang, Y., Jia, Q., Gao, S., Zeng, X., Wang, Y., Angsuesser, S., Liu, Y., Ye, X. and Fei, T. (2019) Extracting human emotions at different places based on facial expressions and spatial clustering analysis. *Transactions in GIS* 23 (3), 450–480.

Ke, G.N., Utama, I.K.A.P., Wagner, T., Sweetman, A.K., Arshad, A., Nath, T.K., Neoh, J.Y., Muchamad, L.S. and Suroso, D.S.A. (2022) Influence of mangrove forests on subjective and psychological wellbeing of coastal communities: Case studies in Malaysia and Indonesia. *Frontiers in Public Health* 10. https://doi.org/10.3389/fpubh.2022.898276.

Mody, M. (2023) Hospitality as the bridge: Advancing transformative service research towards human flourishing. *The Service Industries Journal* 43 (7–8), 423–453. https://doi.org/10.1080/02642069.2023.2197222.

Moratori, P., Wagner, C., Houghton, R.J., Shipp, V., Johal, J., Welch, P. and Ali, S. (2013) Towards a ground truth dataset for affect detection from physiological information. In J.A. Botía and D. Charitos (eds) *Workshop Proceedings of the 9th International Conference on Intelligent Environments* (pp. 128–136). IOS Press.

Moyle, B.D., Moyle, C., Bec, A. and Scott, N. (2019) The next frontier in tourism emotion research. *Current Issues in Tourism* 22 (12), 1393–1399. https://doi.org/10.1080/13683500.2017.1388770.

Picard, R.W. (2003) Affective computing: Challenges. *International Journal of Human–Computer Studies* 59 (1–2), 55–64.

Pu, L., Chen, X., Jiang, L. and Zhang, H. (2022) Spatiotemporal characteristics of coupling and coordination of cultural tourism and objective wellbeing in Western China. *International Journal of Environmental Research and Public Health* 20 (1), 650.

Rayyan (2024) https://www.rayyan.ai/ (accessed 20 March, 2024).

Richardson, R.B., Fernandez, A., Tschirley, D. and Tembo, G. (2012) Wildlife conservation in Zambia: Impacts on rural household welfare. *World Development* 40 (5), 1068–1081.
Rooney, A. (2018) *A história das neurociências.* M. Books.
Salviati, M.E. (2017) *Manual do Aplicativo Iramuteq (versão 0.7 Alpha 2 e R Versão 3.2.3).* Planaltina.
Scott, N. (2020) Cognitive psychology and tourism – Surfing the 'cognitive wave': A perspective article. *Tourism Review* 75 (1), 49–51. https://doi.org/10.1108/TR-06-2019-0217.
Sikora, M., Russo, M., Đerek, J. and Jurčević, A. (2018) Soundscape of an archaeological site recreated with audio augmented reality. *ACM Transactions on Multimedia Computing, Communications, and Applications (TOMM)* 14 (3), 1–22.
United Nations (2015) *The 17 Goals.* Department of Economic and Social Affairs Sustainable Development. https://sdgs.un.org/goals (accessed 20 March 2024).
Valdivielso, M.E. and Houge, M.S. (2022) Climate change and adventure guiding: The role of nature connection in guide wellbeing. *Frontiers in Public Health* 10, 946093.
Wang, Y., Wang, L., Zhou, W. and Ying, Q. (2023) Rural recreation tourism in the Panxi region of China in the context of ecological welfare. *Heliyon* 9 (12), e22384.
Web of Science database (2024) Available at www.webofscience.com (accessed 20 March 2024).
Wiltshier, P. (2020) Health and welfare at the boundaries: Community development through tourism. *Journal of Tourism Futures* 6 (2), 153–164. https://doi.org/10.1108/JTF-05-2018-0021.
Xie, G., Li, W., Xiao, Y., Zhang, B., Lu, C., An, K., Wang, J., Xu, K. and Wang, J. (2010) Forest ecosystem services and their values in Beijing. *Chinese Geographical Science* 20, 51–58.
Ximenes, D., Nogueira da Silva, G., Maglio, I., Chiquetto, J., Amato-Lourenço, L., Vasconcellos, M., Jacobi, P., Coutinho, S., César, V. and Mineiro, T. (2020) A importância dos espaços públicos y áreas verdes pós-pandemia na cidade de São Paulo (sp). *Revista Labverde* 10. https://doi.org/10.11606/issn. 2179-2275.labverde.2020.1722914.
Zeng, L., Li, R.Y.M. and Huang, X. (2021) Sustainable mountain-based health and wellness tourist destinations: The interrelationships between tourists' satisfaction, behavioral intentions, and competitiveness. *Sustainability* 13 (23), 13314.
Zhang, G., Huang, K. and Shen, S. (2023) Impact of spiritual values on tourists' psychological wellbeing: Evidence from China's Buddhist mountains. *Frontiers in Psychology* 14. https://doi.org/10.3389/fpsyg.2023.1136755.

8 Co-Designing Transformative Wellbeing Tourism Experiences for Japanese Tourists to Finland

Kelsey M. Johansen and Henna Konu

8.1 Introduction

This case study focuses on nature-based wellbeing tourism in the Saimaa Lake District of the Finnish Lakeland region. *Wellness* refers to 'the active pursuit of activities, choices and lifestyles that lead to a state of holistic health' (Global Wellness Institute, 2023a: para. 1). *Wellness tourism* is a component of the wellness economy, referring to the activities and expenditures of domestic and international wellness tourists, including those who engage in primary or secondary wellness tourism (Global Wellness Institute, 2023b). Wellness or wellbeing tourism can occur in diverse settings, through a spectrum of service offerings, and with a diverse array of intended outcomes.

Nature connection-centric activities, such as *forest bathing*, can support the development of immersive, intentionally slow, and mindful wellness tourism experiences leading to improved wellbeing and healthy lifestyles (Farkić *et al*., 2021). In turn, these experiences can facilitate psychological transformations, including changes in attitudes, values, beliefs, perspectives or worldviews, leading to behavior changes and individual, societal, and environmental wellbeing (Coghlan & Weiler, 2018; Pung *et al*., 2020; Teoh *et al*., 2021). *Nature-based wellbeing tourism* is therefore comprised of activities that occur in nature or natural settings, that leverage the restorative powers of nature exposure, while fostering positive human–nature connections that drive transformation and achievement of wellbeing outcomes (Johansen & Konu, 2025). Wellness tourism was the top product development theme highlighted in

Visit Finland's *Tourism Roadmap 2015–2025* and is a key component of the Ministry of Economic Affairs and Employment's (2020 July) *Tourism Strategy 2019–2028 and Action Plan 2019–2023*, which aims to rebuild the post-pandemic Finnish tourism sector by focusing on sustainable growth and renewal (TEM, 2020 July; TEM, 2024).

Prior to the pandemic, tourism was an important growth sector in Finland, making considerable contributions to the economy (OECD, 2022). Over the period 2017–2019, tourism demand increased 8%, faster than any other sector, with tourism directly contributing 2.7% of the nation's GDP, providing 133,200 jobs and supporting 28,500 businesses (OECD, 2022). In 2019, international visitor spending totalled €5.6 billion (US $6.97 billion), or 5.1% of total exports, with domestic spending totalling €12.9 billion (World Travel & Tourism Council, 2024). Despite the strength of Finland's domestic market, in 2020 total tourism spending declined 41% at the height of the pandemic (World Travel & Tourism Council, 2024) with international tourist arrivals falling 72.8% (OECD, 2022). In 2023, international tourism arrivals remained 22.3% lower compared to pre-pandemic levels, with Finnish international tourism arrivals expected to return to 2019 levels in 2024 (OECD, 2022; Visit Finland, 2024a).

In the early 2000s, the Finnish Tourism Board (now Visit Finland) first identified wellbeing tourism as a potential growth market (Björk *et al.*, 2011). Since then, considerable efforts have been made to operationalize wellbeing tourism, destination development, and entrepreneurship through regional destination-specific approaches that leverage local resources, including nature, culture, knowledge and technology to create distinctive and genuine wellbeing tourism experiences (Björk *et al.*, 2011; Konu, 2015; Konu & Laukkanen, 2010). As Finnish wellbeing tourism has grown, the importance of natural environments as a source of health and wellbeing has increased (Tyrväinen *et al.*, 2024), largely due to the connection between Finnish wellbeing, outdoor activities like Nordic walking, and wellbeing pursuits like traditional saunas (Björk *et al.*, 2011). This is supported by a recent international survey of nature tourism trends in the Nordic countries which identified the health and wellbeing benefits of nature as an emerging, and commercially significant, avenue for tourism development in Finland (Haukeland *et al.*, 2023).

These health benefits were first marketed in an international campaign run through Visit Finland's 2015–2017 FinRelax program, one of the three growth programs in the *Finnish Tourism 2025 Roadmap*, which aimed to make Finland the leading Nordic wellness tourism destination (Visit Finland, 2020; Visit Finland, 2024b). The program employed strategic marketing initiatives aimed at increasing inbound travel from Japanese, German and Russian markets (Visit Finland, 2024b). Product development competitions in four regions of Finland helped identify suitable Finnish wellbeing products which were awarded the 'Authentic

FinRelax Experience' mark (Visit Finland, 2020); today, these and other subsequently developed products are actively marketed by Visit Finland, capitalizing on the program's success (Visit Finland, 2024b).

In addition to driving personal transformation and fostering connections to the natural world (Coghlan & Weiler, 2018; Pung *et al.*, 2020; Teoh *et al.*, 2021) and economic benefits to local communities (Haukeland *et al.*, 2023), nature-based wellbeing tourism products such as those developed in Finland can contribute to achieving the United Nations sustainable development goals (UN SDGs) (Dillette *et al.*, 2021; Farkić *et al.*, 2020). This includes promoting wellbeing (SDG3); generating jobs/boosting local economies (SDG8); reducing poverty and inequalities (SDGs 1 and 10); developing sustainable cities (SDG 11); and fostering pro-environmental behaviours (SDGs 6, 7, 13, 14 and 15) and responsible consumption and production (SDG12).

Previous studies (e.g. Yang *et al.*, 2023) have called for collaborative research with service providers to identify transformational and eudaimonia-cultivating practices in designing tourism services. Based on key informant interviews with SaimaaLife and its Japanese partner organizations (the Japanese ELÄMÄ project and Eco Conscious Japan), and thematic analysis of secondary business communications, the case study that is the subject of this chapter provides a practical example of how tourism service providers employ sustainable business models to co-design and deliver wellbeing tourism experiences in Finland (see also Johansen & Konu, 2025). It also explores how integrating sustainability and transformative elements into tourism product offerings, along with adopting innovative and collaborative sustainable business models, can produce wellbeing outcomes for customers while addressing tourism micro, small and medium enterprises' (mSMEs) competitiveness and contributing to the achievement of the UN SDGs.

SaimaaLife and its Japanese collaborators were selected for the case study because of their focus on sustainability and wellbeing within and across business practices and because of Visit Finland's focus on Japan as a key in-bound wellness tourism market, along with Visit Finland's strong investments in developing the region's wellness tourism product offerings through the FinRelax program (Visit Finland, 2020). Additionally, the loss of the in-bound Russian market, which was the largest in-bound market share at 12% of visitor arrivals, or 820,888 visitor nights, in 2019, following the post-pandemic border closures stemming from Russia's war against the Ukraine (Visit Finland, 2024a; World Travel & Tourism Council, 2024), necessitates a greater understanding of the Japanese market.

This chapter includes a review of the relevant literature, and a discussion of the methodology employed. A description of the case study follows, including the development of SaimaaLife, the business' philosophy and approach, its collaborative business partnerships, and their joint product development ventures. Findings are discussed within the context of the extant literature prior to the conclusion which explores the case study's limitations and areas for further study.

8.2 Literature Review

The promotion of sustainable tourism is imperative for the future of nations, like Finland, that rely on tourism as a social, cultural and economic phenomenon (Alonso-Muñoz *et al.*, 2022). Tourism businesses, and their ability to develop more sustainable products and services, are the starting point for mainstreaming sustainable tourism (Font *et al.*, 2018). In addition to the UN 2030 Agenda, global issues, such as climate change, financial and energy crises, the COVID-19 pandemic, and ongoing geopolitical conflicts and wars, collectively known by the term *polycrisis* (Lawrence *et al.*, 2024), combined with rapid technology development, have forced tourism businesses to innovate by adopting new business models that proactively address these and other issues (Joyce & Paquin, 2016). The polycrisis has also increased pressure to respond to sustainability concerns, driving interest in business models that are grounded in economic, environmental and social sustainability (Bocken *et al.*, 2014; Joyce & Paquin, 2016).

To be effective, sustainable business models should bring forth value propositions focused on how value is created, delivered and captured (Bocken *et al.*, 2014). These value propositions link to product/service development, customer relationships, value creation and delivery to key activities, resources, channels, partners and technology, and the value capture from cost structures and revenue streams (Osterwalder *et al.*, 2005; Richardson, 2005). In sustainable businesses, value is connected to economic, social and environmental value (Beltramello *et al.*, 2013). Value creation becomes a collaborative process, involving diverse stakeholders, that occurs via formal and informal channels and produces benefits beyond profit (Schaltegger *et al.*, 2015).

Bocken *et al.* (2014: 43) categorized sustainable business models into eight archetypes:

(1) Maximize material and energy efficiency
(2) Create value from 'waste'
(3) Substitute with renewables and natural processes
(4) Deliver functionality rather than ownership
(5) Adopt a stewardship role
(6) Encourage sufficiency
(7) Re-purpose the business for society/environment
(8) Develop scale-up solutions

Tourism businesses can link to several archetypes, especially the 'Adopt a stewardship role' archetype, which includes biodiversity protection and consumer care, and promoting consumer health and wellbeing; and the ‘Encourage sufficiency’ archetype, focused on consumer education, communication and awareness, and responsible product distribution/promotion (Bocken *et al.*, 2014).

Business-model innovation can support tourism businesses, irrespective of size, in making operational, policy, and practice changes to become more sustainable. SMEs are essential to economic growth (Massaro *et al.*, 2016; Narayanan *et al.*, 2020) and can promote innovation, provided they have a supportive policy and funding environment (Veugelers, 2008). Within the European Union, SMEs account for more than 99% of businesses (Massaro *et al.*, 2016) and are recognized as drivers of sustainable and local socioeconomic development (Stojanović & Travar, 2013). Nature-based tourism (NBT) is defined by small, frequently rural, enterprises (Lundberg & Fredman, 2012). In Finland, NBT is dominated by microenterprises, or businesses with less than 10 employees and sales of less than €2 million per year (Vesterinen, 2017).

In the global wellness tourism industry, mSMEs compete with national and multinational companies for market access (Milojković *et al.*, 2021). Tourism mSMEs have difficulty remaining competitive without collaboration (Tuohino & Konu, 2014). In times of crisis, tourism mSME clusters can support individual businesses’ competitiveness in sectors heavily dominated by multinational corporations or large-scale national chains (Milojković *et al.*, 2021). Cluster collaboration can take diverse forms, focusing on product development, service provision and/or shared marketing campaigns. Collaboration can also occur at diverse levels, and for diverse reasons – e.g. the destination or business level – within an interest network, or for a specific purpose (Konu & Smith, 2017). Tourism mSMEs collaboration benefits include the creation of complementary goods and services, increased capacity to leverage resources, increased productivity, enhanced sharing and expanded knowledge bases, the development of joint marketing strategies, fostering entrepreneurship, and affording new business opportunities, including increased innovation (Konu & Smith, 2017).

Against this backdrop, this chapter explores innovative and collaborative approaches to destination development and service delivery through a case study of SaimaaLife, a tourism mSME owned and operated by Mari Ahonen in the Saimaa Lake District of Finland’s Lakeland region. The case study focuses on the development of SaimaaLife, showcasing how a collaborative approach to integrating sustainability and transformative elements into tourism product offerings can produce wellbeing and transformative outcomes for Japanese tourists and tourism operators, address mSME competitiveness, and contribute to achieving the United Nations SDGs.

8.3 Methods

This case study employed a qualitative approach to explore the co-design of nature-based wellbeing tourism experiences in Finland based on thematic analysis of multiple datasets (interviews, and client-facing business communications like blogs, websites and print publications). Data collection occurred between September 2023 and February 2024. Three interviews were conducted; the first with Mari Ahonen (SaimaaLife) was face-to-face at the company's premises in Punkaharju, while the second and third with the Japanese collaborators were online. Information gathered through interview with SaimaaLife by the second author (conducted in Finnish) generated themes for the subsequent interviews with their Japanese collaborators and for the thematic analysis of secondary documents. Thematic analysis of the organizations' websites, led by the first author, identified the following themes: (1) sustainable business models and business development, (2) entrepreneurship and innovation, (3) wellbeing tourism experience and product development, (4) sustainability and the United Nations SDGs, and (5) wellbeing and nature connection.

As the thematic analysis of the organizations' websites pre-dated the second and third interviews, themes generated by it were centered in the interview questions. Semi-structured interviews combine structured questions with unstructured exploration (Wilson, 2014: 23). This ensured that themes germane to the research were addressed, supporting the generation of rich and thick descriptions (Geertz, 1973) while enabling interviewees to emphasize aspects of their collaborative working relationships, product development and business approaches that they deemed most relevant (Creswell & Plano Clark, 2011). Interviews were recorded, transcribed, and thematically analyzed, per Braun and Clarke (2006, 2012). This complemented the thematic analyses of client-facing communications produced by SaimaaLife. Conducted by the first author, thematic analysis provided historical context to the entrepreneur's interview through an analysis of their self-narratives published in blog posts and a book. Tourism entrepreneur names have been retained (with permission) due to their expertise, high profile, and the ease by which they can be re-identified as the owners and operators of the three mSME included in the SaimaaLife case study.

8.4 Case Description and Background

SaimaaLife is a sustainable wellness business, located in the town of Punkaharju in the Saimaa Lake District of Finland's Lakeland region (see Figure 8.1), and owned and operated by Mari Ahonen (formerly Pennanen). Mari is a trained mental health expert and forest bathing nature trainer who graduated from Shinsu Shinanomachi Healing Forest in Nagano, Japan (Pennanen, 2022).

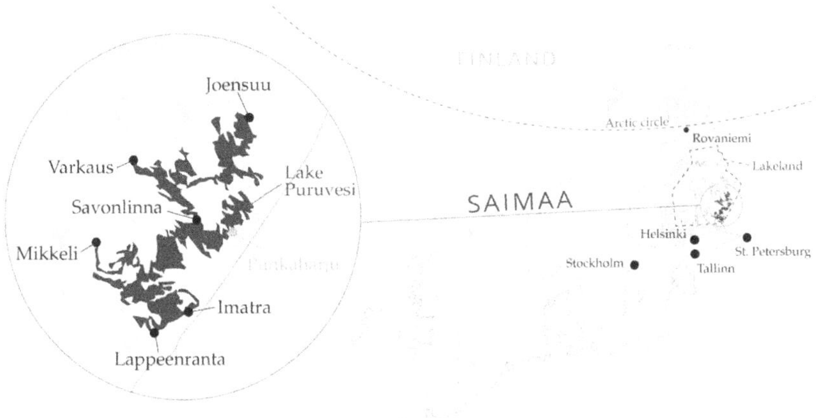

Figure 8.1 The location of SaimaaLife business in Punkaharju
Source: © 2022 SaimaaLife and Mari Ahonen.

SaimaaLife began as a blog in 2012, inspired by Mari's nature-facilitated healing journey during which she used traditional psychotherapy and nature immersion to address burnout, depression, anxiety, exhaustion, and other traumatic experiences (Pennanen, 2022). Through reflection, compassion, trust and kindness, and by embracing a sustainable lifestyle close to nature, Mari healed her connections with self, others, work and food (Pennanen, 2022). Mari's transformative healing journey inspired her to create the blog as a platform to share her insights and to support others (Pennanen, 2022). The blog received international recognition in 2013, which led to publishing a natural wellbeing e-guide in 2014, and offering four-week online courses on nature-facilitated emotional processing in 2015 (SaimaaLife, 2024a). Since then, SaimaaLife has grown considerably. Today, Mari also provides forest therapy and nature immersion workshops to domestic and international participants, and serves as a travel guide and nature trainer, running virtual workshops and providing in-person and remote education services (SaimaaLife, 2024a, 2024b).

8.4.1 Natural wellbeing: The SaimaaLife philosophy

Mari's unique philosophy is a core component of her service delivery model, reflecting lessons learned through her *natural wellbeing* journey. The SaimaaLife natural wellbeing philosophy includes six core dimensions (Pennanen, 2022):

(1) Being physically in nature and spending time outdoors, when possible, or seeking opportunities to experience nature digitally and/or virtually.
(2) Bringing elements of nature into your life (e.g. natural foods, skincare, clothing, and décor made from natural fibers and materials).

(3) Connecting with other people, non-human animals and the natural world through the five senses.
(4) Adopting a less sedentary lifestyle by engaging in movement.
(5) Embracing and cultivating your ability to think, learn and create.
(6) Being true to what is natural to you, reflecting your DNA, body, mind and soul.

Through Mari's workshops and activities, participants are supported in developing and cultivating a natural wellbeing practice that starts by embracing each dimension of the SaimaaLife philosophy before customizing it to ensure it is personally meaningful, locally sustainable and culturally relevant (SaimaaLife, 2024a). This ensures that their practice is sustainable, helps them to find and connect with 'their nature', and supports improved health and happiness (Pennanen, 2022).

8.4.2 Forest bathing with a Finnish twist

The positive effects of forests on individual wellbeing and physical and mental health have been extensively studied by academics (e.g. Lee *et al.*, 2014; Park *et al.*, 2007; Tsunetsugu *et al.*, 2010; Tyrväinen *et al.*, 2018). In Japan, forest bathing was first introduced by the Japanese government in 1982; since then, interest in its benefits – which range from stress reduction to physiological health benefits – has increased (Korpela *et al.*, 2014; Lee *et al.*, 2014; Tsunetsugu *et al.*, 2010). This has led to studies of the benefits of nature, greenspaces and forest environments for wellbeing in both Japanese and Finnish contexts (e.g. Korpela *et al.*, 2014; Park *et al.*, 2007; Tyrväinen *et al.*, 2014).

SaimaaLife's wellbeing philosophy stems from the importance that Mari places on the human–nature connection and its positive wellbeing impacts. After realizing the benefits of this approach, Mari trained as a mental health expert and became the first foreigner to attain certification as a forest bathing nature trainer from Shinshu Shinanomachi Healing Forest in Nagano, Japan (SaimaaLife, 2017, November 17). SaimaaLife forest bathing (see Figure 8.2), or Forest Bathing with a Finnish Twist, is a merger of traditional forest bathing techniques with Mari's personal natural wellbeing philosophy and biophilic approach (SaimaaLife, 2017, November 17). This includes Finnish four-season outdoor lifestyle practices, Finnish cultural elements and access to local natural areas (SaimaaLife, 2017, November 17). The 'Finnish twist' compliments traditional Japanese techniques due to Finnish/Japanese cultural similarities, including a similar mindset, respect for nature and quietness and a love of mushrooms (SaimaaLife, 2017, November 30).

Incorporating elements of Finnish culture, Lake Saimaa nature, and her mental health training allowed Mari to develop personalized

Figure 8.2 Japanese tourists participate in a guided nature-relaxation and forest-bathing experience with Mari from SaimaaLife

Source: © 2023 SaimaaLife, Mari Ahonen, and Marianne Ahonen Photography.

year-round forest bathing trainings and other nature based workshops (see Table 8.1), which she delivers in Punkaharju Nature Reserve and Punkaharju Research Forest, in partnership with local wellness spas, retreats, hotels, and lakeside rental cottage companies (SaimaaLife, 2024c).

Table 8.1 Components of a typical SaimaaLife workshop

• Overview of the wellbeing benefits of nature connection
• Discussion of Finnish approaches to health and happiness, including the role of nature in the pursuit of Finn's happiness
• Forest bathing practices
• Breath work and gentle stretching
• Discussion of the importance of space, healthy boundaries, humanity, self-compassion and emotional processing in personalized healing journeys
• How to connect to your own voice and intuition
• How to focus on being, letting go and remaining calm
• How to achieve more clarity, balance, courage, joy and lightness in your life
• Ways to take nature and eco-psychological practices with you from the forest/workshop locations to use them elsewhere in your life with the aim of relieving stress, haste and anxiety
• Communal tea/coffee enjoyed in wooden *kuksa* mugs
• A copy of Mari's guidebook, *Find Your Nature*

Source: The authors (2024), adapted from SaimaaLife (2022, August 14).

Workshop locations are selected based on participants' age, fitness levels and desired wellbeing outcomes; workshops typically last three hours. These workshops are expanded upon to incorporate additional aspects of Finnish culture and wellbeing practices, including wild food foraging, traditional homestyle Finnish meals, open-water lake swimming, *savusauna* (smoke saunas), as well as mainstream wellbeing practices like journaling, and reflective dialogue, to co-design customized week-long wellbeing tourism experiences in partnership with Japanese collaborators and Finnish businesses based locally in the Saimaa region (see discussion of the co-design process in Johansen & Konu, 2025).

8.4.3 Collaborative partnerships

Mari and SaimaaLife's Japanese collaborations began in 2016. Initial collaborations with Asaka Ito, the Representative Employee and Experience Designer at Kokemus LLC led to the development of SaimaaLife's YouTube channel; this grew into virtual and in-person workshops and virtual travel to Finland, which coincided with the SaimaaLife website's 2017 launch in Japanese (Kokemus LLC, 2024a, 2024b; SaimaaLife, 2017, November 17, 2024a). In 2018, a 360°/VR series was launched prior to the first Japanese tourists' visit to Saimaa (see Figure 8.3).

Travel coordination services started with trips co-designed and co-delivered with Yukie Tonuma, the founder of Eco Conscious Japan, with logistical support from Asaka, and expanded the following year to include Yumi Ishihara, the Representative Director of the Japanese ELÄMÄ project (Yukie Tonuma, personal communication, February 15 2024; Yumi Ishihara, personal communication, February 20 2024).

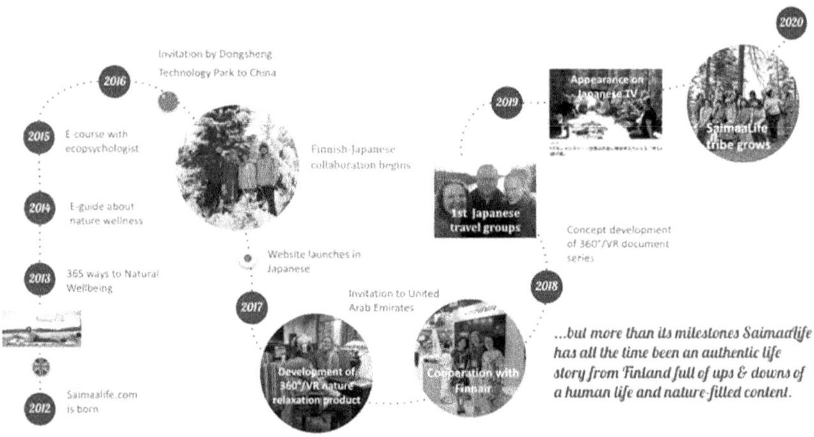

Figure 8.3 SaimaaLife business development timeline

Source: © 2022 SaimaaLife and Mari Ahonen.

8.4.4 Product development

As a part of SaimaaLife's ongoing collaborations with Japanese travel partners, Mari has co-developed more than 10 'Find Your Nature' tourism experiences since 2018. Collaborative product development begins with a product research and regional familiarization tour where Japanese collaborators experience Saimaa Nature relaxation, build the local knowledge needed to market the destination to Japanese tourists, and cultivate a relationship with Mari through shared experiences and homestays (Yukie Tonuma, personal communication, February 15 2024; Yumi Ishihara, personal communication, February 20 2024). Collaborations are possible because of the entrepreneurs' shared interests and values, collaborative and reciprocal approaches to innovation, comparable business sizes, and the similar sustainable business models that each employs as owners and operators of tourism mSMEs (Yukie Tonuma, personal communication, February 15 2024; Yumi Ishihara, personal communication, February 20 2024).

Once designed, the 'Find Your Nature' tourism experience includes interaction with customers both online and onsite. Initially, customers meet Mari and are introduced to SaimaaLife through a video message sent to participants one or two weeks pre-trip. While an essential part of rapport-building with Mari, who will guide their onsite experiences, the video also helps participants direct the focus of the trip and start reflecting on their 'inner trip' (Mari Ahonen, personal communication, September 8 2023). Once in Finland, the trip lasts 3–7 days and includes activities that help participants re-connect with nature and their inner selves through SaimaaLife's natural wellbeing approach, Saimaa Nature Relaxation experiences, and Forest Bathing with Finnish Twist activities (Mari Ahonen, personal communication, September 8 2023). Normally, a day consists of visiting one of the tourist attractions at the destination, such as the Punkaharju Nature Reserve, and includes relaxing activities as well as guided wellbeing workshops (see Table 8.2), with the program designed to ensure participants do not feel rushed (Mari Ahonen, personal communication, September 8 2023).

Central trip components include local food and embodied nature immersion experiences (e.g. swimming in natural waters, forest walking, stretching outdoors, cycling on nature paths, and traditionally Finnish saunas) as well as making something by hand (e.g. handicrafts and cooking with foraged natural ingredients), which emphasize sensory experiences (Mari Ahonen, personal communication, September 8 2023). Nature and natural elements, and contact with nature, have a central role in all activities and time in nature also gives participants space and time to reflect on their experience and life (Yukie Tonuma, personal communication, February 15 2024). At the end of the trip, there

Table 8.2 Components of a typical SaimaaLife 'Find Your Nature' tour

• Post-arrival decompression time, and time to adjust to the time zone change
• Sustainable in-country travel via rail
• Local welcome in Saimaa Lake District, including homemade meal created with local ingredients
• Discussion of local life and lifestyles in the Saimaa region
• Presentation about Mari's personal nature wellbeing and entrepreneurship journeys
• Overview of the wellbeing benefits of nature connection
• Overview of natural wellbeing and nature-based wellness
• Discussion of Finnish approaches to health and happiness, including the role of nature in the pursuit of Finns' happiness
• Rest and relaxation
• Forest bathing and mindful forest walking practices
• Guided wild edible foraging trips (seasonally available local herbs, berries and/or mushrooms)
• Breath work and gentle stretching
• Discussion of the importance of space, healthy boundaries, humanity, self-compassion and emotional processing in personalized healing journeys
• Workshops on: 1. How to connect to your own voice and intuition 2. How to focus on being, letting go, and remaining calm 3. How to achieve more clarity, balance, courage, joy and lightness in your life 4. Ways to take nature and eco-psychological practices with you from the forest/workshop locations to use it elsewhere in your life with the aim of relieving stress, haste and anxiety
• A guided tour of LUSTO, the Finnish Forest Museum
• Personal reflective time, including journaling, self-reflection and independent peaceful movement outdoors
• Communal meals and opportunities for informal dialogue
• Guided discussion on wellbeing outcomes achieved during the trip, and how to maintain individuals' wellbeing practices when they return home
• Pre-departure activities in Helsinki facilitated by Japanese collaborators

Source: The authors (2024).

are reflective individual and group discussions with participants (Mari Ahonen, personal communication, September 8 2023).

These 'Find Your Nature' tourism experiences are co-designed specifically for Japanese tourists served by SaimaaLife's Japanese collaborators, including teachers and principals interested in wellbeing and education, self-identified *ekobito* or eco-conscious people interested in natural wellbeing and nature connection through sustainable lifestyle practices (Yukie Tonuma, personal communication, February 15 2024), and individuals looking to (re)design their lives in ways that enhance happiness through Finnish outdoor lifestyle practices (Yumi Ishihara, personal communication, February 20 2024). These trips always include SaimaaLife's natural wellbeing philosophy and may include as an option visits to local schools, Kerimäki village and church, and organic/sustainable farms and restaurants in Saimaa, as well as trips to the Moomin Museum, Oodi Library, or Lapinlahden Lähde (Finland's first psychiatric hospital that focuses on mental health, wellbeing and culture). Further options include visits to Nuuksio National Park, and/or integration of wellbeing gastronomy experiences in Finnish restaurants in the Helsinki region as secondary wellbeing tourism experiences that serve as transitional periods before or after time with SaimaaLife.

Virtual wellbeing tourism products became an essential part of the SaimaaLife service delivery model during the pandemic and as the tourism industry began to re-open (SaimaaLife, 2020, December 14). Beginning in June 2020, SaimaaLife and Eco-Conscious Japan offered six virtual tours, all of which sold out (Yukie Tonuma, personal communication, February 15 2024). Priced at €20 per person, Japanese tourists travelled virtually to Saimaa from their Japanese homes via video call which supported a guided 360° video, photo and interpretation experience created using a combination of new and existing materials (SaimaaLife, 2020, December 14; YLE.fi, 2020, May 27).

Over the two-hour virtual tour, Yukie guided her tour participants on a virtual flight from Tokyo's Narita Airport to Helsinki, a familiar experience for her based on years of pre-Pandemic collaborative tours with SaimaaLife (Yukie Tonuma, personal communication, February 15 2024). Once in Helsinki, the group boarded a train for Savonlinna, then travelled virtually by boat to Tynkkylän Lomaniemi, a resort with holiday cottages on Lake Saimaa, where the remaining tour elements were guided by Mari and other local tourism entrepreneurs (YLE.fi, 2020, May 27). Each virtual tour covered a two-day, and one-night, visit focused on Saimaa nature relaxation and Finnish culture, including seasonal experiences like nightless winter days and sun-filled summer nights, peaceful immersion in the Saimaa lakeside ambience, Finnish smoke saunas, and birch bark weaving (*tuohityö*) workshops (YLE.fi, 2020, May 27). Moments for quiet reflection were interspersed throughout allowing virtual wellbeing tourists to digest their experiences (YLE.fi, 2020, May 27). Since the resumption of travel, these VR trips have shifted focus, becoming a key part of the marketing and promotion of travel to the Saimaa region (Yukie Tonuma, personal communication, February 15 2024). Through community group meetings and condensed 30-minute tours, Yukie introduces potential tourists to the Saimaa region, with Mari helping to foster visit intention, rapport and trip expectations (YLE.fi, 2020, May 27).

8.5 Discussion

As a result of the polycrisis, increasing pressure to respond to sustainability concerns, and rapid technological development, tourism operators, and mSMEs in particular, have had to adopt innovative sustainable business models to remain competitive while also addressing the United Nations SDGs (Bocken *et al.*, 2014; Joyce & Paquin, 2016; Lawrence *et al.*, 2024). As earlier work highlighted, collaborative tourism clusters comprised of mSMEs operating under sustainable business models and focused on product development, service provision, and/or shared marketing campaigns, can produce diverse benefits through innovative value propositions that create economic, social and environmental value.

The sustainable business model employed by Mari and SaimaaLife aligns with four of Bocken *et al.*'s (2014) sustainable business model archetypes: (1) maximizing material and energy efficiency, (2) adopting a stewardship role, (3) encouraging sufficiency and (4) developing scale-up solutions (see Table 8.3).

SaimaaLife's virtual and in-person workshops and collaborative in-person tours for Japanese tourists drive personal transformation and foster connections to the natural world, while generating economic, environmental and social value for the region's rural communities, paralleling findings by Coghlan and Weiler (2018), Pung *et al.* (2020) and Teoh *et al.* (2021). Furthermore, adoption of sustainable business models, and their accompanying archetypes, helps SaimaaLife, its local partners and

Table 8.3 SaimaaLife's Alignment with Sustainable Business Model Archetypes

(1) Maximize material and energy efficiency	SaimaaLife and its Japanese collaborators maximize material and energy efficiency by generating less emissions through sustainable in-country travel practices, including use of rail services, carpooling, and active transportation; they generate less waste by composting and use less energy by preparing meals communally.
	Existing 360° photos and videos, and VR marketing materials were re-purposed and combined with new materials during the COVID-19 pandemic to help SaimaaLife its Japanese collaborators create innovative, sustainable, wellbeing tourism products, thus remaining competitive within the wellness tourism economy.
(2) Adopt a stewardship role	The SaimaaLife natural wellbeing philosophy is grounded in a biophilic approach that encourages workshop and tour participants to spend time in nature and connect with other people, non-human animals and the natural world.
	SaimaaLife and its Japanese collaborators limit trip group sizes to reduce environmental impacts.
(3) Encourage sufficiency	SaimaaLife workshops and tours help participants to shift their mindset away from consumerism and towards foraging for wild edibles, eating locally and seasonally, and developing an appreciation for natural foods, for skincare, clothing, and for décor made from natural fibres and materials.
(4) Develop scale-up solutions	SaimaaLife and its Japanese collaborators have taken a measured approach to scaling-up their mSMEs and tours. SaimaaLife began as a blog, before branching into online workshops and a YouTube channel, then in-person workshops, prior to welcoming international guests for tours. Through this scaled-up approach, they developed individual sustainable business models, collaborative working relationships and innovative service delivery approaches.
	When the COVID-19 pandemic hit, they pivoted to provide new virtual tourism experiences that aligned with the wellbeing tourism needs of their existing client base, while developing a new market for post-pandemic tours.

Source: The authors (2024) adapted from Bocken *et al.* (2014).

its Japanese collaborators address the United Nations SDGs at local and international levels. This includes promoting good health and wellbeing (SDG 3), decent work and economic growth (SDG 8), reducing poverty and inequalities and building sustainable cities and communities (SDGs 1, 10 and 11), and fostering pro-environmental behaviours (SDGs 6, 7, 13, 14 and 15), as well as responsible consumption and production (SDG 12).

Through workshops and tours, during which they learn about SaimaaLife's natural wellbeing philosophy and acquire the skills to develop their wellbeing practices, domestic workshop participants and international tourists work towards good health and wellbeing, recover from burnout, and (re)design their lives through workshops on work–life balance (SDGs 3 and 8). Furthermore, by healing her relationship with work and committing to cultivating local partnerships and meaningful international collaborations, Mari showcases how to succeed as an entrepreneur without sacrificing one's mental health and wellbeing (SDG 3) and how to promote decent work (SDG 8). Through local partnerships and international collaborations, SaimaaLife promotes economic growth, poverty reduction, reduces inequalities in rural communities and promotes sustainable cities (SDGs 1, 8, 10 and 11).

SaimaaLife's workshops and tours also foster pro-environmental behaviors (SDGs 6, 7, 13, 14 and 15) and responsible consumption and production (SDG 12). Tours stay in locally owned and operated holiday cottages, rather than resorts or multinational hotel chains, and travel in-country via train. Most meals are communal or self-catered, using locally sourced ingredients supplemented with seasonally foraged wild edibles, like herbs, berries and mushrooms, and participants are encouraged to use natural skin-care products and to transition to clothing and décor made from natural fibers and materials. Lastly, participants are guided towards personally meaningful, locally sustainable and culturally relevant practices when designing their own wellbeing practices.

As the case-study description, product-development approaches, and discussion above highlight, Mari's natural wellbeing philosophy and the way she views herself in relationship with nature and people, extends beyond her wellbeing journey, through the development of the SaimaaLife blog and the launch of her workshops and tours, and into each of the unique collaborative partnerships she has cultivated.

8.6 Conclusion

This case study presents a novel exploration of collaborative approaches to co-designing wellbeing tourism products and implementing sustainable business models, including innovative service delivery approaches in response to the global polycrisis. Situated within the context of SaimaaLife, a tourism mSME operating in the Finnish Lakeland region, and its partnerships with Japanese collaborators, this chapter has explored ways to center wellbeing outcomes for tourists and tourism operators as well as for local communities, society and the environment in tourism product development. Simultaneously, this chapter has explored the importance that female tourism operators placed on addressing issues of mSME competitiveness through collaboration as opposed to competition, and how this contributes to achievement of the United Nations SDGs.

While qualitative case studies are a popular approach in tourism studies, as they allow for in-depth exploration of complex phenomena within their real-world context, this approach has limitations. Although this chapter provides new insights into Nordic approaches to wellbeing tourism product development grounded in a natural wellbeing philosophy, culturally relevant Nordic outdoor lifestyle practices, traditional forest bathing techniques and collaborative approaches to tourism product co-design, the lack of generalizability of its findings beyond the businesses and regions focused on here point to the need for additional research. Said research should explore how tourism mSMEs employ sustainable business models as alternative pathways to achieving the UN SDGs and how their outcomes compare to the large-scale corporate social responsibility (CSR) approaches favored by larger, often multinational, corporations.

This case study has highlighted how innovation and resilience, partnered with value propositions focused on economic, social and environmental value, meaningful, collaborative, and reciprocally beneficial business-to-business partnerships and customer relationships, can address mSME competitiveness, and produce benefits beyond profits, in a sector dominated by multinational corporations or large-scale national chains. Additional quantitative and survey research that explores these issues beyond the geographically limited case study region is also needed. Despite these limitations and the need for additional research, this chapter's findings provide a meaningful starting point relevant for academic researchers and advanced tourism students – as well as practitioners – studying or developing and implementing wellbeing tourism services as pathways to sustainable and local socioeconomic development.

References

Alonso-Muñoz, S., Torrejón-Ramos, M., Medina-Salgado, M. and González-Sánchez, R. (2022) Sustainability as a building block for tourism – Future research: Tourism Agenda 2030. *Tourism Review* 78 (2), 461–474. http://dx.doi.org/10.1108/TR-12-2021-0568.

Beltramello, A., Haie-Fayle, L. and Pilat, D. (2013) Why new business models matter for green growth. OECD, 01 (February), 1–107. https://doi.org/10.1787/5k97gk40v3ln-en.

Björk, P., Tuohino, A. and Konu, H. (2011) Wellbeing tourism in Finland. A wide perspective. *Matkailututkimus* [Finnish Journal of Tourism Research] 7 (2), 26–41. https://journal.fi/matkailututkimus/article/view/90859.

Bocken, N.M.P., Short, S.W., Rana, P. and Evans, S. (2014) A literature and practice review to develop sustainable business model archetypes. *Journal of Cleaner Production* 65, 42–56. https://doi.org/10.1016/J.JCLEPRO.2013.11.039.

Braun, V. and Clarke, V. (2006) Using thematic analysis in psychology. *Qualitative Research in Psychology* 3 (2), 77–101. https://doi.org/10.1191/1478088706qp063oa.

Braun, V. and Clarke, V. (2012) Thematic analysis. In H. Cooper, P.M. Camic, D.L. Long, A.T. Panter, D. Rindskopf and K.J. Sher (eds) *APA Handbook of Research Methods in Psychology. Volume 2: Research Designs: Quantitative, Qualitative, Neuropsychological, and Biological* (pp. 57–71). American Psychological Association.

Coghlan, A. and Weiler, B. (2018) Examining transformative processes in volunteer tourism. *Current Issues in Tourism* 21 (5), 567–582. https://doi.org/10.1080/13683500.2015.1102209.

Creswell, J. and Plano Clark, V.L. (2011) *Designing and Conducting Mixed Methods Research* (2nd edn). Sage.

Dillette, A.K., Douglas, A.C. and Andrzejewski, C. (2021) Dimensions of holistic wellness as a result of international wellness tourism experiences. *Current Issues in Tourism* 24 (6), 794–810. https://doi.org/10.1080/13683500.2020.1746247.

Farkić, J., Filep, S. and Taylor, S. (2020) Shaping tourists' wellbeing through guided slow adventures. *Journal of Sustainable Tourism* 28 (12), 2064–2080. https://doi.org/10.1080/09669582.2020.1789156.

Farkić, J., Isailovic, G. and Taylor, S. (2021) Forest bathing as a mindful tourism practice. *Annals of Tourism Research Empirical Insights* 2 (2), 1–9. https://doi.org/10.1016/j.annale.2021.100028.

Font, X., English, R. and Gkritzali, A. (2018) Mainstreaming sustainable tourism with user-centred design. *Journal of Sustainable Tourism* 26 (10), 1651–1667. https://doi.org/10.1080/09669582.2018.1491981.

Geertz, C. (1973) Thick description: Toward an interpretive theory of culture. In C. Geertz, *The Interpretation of Cultures: Selected Essays* (pp. 3–30). Basic Books.

Global Wellness Institute (2023a) *Wellness Definitions* [website]. https://globalwellnessinstitute.org/what-is-wellness/wellness-economy-definitions/.

Global Wellness Institute (2023b) *Wellness Tourism* [website]. https://globalwellnessinstitute.org/what-is-wellness/what-is-wellness-tourism/.

Haukeland, J-V., Fredman, P., Tyrväinen, L., Siegrist, D. and Lindberg, K. (2023) Prospects for nature-based tourism: Identifying trends with commercial potential. *Journal of Ecotourism*. https://doi.org/10.1080/14724049.2023.2178444.

Johansen, K.M. and Konu, H. (2025) Designing transformative nature-based wellbeing tourism experiences: A case study from the Finnish Lakeland Region. *Tourism Recreation Research*. https://doi.org/10.1080/02508281.2024.2443983.

Joyce, A. and Paquin, R.L. (2016) The triple layered business model canvas: A tool to design more sustainable business models. *Journal of Cleaner Production* 135 (November 1), 474–1486. https://doi.org/10.1016/J.JCLEPRO.2016.06.067.

Kokemus LLC (2024a) *Kokemus* について [About Kokemus] [website]. https://kokemus.tokyo/about/.

Kokemus LLC (2024b) フィンランドプロジェクト [Finland Project] [website]. https://kokemus.tokyo/finland/finland-project/.

Konu, H. (2015) Developing a forest-based wellbeing tourism product together with customers – An ethnographic approach. *Tourism Management* 49 (August), 1–16. http://dx.doi.org/10.1016/j.tourman.2015.02.006.

Konu, H. and Laukkanen, T. (2010) Predictors of tourists' wellbeing holiday intentions in Finland. *Journal of Hospitality and Tourism Management* 17 (1), 144–149. https://doi.org/10.1375/jhtm.17.1.144.

Konu, H. and Smith, M. (2017) Cross-border health tourism collaborations: Opportunities and challenges. In M.K. Smith and L. Puczko (eds) *The Routledge Handbook of Health Tourism* (pp. 298–314). Routledge.

Korpela, K., Borodulin, K., Neuvonen, M., Paronen, O. and Tyrväainen, L. (2014) Analyzing the mediators between nature-based outdoor recreation and emotional wellbeing. *Journal of Environmental Psychology* 37, 1–7. https://doi.org/http://dx..org/10.1016/j.jenvp.2013.11.003.

Lawrence, M., Homer-Dixon, T., Janzwood, S., Rockstöm, J., Renn, O. and Donges, J.F. (2024) Global polycrisis: The causal mechanisms of crisis entanglement. *Global Sustainability* 7 (6), 1–16. https://doi.org/10.1017/sus.2024.1.

Lee, J., Tsunetsugu, Y., Takayama, N., Park, B., Li, Q., Song, C., Komatsu, M., Ikei, H., Tyrväinen, L., Kagawa, T. and Miyazaki, Y. (2014) Influence of forest therapy on cardiovascular relaxation in young adults. *Evidence-based Complementary and Alternative Medicine* 2014, 834360. https://doi.org/10.1155/2014/834360.

Lundberg, C. and Fredman, P. (2012) Critical success factors and constraints among nature-based tourism entrepreneurs. *Current Issues in Tourism* 15 (7), 649–671. https://doi.org/10.1080/13683500.2011.630458.

Massaro, M., Handley, K., Bagnoli, C. and Dumay, J. (2016) Knowledge management in small and medium enterprises: A structured literature review. *Journal of Knowledge Management* 20 (2), 258–291. https://doi.org/10.1108/JKM-08-2015-0320.

Milojković, D., Nikolić, M., Čolović, M., Nešić, M. and Ranković, K. (2021) The role of a cluster in creating the competitive spa and wellness tourism products on the global market in a time of crisis. *Spa & Wellness Tourism – Development, Perspectives, and Experiences* [electronic version]: *Proceedings of Singidunum University [VI] International Scientific Conference SITCON* (pp. 22–34). SITCON. https://doi.org/10.15308/Sitcon-2021-22-34.

Narayanan, S., Nadarajah, D., Sambasivan, M. and Ho, J.A. (2020) Antecedents and outcomes of the knowledge management process (KMP) in Malaysian SMEs. *Journal of Small Business & Entrepreneurship* 35 (5), 697–723. https://doi.org/10.1080/08276331.2020.1818540.

OECD (Organisation for Economic Co-operation and Development) (2022) Finland. In *OECD Tourism Trends and Policies 2022* (pp. 161–165). OECD Publishing. https://doi.org/10.1787/447c92c2-en.

Osterwalder, A., Pigneur, Y. and Tucci, C.L. (2005) Clarifying business models: Origins, present, and future of the concept. *Communications of the Association for Information Systems* 16 (July). https://doi.org/10.17705/1CAIS.01601.

Park, B.-J., Tsunetsugu, Y., Kasetani, T., Hirano, H., Kagawa, T., Sato, M. and Miyazaki, Y. (2007) Physiological effects of Shinrin-yoku (taking in the atmosphere of the forest) – Using salivary cortisol and cerebral activity as indicators. *Journal of Physiological Anthropology* 26, 123–128. https://doi.org/10.2114/jpa2.26.123.

Pennanen, M. (2022) *Finding Your Nature – Journey from Stress and Exhaustion to Better Balance, Peace, and Energy*. SaimaaLife.

Pung, J.M., Gnoth, J. and Del Chiappa, G. (2020) Tourist transformation: Towards a conceptual model. *Annals of Tourism Research* 81, 102885. https://doi.org/10.1016/j.annals.2020.102885.

Richardson, J.E. (2005) The business model: An integrative framework for strategy execution. *Social Science Research Network* 144, 133–144. https://doi.org/10.2139/ssrn.932998.

SaimaaLife (2017 November 17) Japanese forest bathing – Shinrin-yoku – with a Finnish twist [blog]. https://www.saimaalife.com/forest-bathing-shinrin-yoku/.

SaimaaLife (2017 November 30) Harmony prevails if people of similar nature meet [blog]. https://www.saimaalife.com/similar-nature-culture/.

SaimaaLife (2020 December 14) Virtual tour frenzy and a recap of the whirlwind that 2020 has been! [blog]. https://www.saimaalife.com/saimaalife-nature-inspired-virtual-tours-to-saimaa-finland/.

SaimaaLife (2022 August 14) Peace and power of mind from the forest – SaimaaLife workshop by Mari [blog]. https://www.saimaalife.com/peace-and-power-of-the-mind-from-the-forest-saimaalife-workshop-by-mari-punkaharju-finland/.

SaimaaLife (2024a) About – Connect with nature, and you connect with yourself [website]. https://www.saimaalife.com/about/.

SaimaaLife (2024b) SaimaaLife – Naturally the best [website]. https://www.saimaalife.com/.

SaimaaLife (2024c) Shinrin-yoku [website]. https://www.saimaalife.com/shinrin-yoku-forest-bathing/.

Schaltegger, S., Hansen, E.G. and Lüdeke-Freund, F. (2015) Business models for sustainability: Origins, present research, and future avenues. *Organization & Environment* 29 (1), 3–10. https://doi.org/10.1177/1086026615599806.

Stojanović, T.M. and Travar, M. (2013) Organizacija i razvoj klastera u Bosni i Hercegovini [Organization and development of clusters in Bosnia and Herzegovina]. *Časopis za poslovnu teoriju i praksu 'Poslovne studije'* [Journal of Business Theory and Practice: 'Business studies'] (9–10), 245–260. https://www.poslovnestudije.com/arhiva/radovi2013/stojanovictrivanovicmirjana_travarmihajlo.pdf.

TEM (Työ- ja elinkeinoministeriö) (2020 July) *Achieving More Together – Sustainable Growth and Renewal in Finnish Tourism: Finland's Tourism Strategy 2019–2028 and Action Plan 2019–2023* [online]. Ministry of Economic Affairs and Employment. https://julkaisut.valtioneuvosto.fi/handle/10024/162136.

TEM (Työ- ja elinkeinoministeriö) (2024) *Finland's Tourism Strategy for 2022–2028* [online]. Ministry of Economic Affairs and Employment. https://tem.fi/en/finland-tourism-strategy.

Teoh, M.W., Wang, Y. and Kwek, A. (2021) Conceptualising co-created transformative tourism experiences: A systematic narrative review. *Journal of Hospitality and Tourism Management* 47 (2021), 176–189. https://doi.org/10.1016/j.jhtm.2021.03.013.

Tsunetsugu, Y., Park, B.J. and Miyazaki, Y. (2010) Trends in research related to 'Shinrin-yoku' (taking in the forest atmosphere or forest bathing) in Japan. *Environmental Health and Preventive Medicine* 15, 27–37. https://doi-org.ezproxy.uef.fi:2443/10.1007/s12199-009-0091-z.

Tuohino, A. and Konu, H. (2014) Local stakeholders' views about destination management: Who are leading tourism development? *Tourism Review* 69 (3), 202–215. https://doi.org/10.1108/TR-06-2013-0033.

Tyrväinen, L., Ojala, A., Korpela, K., Lanki, T., Tsunetsugu, Y. and Kagawa, T. (2014) The influence of urban green environments on stress relief measures: A field experiment. *Journal of Environmental Psychology* 38, 1–9. https://doi.org/10.1016/j.jenvp.2013.12.005.

Tyrväinen, L., Lanki, T., Sipilä, R. and Komulainen, J. (2018) Mitä tiedetään metsän terveyshyödyistä? [What is known about the health benefits of forests?]. *DUODECIM* 134 (13), 1397–1403. https://www.duodecimlehti.fi/xmedia/duo/duo14421.pdf.

Tyrväinen, L., Tuulentie, S. and Konu, H. (2024) Luontomatkailun tutkimus Suomessa – historiasta tulevaisuuden tutkimussuuntiin [Nature-based tourism research in Finland – From the past to the future research directions]. *Matkailututkimus* [Finnish Journal of Tourism Research] 20 (1), 95–116. https://doi.org/10.33351/mt.143811.

Vesterinen, N. (2017) *4 Hyvää Syytä Panostaa Matkailuun* [4 Good Reasons to Focus on Tourism]. Työ-ja elinkeinoministeriö.

Veugelers, R. (2008) The role of SMEs in innovation in the EU: A case for policy intervention? *Review of Business and Economics* 53 (3), 239–262. https://econpapers.repec.org/RePEc:ete:revbec:20080302.

Visit Finland (2020) Hyvinvointimatkailun tuotesuositukset 2020 [Wellness tourism product recommendations 2020]. https://www.visitfinland.fi/4a81f0/globalassets/julkaisut/visit-finland/tutkimukset/2020/hyvinvointimatkailun-tuotesuositukset-2020.pdf.

Visit Finland (2024a) Rudolf tourism statistics dashboard [website]. https://app.powerbi.com/view?r=eyJrIjoiYTVhODhlMTAtMmZiZC00ZjdmLWE2YWUtN2Q0MjJlMGE2ZTNhIiwidCI6IjdjOTRhMjQ4LWVjZjItNDFiNi05YjQyLTkyMzY1MTExNGIwNCIsImMiOjh9.

Visit Finland (2024b) *Hyvinvointimatkailu* [Wellness tourism]. https://www.visitfinland.fi/liiketoiminnan-kehittaminen/tuotekehitysteemat/hyvinvointimatkailu.

Wilson, C. (2014) *Interview Techniques for UX Practitioners: A User-Centered Design Method.*

World Travel and Tourism Council (2024) *Finland – 2024 Annual Research: Key Highlights* [online report]. WTTC. https://researchhub.wttc.org/product/factsheet-finland-travel-tourism-economic-impact.

Yang, W., Zhang, Y. and Wang, Y.-C. (2023) Would travel experiences or possessions make people happier? *Journal of Travel Research* 62 (2), 412–431. https://doi.org/10.1177/00472875211064631.

YLE.fi. (2020) Maksullinen virtuaalimatkailu on korona-ajan uusi ilmiö – ensimmäiset japanilaisryhmät tulevat Saimaalle virtuaalisesti kesäkuussa [Paid virtual tourism is a new phenomenon of the corona era – The first Japanese groups will come to Saimaa virtually in June] [website]. *YLE.fi*, 27 May. https://yle.fi/a/3-11370424.

9 Enhancing Wellness Tourism with Calligraphy-Based Mindfulness Therapy

Mayumi Hieda and Malcolm Cooper

9.1 Introduction

Travel experiences that result in an increase in wellness have always been one of the major contributors to health and wellbeing, but this benefit has often been in the background. Recently, however, many tourists are choosing to go on trips that have the direct aim of improving their health and their sense of wellness (Kazakov & Oyner, 2021). It is the primary goal of this chapter to demonstrate the application of one such technique: wellness tourism based on practicing calligraphy. This activity can be used, like others, to escape from daily affairs, to relieve life pressures and achieve a balance between physical and psychological states – and it is an inexpensive (Buckley *et al.*, 2022; Kazakov & Oyner, 2021; Kessler *et al.*, 2020) part of wellness tourism (Adams *et al.*, 2015; Cooper *et al.*, 2015; Erfurt-Cooper & Cooper, 2009; Guerra *et al.*, 2022; Han *et al.*, 2018).

Wellness tourism meets individual health-related needs by offering resources to the traveler that include, for example, hot springs, spas, yoga, meditation, calligraphy, massage, diet therapy, wellness education and support for medical treatment (Bodecker, 2018; Dini & Pencarelli, 2021; Luo *et al.*, 2018). Importantly, wellness is not a passive or static state but, rather, an 'active pursuit', and these contributions can be medical or leisure-based (Smith & Puczkó, 2015): sports and adventure tourism that can increase physical health and fitness; occupational wellness trips that address work-related issues such as stress-management; spiritual retreats that can balance body, mind and spirit; and relaxation gained through activities such as calligraphy (Farren, 2024; Widemann, 2024). Calligraphy, if directed in the way we propose in this chapter, can provide an important means of stress reduction.

The chapter is organized to provide the necessary background to understanding the role of calligraphy therapy in wellness tourism and to reveal our techniques for making this happen.

Many of the techniques used in wellness tourism are based on recent changes in leisure and lifestyle trends, such as healthier nutrition, self-imposed fitness regimes, mindfulness, or the quest for alternative spirituality (Hettige, 1991; Jones & Lyanage, 2018). There are also shifts in many societies, from curative to preventative healthcare, which require greater knowledge and self-responsibility (Global Mind Project, 2023). In addition, the mainstream tourism industry is also investing heavily in wellness products – for example, the cruise industry – possibly to give a healthy 'feel' to a product traditionally associated with eating and drinking too much. How these contrasting aims can be integrated is the overall subject of this book, and specifically of this chapter.

The tourism industry is responding to society's need for holidays that enhance quality of life and include all domains of wellness (physical, emotional, spiritual, psychological and intellectual), as well as alternative destinations (and solutions) for medical treatment and healthcare (Adams *et al.*, 2015; Bodeker, 2018; Latif *et al.*, 2019). Empirical evidence has shown that wellness tourism is primarily the act of travelling to foreign countries and/or parts of one's own country (very much a Japanese activity; Funck & Cooper, 2013) to seek medical solutions for various health issues, such as cancer treatments, body-parts replacement, fertility, cardiac surgery, orthopaedic therapy and so on (Connel, 2006; Han & Hyun, 2015). Recently, however, there has been a shift in travel patterns towards wellness tourism that focuses on the mind–body therapies such as calligraphy, traditional Chinese medicine, ayurveda, yoga and spa (Connell, 2006; Cooper *et al.*, 2015; Erfurt-Cooper & Cooper, 2009; Hall, 2011; Huang & Xu, 2018; Latif *et al.*, 2019; Smith & Puczkó, 2015; Yu *et al.*, 2021).

Calligraphy is an activity that combines language, art and mental/physical activity. Incorporating the activities of calligraphy into wellness tourism allows for mind–body therapy based on the physical act of brushing ink (John W. Brick Mental Health Foundation, 2022), while practicing meditation and breathing techniques (Banushi *et al.*, 2023) and facing one's feelings. In this chapter, we show how this can be done either in a group or individually; but the most important point is that, after creation, there is time to introduce a participant's own effort to the group and communicate its value. The goal is not to write well, or even to study the often-used Japanese *kanji* or Islamic art that are its basis but rather to value current feelings (state of mind) and emotions while completing the task. Our approach is to use the workshop methodology described in this chapter to enhance visual perception, increase attention and concentration, help those involved to perform controlled actions, remove their inhibitions, manage impulses, improve monitoring ability, strengthen working memory and enhance their ability to execute tasks.

No matter what the challenges confronting the tourism industry are, wellness tourism is here to stay (Dini & Pencarelli, 2021; Global Wellness Institute, 2023; Han *et al.*, 2018; Xie *et al.*, 2021). In this chapter we outline our manifestation of it: calligraphy (arts) therapy (Gaur, 1994). Fancourt *et al.* (2023) and Magsamen and Ross (2023), among others, show that arts engagement impacts positively our mental health and wellbeing, reduces stress, alleviates symptoms of depression and increases our social supports, while protecting against mental health disorders and cognitive decline (Backman *et al.*, 2022; Kansky & Diener, 2017; Keyes, 2014). Calligraphy is an activity that bridges the gap between language processing and artistic expression (Tharp, 2003). This characteristic makes it particularly stimulating for the brain, activating both the left and right hemispheres, and is why we have chosen to explore the use of calligraphy as a support for our contribution to wellness tourism (Dillette *et al.*, 2020). Language processing is a primary function of the left hemisphere (Sousa, 2017). During calligraphy therapy the left hemisphere of the brain is engaged in several ways: decoding the written word or characters being formed, recalling and forming the proper sequence of strokes, and an internal dialogue guiding hand movements for precise letter formation (Christman *et al.*, 2010). At the same time the right hemisphere, known for its role in spatial awareness, visual processing and creativity, is involved in visualizing the desired final form of the calligraphy piece, maintaining spatial relationships between strokes and characters, and coordinating our hand movements for smooth and controlled execution (Christman *et al.*, 2010).

Activities that engage both hemispheres of the brain can enhance cognitive function, improve memory and promote overall wellbeing (Jaeggi *et al.*, 2008). Tharp (2003), however, suggests that building a creative habit incorporating cognitive function, for example, requires daily practice. Incorporating calligraphy therapy into wellness tourism through relaxation in a group or individually, allows for calming the mind by brushing ink, meditating, learning breathing techniques and facing one's feelings through calligraphy. Recent studies have demonstrated that, since calligraphy is an activity that works on the entire cognitive function, it is expected to be effective in relieving stress (Kazakov & Oyner, 2021; Wideman, 2024). By describing our approach to calligraphy therapy in this chapter, we aim to enlighten readers about a cultural and mental/physical activity that can be enjoyed in groups or individually and that will help to maintain physical and mental functions by promoting stress relief and relaxation within wellness tourism (Powell, 2018; Yu *et al.*, 2021).

9.2 The Enduring Link: Exploring the Historical and Cultural Roots of Calligraphy and Wellbeing

From the delicacy of Chinese brushstrokes to the intricacies of Islamic script, calligraphy transcends the act of writing. It is an art form steeped in history, in culture, and it has a profound connection to human wellbeing (Gaur, 1994; Global Council for Happiness and Wellbeing, 2022; Global Mind Project, 2023; Takeda, 2022): the basis for wellness tourism. This section looks at the rich tapestry of calligraphy traditions and shows how, for centuries, the practice has fostered mindfulness, focus and a sense of inner peace (Wei & Long, 2021) and how it is an established source of wellness that we hope to bring to the forefront of wellness tourism.

By way of context, the demand for personal and community wellness is increasing worldwide. The 2023 Global Wellness Economy Monitor showed that the global wellness industry is now growing at 12% per year to a $5.6 trillion market in 2022 (Global Wellness Institute, 2023), with the 'mental wellness' segment growing even more rapidly (12.8%) to US $181 billion. While the recent COVID-19 pandemic temporarily put a stop to this growth, its inherent attractiveness has meant that it has been revitalized since 2021; in Japan, for example, societal interest in such forms of health has increased (European Parliamentary Research Service, 2020).

Calligraphy, by its very nature (Imo, 2024; Wideman, 2024), requires and produces a coordinated effort between the hemispheres of the brain, brought about by considerable practice, and leading to the following benefits:

- The act of concentrating on both the form and meaning of the characters being written can enhance focus and concentration.
- The repetitive and controlled movements involved in calligraphy can improve fine motor skills and hand–eye coordination.
- The freedom to explore different styles and techniques in calligraphy allows for creative expression and problem-solving.

In sections 9.2.1–9.2.3 we discuss the cultural basis of calligraphy that underlies what we are proposing in the wellness tourism context.

9.2.1 East Asia: The art of cultivating harmony

In East Asia, calligraphy holds a particularly esteemed position (Lovett, 2017). The Chinese characters (*hanzi*) and the Japanese characters (*kanji*) are not merely symbols to learn as vocabulary: they are imbued with meaning and history. The practice of calligraphy, known as *shofo* in China and *shodo* in Japan, is viewed as a form of self-cultivation and a path to harmony, rather than considered just an alphabet. The emphasis lies not just on the final product but on the mindful process itself. The slow, controlled movements of the brush require focus and concentration, akin to a form of meditation. Ancient Chinese texts like the *Classic of Calligraphy* by Wang Xizhi (Wei & Long, 2021) emphasize the importance of a tranquil mind and the connection between breath, movement, and character formation. Similarly, Japanese *shodo* emphasizes '*fude no kokoro*', which translates to 'the heart of the brush' – a concept that underscores the importance of channelling one's inner state onto paper (Takeda, 2022).

On 26 January 2024, the UN Agency for Cultural Affairs announced that the Inter-Ministerial Liaison Conference of the *Convention for the Safeguarding of Intangible Cultural Heritage* had decided to propose 'Calligraphy' for inclusion on the UNESCO Intangible Cultural Heritage list, following an earlier meeting at the Intangible Cultural Heritage Subcommittee of the Council for Cultural Affairs on 18 December 2023, where 'Calligraphy' had been selected as a candidate for 2024 UNESCO Intangible Cultural Heritage list. At this point the listing process had taken some nine years (Imo, 2024), pushed by Japan. The UNESCO Intangible Cultural Heritage registration review on this application is expected to take place in 2026. Beyond the meditative and cultural aspects, calligraphy in East Asia is seen as a reflection of personal character: the quality of one's brushstrokes reflects not just skill but also inner qualities like discipline, patience and perseverance. This belief is rooted in the Confucian philosophy that emphasizes self-improvement and moral cultivation (Tan, 2017) and is used in our activity to reinforce the concept of mindfulness when we set the framework for each workshop.

9.2.2 The Islamic world: The art of divine beauty

In the Islamic world, calligraphy also transcends mere writing, becoming a sacred art form intricately linked to faith. Arabic script, with its flowing lines and geometric forms, holds immense beauty and spiritual significance. Islamic calligraphy is often used to adorn mosques, religious texts and everyday objects, serving as a visual representation of the divine word (Butler-Wheelhouse, 2020). The meticulous nature of calligraphy practice fosters a sense of mindfulness and devotion. The calligrapher's concentration mirrors the focus and discipline required for prayer and religious contemplation.

9.2.3 The western world: The legacy of penmanship

While less explicitly linked to wellbeing in comparison to the Eastern and Islamic traditions, calligraphy also holds significance in the western world. The practice of penmanship (defined as calligraphy in this tradition), from the intricate illuminated manuscripts of the Middle Ages to the elegant calligraphy of the Renaissance, demands focus and concentration. This meticulous attention to detail fostered a sense of

Figure 9.1 Beginning the journey
Source: The authors (2024).

order and discipline, valued during a period of significant intellectual and cultural development (Lovett, 2017). Later, the invention of the printing press undoubtedly diminished the practical need for elegant script. However, the art of calligraphy continued to be practiced as a form of artistic expression and a means of preserving cultural heritage. In recent years, there has been a renewed interest in the calligraphic arts, with workshops and classes attracting individuals seeking mind and body wellness through artistic expression (Figure 9.1).

9.3 Incorporating Calligraphy into Wellness Tourism

Beyond its historical and cultural significance, calligraphy offers a surprising array of psychological benefits (Wideman, 2024). The act of transforming ink into beautiful characters on paper can be a powerful tool for promoting mindfulness, fostering creativity and enhancing overall wellbeing. The historical and cultural connection between calligraphy and wellness finds support in recent scientific research. The practice offers a multitude of benefits, including stress reduction, where the repetitive motions and focused concentration required for calligraphy can induce a state of relaxation, similar to meditation. This can lead to a reduction in stress hormones and feelings of anxiety (Farren, 2024). Other benefits include improved focus and attention. A word of caution here: our primary motive is relaxation and communication; we are not teaching calligraphy. We are promoting an alternative form of wellness based on the feeling of accomplishment, which has 'wellness' value in all communities.

For our purposes the essence of calligraphy therapy lies in what is happening in the present. Each brushstroke demands focused attention on breath control, posture, and the intricate dance between brush and paper. This mindful state mirrors practices like meditation, reducing mental clutter and promoting a sense of calm. Mindfulness practices can lead to decreased stress hormones, improved emotional regulation and enhanced focus (Kriakous *et al.*, 2021). The repetitive nature of calligraphy further contributes to mindfulness. The rhythmic movements of the brush create a sense of flow, a state of complete absorption in the activity that can lead to feelings of joy and satisfaction (Csikszentmihalyi, 2003).

The repetitive nature of calligraphy also fosters a state of focused attention. The mind becomes absorbed in the controlled movements of the hand, reducing mental clutter and promoting a sense of being present in the moment. This resembles mindfulness meditation, where focusing on repetitive actions like breathing helps quiet the mind and achieve a state of calm. The repetition ingrained in calligraphy practice also leads to the development of muscle memory. Over time, the body remembers the precise movements required to form characters, allowing for smoother and more controlled strokes (Csikszentmihalyi, 2003). This progression fosters a sense of mastery and accomplishment, further contributing to wellbeing. However, calligraphy in the fullest sense is a journey, not a destination. It requires patience and dedication to master the art form. The slow, deliberate movements cultivate a sense of perseverance and an ability to focus on the present moment without succumbing to frustration. This fosters a mindset of growth and the appreciation of delayed gratification. We use part of this to develop our mindfulness content in our wellness tourism workshops, taking care to begin the workshop with relaxation exercises to assist this process.

The discussion so far points to the conclusion that calligraphy can be a powerful tool for promoting wellness (Table 9.1). All in all, it offers a unique combination of mental and physical benefits that can significantly contribute to overall wellbeing. Importantly, however, the ancient art of calligraphy is finding a new lease of life within the burgeoning field of wellness tourism (Kriakous *et al.*, 2021). Wellness retreats, workshops and tours are increasingly incorporating calligraphy and similar activities into their offerings, recognizing their potential to enhance wellbeing and offer a unique cultural experience for travelers (Adams *et al.*, 2015). In the sections that follow, we explore how calligraphy is integrated into wellness tourism in our workshops, who this approach might appeal to, and further tease out the benefits of combining travel and calligraphy therapy.

Wellness retreats focused on mindfulness, stress reduction or creativity are incorporating calligraphy workshops into their programs. These workshops can range from beginner-friendly sessions to those aimed at more advanced practitioners. Beginner workshops might focus on basic brush techniques, stroke formation of simple characters, and the fundamentals of creating a balanced composition. Advanced workshops can delve deeper into specific calligraphy styles (e.g. Chinese brushwork, Islamic geometric

Table 9.1 The benefits of incorporating calligraphy therapy into wellness tourism

Benefit	**Description**
Mindfulness and focusing	The repetitive motions and concentration required for calligraphy encourage mindfulness. It allows the participant to be present in the moment, focusing solely on the formation of each stroke. This can be a great way to quiet the mind and reduce stress and anxiety.
Improved motor skills and coordination	Practicing calligraphy exercises fine motor skills and hand–eye coordination. This can be beneficial for people of all ages, but especially for those looking to improve dexterity or recovering from injuries.
Self-expression and creativity	Calligraphy allows creative expression through different styles, letterforms and colors. This creative outlet can be very therapeutic and promote a sense of accomplishment.
Flow state	The repetitive nature of calligraphy can induce a state of flow, where participants become completely absorbed in the activity and lose track of time. This state of flow is associated with feelings of joy, satisfaction and peak performance.
Enhanced self-esteem	Completing a calligraphy piece, whether it's a simple word or a more elaborate design, can provide a sense of accomplishment and satisfaction, while seeing calligraphy skills improve over time can boost confidence and self-esteem.
Group and community trust building	Calligraphy classes or workshops can be a great way to connect with others who share your interests. This social interaction can further contribute to overall wellbeing.
Relaxation and stress relief	The rhythmic and focused nature of calligraphy can be very calming and promotes relaxation. It can be a form of meditative practice, helping participants to detach from daily worries.

script), explore personal expression through calligraphy, or provide practice time with personalized guidance from experienced instructors. Our goal, however, is to use the mindfulness benefits to enhance wellness, not to learn the meaning of the characters themselves (Butler-Wheelhouse, 2020).

An expansion of this can be seen in calligraphy-themed tours. Travel companies are offering tours that integrate calligraphy experiences with cultural immersion. These tours visit historical sites or museums dedicated to calligraphy traditions, provide opportunities to learn from master calligraphers, and even allow participants to try their hand at the art form in a culturally significant setting (Buckley *et al.*, 2022). For example, a tour of China or Japan could include visits to renowned calligraphy schools, attendance at workshops on traditional brushwork techniques, and opportunities to observe and interact with master calligraphers (Han *et al.*, 2018). On the other hand, a tour through Turkey or Morocco could explore mosques with magnificent examples of Islamic calligraphy, providing opportunities to learn about the cultural significance of the art form. Finally, Artist Retreats are a specialized form of art activities. Some programs offer retreats that combine calligraphy practice with other wellness activities like yoga, meditation or nature walks. These programs provide dedicated time for focused calligraphy practice alongside opportunities for relaxation and rejuvenation, often in a beautiful setting (Xie *et al.*, 2021).

The use of calligraphy in wellness tourism can thus cater to the diversity of tourists seeking various wellness benefits. Those visitors seeking tools for stress management and relaxation can find calligraphy's repetitive motions, focus on breath, and meditative qualities to be particularly beneficial (our approach is based on this). Other people may be interested in artistic exploration, as calligraphy provides a creative outlet for individuals seeking new ways to express themselves visually (Wideman, 2024). The opportunity to explore different styles and techniques can be a source of self-discovery and artistic growth. For those interested in experiencing different cultures through cultural immersion, incorporating calligraphy into their travels offers a unique opportunity to learn about historical traditions, symbolic meanings behind characters, and the cultural significance of the art form.

There are several additional benefits to combining travel with calligraphy therapy (Luo *et al.*, 2018; Yu *et al.*, 2021). These benefits include:

(1) Change of scenery and disconnection from routine, because travelling to a new environment provides a welcome break from daily routine, allowing participants to immerse themselves fully in the practice. This change of scenery can enhance relaxation and promote mindfulness.
(2) Cultural immersion and deeper understanding, because learning calligraphy in its cultural context provides a deeper appreciation for the art form and its historical significance. This enriches the experience and fosters a sense of connection with a different culture.
(3) Social connection and community building, because participating in workshops or retreats alongside others allows for social interaction and a sense of community with like-minded individuals.

9.4 Challenges for Calligraphy Therapy in Wellness Tourism

Calligraphy therapy thus offers a unique and promising addition to the wellness tourism industry. However, there are certain challenges that need to be addressed to ensure its wider adoption and successful integration. These include:

(1) Calligraphy supplies and instruction might not be readily available at all wellness destinations. This can be a barrier for tourists who are interested in trying it but haven't planned ahead.
(2) Finding qualified instructors who can effectively combine calligraphy practice with wellness principles requires specific training. Not all calligraphy teachers are equipped to handle the therapeutic aspect, so developing training programs for calligraphers that incorporate wellness principles may be needed to bridge the instructor qualification gap. This could involve collaborating with psychological counsellors, physical therapists, yoga instructors, or meditation teachers.

(3) Integrating calligraphy workshops seamlessly into existing wellness programs requires careful planning. The duration, intensity and focus of the calligraphy sessions should complement the overall goals of the wellness retreat or program. A program of structured workshops that combines calligraphy practice with mindfulness exercises, guided breathing or meditation can enhance the therapeutic benefits. This would create a more holistic experience for wellness tourists.

(4) Be mindful of cultural preferences. We offer a variety of calligraphy styles from different cultures and incorporate elements from the destination country's calligraphy traditions.

(5) While our program offers a structured framework, we should consider incorporating flexibility to cater to individual needs. This could involve offering one-on-one sessions with a therapist or allowing participants to choose their focus areas.

9.5 Calligraphy Therapy and Creating Wellness in a Group

By addressing these challenges and capitalizing on the opportunities revealed in this chapter, the calligraphy activity that is at present usually a form of precision writing can become a sought-after and valuable addition to the wellness tourism industry as a form of therapy. The group therapy described here offers a unique way for tourists to combine cultural immersion, creative exploration and stress reduction during their travels and is the basis of our initiative: the creation of a new 'calligraphy therapy'. We utilize a workshop format that allows for scalability, depending on interest, but retains the interpersonal closeness that this experience is best suited to (Figures 9.2, 9.3, 9.4 and Table 9.2). Each workshop is allocated

Figure 9.2 Advertising and beginning the group therapy
Source: The authors (2024).

Figure 9.3 Workshops in operation
Source: The authors (2024).

Figure 9.4 The completed sessions
Source: The authors (2024).

Table 9.2 Schedule for therapy sessions

Time	Activity
5 minutes	The purpose and structure of this therapy session. Reveal the work process of 'Plan → Execute → Review → Correction → Repeat'
10 minutes	Presentation on the theory and practice of calligraphy and mindfulness: • impact of the physical activity of calligraphy, mindfulness and breathing • enhances visual perception • corrects posture • improves concentration • how we feel refreshed and experience stress reduction • how to activate the brain, by calmly focusing on the tip of the brush and cultivating concentration; the brain will be stimulated and trained. We want participants to see that by practicing calligraphy, they can gradually experience positive effects on their lives and remove the problems in daily life
10 minutes	Mindfulness practice: • practicing meditation and breathing techniques • facing one's feelings • and after calming the mind • work on calligraphy
10 minutes	Rub down an ink stick and further practice mindfulness (relaxation), calming the mind by practicing brushing ink
45 minutes	Calligraphy practice (Figures 9.2–9. 4): • learn to perform controlled actions • removes inhibitions, curbs impulses (stress management) • improves monitoring ability, judging whether the font is good or bad and correcting it • strengthens working memory • drawing while comparing the model (own style) • enhancing execution capability using the work process of 'Plan → Execution → Review → Correction → Repeat'
25 minutes	Discussion about the activity. Since calligraphy therapy is done in a group, there will be time to introduce members' own work and communicate how they felt. The goal is not to write well but to practice drawing while evaluating current feelings (state of mind) and emotions
15 minutes	Clean tools and finish

90 minutes to two hours and materials and workspaces are provided (a small fee is charged for materials). We have trialled this form of therapy at arts and street markets in New Zealand (Christchurch, Lake Tekapo), Switzerland (Interlaken, Geneva), Thailand (Bangkok, at the conference this book is a product of), and Oita Prefecture, Japan (Kitsuki, Oita City and Beppu City) and it proved to be very interesting and productive to passers-by and those who answered our advertising. Also, this workshop is easily combined with other forms of wellness tourism to produce a very attractive set of activities for the wellness traveller.

Our workshop is a concept that merges our expertise in tourism and psychology to create a unique and potentially transformative experience for wellness travelers. By combining established therapeutic techniques like mindfulness and calligraphy within a travel setting, we cater to a growing market seeking fresh approaches to wellness. This particular approach addresses the mind–body connection.

9.6 Conclusions

This chapter has revealed that calligraphy-based therapy has the potential to promote wellbeing within the context of wellness tourism. We presented a conceptual approach that integrates calligraphy practice in a workshop with mindfulness techniques and can be scaled to suit the circumstances of the tourists and the destination. This is based on the fact that wellness tourism offers individuals a chance to escape daily routines and achieve a balance between physical and psychological states. In this initiative, we created a 'calligraphy therapy workshop' that combined our years of experience in tourism management and clinical psychology as an input into wellness tourism. This is a sharing concept: calligraphy activities that are combined with psychotherapy are a new approach in the field of wellness tourism. In this approach we incorporate: (1) relaxation methods (calming the mind by brushing ink, practicing meditation and breathing techniques), facing one's feelings and, after calming the mind, (2) receiving guidance on and practicing calligraphy, and (3) reinforcing the relationship between calligraphy and brain function, activating both the right and left hemispheres of the participant's brains. Various studies have demonstrated that calligraphy is an activity that works on the entire cognitive function. In addition, we provide mindfulness and meditation along with calligraphy, thus turning this activity into a form of therapy which, when combined with travel, has the potential to be a central part of wellness tourism.

On the tourism side, travel experiences that result in an increase in wellness have always been one of the major contributors to health and wellbeing, but this benefit has often been in the background. Recently, however, many tourists are choosing to go on trips that have the direct aim of improving their health and their sense of wellness, and travel companies are offering tours that integrate calligraphy experiences with cultural immersion. These tours visit historical sites or museums dedicated to calligraphy traditions, provide opportunities to learn from master calligraphers, and even allow participants to try their hand at the art form in a culturally significant setting. It was the primary goal of this chapter to demonstrate the application of this activity. This activity can be used, like others, to escape from daily affairs, relieve life pressures, and to achieve a balance between physical and psychological states. Furthermore, it is inexpensive. Wellness tourism meets individual health-related needs by offering resources to the traveler that include, for example, hot springs, spas, yoga, meditation, calligraphy, massage, diet therapy, wellness education and support for medical treatment. Importantly, wellness is not a passive or static state but, rather, an 'active pursuit'; furthermore these contributions can be medical or leisure-based. Calligraphy, if directed in the way we have proposed in this chapter, can provide an important means of stress reduction in association with other activities.

However, while calligraphy therapy offers a unique approach to wellbeing, it is important to consider its limitations. While studies show promise, calligraphy therapy is a relatively new field. More research is needed to confirm its effectiveness for various conditions. Importantly, calligraphy styles and tools can be culturally specific: this can be a barrier for some participants. Furthermore, mastering calligraphy takes time and practice. This initial hurdle could be discouraging for those seeking immediate results so, while calligraphy offers benefits, it is likely to be most effective when combined with other established therapeutic approaches. In conclusion, calligraphy therapy holds promise as a tool for improving mental and emotional wellbeing. However, acknowledging its limitations can help manage expectations and ensure that it is used appropriately within a broader therapeutic framework.

References

Adams, K., Snyder, J., Crooks, V. and Johnston, R. (2015) Tourism discourse and medical tourists' motivations to travel. *Tourism Review* 70 (2), 85–96.

Backman, S.J., Huang, Y.C., Chen, C.C., Lee, H.Y. and Cheng, J.S. (2022) Engaging with restorative environments in wellness tourism. *Current Issues in Tourism* 26 (5), 789–806.

Banushi, B., Brendle, M., Ragnhildstveit, A., Murphy, T., Moore, C., Egberts, J. and Robison, R. (2023) Breathwork interventions for adults with clinically diagnosed anxiety disorders: A scoping review. *Brain Sciences* 13 (2), 256.

Bodeker, G. (2018) *Mental Wellness: Pathways, Evidence, and Horizons*. Mental Wellness Initiative, Global Wellness Institute.

Buckley, R., Cooper, M., Chauvenet, A. and Zhong, L. (2022) Theories of experience value & mental health at tourism destinations: Senses, personalities, emotions and memories. *Journal of Destination Marketing & Management* 26, 100744.

Butler-Wheelhouse, A. (2020) *The Rhythm of the Pen and the Art of the Book: Islamic Calligraphy from the 13th to the 19th Century*. Paul Holberton Publishing.

Christman, S.D., Propper, R.E. and Rauch, S.L. (2010) Functional asymmetry in the human prefrontal cortex during working memory tasks. *Neuropsychologia* 99, 174–185.

Connell, J. (2006) Medical tourism: Sea, sun, sand and... surgery. *Tourism Management* 27 (6), 1093–1100.

Cooper, M., Vafadari, K. and Hieda, M. (2015) *Current Issues and Emerging Trends in Medical Tourism*. IGI Global Press.

Csikszentmihalyi, M. (2003) *Good Business: Leadership. Flow, and the Making of Meaning*. Penguin Books.

Dillette, A.K., Douglas, A.C. and Andrzejewski, C. (2020) Dimensions of holistic wellness as a result of international wellness tourism experiences. *Current Issues in Tourism* 24 (6), 794–810.

Dini, M. and Pencarelli, T. (2021) Wellness tourism and the components of its offer system: A holistic perspective. *Tourism Review* 77 (2), 394–412.

Erfurt-Cooper, P.J. and Cooper, M. (2009) *Health and Wellness Tourism: Spas and Hot Springs*. Channel View Publications.

European Parliamentary Research Service (2020) *Japan's Aging Society*. EPRS.

Fancourt, D., Bone, J.K., Bu, F., Mak, H.W. and Bradbury, A. (2023) *The Impact of Arts and Cultural Engagement on Population Health: Findings from Major Cohort studies in the UK and USA 2017–2022*. The Social Biobehavioural Research Group, University College London.

Farren, D.E. (2024) *The Beginner's Guide to Meditation and Mindfulness: Reduce Stress, Decrease Anxiety, and Improve Mental Health through Meditation and Mindfulness*. Independently published. Kindle Edition.

Funck, C. and Cooper, M. (2013) *Japanese Tourism*. Berghahn Books.
Gaur, A. (1994) *A History of Calligraphy*. British Library.
Global Council for Happiness & Wellbeing (2022) *Global Happiness and Wellbeing Policy Report 2022*. Sustainable Development Solutions Network.
Global Mind Project (2023) *Mental State of the World in 2023: A Perspective on Internet Enabled Populations*. Sapien Labs.
Global Wellness Institute (2023) *Global Wellness Economy Monitor 2023*. Global Wellness Institute.
Guerra, R., Santos, N. and Gonçalves, E. (2022) Health and wellness tourism: Contributions to a local sustainable development strategy. In M.D. Vujicic., A. Kasim., S. Kostopoulou., J. Chica Olmo. and M. Aslam (eds) *Cultural Sustainable Tourism: Advances in Science, Technology & Innovation*. Springer.
Hall, C.M. (2011) Health and medical tourism: A kill or cure for global public health? *Tourism Review* 66 (1/2), 4–15.
Han, H. and Hyun, S.S. (2015) Customer retention in the medical tourism industry: Impact of quality, satisfaction, trust, and price reasonableness. *Tourism Management* 46, 20–29.
Han, J.-S., Lee, T.J. and Ryu, K. (2018) The promotion of tourism products for domestic tourists. *International Journal of Health Tourism Research* 20 (2), 137–146.
Hettige, S.T. (1991) Western and Ayurvedic systems of medicine in Sri Lanka: Some preliminary observations. *Journal of Social Science* 5 (1), 27–54.
Huang, L. and Xu, H. (2018) Therapeutic landscapes and longevity: Wellness tourism in Bama. *Social Science & Medicine* 197, 24–32.
Imo, K. (2024) *Japanese Calligraphy Cultural Association comment on the registration of Calligraphy on the UN Intangible Heritage List*. JCCA.
Jaeggi, S., Buschkuehl, M., Jonides, J. and Shah, P. (2008) Improving fluid intelligence with training on working memory. *Proceedings of the National Academy of Sciences* 105 (38), 16768–16773.
John W. Brick Mental Health Foundation (2022) Move your mental health: A review of the scientific evidence on the role of exercise and physical activity in mental health. https://www. johnwbrickfoundation.org/move-your-mental-health-report/
Jones, M. and Liyanage, C. (2018) Traditional medicine and primary healthcare in Sri Lanka: Policy, perception and practice. *Asian Review of World Histories* 6, 157–184.
Kansky, J. and Diener, E. (2017) Benefits of wellbeing: Health, social relationships, work, and resilience. *Journal of Positive Psychology and Wellbeing* 1 (2), 129–169.
Kazakov, S. and Oyner, O. (2021) Wellness tourism: A perspective article. *Tourism Review* 76 (1), 58–63.
Kessler, D., Lee, J.H. and Whittingham, N. (2020) The wellness tourist motivation scale: A new statistical tool for measuring wellness tourist motivation. *International Journal of Spa and Wellness* 3 (1), 24–39.
Keyes, C.L.M. (2014) Mental health as a complete state: How the salutogenic perspective completes the pictures. In G.F. Bauer and O. Hämmig (eds) *Bridging Occupational, Organizational and Public Health: A Transdisciplinary Approach* (pp. 179–192). Springer.
Kriakous, S.A., Elliott, K.A., Lamers, C. and Owen, R. (2021) The effectiveness of mindfulness-based stress reduction on the psychological functioning of healthcare professionals: A systematic review. *Mindfulness* 12 (1), 1–28.
Latif, R.A., Zubir, A.Y., Asbollah, A.Z. and Som, E.M. (2019) Development of wellness-village tourism: An exploratory study of a small town. *International Journal of Innovation, Creativity and Change* 6 (3), 417–432.
Lovett, P. (2017) *The Art and History of Calligraphy*. British Library.
Luo, Y., Lanlung, C., Kim, E., Tang, L.R. and Song, S.M. (2018) Towards quality of life: The effects of the wellness tourism experience. *Journal of Travel & Tourism Marketing* 35 (4), 410–424.
Magsamen, S. and Ross, I. (2023) *Your Brain on Art: How the Arts Transform Us*. Canongate Books.

Powell, A. (2018) When science meets mindfulness. *The Harvard Gazette*, 9 April. https://news.harvard.edu/gazette/story/2018/04/harvard-researchers-study-how-mindfulness-may-change-the-brain-in-depressedpatients/

Smith, M. and Puczkó, L. (2015) More than a special interest: Defining and determining the demand for health tourism. *Tourism Recreation Research* 40 (2), 205–219.

Sousa, D.A. (2017) *How the Brain Learns* (5th edn). Corwin.

Takeda, R. (2022) *Shodo: The Practice of Mindfulness through the Ancient Art of Japanese Calligraphy*. Watkins Publishing.

Tan, C. (2017) Confucianism and education. In G. Noblit (ed.) *Oxford Research Encyclopedia of Education* (pp. 1–18). Oxford University Press.

Tharp, T. (2003) *The Creative Habit: Learn It and Use It for Life*. Simon & Schuster.

Wei, L. and Long, M. (2021) Entexted heritage: Calligraphy and the (re)making of a tradition in contemporary China. *China Perspectives* 2021 (3), 41–51.

Wideman, R. (2024) *The Psychology of Calligraphy: A Path to Mindful Relaxation and Creativity*. Calligrascape.

Xie, L., Guan, X., He, Y. and Huan, T.C. (2021) Wellness tourism: Customer-perceived value on customer engagement. *Tourism Review* 77 (3), 859–876.

Yeung, O. and Johnston, K. (2020) *Defining the Mental Wellness Economy*. Global Wellness Institute.

Yu, J., Smale, B. and Xiao, H. (2021) Examining the change in wellbeing following a holiday. *Tourism Management* 87, 1–12.

Theme 3
Wellness Tourism Destination Development and Management

10 The Prospects of Ethno-Botanical Wellness Tourism through a Destination Stewardship Approach: Evidence from India

Sushma Maligi and Jagadeesh Kivudanavar

10.1 Introduction: Environment and Wellness Tourism

Nature – with its diverse and vital offerings, like water, oxygen and biodiversity – sustains life. All spheres of life are somehow connected to the wild or to the domesticated component of biodiversity. The edible parts account for the major source of food and medicine. Their value is apparent in the fields of agriculture, building, furniture, paper making, textiles, dyes, oils, perfumes and various other spheres.

The living environment significantly influences the shaping of human cultures where it is revered as source of life; and, eventually, humans also influence their environment. The need to conserve the biological resources of the environment, and the restrictions that this imposed on people, required an awareness of the need to share resources and required conscious decision-making to implement it. Eventually, with time, these conscious restrictions were ingrained as values. These values are reflected in religious beliefs, land-management practices, dietary considerations, art forms, social structures, and even language in various cultures (Sharma & Sharma, 2009).

Ethno-botany is a discipline that addresses the relationships between humans and plants as an interface of natural and social sciences (Fuller, 2013). Ethno-botanical knowledge and information have proven to have significant and diverse contributions to make toward human health and wellbeing. Thus, ethno-botany studies the traditional use of plants by humans, especially Indigenous peoples, which structures traditional ecological knowledge (TEK) linking it to human wellbeing (Berkes *et al.*, 2000).

Since time immemorial, India has revered the environment as a transcendental entity that is sacred and divine, something attested to by Indian philosophy through Vedantha and the Vedas. Indian philosophy emphasizes that people have a participatory life with the environment, and they play a momentary role before they attain their solace in the five elements: water, earth, sky, air and fire (James, 2013). The abundant land of India is blessed with rich medicinal plants. It has been the sought-after destination for authentic traditional wellness offerings and experiences offering nature-based alternatives such as ayurveda and plant-based folk medicine systems (Mishra, 2020). The *Global Wellness Economy Monitor 2023* ranks India as the seventh top performer amongst wellness economy markets in the world.

This chapter proposes an ethno-botanical wellness tourism (EWT) model where TEK is combined with modern management techniques of destination stewardship to bring about a potentially regenerative way of integrating ethno-botany, wellness and tourism. This study defines Ethno-botanical Wellness as 'travel to ethno-botanical areas to maintain or improve wellbeing through traditional wellness techniques'. This definition is adapted from the wellness tourism definition of the Global Wellness Institute (2017).

The study uses evidence from Kappathagudda, a rich habitat of 'medicinal and aromatic plants' (MAPs) located in Karnataka, India, as an ethno-botanical wellness destination (see Figure 10.1). The study area is at a crossroads as it is an offshoot of the Western Ghats, partly declared to be a wildlife sanctuary to protect the flora and fauna. Nonetheless, much of the eco-sensitive area is exposed to mining and other unsustainable forms of economic development (Ramachandra *et al.*, 2018). The local community has long established a unique relationship between the flora and fauna of the area. Owing to their beliefs and local wisdom, the people have a unique culture, often expressed through practices, customs, crafts, food, costumes, etc. Conservation of such invaluable heritage could be at risk through non-traditional and unsustainable forms of development. Unplanned and *ad hoc* development will erode the ecology and the wisdom, so immediate attention is required. The growing need for sustainable lifestyle and wellness retreats creates an opportunity to develop MAP destinations as Ethno-botanical Wellness destinations (Jacob *et al.*, 2024). The scope is immense in creating equal opportunities for ecological conservation, sustaining and regenerating folk medicine while ensuring economic gains and checking unhealthy development.

This chapter thus explores the phenomenon of ethno-botanical tourism and wellness tourism in a MAP-based destination and the key drivers and challenges of implementing ethno-botanical wellness tourism based on the destination stewardship model.

10.2 Literature Review

10.2.1 Medicinal and aromatic plants

India is one of the 17 mega biodiversity-rich countries, and harbors 4 of the world's biodiversity hotspots, which account for 7% of the world's biodiversity (IUCN, 2024). The country is one of the world's richest sources of medicinal plants, with more than 45,000 species according to the National Medicinal Plant Board. It is a rich reservoir of MAPs containing a wealth of valuable genetic resources. It is blessed with diverse geographic and agro-climatic zones and possesses a culture rich in folklore and traditional knowledge. Kappathagudda is a treasure trove of medicinal and aromatic plants (Katrahalli, 2010; Kshirsagar & Vrishni, 2021). The use of this knowhow in healthcare has resulted in the application of MAPs in large numbers via our traditional systems of medicine, called Indian systems of medicine (ISM), which include ayurveda, siddha, unani and homoeopathy, and therapies such as yoga and naturopathy. Practitioners and scholars of traditional medicine often say, 'Nanaushadhi Bhootam Jagat Kinchit', i.e. 'There is no plant in the world which does not have medicinal properties', indicating that every plant species possesses medicinal benefits. It is no exaggeration to say that the use of plants for human health is probably as old as humanity itself (Babu *et al.*, 2017). The World Health Organization has stated that medicinal plants are accessible, affordable and culturally appropriate sources of primary healthcare for more than 80% of Asia's population (Bodeker *et al.*, 2005).

Yet, despite the availability of these resources, application and development of folk medicine and knowledge of it has been limited. Instead, fast-paced, ill-sighted developments have exposed MAPs to greater risk of extinction (Das *et al.*, 2016). While few species eventually fade out from natural causes, the threat to MAPs is accentuated and multiplied due to human intervention (Bhattarai & Karki, 2004). Studies also back the need for conservation and the sharing of knowledge to encourage learning, in order to avoid the loss of folk knowledge on medicine and wellbeing (Jacob *et al.*, 2024; Kumar *et al.*, 2021). The involvement of all stakeholders, i.e. collectors, traders, manufacturers and consumers, through the sharing of benefits, can help a great deal in the conservation of resources, which is so vital for human health and survival. Although full participation of local communities in the conservation and management of MAPs is desirable in regenerating and maintaining a viable population of medicinal plants in natural habitats, including forests (Tiwari *et al.*, 2004), studies have found it challenging, due to the diverse interests, to find a standard solution involving multiple stakeholders (Ferreira *et al.*, 2020; Kazadi *et al.*, 2016; Paine & Roe, 2018).

At the community level, local people are the actual resource managers. Although they depend heavily on these natural resources, they might be misled by commercial interests that seek to exploit their poverty and/or due to ignorance, which might give rise to severe problems for the environment and their livelihoods. Hence, it is suggested that the approach taken to conserving wild medicinal plants for sustainable exploitation should be targeted at different levels, involving all stakeholders, from improving living standards to changing people's attitudes (Kumar *et al.*, 2021). Evidence from Namdapha National Park in Arunachal Pradesh, and from Kaziranga National Park and Manas wildlife sanctuary in Assam, warn of the rise and fall of ecotourism joint ventures. The government has said that the disadvantages of developing tourism outweigh any economic advantages (Shackley, 1995). Adoption of the destination stewardship approach thus balances the needs of multiple stakeholders within the legislative framework, avoiding any negative tourism development consequences.

10.2.2 Ethno-botany, wellness and tourism

The study of the association, interaction and interrelationships of ethnic human societies (mainly tribal and Indigenous communities) with the surrounding flora is termed 'ethno-botany' or aboriginal botany. Harshberger, one of the fathers of economic botany in America, is credited with the term ethno-botany in 1896. There are many sub-disciplines of ethno-botany dealing with various aspects of tribal plants, such as ethno-agriculture, ethno-taxonomy, ethno-medicobotany, ethno-ecology, ethno-mycology, ethno-gynecology, ethno-toxicology, ethno-pharmacology, ethno-phytotaxonomy, ethno-veterinary medicine, etc. (Vedavathy, 2004). Ethno-botanical surveys are conducted to locate culturally important, regionally scarce, and disappearing medicine plants, and the studies back the use of MAPs in healing and wellness leading to health promotion and ecological integrity (Dean, 2024; Pesek *et al.*, 2009; Pforr & Locher, 2003; Putri *et al.*, 2015; Ruhanen, 2009; Setiadi & Siringoringo, 1970).

The intertwining benefits of travel and the natural habitat could be experienced through ethno-botanical wellness tourism. As with any other tourism destination that strives to create a competitive edge, wellness destinations worldwide have created their niche from their unique geography, culture, diet and traditional wellness techniques by offering sand baths, yoga retreats, Turkish baths, hot springs or urban spas. Thus, ethno-botany and wellness through yoga, meditation, ayurveda, and nature-based medicines create a unique opportunity for the wellness seeker to immerse themselves in ethno-botanical wellness tourism.

Many studies have backed the benefits of embracing ethno-botanical tourism (Hakim, 2021; Ibo & Arimukti, 2019). The destinations, with their rich cultural and ecological heritage, have started integrating agriculture, culture and economy through tourism ventures to sustain the people's culture and livelihoods, as in Bali (Dewa *et al.*, 2024). Ethno-botanical knowledge has increased the socioeconomic status of the regions through tourism development (Mansfield & Potočnik Topler, 2021; TERRA, 2023). Studies have been conducted in well-established religious tourism destinations in Madura islands, seeking to evaluate the local wisdom towards the use value of the species and their need in the well-established religious tourism destinations in Madura islands (Putri & Bashri, 2019). There is evidence that some tourism destinations have developed ethno-botanical tourism in the Banyak Islands of Indonesia, making use of Halobanese oral traditions (Andriany *et al.*, 2022). Conservation and sustainable utilization of MAPs have been integrated with ecotourism development strategies to promote rainforest eco-lodges and ethno-botanical tourism in Indonesia (Ridwan *et al.*, 2023). And Izmir, in Turkey, facing the problems of a reduction in agricultural land and migration to the cities, has opted for ecotourism and cultural tourism to check the depletion of resources and the migration of the people to the urban areas (Emekli & Baykal, 2011).

10.2.3 Indian philosophy and the destination stewardship approach

The environment, and the life around it, are closely intertwined in Indian Hindu philosophy (Awasthy & Gupta, 2021): living and non-living entities are equally revered and are in harmony with day-to-day activities. Hindu philosophy emphasizes safeguarding the biotic and abiotic worlds, which sustain life. Various rituals have been institutionalized in an attempt to safeguard the unique environmental species (Pattnaik, 2024). The concepts of sacred forests and groves (Rath & Ormsby, 2020) and the elements of earth, water, air and fire (Hopkins, 2020) have been assigned the greatest importance and have been worshiped since time immemorial in India. Associated with local deities, flora and fauna have been revered as an essential part of religious rituals fostering conservation and regeneration. The sacredness of a site reflects a vital link between community wellbeing and nature conservation (Delgado *et al.*, 2010; Maru *et al.*, 2020).

In today's dynamic and culturally diverse environment, there is an increased need for a legal structure that ensures conservation (Martin *et. al.*, 2013, 2016). A regulatory framework identifies eco-sensitive areas as reserved areas, protected areas, and nationally significant parks. The area of our study is designated a Wildlife Sanctuary. Any area within any reserved forest, or any part of the territorial waters considered adequately significant from an ecological, faunal, floral, geomorphological, natural or zoological point of view, can be designated a sanctuary under the provisions of Section 26A of the Wild Life (Protection) Act 1972, to protect, propagate or develop wildlife or its environment (Karnataka Forest Department, 2024). While fully protected areas are subject to strict checks on unsustainable activities, the regulations covering partially protected areas are widely variable and allow many activities, like collecting wood, fishing, etc., resulting in questionable stewardship of ecological and social factors (Turnbull *et al.*, 2021a, 2021b). The need for stewardship aroused concerns among a significant part of the local community, who countered the government's move to declare the area as reserved forests and sanctuaries since the sole source of their livelihood derived from forests and agriculture. The protected tag restricts the movements and access of the locals, causing a conflict of interest (Sawkar & Hegde, 2013).

Sustaining and safeguarding the resources that sustain life in an area, while keeping it open for public access and economic benefits, seems possible through the contemporary framework of destination stewardship. The concept attests to taking responsibility for protecting, caring for, and using the environment for positive ecological and social outcomes (Bennett *et al.*, 2018; Lerner, 1993). Destination stewardship is an approach to destination governance that seeks to balance, and meet, a destination's economic, environmental and social/cultural needs while operating within a legitimate governance model with active participation from the public and private sectors, as well as the local community (Day, 2024; Galant & Golja, 2015). The pandemic has forced us to rethink and re-strategize destination planning based on a social and environmentally conscious approach and governance backed by ethical considerations. This calls for a collaborative approach asserting co-management of shared resources, such as natural and cultural resources, while catering to the market expectations and the needs of the local communities (WTTC, 2021). The destination stewardship approach is specifically beneficial for the area of study as it furthers the cause of sustainable development and social inclusion, encouraging proactive governance and co-creation – the primary global goals set forth by the United Nations.

While there has been significant evidence of wellness based on MAPs, scant research has been undertaken, or attempts been made, to tailor the ethno-botanical approach to deliver benefits to more prominent beneficiaries. Despite extensive research on destination planning and a collaborative approach, there is little evidence of a destination stewardship model. The current study is one of the preliminary attempts at conceptualizing wellness tourism based on ethno-botanical resources while considering a destination stewardship approach. This study thus proposes one solution for *in situ* conservation of the sensitive areas, integrating public–private–community collaboration to regenerate destination resources and enhance the economic benefits but with due care taken to minimize negative impacts.

10.3 Research Methodology and Data Collection

The current study is structured using a case study approach. It interprets the phenomenon of destination stewardship in conserving and sustaining a place's ethno-botanical resources through the qualitative techniques of interpretive phenomenology. Interpretative phenomenological analysis (IPA) is a method of qualitative inquiry that centers on comprehending individual personal lived experiences (Noon, 2018). It prioritizes the exploration of intricate experiences before forming broad assertions and is advantageous for investigating intricate, uncertain, and emotionally charged subjects (Alase, 2017; Lima *et al.*, 2020; Smith & Nizza, 2022). IPA strives to present descriptions of lived experiences without enforcing pre-existing theoretical frameworks. The commitment shared by the place's stakeholders and their feelings towards development are crucial to developing a destination and the policies affirming it.

The ethno-botanical sphere of the place was understood using secondary data sources. Data collection on destination stewardship was prompted by the Destination Stewardship Diagnostic Framework (WTTC, 2021) put forth by the World Tourism and Travel Council (WTTC). It guides scrutiny of the status and prospects of wellness tourism development and meets the needs of the destination. The analysis should provide a better understanding of the governance structure and the stakeholder involvement at the initial stages of development to support more outstanding destination stewardship. The framework explores the aspects of governance directed towards multiple stakeholders, including the public sector, the private sector and the community.

The Destination Stewardship Diagnostic Framework suggests reviewing the destination needs, governance system, and stakeholders involved (Public, Private, Third, and Community). As indicated in Table 10.1, the open-ended research questions were sourced and adapted from the diagnostic framework.

10.3.1 Recruiting participants and data collection

The current study enquires about the dimensions of the local tourism administration and the forest department (public sector), local businesses (private sector) and the local communities. During the initial visits, the local tourism administration and the forest department were interviewed to ascertain the current status of vigilance, conservation and developmental plans. To ascertain the perspective of the local community, in-depth interviews of 10 well-informed locals were conducted, coupled with observation, in the study area. The interviews

Table 10.1 List of questions adapted for the in-depth interviews with the multiple and interconnected stakeholders

Question number	Interview questions
(1)	How do the stakeholders describe Kappathagudda as an ethno-botanical destination?
(2)	What contexts or experiences have influenced their feeling of destination stewardship and belongingness?
(3)	How are you involved in propagating, conserving and sustaining the ethno-botanical resource of Kappathagudda?
(4)	What are the visitor motivation and visitor segmentation in Kappathagudda?
(5)	What are the needs and vision for development at Kappathagudda?
(6)	What is the existing institutional framework for implementing the destination development plan?
(7)	What form of collaboration would benefit sustainable and regenerative destination development?
(8)	Have the resources been utilized effectively with transparent and efficient protocols in place?
(9)	Who influences destination conservation and development? Furthermore, who, according to you, should lead the process?
(10)	Do you feel there is a need for rightful and lawful actions guided by the principles of integrity, accountability and transparency?
(11)	Do you feel there is enough data collection, analysis, reporting, and sharing of knowledge related to ethno-botanical resources and the prospects of sustainable livelihoods through sustainable tourism?

lasted about 1 hour and 40 minutes and used the judgmental sampling technique to involve the various community segments. Residents of the area who had been associated with the development and/or conservation, or who have known the area for two decades, were preferred to facilitate the insights. The interviews were conducted in the local language, Kannada, to facilitate better understanding and information exchange.

10.3.2 Data analysis

The semi-structured interviews were recorded using voice and video recorders and later transcribed for further analysis. The original transcripts were read in detail and exploratory notes were prepared along with highlighting the experiential statements indicating the participant's level of association with the destination and its resources. Significant statements were highlighted for each case and cross-case analysis was undertaken to synthesize and integrate the views of multiple stakeholders with the pre-determined questions to develop a cluster of meanings.

10.4 Area Under Study: Kappathagudda

The study area is located between 15°16′ and 16°55′ N latitude and 75°10′ and 75°55′ E longitude (Figure 10.1).

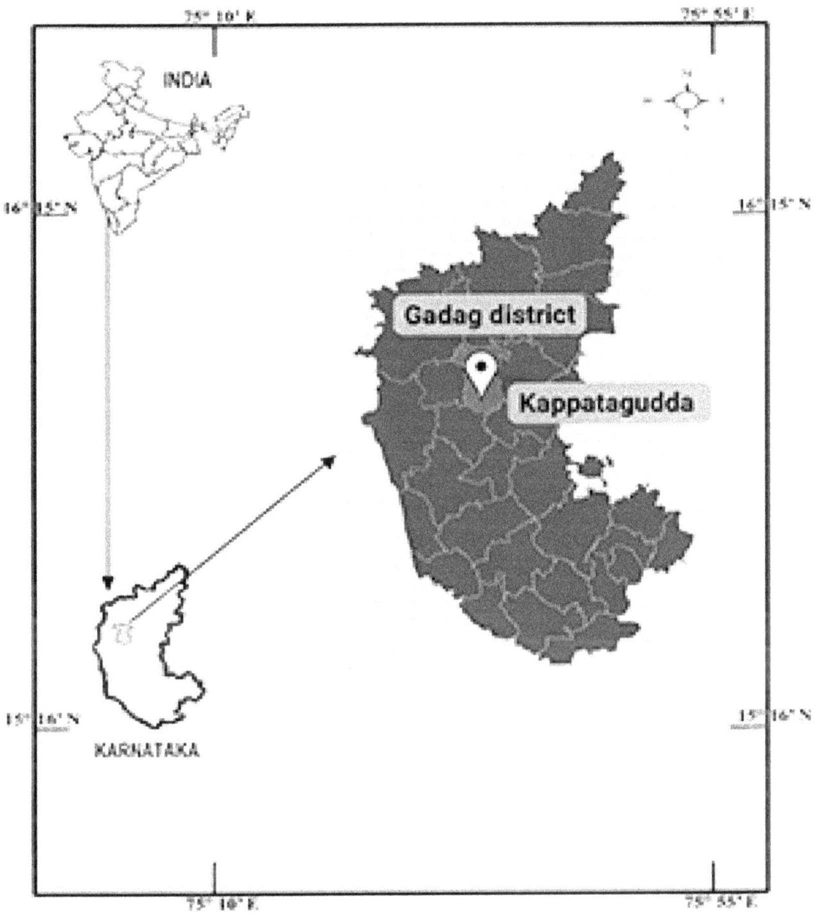

Figure 10.1 Location of the Kappathagudda Hills, Gadag, Karnataka, India

The Kappathagudda Hills, about 63 km in length and about 15 km in width, are an oasis in the dry, drought-prone lands of Gadag District, situated in the northern part of Karnataka State. References date back to the times of the Hindi epic *Ramayana*, where Hanuman is believed to have crossed this land at Sanjivini Parvat, the mountain of life-reviving herbs that brought Lakshmana's life out of danger during the final war with Ravana. It is a treasure trove of medicinal and aromatic plants and is also well known for its gold reserves and abundant wind energy. The inscriptions in the temples and tanks of Gadag District ascribe the hill as *Drona parvatha* (ASI, 1965). This indicates a few of the gardens and the tanks as *sarvamanya*, meaning most precious and dear to the deities, which means they were not utilized for economic gain.

Only a part of the Kappathagudda hills was declared a 'Conservation Reserve'; and, in due course, that decision had to be recalled owing to pressure from the mining companies. Much later, in May 2019, a part of it was declared a Wildlife Sanctuary by the state government. The landscape is unique and is a classic example of a dryland ecosystem. The sanctuary also has certain valleys and depressions containing a good mix of dry deciduous and riverine forests. It is the only Wildlife Sanctuary declared in the state with the objective of conservation of wild flora. The landscape hosts a wide range of fauna, including leopards, hyenas, wolves, foxes, jackals, four-horned antelopes, blackbucks, monitor lizards, jungle cats and various reptiles and birds. The sanctuary forms the central catchment for the Tungabhadra River in the district, as well as containing various tanks and ponds over the entire Gadag District. The sanctuary runs a length of 45 km from north to south and 25 km from east to west in four blocks. The total area of the sanctuary is 244.15 km^2, and it has an eco-sensitive zone of 595.77 km^2.

The sanctuary comes to life during the monsoon season with its green carpet of medicinal herbs and grasses, a wonderful treat for trekkers and hikers. The sanctuary is highly fragmented and faces immense anthropogenic pressure due to encroachments, grazing, illegal firewood collection and poaching. This poses a challenge to the park managers in preserving this unique ecosystem.

10.5 Findings and Discussion

Table 10.2 records the demographic details of the local respondents. Ten locals – 9 males and 1 female – were interviewed.

Their ages ranged from 30 to 90 years. The years of association indicate the local community's involvement level in understanding, interpreting, conserving and sustaining the region's natural capital. The discussion below is guided based on the Destination Stewardship Diagnostic Framework.

Table 10.2 Demographic information on the informed locals

Respondent number	Gender	Occupation	Age	Years of association
(1)	Male	Vanaspathi (herbal) practitioner	46	22
(2)	Male	Vanaspathi (herbal) practitioner	90	80
(3)	Male	Local business	45	15
(4)	Male	Seer	70	21
(5)	Male	Retired academician	65	55
(6)	Male	Informed local	70	60
(7)	Male	High school teacher	55	45
(8)	Male	Social worker	45	30
(9)	Male	Local guide	30	20
(10)	Female	Informed local	50	25

10.5.1 Ethno-botanical resource and destination association

The ethno-botanical analysis of the place has identified a unique, rare and endemic ecosystem deserving the highest protection available under the extent of the law. The ethno-botanical survey undertaken at the villages of the Kappa Hills indicated 322 species belonging to 234 genera and 90 families accounting for more than 21,000 medicinal plants. The medicinal value of the species was evident in the locals (respondents R1, R4 and R7) recalling the colloquial saying, '*Yeppattha Gudda Nodakkintha Kappathagudda Nodu*', which could be interpreted as 'It's worth visiting just Kappathagudda rather than to visit the 70 other hills'. The locals believe every single plant has one or other usage, leading to improved and sustained wellbeing. One of the herbal practitioners (Respondent 1) deliberated:

> About 27 types of ailments, including fever, diarrhea, piles, indigestion, back pain, chest pain, abdomen pain, could be cured using the herbs; and never has he ever taken any western medicine so far.

Kappathagudda is endowed with a rich abundance of the medicinal herbs (Vanaspati). Herbal healers are quite evident in the area and have been involved in ethno-botanical wellness for generations. One of the respondents recollected his great-grandfather as his first teacher. At the age of 90, the eldest respondent has 80 years of experience with medicinal herbs. Due to their expertise and age, the herbal healers are addressed as *Ajjayyas*, meaning 'the elderly' in the local dialect. Although enormous textual resources are available on medicinal herbs and aromatic plants in the ancient Indian texts such as the Vedas, Upanishads, and the Samhitas (compilations) on ayurveda and yoga, the traditional ecological knowledge forming the folk medicine system is passed down the generations through oral tradition mostly and there is no formal written documentation. The younger generation of the community are guided and mentored by the older practitioners in identifying the plants and ailments and in preparing the prescribed medicines. Learners are advised to work on identifying and understanding the MAPs based on their appearance, fragrance and the season in which they grow.

Ethno-botanical reports conducted by the forest department, universities and researchers are available in print and online. Respondent R4 (the seer) highlighted nature's modesty and selflessness by his quoting '*Hesarrillada, Hesarollada Gidagalu*', which means that several 'unidentified, unnamed plant species don't even demand a name but are highly potent and of great utility'.

All respondents agreed to wellness tourism initiatives based on the area's MAPs. The abundance of iron ore, manganese, limonite, gold, manganese and copper concentrations accentuates the effectiveness of the medicinal plants (Bandiera *et al.*, 2016; Pietrelli *et al.*, 2022). Thus, Kappathagudda is synonymous with a natural medicine system that has a multitude of benefits for almost all common ailments and general wellbeing. The community has standardized the process of preparing medicines, which demands meticulous planning to ensure their safety, efficacy and quality. The preparation follows the procedure of harvesting, part selection, cleaning, drying, storage, extraction (decoction/infusion/soaking/cold press), using solvents, dosage, preservation of medicine, and quality sustenance. Quality accreditations are preferred both to standardize the services and provide quality assurance.

10.5.2 Visitor segmentation

The study indicated that the place is well visited by traditional medicine practitioners and healers for the collection of medicinal roots, shoots, leaves, etc. Respondent 1 indicated:

> ...herbal healers who had searched for specific herbs from the Himalayas. They are regarded and welcomed by religious shelters like Mathas or temples, or they will be hosted by communities well-versed in the traditional medicine system....

Kappathagudda attracts both nature enthusiasts and researchers. With the growing number of updates on social media, domestic tourists go to the hills to indulge in trekking, birdwatching and camping. Entry to the hill is governed exclusively by the authorities.

10.5.3 Level of stewardship

The utility levels of the botanical resource together with the Indigenous culture of the people, who equate ecology with the highest power, and which has brought about the conservation and preservation of the flora and fauna, which has fueled destination stewardship. The various religious establishments (*mathas*), including Kappata Malleshwara temple of nature, hold nature to be at the core of worship. Safeguarding the ecology and disbursing the benefits of the ecology through folk medicine is a religious undertaking. It indicates manifold and fragmented efforts to preserve the MAPs of the area. Respondent R7 felt:

> The locals are part of the problem, and they alone can be part of the solution too... owing to unsustainable lifestyles and cooking, which barrens and burdens the ecology by collecting wood or plucking off the wild berries....

The locals revere the resources and have been deriving their livelihoods from them; hence, they have a yearly plantation tradition. They also have days on which they do not access certain herbs, indirectly indicating the community's level of stewardship. The community also faces the threat of crop loss due to the blackbuck antelopes; and yet, there have been no reports of killing as they worship it as part of their culture. The involvement level of the informed locals in safeguarding the resources is praiseworthy, as they team up to reach all corners of the villages to encourage the locals to adopt sustainable livelihoods and lifestyles through street plays.

Respondent R7 recollected the first time he was part of the play 25 years ago and how he is continuing to this day. The informed locals intend to keep their traditional knowledge and traditions alive by creating awareness and advocating the benefits of MAPs to the larger public. Making schoolchildren aware of the value of MAPs is undertaken as an annual activity by the schools nearby. This begins with an early morning trek into the hills initiated by the *mathas* and guided by the herbal experts. The trek also involves sessions by folk artists and the shepherd community, who make the children aware of the flora and fauna and of the common ailments of domesticated animals. The children are also encouraged to recite a poem or to narrate a story about nature that shows reverence for it. Learning happens outside the classroom and thus has a significant impact on young minds.

10.5.4 Destination need

The scope of the study, and the need of the destination, is to understand the usability of the shared pool of resources and the MAPs of the Kappathagudda hills. The 80,000 acres of the area are uninhabited, which provides room for excellent conservation activities. Nevertheless, owing to political pressures and business inclinations, the destination is under threat from the swaying sword of deforestation. Mining, poaching and the unlawful collection and processing of herbs and forest produce, have been pressing issues for the destination. While the government's efforts are credible in safeguarding the ecosystem, efforts to increase community awareness are needed. Non-use is treated as disrespect for the resource. Respondent R4 deliberated '*Kappathagudda Ulisi, Belesi, hagu balasi*' – the 'conservation, regeneration, and usage' of the medicinal herbs as the sole need. Sustainable and mindful consumption is professed instead.

10.5.5 Governance system

Analyzing the aspects of governance indicates that the public sector is firmly committed to protecting the unique ecosystem. However, it lacks a collaborative and consensual mode of implementation owing to the political pressures created by unethical business proposals. The destination calls for formal and informal networks of collaboration involving the religious establishments, the community, the private sector, the public sector and the tertiary sector. The tertiary services provide the required attention and services to benefit visitors by creating accessibility and experience. While the idea of herbal gardens and eco-parks is well conceptualized, in practice the necessary facilities are either not functioning or are inactive. The facilities need to create value by disseminating information and creating an immersive experience.

10.5.6 Resource mobilization

Traditional ecological knowledge needs to be well integrated with traditional healing systems and backed by ethical product development, ensuring optimum usage of the resources available. The involvement of NGOs and educational organizations such as universities could be beneficial in terms of knowledge, skill and resource sharing. All stakeholders have made fragmented efforts in an isolated form. The Nandiveri *matha*, in Gadag District, organizes a two-day fair, of importance both culturally and as a mark of the importance of nature. It celebrates the deity in the form of nature, and is a one-of-a-kind initiative. The government also organizes the Nature Tourism Festival. The rural university in the area has a thematic botanical garden with trees planted as per the zodiac signs. It is believed by the locals, as shared by respondent R2, that:

> Every zodiac sign has some favorable tree species, and walking through it and planting it would benefit the individuals in manifold as per the scriptures….

This indicates a regenerative form of ethno-botanical tourism. Certain plant species could be planted in sacred areas or public access areas, which would increase the area's oxygen level and provide rejuvenating shade. Simply sitting underneath trees such as *shami*, *bilwa* and *neem* could induce good health for all. The destination indicates a relatively high level of resource mobilization and an optimum level of green investment.

10.5.7 Influence

The commitment towards destination stewardship needs to be documented and shared through the community leaders and the other potential stakeholders, such as the students and the NGOs, as they have a huge impact on ensuring and enabling destination stewardship. Owing to the loss of about 765 hectares of the Kappathagudda forest area (out of 32,346.5 hectares) from illegal encroachments and wildfires, the religious establishment – along with the forest department, school and college-going students, and other environmental stewards – have planted 249,000 saplings. Respondent R10 indicated:

> Forest fires, once upon a time a regional concern, have elevated to be an international concern owing to the media and declaration by the government as a Wildlife Sanctuary....

10.5.8 Legitimacy

The mandate for the protection of the ecological resources and the development of the region for the better prospects of the stakeholders must be prioritized. Thus, continued scientific research collaborations and community engagement backed by political support is called for. Legal enforcement needs to be transparent and inclusive. Public funds need to be utilized for resource conservation and community upliftment while being accountable and accessible. Quality accreditations and certifications could benefit in the longer run to provide assurance. Media coverage and involvement would provide greater reach, legitimacy and impact.

10.5.9 Data- and knowledge-sharing

Data- and knowledge-sharing across the stakeholders is imperative to creating a unique and competitive wellness experience. The study indicates that 80% of the respondents were unaware of ethno-botany or ethno-botanical wellness. MAPs are well known but the collaborative development of new products and an understanding of emerging tourism trends are lacking across different segments. The government must proactively understand market needs and trends by investing in staff, skills and research. Digital aids would assist in visitor and resource management.

The destination stewardship model provides four plausible and possible scenarios based on the level of involvement of the multiple stakeholders in destination development and the level of interest towards stewardship. The study places Kappathagudda as the best fit for ‘Scenario 2’ of the destination stewardship model, indicating ‘Top–Down Steering’ having high public and community engagement in destination stewardship and low engagement of the private sector in destination stewardship.

The study indicates that Kappathagudda needs to address the following issues in developing of ethno-botanical wellness tourism:

- Fragmented approach.
- Focussing on value rather than volume.
- Narrowing the gaps between local governance, state governance, and central governance for the safety of the ecology and the livelihoods of the community.
- Adopting a proactive approach in researching, analyzing and disseminating knowledge.

10.6 Limitations and Conclusion

The study was limited to assessing Kappathagudda's prospects toward achieving sustainable destination development and planning, through the lens of a destination stewardship model. The ethno-botanical dimension of the location demands a detailed inquiry. Studies linking culture and sustainability would provide more meaningful, achievable and appropriate techniques for sustaining resources and livelihoods.

Despite limitations, ethno-botanical wellness tourism is one of the best ways to conserve and regenerate eco-sensitive MAP destinations while preserving natural healing methods. The current study adds to the body of knowledge by elaborating on ethno-botanical wellness and Indigenous philosophy as a means of sustaining ecological resources and destination stewardship. Such engagement has to date been one-sided, solely driven by the cultural and religious establishment backed by the public sector; however, community involvement is encouraged to co-create products and experiences.

Highlighting the practical implications, the study suggests sustainable economic models through green investments and green entrepreneurship avenues. The destination has promising prospects through inclusive entrepreneurial opportunities through wellness tourism retreats offering healthy routines, medicinal therapies, herbal botanical gardens, medicinal trails, healthy diet workshops, gastronomical experiences and gardening sessions, to foster regeneration. Destination assessment proves to be vital for the development of sustainable, inclusive and resilient destinations. The study places destination wellbeing through destination stewardship at the core of matters, rather than destination competitiveness, as it assures enhanced destination image, improved liveability, and accountability for shared resources. The chapter deliberates on conscious planning and green entrepreneurship through holistic wellbeing and traditional medicine systems.

Drawing attention to the social implications, this chapter strongly emphasizes harmonizing Indigenous philosophy, community wisdom, academic insights and industry outlooks, backed by a legal framework to protect the natural and cultural assets of value through regenerative strategies for ethno-botanical wellness tourism.

References

Alase, A. (2017) The interpretative phenomenological analysis (IPA): A guide to a good qualitative research approach. *International Journal of Education and Literacy Studies* 5 (2), 9–19.

Andriany, L., Lubis, T., Amalia, A., Abus, A.F. and Delima, D. (2022) Shaping ethno-botanical tourism on the coastal landscape through Halobanese oral traditions at

Banyak Island. *IOP Conference Series: Earth and Environmental Science*. https://doi.org/10.1088/1755-1315/1115/1/012103.

ASI (1965) *South Indian Inscriptions Vol. XV (Bombay–Karnataka Inscriptions Vol. II)*. Archaeological Survey of India.

Awasthy, R. and Gupta, R.K. (2021) Unravelling the layers of Indian culture and worldview: An exploratory study. *International Journal of Indian Culture and Business Management* 22 (1), 137–166.

Babu, N., Srivastawa, S.K., Prusty, M. and Sahoo, T. (2017) *Medicinal and Aromatic Plant Production Technologies*. ICAR- Central Institute for Women in Agriculture.

Bandiera, M., Dal Cortivo, C., Barion, G., Mosca, G. and Vamerali, T. (2016) Phytoremediation opportunities with alimurgic species in metal-contaminated environments. *Sustainability* 8 (4), 357.

Bennett, N.J., Whitty, T.S., Finkbeiner, E., Pittman, J., Bassett, H., Gelcich, S. and Allison, E.H. (2018) Environmental stewardship: A conceptual review and analytical framework. *Environment Management* 61 (4), 597–614.

Berkes, F., Colding, J. and Folke, C. (2000) Rediscovery of traditional ecological knowledge as adaptive management. *Ecological Applications* 10 (5), 1251–1262.

Bhattarai, N. and Karki, M. (2004) Medicinal and aromatic plants: Ethnobotany and conservation status. In J. Burley (ed.) *Encyclopedia of Forest Sciences* (pp. 523–532). Elsevier. https://doi.org/10.1016/B0-12-145160-7/00255-6.

Bodeker, G., Burford, G., Grundy, C., Ong, C.-K. and Shein, K. (2005) *WHO Global Atlas of Traditional, Complementary and Alternative Medicine*. World Health Organization.

Das, M., Jain, V. and Malhotra, S.K. (2016) Impact of climate change on medicinal and aromatic plants. *The Indian Journal of Agricultural Sciences* 86 (11), 1375–82.

Day, J. (2024) Destination stewardship and sustainable urban tourism. In C. Maxim, A.M Morrison, J. Day and J. Andres Coca-Stefaniak (eds) *Handbook on Sustainable Urban Tourism* (pp. 276–290). Edward Elgar Publishing.

Dean, M. (2024) Exploring ethnobotanical knowledge: Qualitative insights into the therapeutic potential of medicinal plants. *Golden Ratio of Data in Summary* 4 (2), 154–166.

Delgado, F., Escobar, C., Verschuuren, B. and Hiemstra, W. (2010) Sacred natural sites, biodiversity and wellbeing: The role of sacred sites in endogenous development in the COMPAS network. In B. Verschuuren, R. Wild, J. McNeely and G. Oviedo (eds) *Sacred Natural Sites* (pp. 188–197). Earthscan and the International Union for Conservation of Nature (IUCN).

Dewa, I., Agung, G., Putra, D. and Adhika, I.M. (2024) The traditional village as a part of a cultural landscape: The development of cultural agriculture tourism in Catur, Bali. *Sinergi* 28 (1) 43–54. https://doi.org/10.22441/sinergi.2024.1.005.

Emekli, G. and Baykal, F. (2011) Opportunities of utilizing natural and cultural resources of Bornova (Izmir) through tourism. *Procedia – Social and Behavioral Sciences* 19, 181–189.

Ferreira, V., Barreira, A.P., Loures, L., Antunes, D. and Panagopoulos, T. (2020) Stakeholders' engagement on nature-based solutions: A systematic literature review. *Sustainability* 12 (2), 640.

Fuller, R. (2013) Ethnobotany: Major developments of a discipline abroad, reflected in New Zealand. *New Zealand Journal of Botany* 51 (2), 116–138. https://doi.org/10.1080/0028825X.2013.778298.

Galant, A. and Golja, T. (2015) Towards destination stewardship: Forecasting financial performance of responsible tourism on a selected Croatian destination. In M.H. Bilgin, H. Danis, E. Demir and C.K.M. Lau (eds) *Innovation, Finance, and the Economy: Proceedings of the 13th Eurasia Business and Economics Society Conference* (pp. 157–170). Springer International Publishing. https://doi.org/10.1007/978-3-319-15880-8_13.

Global Wellness Institute (2017) Global Wellness Economy Monitor. Retrieved from https://globalwellnessinstitute.org/wp-content/uploads/2018/06/GWI_Wellness EconomyMonitor2017_FINALweb.pdf.

Hakim, L. (2021) Coffee: Ethnobotany, tourism and biodiversity conservation in East Java. *IOP Conf. Ser.: Earth Environ. Sci.* https://doi.org/10.1088/1755-1315/743/1/012063.

Hopkins, E.W. (2020) *The Religions of India*. BoD–Books on Demand.

Ibo, L.K. and Arimukti, S.D. (2019) Ethno-botanical study of Batak Toba sub-ethnic community in Martoba Village, Samosir District, North Sumatra. *Prosiding Seminar Nasional Masyarakat Biodiversitas Indonesia* 5 (1), 34–41 https://doi.org/10.13057/psnmbi/m050216.

IUCN (2024, August) *India*. https://iucn.org/: https://iucn.org/our-work/region/asia/countries/india.

Jacob, D.E., Nelson, I.U. and Izah, S.C. (2024) Healing trails: Integrating medicinal plant walks into recreational development. In S.C. Iza, M.C. Ogwu and M. Akram (eds) *Herbal Medicine Phytochemistry: Applications and Trends* (pp. 2049–2102). Springer International Publishing.

James, G.A. (2013) *Ecology is Permanent Economy: The Activism and Environmental Philosophy of Sunderlal Bahuguna*. SUNY Press.

Karnataka Forest Department (2024, March) Kappathagudda Wildlife Sanctuary. https://aranya.gov.in/aranyacms/(S(0eyio4ktl0dmedqaodzt3gwz))/English/WildLifeSanctuary.aspx.

Katrahalli, K.S. (2010) Wild medicinal plants of Kappat Hills, Gadag District, Karnataka. *Research and Reviews in Biomedicine and Biotechnology* 1, 111–118.

Kazadi, K., Lievens, A. and Mahr, D. (2016) Stakeholder co-creation during the innovation process: Identifying capabilities for knowledge creation among multiple stakeholders. *Journal of Business Research* 69 (2), 525–540.

Kshirsagar, Y. and Vrishni, S. (2021) *Kappathagudda: A Repertoire of Medicinal Plants of Gadag*. KFD.

Kumar, A., Kumar, S., Komal, Ramchiary, N. and Singh, P. (2021) Role of traditional ethno-botanical knowledge and Indigenous communities in achieving sustainable development goals. *Sustainability* 13 (6), 3062.

Lerner, S.C. (ed.) (1993) *Environmental Stewardship: Studies in Active Earthkeeping*. University of Waterloo.

Lima, I., Trujillo, C.A., Tapia, K.R.L., Padrón, O.J.M., Arciniegas, T.G. and Toro, M.E.N. (2020) Biodiversity and Culture' Theme Park: An educational–environmental and tourism strategy, La Paz Parish, Carchi Province. In A. Basantes-Andrade, M. Naranjo-Toro, M. Zambrano Vizuete and M. Botto-Tobar (eds) *Technology, Sustainability and Educational Innovation (TSIE)* (pp. 432–444). Springer. https://doi.org/10.1007/978-3-030-37221-7_36.

Mansfield, C. and Potočnik Topler, J. (2021) Building the ethnopôle: Eliciting and sharing ethnobotanical knowledge in tourism development. *Annals for Istrian and Mediterranean Studies* 31 (2), 197–208. https://doi.org /10.19233/ashs.2021.13.

Martin, A., McGuire, S. and Sullivan, S. (2013) Global environmental justice and biodiversity conservation. *The Geographical Journal* 179 (2), 122–131.

Martin, A., Coolsaet, B., Corbera, E., Dawson, N.M., Fraser, J.A., Lehmann, I. and Rodriguez, I. (2016) Justice and conservation: The need to incorporate recognition. *Biological Conservation* 197, 254–261.

Maru, Y., Gebrekirstos, A. and Haile, G. (2020) Indigenous ways of environmental protection in Gedeo community, Southern Ethiopia: A socio-ecological perspective. *Cogent Food & Agriculture* 6 (1), 1766732.

Mishra, K. (2020) *The Indic Quotient: Reclaiming Heritage through Cultural Enterprise*. Bloomsbury.

Noon, E.J. (2018) Interpretive phenomenological analysis: An appropriate methodology for educational research? *Journal of Perspectives in Applied Academic Practice* 6 (1), 75–83.

Paine, M.F. and Roe, A.L. (2018) 'Green medicine': The past, present, and future of botanicals. *Clinical Pharmacology & Therapeutics* 104 (3), 410–415. https://doi.org/10.1002/cpt.1168.

Pattnaik, B.K. (2024) Environmental and ecological bases of Indian traditions: Search for an Indigenous vision. In B.K. Pattnaik (ed.) *Environmental and Ecological Sustainability through Indigenous Traditions: Perspectives from the Global South* (pp. 57–94). Springer Nature Singapore.

Pesek, T., Abramiuk, M.A., Garagić, D., Fini, N., Meerman, J.C. and Cal, V. (2009) Sustaining plants and people: Traditional Q'eqchi' Maya botanical knowledge and interactive spatial modeling in prioritizing conservation of medicinal plants for culturally relative holistic health promotion. *Ecohealth* 6, 79–90. https://doi.org/10.1007/s10393-009-0224-2.

Pforr, C. and Locher, C. (2003) Indigenous tourism and ethnopharmacology: A new strategic alliance for a sustainable future? *Null*. https://doi.org/null.

Pietrelli, L., Menegoni, P. and Papetti, P. (2022) Bioaccumulation of heavy metals by herbaceous species grown in urban and rural sites. *Water, Air, & Soil Pollution* 233 (4), 141.

Putri, E.K. and Bashri, A. (2019) Ethno-botanical study of plant in historical–religious tourism area and the sacred place at Sumenep, Madura. *Biotropika: Journal of Tropical Biology* 7 (3), 102–111. https://doi.org/10.21776/ub.biotropika.2019.007.03.3.

Putri, R.I., Supriatna, J. and Walujo, E.B. (2015) Ethno-botanical study of plant resources in Serangan Island, Bali. *Asian Journal of Conservation Biology* 3 (2), 135–148.

Ramachandra, T.V., Bharath, S., Subash Chandran, M.D. and Joshi, N.V. (2018) Salient ecological sensitive regions of central Western Ghats, India. *Earth Systems and Environment* 2, 15–34.

Rath, S. and Ormsby, A.A. (2020) Conservation through traditional knowledge: A review of research on the sacred groves of Odisha, India. *Human Ecology* 48 (4), 455–463.

Ridwan, R., Zahrah, M. and Rahmawaty, R. (2023) Ethno-botanical study and conservation strategy of medicinal plants in the ecotourism area of Kedah Rainforest Lodges in Aceh, Indonesia. *Biodiversitas: Journal of Biological Diversity* 23 (12), 6227–6237. https://doi.org/10.13057/biodiv/d231218.

Ruhanen, L. (2009) Stakeholder participation in tourism destination planning another case of missing the point. *Tourism Recreation Research* 34 (3), 283–294. https://doi.org/10.1080/02508281.2009.11081603.

Sawkar, R.H. and Hegde, V.R. (2013) Development potential of Kappatagudda hill ranges in Gadag District, Karnataka. *Journal of the Geological Society of India* 82 (5), 447–454. https://doi.org/10.1007/s12594-013-0175-7.

Setiadi, I.G.W. and Siringoringo, R.L. (1970) Ethno-botanical tourism potential in Bali Botanical Garden. *Jurnal Master Pariwisata (JUMPA)* 3 (2), 387–396. https://doi.org/10.24843/jumpa.2017.v03.i02.p13

Shackley, M. (1995) Just started and now finished: Tourism development in Arunachal Pradesh. *Tourism Management* 16 (8), 623–625.

Sharma, P.D. and Sharma, P.D. (2009) *Ecology and Environment*. Rastogi Publications.

Smith, J.A. and Nizza, I.E. (2022) *Essentials of Interpretative Phenomenological Analysis*. American Psychological Association.

TERRA. *Journal of Local Development* 12 (2023), 126–149. https://doi.org/10.7203/terra.12.25651.

Tiwari, B., Tynsong, H. and Rani, S. (2004) Medicinal plants and human health. In J. Burley (ed.) *Encyclopedia of Forest Sciences* (pp. 515–523). Elsevier. https: //doi.org/10.1016/B0-12-145160-7/00256-8.

Turnbull, J.W., Clark, G.F. and Johnston, E.L. (2021a) Conceptualising sustainability through environmental stewardship and virtuous cycles – A new empirically-grounded model. *Sustainability Science*, 1475–1487. https://doi.org/10.1007/s11625-021-00981-4.

Turnbull J.W., Johnston E.L. and Clark, G.F. (2021b) Evaluating the social and ecological effectiveness of partially protected marine areas. *Conservation Biology* 35 (3), 921–932. https://doi.org/10.1111/cobi.13677.

Vedavathy, S. (2004) Tribal medicine and medicinal plants. In J. Evans, J. Burley and J.A. Youngquis (eds) *Encyclopedia of Forest Sciences* (pp. 532–538). Elsevier.

World Tourism and Travel Council (2021, July) *Towards Destination Stewardship: Achieving Destination Stewardship through Scenarios & a Governance Diagnostics Framework*. WTTC. https://researchhub.wttc.org/product/towards-destination-stewardship.

11 Thermal Tourism in Europe: Exploring the Wellness Dimension

Dália Liberato, Joana A. Quintela, Paulo Neto, Pedro Liberato and Filipa Brandão

11.1 Introduction

Health tourism is considered a strategic product for the development of many tourist destinations with thermal resources (Pereira *et al.*, 2023). Europe has one of the richest and best-documented areas of thermal waters – the use of which dates to Greek and Roman cultures where they formed part of everyday life – being one of the most ancient forms of western therapy (Solimene, 2020). In recent decades, health and wellbeing have become essential motivations for consumption (Kervankıran, 2016), drawing the interest of researchers from various disciplines (Río-Rama *et al.*, 2018). However, one of the current challenges for academic research and the wellness tourism industry is the conceptual development related to the critical term 'wellness'. Wellness is one of the new trends, not only in health tourism but also in modern tourism. It is a 'state of complete physical, mental and social wellbeing and includes attitudes and actions that prevent diseases, improve health and quality of life, and lead to physical and mental balance' (Šušić & Dimitrijević, 2015: 69).

In recent years, in Europe, classical thermalism – mainly focused on the 'curative' dimension – has been replaced by modern thermalism, mostly based on the 'wellness' dimension, where the offer is more focused on therapeutic motivations of a preventive nature, combined with recreational and tourist aspects (Brandão *et al.*, 2021). Following this trend, spas are beginning to regain a certain dynamism by investing in a diversified offer that considers not only therapeutic treatments but also a holistic perspective that includes both health and wellness services.

The global economic crisis caused by the COVID-19 pandemic severely affected the tourism industry. Several measures, such as social isolation, were adopted to combat and reduce contagion, which significantly impacted people's lives, contributing to financial, psychological and family imbalances (Corbari & Grimm, 2020). During the pandemic, the search for health and wellness destinations was motivated by fear, which increased stress and anxiety levels in healthy people and aggravated symptoms in those with pre-existing mental disorders (Oliveira *et al.*, 2020). The main aim of this study is to investigate how wellness has reshaped the thermalism sector. The specific goals of the study include examining whether supply has adapted to current demand and providing a critical analysis of the changes in traditional thermalism today. To achieve these research goals, a qualitative study was developed. A total of five European countries with a tradition of thermalism were included in the study.

The chapter begins with a literature review on the evolution of thermalism in Europe. The methodology focuses on the research design, highlighting the objectives of the study. This section also describes the empirical study process, including the research instrument, the primary data-collection procedure, and data analysis. The results are then discussed, and the study's limitations and proposals for future research are highlighted. Finally, the main conclusions of the study are indicated, as well as its theoretical and practical contribution.

11.2 Evolution of Thermalism

The concept of thermalism, derived from the Roman word 'thermae', has been used for 2000 years to describe a series of relaxation, bathing and social activities in which water is an indispensable natural resource (Britannica, 2021). To this end, the spas of classic antiquity also included educational facilities such as libraries, lecture theaters and public areas for art exhibitions. Over time, different perspectives on thermalism have emerged (Stevens *et al.*, 2018). According to Miranda and Vieira (2021), thermalism is the use of springs, rivers or seawater at specific temperatures for medicinal purposes, and is one of the oldest wellbeing practices in Europe. For Rodríguez-Sánchez (2017), thermalism also refers to the study of water for therapeutic purposes due to its temperature or chemical composition. Thermalism therefore explores different ways of using mineral water to treat the body and applies techniques such as immersion baths, saunas and inhalation therapy, among others.

Hellman and Drago (2018) concur, stating that the therapeutic use of water can have different names depending on the type of water and the temperature used, and can include thermal, curative, thalassic, and balneal therapy. In some countries like Portugal, 'thermalism' is the most commonly used term, while balneotherapy, which ends up being a synonym, is used more in countries like Germany. Nonetheless, there are different modalities and uses of water, such as thalassotherapy. Although there are similarities in the techniques of thermalism/balneotherapy and thalassotherapy, the former uses mineral medicinal waters for its treatments while thalassotherapy uses seawater or ordinary water (Hellmann & Drago, 2018; Munteanu & Munteanu, 2019; Río-Rama *et al.*, 2018).

The scientific development of our understanding of the curative properties of thermal waters has contributed to the broader dissemination of this concept. Recent literature has highlighted the potential of thermalism to improve the wellbeing of individuals and local communities (Bandeiras, 2019; Pereira *et al.*, 2021). Currently, thermalism plays an important role in promoting health and well-being, offering benefits such as stress reduction, relief from depression, and energy restoration. In addition to its recognized therapeutic effects, thermalism is increasingly valued for its preventive potential and its influence on lifestyle changes. As such, it can be understood as a key factor in enhancing quality of life and improving sleep, extending beyond its traditional therapeutic function to embrace a broader, preventive approach focused on health promotion and the prevention of future illnesses (Pereira *et al.*, 2021).

Today, thermalism has lost some of its power due to the evolution of medical science, which has created better, more consistent and faster therapies, replacing those provided by mineral waters (Keyes, 1998). 'Modern' thermalism has led to a decrease in elderly visitors (Tzedopoulos *et al.*, 2018). However, younger demographic groups are increasingly attracted to wellness services that promote care and harmony between body and mind (Tzedopoulos *et al.*, 2018). Studies of Portuguese thermal institutions by Rocha and Brandão (2014) and Quintela *et al.* (2016) help to further distinguish between these two distinct thermalism market segments, classical thermalism and wellness/modern thermalism. The first market segment is motivated by therapeutic outcomes, and seeks to alleviate, or bring about recovery from, identified pathologies (Quintela *et al.*, 2016; Rocha & Brandão, 2014). In contrast, the second market segment's primary motivation includes a combination of leisure, tourism and/or therapeutic recreation outcomes.

According to Israelowich (2016) and Pereira *et al.* (2021), thermalism's long history shows that it has evolved, becoming a commercialized product deeply rooted in the sociocultural habit of the European Community (Tzedopoulos *et al.*, 2018). This commercialization includes the development of thermal tourism, which, according to Bandeiras (2019), exists when a thermal spring is used for medicinal or therapeutic purposes. As described by Gianfaldoni *et al.* (2017), one of the significant innovations in the concept was the extraordinary connection of the classical concept of thermalism to wellness through the ever-increasing activities in this new form of spa tourism. This approach has led to different associations with the activities practised in thermal water areas and spas, as described in Figure 11.1.

Today, thermal tourism has adapted to the interests of communities, developing new treatments and techniques, and investing in thermal infrastructures in line with the new demands of the market and

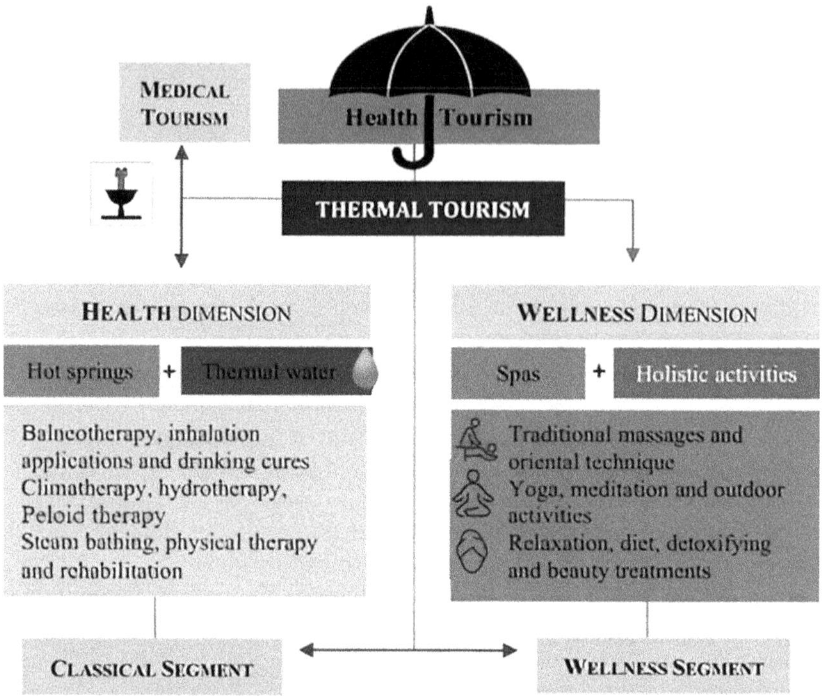

Figure 11.1 Visual representation of the definition and conceptual framework of thermal tourism as articulated by Quintela (2022)

lifestyles. Restructuring classic spas according to emerging trends and current demands represents a 'duality between health and leisure'. The revolution in health tourism services – offering greater specialization through new technologies – has also enabled spas to offer higher quality experiences to travellers who wish to improve their wellbeing (Gómez Pérez *et al.*, 2019; Tzedopoulos *et al.*, 2018). Despite the importance that spas have gained, it is essential to recognize that spas have traditionally been a geological resource for wellbeing and should not be marketed as a commodity aimed at the affluent markets of society (Bandeiras, 2019). Our research is therefore fundamental to exploring this transformation and the evolution of what the concept of thermalism represents today, including its greater focus on wellness.

11.3 Thermalism in Europe

Since the late 2010s, spas have been increasingly recognized for the curative properties of their waters and their essential role in the prevention of illnesses (Nistoreanu & Aluculesei, 2021). Touristic activities now have a positive impact on the economies of countries worldwide. Internationally, countries such as Japan, New Zealand, Turkey, France, Spain, Greece, Tunisia, Italy, Germany, Iceland, the Czech Republic, Hungary and Portugal are some of those with a more robust tradition of using mineral waters for the treatment of various pathologies (Costa, 2020). It is estimated that there are around 34,099 thermal/mineral spring establishments in the world, operating in 130 countries, with a turnover US$ 64.0 billion in 2019 and US$ 39.1 billion in 2017 (GWI, 2019). Hungary stands out as one of the countries with the richest water resources in the world. Budapest is renowned as the city of spas, with a history dating back to the 16th and 17th centuries. In contrast, Italy currently boasts 380 spas, offering activities that are crucial for the health and well-being of its citizens (Costa, 2020).

Since the 21st century, particularly in Europe, thermalism has gained significant attention in tourism. The European Parliament's resolution of 29 November 2007, specifically addressed thermal tourism in one of its chapters, recommending the use of European programs to promote it and emphasizing the importance of cross-border cooperation in defining financing solutions for this tourism product (Gonçalves & Guerra, 2019). In 2011, the European Parliament's resolution of 27 September introduced a new policy framework for tourism in Europe, highlighting that demographic changes in Europe are expected to drive growth in health tourism, particularly in the spa sector (Gonçalves & Guerra, 2019).

According to the Global Wellness Institute (GWI, 2021a), the thermalism sector showed strong growth between 2017 and 2019, with an annual growth of 6.8%. In 2020, with the onset of the COVID-19 pandemic, which had a substantial impact on economies, the industry's revenues declined (Mota *et al.*, 2023). However, it has been trying to recover in recent years in what concerns to safety (Oliveira *et al.*, 2022) and marketing and communication strategies (Antunes *et al.*, 2023). Before 2020, the sector showed rapid and robust growth, with investments in many countries. The same study also mentions that in the years preceding the pandemic, around 115 new centers were opened and that in the year of the pandemic, despite the crisis, 17 centers were opened. Currently, there are new projects in the pipeline, the aim of which is to improve the growth of this sector.

11.4 Methodology

The spa industry is highly concentrated in Europe, which accounts for more than 90% of all establishments worldwide (GWI, 2024a). There has been an increase in the number of establishments in recent years, demonstrating the importance of the sector and the demand for its services, with a slight decline in 2020 due to the COVID-19 pandemic crisis (Ma *et al.*, 2020). Currently, many countries have been offering vouchers to citizens to boost the sector, which like many others, has suffered from this crisis (GWI, 2021b). In Europe, according to GWI (2019), the TOP 10 spa establishments for the year 2017 were Germany in first place followed by Russia, Italy, Austria, Hungary, Spain, Poland, Turkey, the Czech Republic and, in tenth place, France. Using this analysis, it was possible to determine and select the countries that would provide added value for this study. A key factor in the selection of the countries for the study was a shared cultural history around ancient thermalism. Five European countries share such a history: Portugal, Spain, Italy, France and Hungary (Crecente *et al.*, 2018). All these countries are considered important markets in Europe, with investments in the area and services directed towards wellness (Farinha, 2022).

The general purpose of this study is to understand and explore how wellness has transformed the thermalism sector, as well as to understand the adaptation of supply to meet demand, and to establish a critical note on the changes of classical thermalism nowadays. Bearing this in mind, the empirical study was designed based on a qualitative approach. To this end, a semi-structured interview script was drawn up which, in addition to providing a script with previously defined questions, allowed freedom to modify the order or change the form of the questions. The questions were formulated according to the main purpose and the specific objectives of the study.

The target of this research is all organizations in the spa sector located in the countries under study: Portugal, Spain, Italy, Hungary and France. Two interviews were conducted in each of the five countries considered in the study. The interviews were therefore aimed at employees of thermal establishments who, directly or indirectly, had responsibility for promoting wellness services. The selection of stakeholders with greater experience and knowledge of the evolution and transformation of the wellness sector was one of the key criteria for the development of this research, as well as the inclusion of those who were prepared to describe the challenges caused by COVID-19 in this sector.

A total of 10 interviews were collected between October 2021 and June 2022 among thermal spa establishments. With regard to the sociodemographic profile of the interviewees, each had a minimum of 12 years professional experience in the thermal sector and up to 30 years, and all had higher education qualifications and were primarily directors (Table 11.1).

Following the trend in tourism research (Stalmirska & Camprubí, 2022), the treatment of the data was based on content analysis techniques.

11.5 Results

All interviewees reported offering a range of services, some of them innovative, aimed at diversifying and attracting a wider audience.

Table 11.1 Sociodemographic profile of the participants

No.	Role of the interviewee	Age	Professional experience (years)	Academic qualifications
I-1	Thermal spa director	58	22	Bachelor's degree
I-2	Associate professor in tourism management	NA	23	Doctoral degree
I-3	Hotel director	54	30	Postgraduate
I-4	Thermal spa director	NA	20	Bachelor's degree
I-5	Thermal spa director	42	18	Bachelor's degree
I-6	HTWWLife CEO	NA	28	Doctoral degree
I-7	Tourism organization director	44	15	Bachelor's degree
I-8	Spa manager	30	12	Postgraduate
I-9	Hotel manager	NA	23	Bachelor's degree
I-10	President of Thermal Baths of Portugal	51	18	Master's degree

11.5.1 Adapting supply to demand

As demand behavior has already been observed over time, it is important to understand whether supply has adapted to demand. The interviews focused on new strategies and innovative services, where 'the spa offer is being expanded to be more attractive to wellness clients' (I-4). The strategies are about the generation of new products, as can be seen from the statements of several interviewees (Table 11.2).

In general, all the interviewees revealed the adoption of a range of innovative services, which diversified their experience offerings in an attempt to attract a wider market base. It is worth noting that the impact of COVID-19 has led some thermal establishments to 'come back with the same offer as in 2019' (I-5), as 'the cost of raw materials has increased by about 63%, making it difficult to renovate spaces' (I-1).

Table 11.2 Main findings regarding adapting supply to demand

Innovative products	New strategies	Challenges
'Skin clinic'	Creation of several thematic baths, new treatment circuits and the creation of a thermal cosmetics line	Permanent adaptation to the market
Take advantage of the properties of hyposaline waters, offering a treatment service for holistic skincare services for skin diseases, cooperating with a nutritionist, psychologist and dermatologist	Thermal establishments that offer preventive and holistic health prevention services	Alternative ways of circumventing price increases
Several leisure activities, especially sports, such as eco bike rides, and an electric bicycle	New products created to complement the thermal cure associated with nature and wellbeing, bio-healthy menus, tourist routes, exercise plans	Innovating to compete, framing benchmarking analyses

As a result of the economic hardship brought about by the pandemic, the associated service businesses need to create new strategies and projects to remain solvent.

The importance and need for change were also evident in most interviews. For example, interviewee (I-1) highlighted the range of services available, such as 'nutrition, physical exercise, psychological support, yoga, Pilates and a special offer for children'. The same interviewee referred to the importance that 'water can have because of its properties and that it provides answers to certain pathologies, with values that go beyond therapeutic indications, with relaxing effects'. Water has other critical complementary services, as emphasized by other interviewees: 'the aim is not only to bring a client to treat his illness but also to make him aware of all the other things that a spa can offer him, showing that not only a 60-year-old person should come' (I-3).

Interviews revealed that more strategies were being used to open up new markets, including cooperation between sports, nutrition, and even medical experts, whether psychological or physical, following the trends of demand (Hekmat *et al.*, 2022; Koskinen & Wilska, 2018). The interviewees' line of thought is that without cooperation between these different fields, it would be difficult to offer more complete packages. In the case of an idea presented by interviewee (I-4): 'a "skin clinic" is also being developed to take advantage of the properties of hyposaline waters, offering a treatment service for skin diseases, more complete, in cooperation with a nutritionist, psychologist and dermatologist'. The opportunities offered creating body and mind wellbeing activities are important and should not be wasted. It is also essential to 'create new products every year. For example, have a doctor as a consultant and continuously work with him or her. Training staff and introducing some of this concept to younger people familiar with our product, for example, for children' (I-3).

11.5.2 Changes in classical thermalism

According to interviewees, progressive modernization and the creation of new services have transformed classical thermalism into a more up-to-date and customer-orientated concept referred to as modern thermalism. These new services have been attracting an increase in wellness demand to the detriment of classical thermalism. 'Modern thermalism', with its greater emphasis on wellness, is the new reality, present in all the thermal establishments interviewed and it is a concept that was addressed by almost all interviewees (Table 11.3).

Nonetheless, this trend can hinder the development of thermal spas, as well as the development and growth of thermal tourism. Interview results identified some limitations: 'The biggest of all is the often-absurd regulations, which limit the activity in a completely senseless way and, another [constraint is] finding trained professionals to ... hire' (I-9).

Table 11.3 Main findings regarding the changes in classical thermalism

Limitations	Partnerships	Seasonality	Holistic perspective
Wellness services are not subsidized by the government, and spas are luxury services that are not affordable to all segments	Partnerships with hotels, tourism associations and festivals	Seasonality is becoming progressively less relevant in the spa sector compared with other sectors	Wellbeing and health are inclusive and the holistic approach is at their root
Regulations limiting activity, high maintenance costs, machinery and installation problems that require annual renovation	Inclusion of different types of services and complementary products, offering diverse experiences	Thermal baths offer good experiences at different times of the year because they allow for indoor activities	Position thermalism in the dimension of wellness and health prevention, namely among health professionals

Alternative pathways to overcome the less positive effects, and attract more visitors, must be found. Interviews revealed an increasing tendency among the health and wellness industry representatives to value the inclusive and holistic nature of spas (Liao *et al.*, 2023). Although there is a need to position and value the preventative dimension of thermalism, new products and partnerships were being created to combat the current difficulties and trends. Hence the importance of working with various partners and entities, as stated some of the interviewees: 'Surely partnerships are worthwhile' (I-1); 'Tourism products must be increasingly integrated' (I-10); 'Partnerships with hotel units, tourism associations, holding festivals, among others' (I-4).

According to two of the interviewees, partnerships provided great support, making experiences more complete and more valued:

> We advocate partnerships and the inclusion of complementary services, and products. We believe that any activity may improve the wellbeing of the customer. All we need to do is to orchestrate the experiences and the service provision accordingly. (I-6)
>
> [The creation of new products/services becomes the] main challenge for the thermal service, which is to affirm its different offers. It is to make the customer know that thermal spas have special characteristics, and that is why they are good for health and for everything, and that is why you have to pay a different price for them. (I-3)

During the interviews, the impact of seasonality was also discussed, with interviewees stating that: 'Seasonality is not relevant to us as it is to actual thermal facilities' (I-6) and 'there is less seasonality in spas than in other sectors because they make good wet weather experiences' (I-2). Others stated: 'In the past, thermal tourism was very concentrated in three months, and nowadays thermal tourism does not present high peaks, and there is a more uniform demand throughout the year, ending the seasonality' (I-1).

Health and wellness is increasingly a cross-cutting theme in thermal tourism, with activities and dimensions from a more holistic perspective:

> The customer has changed, and we also have to change and explain the changes. We must take advantage of the resources we have, but also enter into market segments that sometimes don't look for treatment daily, they only look for 2 days in a spa. Unite experiences, look for global experiences. (I-3)

Modern thermalism is positioned increasingly as more of a wellness pursuit and is a new reality that all thermal establishments must address, as expressed by almost all interviewees. Some even stated:

> wellness or health have always been inclusive, and the holistic perspective is not new either. What is new is that this has become more mainstream and seems to be monetised more. We were among the first ones who campaigned for a more inclusive approach. For us, this is nothing new. (I-6)

The idea is, instead, that the spa concept has evolved over the generations, adapting to current demand, with offerings more aimed at 'wellness customers' (I-4).

Establishments must innovate to attract new customers; otherwise, they will lose out on other markets. However, in most cases, interviewees revealed a certain uniformity in their perceptions of the spa management limitations associated with expanding to serve wider audiences. Interviewees emphasized their commitment to diversifying service offerings through partnerships that create composite products and more enriching experiences. Interestingly, in terms of service or product innovation, interviewees also gave examples of other European countries, excluded from the study, who have created and introduced new experiences in response to the economic pressures associated with the COVID-19 pandemic.

The introduction of new strategies and innovative products has confirmed the importance of adapting supply to demand. However, the thermal spa sector still faces some challenges due to a lack of investment. On the one hand, due to the precarious global economic situation, some establishments have experienced difficulties related to the maintenance of their premises. On the other, some establishments have expanded their premises due to the high demand for wellness-related services.

11.6 Discussion

Today, according to Branco (2019), younger generations are increasingly concerned with health at an earlier stage of their lives, and the creation of new projects linked to continuous prevention and not only to the treatment of a disease is essential to attracting them, thus changing the paradigm of thermal baths being associated with elderly people with major problems, as shown by Smith *et al.* (2020), and demonstrating the importance of including all age groups in this activity sector. Despite the tendency for changes in the profile of visitors, one of the great innovations in the concept, according to Gianfaldoni *et al.* (2017), has been the extraordinary combination of the classical concept with the concept of wellness, with an ever-increasing number of activities in this new thermal tourism.

In terms of length of stay, one of the most important characteristics of thermal tourism and health tourism is that this is a segment where the length of stay exceeds that of any other type of tourism, and it can 'boost the local economy' as this segment is usually located outside large urban centers (Brandão *et al.*, 2021) and requires a longer period, 2–3 weeks, for traditional medical treatment. It is necessary to create a range of services and products that allows visitors to enjoy themselves more and to stay longer, beyond what they spend on a treatment. Thermal establishments must be able to integrate other tourism products or partnerships so that a person with a long average stay of 10/12/14 days can visit other places and experience other tourism products.

As mentioned in the literature review, in recent decades, especially in the 21st century, thermal establishments have been reinstated, with new concepts and services adapted to current needs, such as physical and psychological wellbeing. Hotels and resorts have become important wellness centers, betting on thermal facilities, whose goal is to attract more customers by offering quality therapies at reasonable prices. The traditional health services of thermal establishments have been replaced by the popularity of services that seek to establish a balance and satisfy healthy lifestyles, such as reducing stress and counteracting the problems of today's society (Anaya-Aguilar *et al.*, 2021). Analysis of the interviews reveals the importance of creating new services in the face of current demand, with strategies to attract new markets, and more cooperation between areas such as sports, nutrition, and even medical fields, either psychological or physical.

Thermalism has assumed a decisive role in the quality of life and sleep, and nowadays it is not only associated with a therapeutic component, a 'classical thermalism', but also comprises a more preventative approach aimed at health promotion and prevention of future diseases, a 'wellness thermalism' (Pereira *et al.*, 2021). While classical thermalism is mainly for older spa-goers looking for curative/therapeutic benefits, wellness thermalism is mainly for younger spa-goers interested in holistic wellness benefits and preventative approaches (Quintela *et al.*, 2023). The wellness concept allowed thermal establishments to reformulate and improve their image, sometimes associated with therapies and treatment of patients, and to become important destinations for wellness tourism. In addition, the concept of wellness is currently considered one of the methods of preventing future diseases in increasingly ageing societies and it aggregates a holistic approach that aims at the mental and spiritual harmony of the human being (Šušić & Dimitrijević, 2015).

Establishments must innovate to attract new customers; otherwise, they will lose out on other markets. However, in most cases, interviewees revealed a certain uniformity in their perceptions of the thermal establishments' management limitations associated with expanding to serve wider audiences. Interviewees emphasized their commitment to diversifying service offerings through partnerships that create composite products and more enriching experiences. Interestingly, in terms of service or product innovation, interviewees also gave examples of other European countries excluded from the study, who have created and introduced new experiences in response to the economic pressures associated with the COVID-19 pandemic.

The introduction of new strategies and innovative products has confirmed the importance of adapting supply to demand. However, the thermal sector still faces some barriers due to a lack of investment. On the one hand, due to the precarious global economic situation, some establishments have experienced difficulties related to the maintenance of their premises. On the other, some establishments have expanded their premises due to the high demand for wellness-related services. These trends are aligned with the significant changes in the wellness market reported by the Global Wellness Institute (GWI, 2024b), marking a departure from the trends of the past 20 years. The market has experienced a substantial boost, with a clear shift in demand. This has led to market segmentation into hard care (hyper-medical, high-tech) and soft care (more straightforward, less expensive, and self-optimized, focusing on emotional and social wellbeing). The market focus has expanded to include relaxation, weight loss, postpartum recovery, post-operative recovery, longevity and complimentary fitness offers, among others.

11.7 Conclusion

This study has allowed us to understand how wellness has transformed the thermalism sector in the last decade. It has also revealed there is a need to adapt supply to demand, including meeting the needs of both older and younger spa-goers. Currently, health and wellness tourism is in a phase of rejuvenation, with increasingly diversified offerings appearing, and the emergence of innovative partnerships and new investments in the sector. It is therefore essential to ensure that supply includes infrastructure and complementary products specialized in both classic and wellness thermalism, targeting the two main segments of thermalism nowadays.

The interviewees mention that adapting supply to meet demand has led to the creation of various services and products aimed at attracting new markets. Examples include projects like the establishment of a 'skin clinic', combining cosmetics with thermal treatments, which leverage the healing properties of water for illness treatment and preventive care, offering significant benefits. In addition to the projects, creating new products linked to sport, nature and nutrition has complemented the thermal offerings. The main aim is to attract market segments increasingly interested in physical activity, healthier eating habits and a better quality of life. This adaptation was identified by the interviewees, in line with the literature (Brandão *et al.*, 2021; GWI, 2023), which suggests that, in the 21st century, the spa has been reinvented with new concepts and services adapted to current needs, such as physical and psychological wellness, to reduce the recent problems of contemporary society.

Although the sample size represents one of the main limitations of this study, precluding generalising the results, this chapter makes meaningful theoretical and practical industry contributions. The analysis of thermalism on a European scale addresses a gap in the literature owing to the limited number of studies employing this approach. Furthermore, it highlights demand trends and the changing consumer profile in Europe, revealing successful adaptation strategies and the shift towards a younger market, with more specialized service demands focused on physical and psychological wellbeing.

The importance of partnerships and modernization of services highlights mechanisms for innovation, including how to offer more opportunities for consumers to enjoy better-quality experiences with other holistic spa package options beyond the so-called 'classic' thermal experience. The findings also included insights that can support industry in better preparing for future challenges in the health and wellness sector. Future research should include comparative and longitudinal studies in the countries studied and should extend the study to other European countries. In this way, it will be possible to monitor the evolution of the wellness sector as an extension of modern thermalism.

References

Anaya-Aguilar, R., Gemar, G. and Anaya-Aguilar, C. (2021) Challenges of spa tourism in Andalusia: Experts' proposed solutions. *International Journal of Environmental Research and Public Health* 18 (4), 1829. https://doi.org/10.3390/ijerph18041829.

Antunes, V., Gonçalves, G. and Estevão, C. (2023) A theoretical reflection on thermalism and communication: Future perspectives in times of crisis. *Journal of Hospitality and Tourism Insights* 6 (4), 1618–1638. https://doi.org/10.1108/JHTI-08-2021-0231.

Bandeiras, L.P.W. (2019) Da memória dos banhos romanos às novas arquiteturas termais: Proposta de uma estância termal na Quinta das Janelas em Óbidos. Master's dissertation, Faculty of Architecture, University of Lisbon.

Branco, C.M.F. (2019) O turismo da saúde e bem-estar em Portugal. Master's dissertation, ISCTE, University of Lisbon. https://repositorio.iscte-iul.pt/handle/10071/19356.

Brandão, F., Liberato, D., Teixeira, A.S. and Liberato, P. (2021) Motives for thermal tourism: An application to North and Central Portugal. *Sustainability* 132, 2688. https://doi.org/10.3390/su132212688.

Britannica (2021) Thermae. Available at: https://www.britannica.com/technology/thermae.

Corbari, S.D. and Grimm, I.J. (2020) A pandemia de Covid-19 e os impactos no setor do turismo em Curitiba (PR): Uma análise preliminar. *Ateliê do Turismo* 4 (2), 1–26. https://periodicos.ufms.br/index.php/adturismo/article/view/11284.

Costa, A.M.P. da. (2020) Turismo termal: A segmentação por fatores motivacionais. Master's disseration, ISCTE, University of Lisbon. Available at: https://repositorio.iscte-iul.pt/handle/10071/21406.

Crecente, M., González Soutelo, M.S. and Simons, P. (2018) *Thermal Tourism and Spa Heritage in Europe: The case of EHTT.* European Historic Thermal Towns Association. Available at: https://historicthermaltowns.eu/downloads/ThermalTourismAndSpaHeritageEurope-ehtta.pdf.

Farinha, C. (2022) *Cultural Routes of the Council of Europe. Evaluation Cycle 2021-2022. Independent Expert Report. European Route of Historic Thermal Towns.* Cultural Routes of the Council of Europe. Available at: https://rm.coe.int/report-ehtta-en/1680a6f91a.

Gianfaldoni, S., Tchernev, G., Wollina, U., Roccia, M.G., Fioranelli, M., Gianfaldoni, R. and Lotti, T. (2017) History of the baths and thermal medicine. *Open Access Macedonian Journal of Medical Sciences* 5 (4), 566–568. https://doi.org/10.3889/oamjms.2017.126.

Gómez Pérez, C.P., González Soutelo, S., Mourelle Mosqueira, M.L. and Legido Soto, J.L. (2019) Spa techniques and technologies: From the past to the present. *Sustainable Water Resources Management* 5 (1), 71–81. https://doi.org/10.1007/s40899-017-0136-1.

Gonçalves, E.C. and Guerra, R.J. da C. (2019) O turismo de saúde e bem-estar como fator de desenvolvimento local: Uma análise à oferta termal portuguesa. *PASOS. Revista de Turismo y Patrimonio Cultural* 17 (2), 453–472. https://doi.org/10.25145/j.pasos.2019.17.030.

GWI (2019) *Understanding Wellness: Opportunities and Impacts of the Wellness Economy for Regional Development.* Global Wellness Institute. Available at: https://globalwellnessinstitute.org/wp-content/uploads/2019/07/Understanding-Wellness-Four-Global-Forces-Driving-the-Growth-of-the-Wellness-Economy_Rev6.pdf.

GWI (2021a) *The Global Wellness Economy: Looking Beyond COVID.* Global Wellness Institute. Available at: https://globalwellnessinstitute.org/wp-content/uploads/2021/11/GWI-WE-Monitor-2021_final-digital.pdf.

GWI (2021b) *Wellness Tourism Spas as Thermal/Mineral Springs: The Global Wellness Economy: Looking Beyond COVID.* Global Wellness Institute. Available at: https://globalwellnessinstitute.org/wp-content/uploads/2022/02/GWI-WE-Monitor-2021_Wellness-Tourism.pdf.

GWI (2023) *Global Wellness Economy Monitor 2023 – November 2023.* Global Wellness Institute. Available at: https://globalwellnessinstitute.org/wp-content/uploads/2023/11/GWI-WE-Monitor-2023_FINAL.pdf.

GWI (2024a) *2024 Global Wellness Trends Report: The Future of Wellness.* Global Wellness Institute. Available at: https://www.globalwellnesssummit.com/product/2024-global-wellness-trends-report-the-future-of-wellness-pre-order/.

GWI (2024b) *The Global Wellness Economy: Country Rankings Data for 2019–2022.* Global Wellness Institute. Available at: https://globalwellnessinstitute.org/wp-content/uploads/2024/01/2024GWI-Country-Rankings01212024.pdf.

Hekmat, N., Ramazanova, M., Marques, J. and Quintela, J.A. (2022) Wellness tourism experience on the rise post-COVID: Behavioural demand trends and expectations. In R.A. Costa, F. Brandão, Z. Breda and C. Costa (eds) *Planning and Managing the Experience Economy in Tourism* (pp. 215–238). IGI Global. 10.4018/978-1-7998-8775-1.ch012.

Hellmann, F. and Drago, L.C. (2018) Termalismo e Crenoterapia: Potencialidades e desafios para a saúde coletiva no Brasil. *Journal of Management & Primary Health Care* 8 (2), 309–321. https://doi.org/10.14295/jmphc.v8i2.541.

Israelowich, W.C.I. (2016) Patients and healers in the High Roman Empire. *Journal of History of Medicine and Allied Sciences* 71 (3), 345–347. https://doi.org/10.1093/jhmas/jrv050.

Kervankıran, I. (2016) Between traditional and modern: Thermal tourism in Turkey. In I. Egresi (ed.) *Alternative Tourism in Turkey: Role, Potential Development and Sustainabilty* (pp. 109–124). Springer. https://doi.org/10.1007/978-3-319-47537-0_7.

Keyes, C.L.M. (1998) Social wellbeing. *Social Psychology Quarterly* 61 (2), 121–140. https://doi.org/10.2307/2787065.

Koskinen, V. and Wilska, T.A. (2018) Identifying and understanding spa tourists' wellness attitudes. *Scandinavian Journal of Hospitality and Tourism* 19 (3), 259–277. https://doi.org/10.1080/15022250.2018.1467276.

Liao C., Zuo, Y., Xu, S., Law, R. and Zhang, M. (2023) Dimensions of the health benefits of wellness tourism: A review. *Frontiers in Psychology* 13, 1071578. https://doi.org/10.3389/fpsyg.2022.107157.

Ma, S., Zhao, X., Gong, Y. and Wengel, Y. (2020) Proposing 'healing tourism' as a post-COVID-19 tourism product. *Anatolia* 32 (1), 136–139. https://doi.org/10.1080/13032917.2020.1808490.

Miranda, G.U. and Vieira, C.R. (2021) Práticas Integrativas e Complementares como possibilidade de cuidado em saúde mental. *Research, Society and Development* 10 (10), e368101018917. https://doi.org/10.33448/rsd-v10i10.18917.

Mota, M., Nossa, P. and Oliveira Moreira, C. (2023) The impact of health and wellness tourism in the regional economy of Estrela UNESCO Global Geopark, Portugal. *Sustainability* 15, 15151. https://doi.org/10.3390/su152015151.

Munteanu, C. and Munteanu, D. (2019) Thalassotherapy today. *Balneo Research Journal* 10 (4), 440–444. https://doi.org/10.12680/balneo.2019.278.

Nistoreanu, P. and Aluculesei, A.-C. (2021) Can spa tourism enhance water resources and turn them into a national brand? A theoretical review about the Romanian case. *Information* 12, 270. https://doi.org/10.3390/info12070270.

Oliveira, G.S. de, Monteiro, L. de S., Carvalho, M. de F.A.A. and Freire, A.K. da S. (2020) Saúde Mental em tempos da Pandemia da COVID-19: Concepções dos trabalhadores da Atenção Primaria a Saúde. *Research, Society and Development* 9 (10), e9449109339. https://doi.org/10.33448/rsd v9i10.9339.

Oliveira, I., Nogueira, F. and Marques, I. (2022) Thermalism in Portugal: Corporate response to the COVID-19 pandemic: Strategy, safety, human resources and marketing approach. *New Trends in Qualitative Research* 11, 4–15. https://doi.org/10.36367/ntqr.11.e533.

Pereira, R., Costa, V. and Gomes, H. (2023) Health and wellness tourism: An overview of thermal tourism in Portugal. *Journal of Tourism, Sustainability and Wellbeing* 11 (3), 136–147. https://doi.org/10.34623/e2bm-8030.

Pereira, S., Silva, J., Marques, C., Galvão, A. and Alves, M.J. (2021) Thermalism as a determinant of quality of life and sleep: A novel approach to the sector using SF-36v2 and Pittsburgh Index. *Frontiers in Medical Case Reports* 02 (05). https://doi.org/10.47746/FMCR.2021.2505.

Quintela, J.A. (2022) Thermal tourism. In D. Buhalis (ed.) *Encyclopedia of Tourism Management and Marketing* (vol. 4, pp. 375–378). Edward Elgar Publishing.

Quintela, J.A., Costa, C. and Correia, A. (2016) Health, wellness and medical tourism: A conceptual approach. *Enlightening Tourism: A Pathmaking Journal* 6 (1), 1–18.

Quintela, J.A., Costa, C. and Correia, A. (2023) Health and wellness tourism in the pursuit of quality of life: A case study approach for Portugal and Hungary. In O. Doğan (ed.) *Global Perspectives on the Opportunities and Future Directions of Health Tourism* (pp. 138–164). IGI Global. https://www.igi-global.com/chapter/health-and-wellness-tourism-in-the-pursuit-of-quality-oflife/317656.

Río-Rama, M. de la C. del, Maldonado-Erazo, C.P. and Álvarez-García, J. (2018) State of the art of research in the sector of thermalism, thalassotherapy and spa: A bibliometric analysis. *European Journal of Tourism Research* 19, 56–70. https://doi.org/10.54055/ejtr.v19i.325.

Rocha, A.S.S. and Brandão, A. (2014) On developing wellness and medical tourism: The characterization of a national thermal network. *International Journal of Healthcare Management* 7 (4), 226–236. https://doi.org/10.1179/2047971914Y.0000000075.

Rodríguez-Sánchez, J.A. (2017) Cambiar para perdurar: Evolución del termalismo y los establecimientos de águas minero-medicinales. *Dynamis* 37 (2), 517–528.

Smith, M.K., Jancsik, A. and Puczkó, L. (2020) Customer satisfaction in post-socialist spas: A case study of Budapest, City of Spas. *International Journal of Spa and Wellness* 3 (2–3), 165–186. https://doi.org/10.1080/24721735.2020.1866330.

Solimene, U. (2020) A modern concept of thermalism applied to health and wellbeing. *Bulletin of Rehabilitation Medicine* 1 (95). https://www.elibrary.ru/item.asp?id=42456760.

Stalmirska, A.M. and Camprubí, R. (2022) Conducting a systematic qualitative content analysis in hospitality and tourism research. In F. Okumus, S.M. Rasoolimanesh and S. Jahani (eds) *Contemporary Research Methods in Hospitality and Tourism* (pp. 127–141). Emerald Publishing. https://doi.org/10.1108/978-1-80117-546-320221009.

Stevens, F., Azara, I. and Michopoulou, E. (2018) Local community attitudes and perceptions towards thermalism. *International Journal of Spa and Wellness* 1 (1), 55–68. https://doi.org/10.1080/24721735.2018.1432451.

Šušić, V. and Dimitrijević, D. (2015) Wellness spa – A specific form of health tourism. *Facta Universitatis* 12 (1), 69–81.

Tzedopoulos, Y., Kamara, A., Lampada, D. and Ferla, K. (2018) Thermalism in Greece: An ancient cultural habitus in crisis. *International Journal of Professional Business Review* 3 (2), 205–219. https://doi.org/10.26668/businessreview/2018.v3i2.83.

12 How Can Health and Wellness Tourism Boost Regional Development? Unhais da Serra, Portugal: A Potential Answer

Mónica Brito, Margarida Mota and Paulo Nossa

12.1 Introduction

The tourism literature has been witnessing an increase in studies, both theoretical and empirical, on the concept and practices of health and wellness tourism (HWT), as well as the role that this specific sector plays in sustainable regional development, especially in lesser developed areas. It has been demonstrated that enhancing the quality of tourism services within the HWT sector is conducive to the promotion of these regions, thereby attracting more sophisticated customers with greater purchasing power (Medeiros & Cavaco, 2008; Peris-Ortiz & Álvares-García, 2015; Smith & Puczkó, 2009). Between the 18th and the early 20th century, only the wealthiest citizens had access to health and wellness services. These elites oftentimes travelled to other parts of Europe or the US to gain access to quality medical treatments as well as to take advantage of beneficial climate conditions. This trend began to reverse at the end of the 20th century and even more so in the 21st century, as technological developments, namely in communication and transport, made travel more accessible, leading to the democratization of tourism (Fetscherin & Stephano, 2016).

In the case of Portugal, Madeira and Serra da Estrela became among the most recognized climatotherapy destinations in the world, widely used for curative purposes in the second half of the 19th century by tuberculosis patients (Vieira, 2013, 2019) and their families seeking relief at health resorts (Nunes, 2022: 115). Likewise, at various levels of demand and sophistication, national and European thermal resorts have been gaining prestige not only as medical but also as healing and leisure sites, owing either to the quality of the built heritage or to attractive surroundings where social activities can be enjoyed in the hotels and adjacent parks, or on tennis courts, in swimming pools and casinos, and in golf clubs. The golden age of Portuguese thermal spas stimulated development in their home regions (Medeiros & Cavaco, 2008: 26). This was because, in order to satisfy the elite and demanding clients of the period, the spa locations had to be equipped with the urban facilities this clientele was accustomed to, including: sewage disposal, city water, refuse collection, electricity, post offices and telegraphs, as well as sports and leisure facilities. The change in the biomedical paradigm, with a stronger focus on preventive processes and upon health-promoting practices, with an emphasis on an active attitude on the part of the user, as discussed below, has created the opportunity for territories with a lower level of touristification to value their resources, namely by complementing thermal springs with landscape resources, associating new forms of active leisure and preventive practices that were formerly less valued in terms of health destinations. For this reason, the popular view of HWT has changed. Less emphasis is now placed on the thermal waters that used to attract privileged clients and a more holistic approach has taken over in which health promotion is designed to attract tourists willing to invest significantly. This high-end market is currently a niche, but one that promises to expand considerably.

In addition, technological developments in the field of transport and communication have played a crucial role in the democratization of tourism and, as a result, have stimulated the growing demand for health tourism services. In the case of Portugal, the significant modernization of the national road network between 1995 and 2005 significantly reduced travel time and expenses. This helped attract a greater number of traditional spa users and new spa clients to low-density areas that were traditionally less accessible (Medeiros & Cavaco, 2008). At the same time, advances in digital communication, particularly the internet and social networking, have changed the way information reaches potential users. Today, it is possible to obtain detailed information about health and wellness destinations, compare prices, read reviews from other customers and make online reservations with great ease. This access to information has empowered consumers, allowing them to make more informed decisions and plan their trips more efficiently.

At the same time, the democratization of access has made the health tourism market more dynamic. Service providers have improved the quality and variety of their offerings to attract a wider and increasingly informed clientele. This has led to innovations in treatment, improvements in infrastructure, and a greater emphasis on holistic

Table 12.1 Wellness economy (2017–2020)

	Value (US$ trillions)				Average annual growth rate (%)	
	2017	2018	2019	2020	2017–2019	2019–2020
World	4.3	4.5	4.9	4.369	5%	−11.4%
Europe	1.1	0.9	1.2	1.1	6.6%	−11%

Source: Global Wellness Institute, December 2021.

experiences that combine health, wellbeing and leisure (Cristobal-Fransi *et al.*, 2023; Turanci, 2019).

Despite the worldwide economic disruption caused by COVID-19, the Global Wellness Institute (2021) calculated that the 2020 'wellness economy' was worth US $4.4 trillion (Table 12.1), with 38.3% of revenue directly associated with physical activity, healthy eating and nutrition and weight loss.

In Portugal, HWT client numbers consistently outweigh those of classical thermalism despite the plunge in revenues caused by the 2020 pandemic. But despite the dramatic dip between 2019 and 2021, classical thermalism reported a 2021 turnover of €58,489,000 (represents 77% of income), while HWT brought in €17,353,000 (or 23% of total revenue) (Associação das Termas de Portugal, 2022). It is known that 93% of 2021 HWT clients averaged just one day at facilities, spending €45.48, while traditional spa clients spent an average of €273.43. Global statistics point to a moderate recovery of the HWT sector in 2021. This is particularly true in the Portuguese Central Region, which accounts for 52% of total Portuguese HWT clients and 56% of classical thermalism users (Associação das Termas de Portugal, 2022). This chapter presents a case study carried out precisely in this part of the country.

Thermal spas function as catalysts for development at both local and regional levels, generating spillover effects within the economic and social structures. It is evident in such instances that the contributions of these actors are instrumental in enhancing the quality of life within local communities and in mitigating regional disparities. Furthermore, they advocate for the strategic positioning of inland destinations, particularly in the North and Centre regions, where the majority of national thermal springs are concentrated, within a developing paradigm that emphasizes the potential of inland areas (Costa *et al.*, 2015). When the number of spas fell in the 20th century, the income of many of the municipalities located in these regions, which used to rely on spas as an anchor for economic growth, was reduced and contributed to their impoverishment. However, the very territorial positioning of the Centre of Portugal can currently be considered a competitive advantage in terms of quality, innovation and entrepreneurship, both due to the benefits associated with improved accessibility and the positive discrimination of new investments in the field of tourism that has rewarded the more inland territories. In this context, it is observed that a virtuous investment cycle is underway, combining increased investment in infrastructure and human resources with the territory's natural advantages, particularly in health and spa tourism. These territories benefit from less congested demand and an almost untouched landscape (Araújo *et al.*, 2015).

Any analysis of HWT trends must take into account the COVID-19 context, when concerns with biosafety were heightened substantially to levels which had only previously been witnessed in developing countries. This period also saw client preferences change, with greater concern for destination sustainability, growing interest in health and wellness activities, and desire for greater contact with nature, which in turn, led visitors to seek out locations with smaller populations and lower levels of tourist density (Damijanić, 2020; Guo *et al.*, 2024). HWT is not compatible with mass tourism, as by nature it prizes conditions limited to low population density regions. Client demand, on the other hand, has tended to become less seasonal, while the visitor profile is tending toward more ethically, socially and environmentally responsible clients. This lends the sector greater sustainability and increases the attractiveness of those regions that share this view. Thus, this type of tourism may simultaneously promote visitors' health and wellbeing while also encouraging sustainable regional development. It may result in a tourist experience that is out of the ordinary and also contributes to the improving host community's quality of life. This process, with its prospective positive outcomes to be distributed equitably to the various parties, is a challenge pertaining to each individual region.

With this in mind, this chapter discusses the contributions that HWT has made toward the sustainable development of low-population regions and applies the knowledge accrued to the particular case of Unhais da Serra, Portugal.

12.2 Health, Wellness and Tourism: How Are They Related?

In order to answer this question, we must clarify the definition of health used in the World Health Organization Constitution (WHO, 1948): 'a state of complete physical, mental and social wellbeing rather than the mere absence of disease'. This definition assumes that health prevention and promotion initiatives should not be directed exclusively toward disease control, decreased mortality or increased life expectancy, but should also further wellbeing and quality of life. In 1984 the concept was revised, and a more positive approach to health was adopted and began to refer to the extent to which individuals or groups are able to realize their aspirations, satisfy needs and change or cope with the environment. Health was now to be perceived as an everyday resource rather than a life goal (WHO, 1986).

Rather than the previous focus on prophylaxis and treatment, a proactive stance to health is currently encouraged, in which health maintenance efforts are shared by subjects and health institutions, in a consciously collaborative method. This is the result of Aaron Antonovsky's concept of salutogenisis (Antonovsky, 1979), or a positive health paradigm, in counterpoint to the pathogenic approach, which merely focused on disease causality.

> According to The Ottawa Charter for Health Promotion (WHO, 1986), health promotion is a process aimed at creating conditions enabling individuals and groups to control their health. To this end, it is important to empower individuals to identify and fulfil their aspirations, to meet their individual needs and to acquire the skills to deal with their environment (Loureiro & Miranda, 2010). In addition, the UN Conference on Environment and Development in Rio de Janeiro (1992) stressed the importance of a holistic approach to development, focusing on all aspects of life: spirituality, empowerment, society, the environment and the economy. The individual's participation and investment in their health began to be increasingly emphasized as the Jakarta Declaration on Leading Health Promotion into the 21st Century (WHO, 1997) stressed the need to train subjects to promote their own health. As Loureiro & Miranda (2010: 38) pointed out: '...the health of an individual or group is seen as an ongoing process, through self-regulation, in balance with the socio-ecological context'. Thus, among other issues, the Health Development Model (Bauer *et al.*, 2003), recommends: empowering individuals and communities to take greater control over personal, socioeconomic and environmental factors affecting their health; encouraging participation; and employing holistic approaches that encourage people's physical, mental, social and spiritual health (Loureiro & Miranda, 2010).

Meanwhile, an epidemiological transition is underway whereby the predominance of chronic degenerative diseases has increased simultaneously with an exponential rise in psycho-behavioral pathologies. These changes have heightened the need for novel forms of knowledge production and reproduction. The emphasis has shifted from disease to health promotion, from patient hospitalization and institutionalization to community integration, from cure to prevention, and from patient to person (WHO, 2015).

Aligned with the goals of empowerment and self-responsibility, the notion of wellbeing has emerged, a term that Cunha (2006) explains as the fusion of the related concepts of wellness and physical fitness (Dunn, 1961). Dunn posited a distinctive state of health that correlates with overall human wellbeing, encompasses both physical and mental facets, and is dependent on the immediate environment (Dunn, 1959). In this context, the delineation of the construct of wellbeing has been predominantly associated with an abstract notion of contentment and individual satisfaction, rendering it inherently subjective and psychological. Wellbeing activities are an integral part of the holistic paradigm of health, which aims to maintain a robust mind and body, to shape and/or redirect lifestyles, and to conceive of the individual as a whole rather than merely as a patient with an ailment to be cured. Today's concept of wellbeing goes beyond the need to be free of disease: rather, it is intrinsically linked to an individual's physical and emotional satisfaction and positive self-image, which is increasingly independent of biological age. Medeiros and Cavaco (2008: 34) refer to a context in which urban populations of all age groups are growing up in an uninhibited, individualistic and narcissistic way, paying increasing attention to the importance of personal appearance, with an aesthetic marked not only by icons and brands but also by seduction games involving adults of all age classes. The postmodern concept of health is characterized by a social focus on various aspects of the body. The 'new body' is a central aspect of everyday life. A positive or negative image of one's own body can result in an increase or decrease in wellbeing, self-confidence and self-esteem, all of which are essential for the relationships and social performance of individuals (Gustavo, 2010: 117).

Additionally, Tavitiyaman and Saiprasert (2020: 2) provide a definition of psychological wellbeing. Psychological wellbeing is defined as the individual's assessment of feelings of happiness and satisfaction with life. It is understood that this interacts with their emotional states of happiness, joy, satisfaction, and is supported by determinants such as competence, relationship, and health, income, personal values and freedom of choice. In this context, the perception of wellbeing is equivalent to the concept of quality of life, wellbeing, and happiness (Nossa & Caldeira, 2014). In their 2016 study, Hartwell *et al.* acknowledged that consumers' primary objective is to obtain services and experiences that facilitate the attainment of desired states of health and wellbeing. This pursuit is based on a comprehensive equilibrium between the physical, mental and spiritual dimensions of the human being. According to Dillette *et al.* (2021: 798):

> Wellness has been closely associated with prevention of disease and health amongst many scholars and organizations. Wellbeing, on the other hand, has been more closely associated with the intangible concept of happiness and is both subjective and psychological in nature.

On the other hand, as life expectancy increases and societies age in a desirably active way, older adults in affluent societies are often seen as 'tourists by necessity' (Koskinen, 2019). Their access to time and information enables them to invest in their health, to which Koskinen *et al.* (2017) ascribe a growing interest on the part of the elderly in self-development and experiential consumption in this field. 'The most important leisure benefit for people who had recently retired was the benefit of "essentiality", which also turned out to be the only leisure benefit that had a significant contribution to the overall life satisfaction' (Nimrod, 2007: 74).

This association between the 'new goals' in health, the multidimensional appreciation of wellbeing and tourism specialized in serving these purposes, has created novel synergies, stimulating the quality of tourist activities and prompting new business models that enhance sustainable tourism practices, namely in the economic and social aspects to be discussed (Pyke *et al.*, 2016). According to the World Tourism Organization and European Travel Commission (2018: 1–2):

> Wellness tourism is a type of tourism activity which aims to improve and balance all the main domains of human life including physical, mental, emotional, occupational, intellectual, and spiritual. The primary motivation for the wellness tourist is to engage in preventive, proactive, lifestyle enhancing activities such as fitness, healthy eating, relaxation, pampering and healing treatments.

Although proactive behavior in health is generally regarded as beneficial, it is important to recognize that individual accountability not only emphasizes disease self-management but can also lead to the stigmatization of individuals for their poor health (healthism), as well as overlooking the impact that social determinants of health have at the individual and community levels (Nossa & Caldeira, 2014). Moreover, this type of argumentation has facilitated the implementation of neoliberal policies that justify reductions in public health system investment (Nossa, 2020).

The growing emphasis on preventive health practices has led to a rise in investment in an active and healthy lifestyle, which has involved the utilization of services associated with health and wellness tourism. Simultaneously, the increasing prevalence of chronic diseases related to population ageing, such as arthritis, osteoporosis, and cardiovascular diseases, has led to a greater demand for thermal services as an integral part of a healthier and more integrative healthcare plan. The thermal environment offers a tranquil and relaxing refuge for those seeking to escape the stress and pressures of daily life, which contributes to the improvement of their health indicators (Kubo *et al.*, 2014).

The case study presented in this chapter illustrates the growing recognition of the concept of wellness among individuals from diverse age groups. These individuals are investing in improving their health while seeking novel experiences beyond the typical tourist destinations. They value the natural beauty of the landscape and the introduction of innovative services (Lopes, 2016).

12.3 Wellness Tourism and Sustainable Regional Development

Portuguese HWT facilities, namely thermal resorts, are mostly located inland in lesser developed regions, and they often serve as an important engine for local development insofar as they are not self-sufficient but play the role of anchor product, promoting other, complementary tourist businesses (Guerra *et al.*, 2022).

HWT, in fact, can represent a model of sustainable regional development. It promotes health and healthy lifestyles and combines nutrition, physical activity and contact with nature, all of which are in alignment with the sustainability paradigm. The motivations and objectives of HWT not only eschew mass tourism (Dillette *et al.*, 2021) but their demand extends throughout the year, thereby mitigating seasonality. In their role as anchor products, HWT facilities complement other tourism products, increasing the range of activities for tourists to choose from in low-density regions, with the goal of lengthening tourist stays and providing distinctive and memorable experiences (Buckley *et al.*, 2022; Pine & Gilmore, 2013).

This product offers a range of water-related activities, in conjunction with other natural and endogenous resources of the regions. Demand for these services has been growing and increasing in sophistication, leading to marked levels of innovation. Be it a reactive response to the needs and desires of clients, or a proactive anticipation of trends, bringing together complementary, endogenous resources promises to contribute to the sustainable development of more remote, inland regions (Croes *et al.*, 2020; Fazenda *et al.*, 2009).

Insofar as investment is concerned, HWT requires both tangible and intangible investments, in policies and in practices, in infrastructure and equipment, which may enhance the promotion of health and wellbeing of resident communities and, consequently, their quality of life. Being as how most HWT facilities are located in underdeveloped regions, it may be concluded that they promise to make an important contribution to their area's sustainable development. These regions are traditionally poorly served in terms of healthcare, due to their distance from political and economic decision-making centers, as well as the uneven distribution of facilities; but, above all, due to the limited number of qualified health professionals (Dwyer, 2022). At the same time, we would like to highlight HWT's potential for generating direct jobs, both seasonal or permanent, in addition to indirect jobs in related sectors, which are of utmost importance in these regions which are characterized by unemployment and depopulation. This regenerative potential may serve to attract and settle residents, generating local wealth and mitigating regional asymmetries by attracting consumption and investment, either directly in the core activity or in support services. A multiplier effect is to be expected that should benefit local economic agents (Croes *et al.*, 2020; Fazenda *et al.*, 2009).

Let us conclude this section by re-emphasizing the characteristics of the demand profile of this type of tourism. Health and wellness tourists generally have a 'greener profile' than average (with higher levels of income and education and more sophisticated lifestyles), which manifests itself in terms of longer average stays (Croes *et al.*, 2020). The characteristics listed so far, associated with the demand profile, have contributed to HWT's expanding role as a catalyst for sustainable regional development, a trend particularly highlighted during the COVID-19 pandemic.

12.4 Case Study: Unhais da Serra, Portugal

Unhais da Serra was chosen for this case study for three reasons:

(1) The richness and uniqueness of its natural and landscape heritage, particularly its geothermal resources located within the Estrela UNESCO Global Geopark.
(2) The historical association of the territory with the concept of HWT.
(3) Its current innovative and differentiated approach to HWT, not only in terms of its operations but also its model of community relations and its impact on the locale, which constitute essential grounds for obtaining and maintaining a UNESCO classification.

Unhais da Serra is a civil parish with an area of with 29.93 km^2 in the municipality of Covilhã, Portugal, and a population 1050 inhabitants (2021). Its history reflects the importance of HWT in regional development. Located at the foot of Serra da Estrela (Figure 12.1), in addition to its geothermal resources, it offers a privileged location with outstanding natural and landscape features that complement the HWT facilities. The municipality of Covilhã, in turn, covers the largest share of the Estrela UNESCO Global Geopark (497 km^2, representing 22% of the site).

Serra da Estrela, where Unhais da Serra is located, is the classic mountain resort in Portugal (Mota, 2022: 10). It boasts myriad features that support this role: physical and forest landscapes, the climate (cold oceanic climate, with cool summers, high rainfall and frequent snowfall), attractive patterns of ancestral land occupation and usage, noteworthy historical architectural features, vegetation (distinguished by the presence of species that are endemic to the Mediterranean and alpine regions, representing a distinctive feature within Portugal and the Iberian Peninsula), and water resources, with ancestral human activity shaping the landscape and creating a mosaic of inestimable cultural value:

> The history of the relationship between communities and the mountain represents an ancestral legacy that formed a marked identity in the people of Serra da Estrela, who, for hundreds of years, have herded livestock in the region seasonally, during the summer and early autumn. (Mota, 2022: 19)

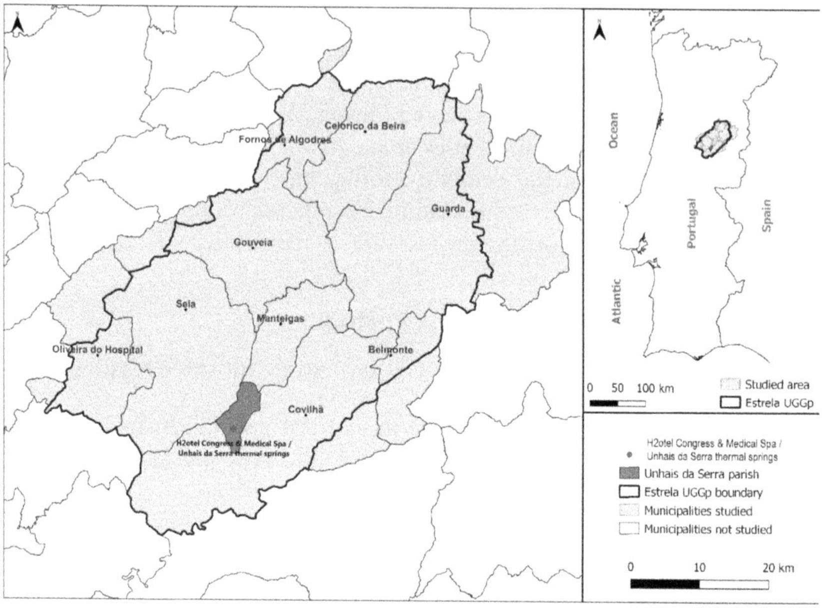

Figure 12.1 Unhais da Serra thermal spring and H2otel Congress & Medical Spa within the Estrela UNESCO Global Geopark perimeter

Source: Estrela Geopark Association.

Tourism developed in Unhais da Serra in the late 19th and early 20th century, due to the availability of its thermal waters and associated services. It later fell into disrepair resulting from a lack of maintenance and a change in tourist attitudes toward spas. Between 1980 and 2000, it came to be frequented by an older, less demanding and less wealthy clientele. This decline was interrupted in 2008 with the building of the H2otel Congress & Medical Spa. This facility aimed to address the lack of quality hotel accommodation in the Serra da Estrela area. It was an innovative concept, the first mountain spa in Portugal. The first step was to renovate the traditional spa, Aquatermas, which continues in autonomous operation and is open to the general public (Table 12.2). It combines medical mineral water

Table 12.2 Mineral–medical characteristics of the Unhais da Serra thermal spring

	Municipality	Chemical properties	Water temperature	Therapeutic benefits	Tourist facility
Unhais da Serra thermal spring	Covilhã	Waters with total mineralization of 280 mg/l, and a pH of 8.5 derived from the Vilariça Fault	37.5°C	Circulatory system Digestive system Respiratory system Rheumatics Musculoskeletal	H2otel Congress & Medical Spa

Source: Adapted from Mota (2022: 25)

with wellness treatments and offers outstanding accommodation in addition to services and activities related to prevention, health promotion and wellbeing, including a medical spa (combating pathologies associated with stress, sedentary lifestyle and addiction) based on the principles of medical hydrology located in the Aquadome. In order to attract both family and corporate sectors, the Aqualudic unit includes a set of indoor and outdoor hydrodynamic pools. Luís Veiga, the CEO, explained their holism strategy:

> We believe that health tourism is a growing trend, and we want to position ourselves, because in non-urban regions, a resort has no other choice than to make use of some sort of thematic concept, regardless of the type. (Veiga, 2009)

To this end, roughly €100,000 were invested in October 2020 for the 'remodelling and updating of the thermal spa', with a view to 'preventing, containing and mitigating the risks associated with the spread of the new coronavirus' (Publituris, 2020).

In 2021, it received, for the 12th consecutive time, the Golden Key of the Boa Cama Boa Mesa Guide (Regina, 2021). The facility also received the Innovative Medical Spa Award at the Congress of the European Spas Association in 2017, certified by the TÜV Rheinland Portugal Certification Body (Environmental Certification ISO 14001 and 9001), gaining both the appellation Eco-Hotel as well as Bio-Friendly Hotel certification.

Overlooking part of the village of Unhais da Serra and the Alforfa glacial valley, the H2otel Congress & Medical Spa has a wellness facility offering a wide range of services, including massages, rituals and face care. Simultaneously, medical services at the Aquadome include a thermal swimming pool with hydromassage, a walking corridor, hot tubs, Vichy showers, hydro-pressotherapy, Bertholaix, airway rooms, steam greenhouses and even a Scottish shower. In order to harmonize with nature and the rural surroundings, the facility was designed to resemble a mountain chalet, and local materials were used both in construction and in decoration. To date, infrastructure investment has been partly financed by the European PITER programme (Integrated Tourist Programmes of Structural Interest and Regional Base). The facility has 90 rooms and its capacity of 188 beds accounts for 8.6% of Covilhã's total accommodation capacity. H2otel Congress & Medical Spa accounts for 20% of the municipality's 4-star accommodations. Figure 12.2 shows that the facility's share of the 4-star accommodation capacity in Covilhã fell 8.5% between 2017 and 2021. This suggests that investment has led to the opening of more facilities in this class, especially post COVID-19.

A study conducted by Lopes (2016) identified the principal differentiating factors of this hotel unit, which encompasses a thermal and spa complex, along with active leisure services. These factors

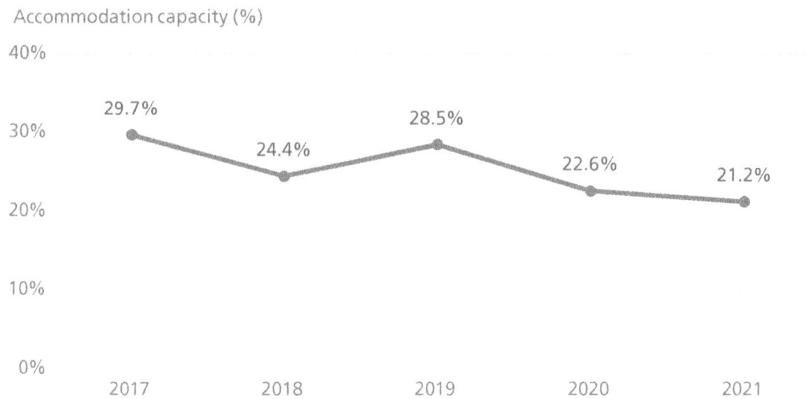

Figure 12.2 Accommodation capacity of H2otel Congress & Medical Spa relative to the total Covilhã 4-star accommodation capacity, 2017–2021

Source: The authors (2024).

include: (1) encouragement for outdoor activities, which provides environmental education to guests through guided interaction with the surrounding ecosystem; (2) designation as a 'Bike Friendly' unit, offering routes guided by trails selected by qualified monitors; and (3) organization of hikes and educational activities for children, which is a differentiating factor noted by clients who stay with their families.

12.5 Methodology

This case study used qualitative techniques to collect empirical data about real contexts from a wide range of sources, which have been analyzed mostly inductively but also deductively (Eisenhardt, 1989). A case study is 'empirical research that investigates a contemporary phenomenon within its real-life context, when the boundaries between the phenomenon and the context are not clearly evident and in which multiple sources of evidence are used' (Yin, 1989: 23). According to Yin (1989), 'case' can be a plurality of units or situations, ranging from the individual to a regional unit coinciding with a country, but it can also be a process, a policy or a practice. The case study method has the advantage of adapting to both quantitative and qualitative data sources, demonstrating a flexibility that is not evident in most other methodological alternatives (Jennings, 2000).

The case study method was thought to be the most appropriate for this project due to its eclectic nature and the fact that it enables researchers to compare qualitative and quantitative data. The case is defined as the civil parish of Unhais da Serra and the relationship between HWT and sustainable regional development.

The impact of HWT on the regional economy of Estrela UGGp will be analyzed by studying the direct effects of this demand segment of tourism (Vellas, 2011) on Unhais da Serra. In this way, the direct impacts on leisure and entertainment services and accommodation will be studied, both from the perspective of tourism supply and demand (Mota, 2022; Mota *et al.*, 2023) by analyzing:

(1) The evolution of the number of jobs in Sociedade Termal de Unhais da Serra, S.A., between 2014 and 2021, with data provided by Informa D&B. (Job creation is an important indicator of the performance of the tourism sector in general, and can also be taken as a measure of the economic importance of the tourism enterprises analyzed in the HWT segment in the Estrela UGGp territory.)
(2) The evolution of the number and value of registrations for thermal attendance at the territory's thermal resorts between 2014 and 2021, with data provided by the Directorate-General for Energy and Geology.
(3) The changes in the estimated number of overnight stays at the H2otel Congress & Medical Spa between 2014 and 2021, with data taken from Statistics Portugal and Tourism of Portugal. (As an important indicator of a destination's performance in terms of its ability to attract tourists, the number of overnight stays is an important element to be analyzed in the context of the direct effects of tourism in Unhais da Serra.)
(4) The evolution of Revenue per Available Room (RevPAR), Total Revenue per Available Room (TRevPAR) and the difference between the two in selected tourist resorts in the territory between 2014 and 2021, in all Covilhã 4-star Hotels (data obtained from Statistics Portugal and Tourism of Portugal).

RevPAR and TRevPAR are indicators used in revenue management practice, which, in turn, has as its main object of study, in the accommodation sector, the management of prices and the physical capacity of a company to maximize its turnover, optimising decision-making at a commercial level and taking into account the intangibility of services and the restrictions of the fixed capacity of each company (Rolim *et al.*, 2019).

12.6 Data Analysis

The impact of HWT on the economy and local development in Unhais da Serra was assessed based on tourism supply and demand.

12.6.1 Supply side: Number of jobs

Sociedade Termal de Unhais da Serra, S.A is the entity responsible for H2otel Congress & Medical Spa operations, and this is its only tourist facility. For this reason, the 2017–2021 Informa D&B data are believed

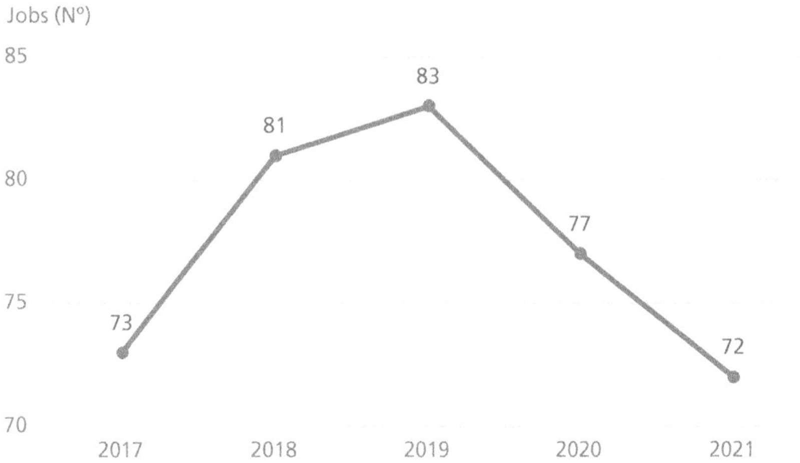

Figure 12.3 Number of jobs at Sociedade Termal de Unhais da Serra, S.A., 2017–2021
Source: The authors (2024).

to correspond with a high degree of confidence only to H2otel Congress & Medical Spa. Figure 12.3 illustrates a constant increase in jobs until 2019. This period corresponded to a large growth in tourist demand nationally, which peaked in that same year. In 2020, a drop of nearly 7.2% occurred and continued in 2021, which was most likely caused by the COVID-19 pandemic hotel crisis.

12.6.2 Demand: Thermal and wellness visits

The Directorate-General for Energy and Geology provided the data for thermal visits, visitor age distribution and the monetary value of Unhais da Serra visits. Figure 12.4 displays the demand for HWT at the Unhais da Serra Spa, by motive: leisure, recreation and/or relaxation. From 2017 to 2021, this type of demand was 2.5 to 3.9 times higher than that of classical thermalism treatments. Significant dips occurred for both segments at the beginning of the COVID-19 pandemic (54% for HWT and 68% for classical thermalism). The year 2021 witnessed some turn around for both segments, although the figures did not recover to their 2017–2019 levels.

The trends differed considerably by age group, for classical and wellness services. Classical spa baths were predominantly sought by seniors, 66–74 years of age, for each year. Although less significant, those aged 45–65 years also marked their presence. Despite significant dips in 2020 demand due to the pandemic, both cohorts recovered in 2021, much more so than any other group of classical thermal spa users.

HWT bookings were predominantly represented by visitors between 45 and 65 years of age. Visitors aged 36–44 made significant numbers of

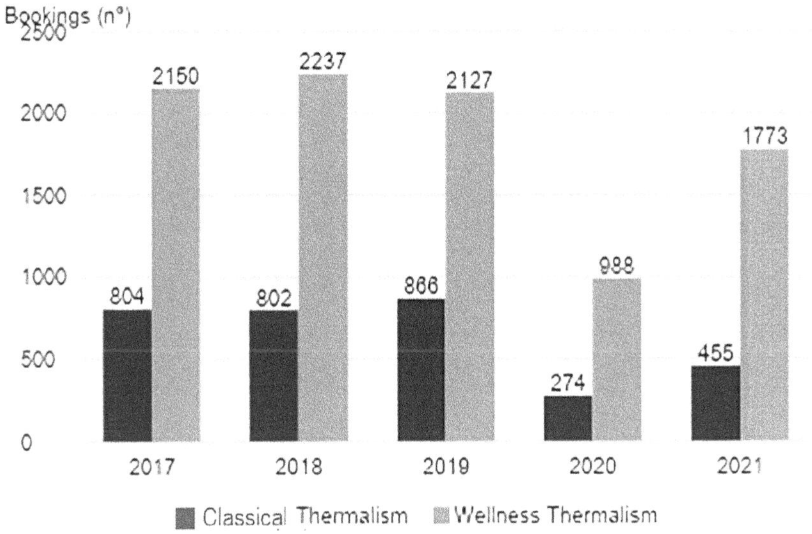

Figure 12.4 Classical and wellness thermalism visits in Unhais da Serra, 2017–2021
Source: The authors (2024).

visits, followed immediately by the 26–35 age group. All these age groups reduced their demand for treatments considerably during COVID-19. However, their recoveries took different forms. While bookings for those aged 45–65 years jumped to numbers above those of 2019, bookings for the group aged 36–44 years increased more moderately, the 26–35 cohort made fewer bookings. Currently, in this post-pandemic period, senior-citizen (66+) demand has begun to draw attention, with numbers very similar to those of classical spa visits.

The monetary value of thermal spa visits at Unhais da Serra thermal spa follows a similar trend to that of visit numbers, both in the classical spa and HWT visits, although without a recovery in 2021 (Figure 12.5). It is therefore important to analyze conjointly the booking variation and their monetary values throughout the period (Figure 12.6).

The 2018 number of visits varied less than their monetary value did, relative to the previous year, while the 2019 variation was the opposite. This trend may denote a HWT demand growth for 2018, while the figures for 2019 may reflect an increase in the purchasing power of thermal clients, since that year witnessed the highest GDP per capita nationally since 1960. This might explain users' predisposition to seek more expensive treatments. The year 2020 witnessed a sharp drop both in booking numbers and their value relative to the previous year, due to the pandemic and consequent restrictions on thermal facility use. Visits increased significantly in 2021, while expenditure on them fell. This may be explained by an increased demand for classical spa visits,

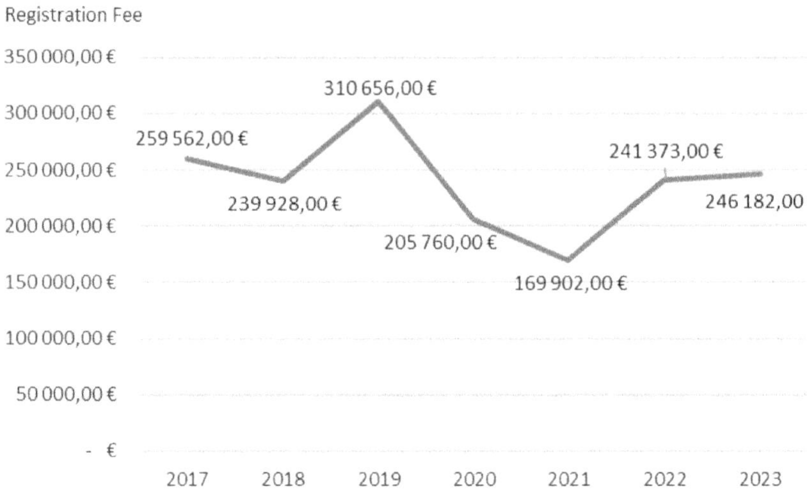

Figure 12.5 The total value of visits to Unhais da Serra thermal spa, 2017–2023
Source: The authors (2024).

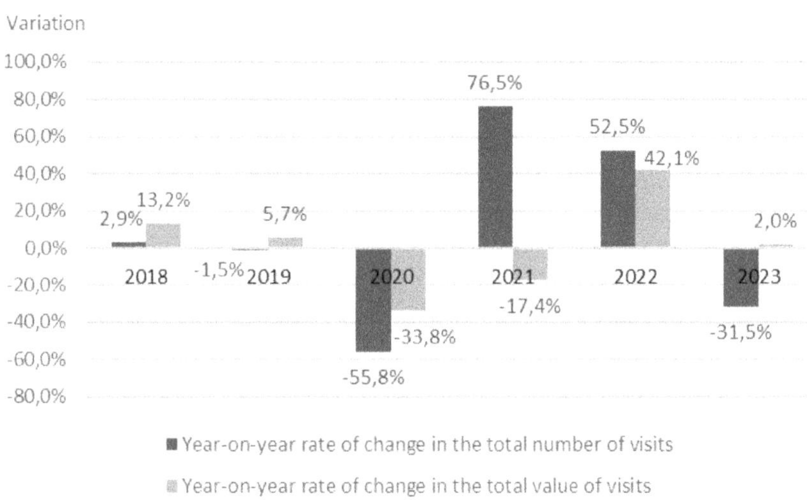

Figure 12.6 Year-on-year rate of change in the total number and the value of visits to Unhais da Serra thermal spa, 2018–2023
Source: The authors (2024).

which are subject to reimbursement through the national health system and, therefore, reflect lower costs for users. After a slight slowdown in the growth in the number of visits in 2022, there is a sharp drop in 2023, accompanied by almost no variation in the value of visits in that year, which may be associated with the attraction of a market segment more geared towards therapeutic treatments, most of which are reimbursed.

12.6.3 Overnight stays

Figure 12.7 compares overnight stays per annum at H2otel Congress & Medical Spa, 2017–2021, with the total 4-star stays for Covilhã, in order to estimate the annual H2otel Congress & Medical Spa stays. The occupancy rate was assumed to be equal across all Covilhã 4-star hotels and constant throughout the period. Overnight stay trends generally accompanied those of thermal visits, with an increase until 2019, a significant dip in 2020, followed by a tenuous recovery in 2021. These numbers have yet to recoup their pre-pandemic values.

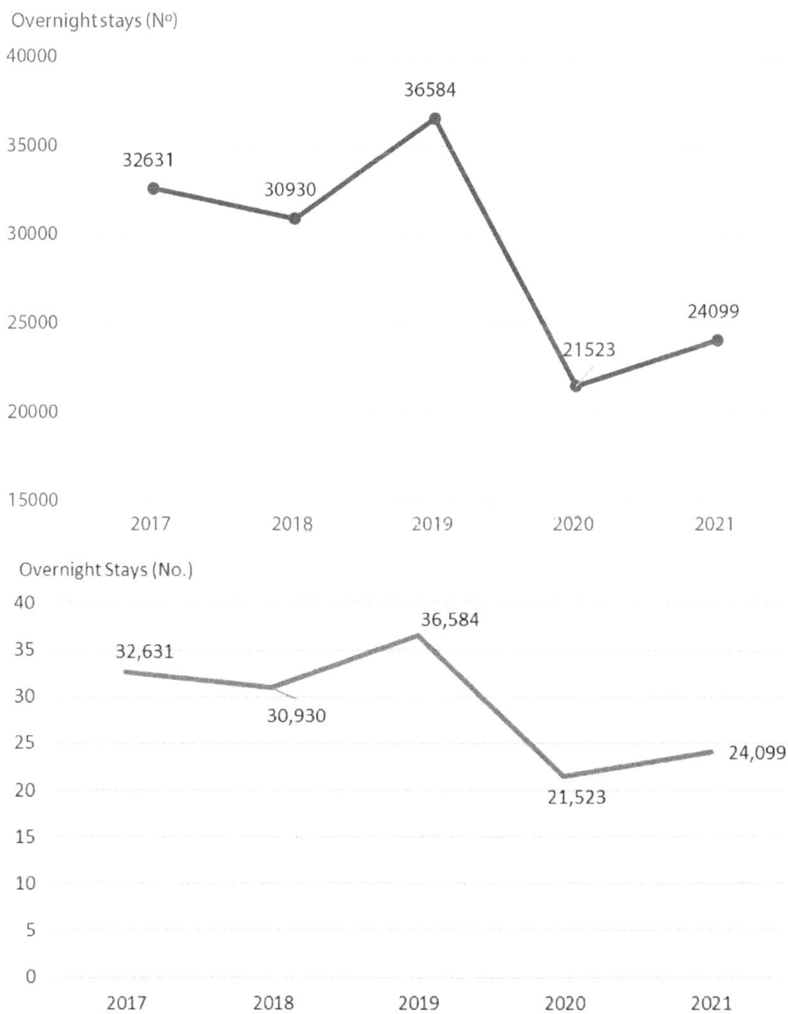

Figure 12.7 Estimated overnight stays at H2otel Congress & Medical Spa, 2017–2021
Source: The authors (2024).

12.6.4 Difference between TRevPAR and RevPAR(€)

Revenue per Available Room (RevPAR) compares the turnover of occupied rooms and available rooms of a facility in a given period, measuring the resort's performance regarding its price management and revenue maximization (Abranja *et al.*, 2020). In turn, the Total Revenue per Available Room (TRevPAR) takes into account all the facility's income including food and beverage, meeting spaces, parking, telephone and/or internet service, and spa and wellness services. Constant monitoring of these figures helps managers identify not only underperforming revenue sources but also profit-generating opportunities, especially when overnight stay rates are disappointing (Lacalle, 2021). The difference between these two indicators results in the revenue per resort from all segments except accommodation. This is the best possible assessment of the value of the spa and wellness services at Covilhã's 4-star hotels and, within these, the H2otel Congress & Medical Spa. RevPAR and total income Covilhã 4-star hotel revenue figures were obtained from the National Institute of Statistics. The TRevPAR was calculated using the ratio between total income and occupied accommodation units (Rolim *et al.*, 2019), the latter obtained from Tourism of Portugal. Occupancy rates were calculated by the ratio between estimated annual overnight stays (i.e. total number of beds occupied during the year) (Figure 12.8) and the accommodation capacity per unit at H2otel Congress & Medical Spa, which was set at 2.1 (occupancy of 188 beds, in 90 rooms). Table 12.3 shows all the data and estimates.

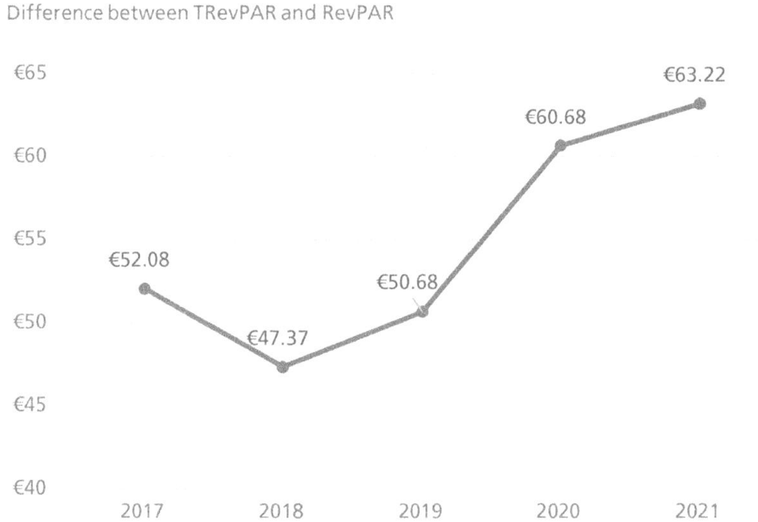

Figure 12.8 Difference between TRevPAR and annual RevPAR for Covilhã's 4-star hotels, 2017–2021

Source: The authors (2024).

Table 12.3 Total revenues, estimated TRevPAR and RevPAR of Covilhã's 4-star hotels and estimated number of occupied units at H2otel Congress & Medical Spa

Year	Total revenue (€)	Estimated no. of units occupied	Estimated TRevPAR (€)	RevPAR (€)
2017	1,497,763.03	15,621	95.88	43.80
2018	1,486,153.45	14,807	100.37	53.00
2019	1,831,575.76	17,514	104.58	53.90
2020	1,039,423.08	10,304	100.88	40.20
2021	1,209,268.62	11,537	104.82	41.60

Source: The author (2024).

The difference between TRevPAR and RevPAR shows a trend contrary to that of other indicators (as shown in Figure 12.8), more similar to that of housing, which may denote a greater resilience of the extra-housing component. As we are evaluating the H2otel Congress & Medical Spa, there is a strong possibility that this value is related to the hotel's spa and wellbeing services.

Another equally relevant fact is that H2otel favors hiring local labor, which helps to attract and secure the population. Both returning residents who had previously been in search of work and recently trained local youth find opportunities here. It also partners with local producers, sourcing food, wine and additional tourist services nearby.

12.7 Discussion

Sociedade Termal de Unhais da Serra, S.A., specifically the H2otel Congress & Medical Spa, saw a dramatic drop in the number of overnight stays (Figure 12.7) and the number of jobs (Figure 12.3) in the period 2019–2021, as did the general travel and tourism sector and, particularly HWT, in which overnight stays decreased by 58.8%. In the Portuguese case, the COVID-19 pandemic was met firstly with a compulsory lockdown on 12 March 2020 followed by a state of emergency declared six days later that applied severe restrictions on the mobility of people and goods, having a progressively negative effect on the economy. In addition to highly restrictive civil and health protection measures, European countries closed their borders and imposed progressive economic lockdowns that severely restricted leisure and tourism, while also disrupting land, sea and air passenger transport. According to UNWTO (2021: 1):

> Global tourism suffered its worst year on record in 2020, with international arrivals dropping by 74% according to the latest data from the World Tourism Organization. Destinations worldwide welcomed 1 billion fewer international arrivals in 2020 than in the previous year, due to an unprecedented fall in demand and widespread travel restrictions. This compares with the 4% decline recorded during the 2009 global economic crisis.

The sharp reduction in economic activity, with the total closure of Portuguese hot springs and spas, lasted until mid-2021, with a gradual reopening and lifting of various restrictions. Thus, the figures cited for the H2otel Congress & Medical Spa followed the national trend of a decrease in tourism jobs.

In 2021, however, Pinos Navarrete and Shaw predicted that greater safety would translate into increased demand for thermal spas:

> In the current context of the COVID pandemic, the value and social importance of spas is mainly motivated by their curative aspect regarding a medical role. It is precisely this dimension that gives them their uniqueness and allows them to differentiate themselves from new establishments that use tap water. This difference is important because, at the time of the reopening of tourist establishments, customers are going to look for quality and safety in facilities and services. Those centres and destinations of mass tourism that cannot guarantee these two dimensions may have a difficult time surviving in the post-pandemic market. (Pinos Navarrete & Shaw, 2021: 248)

In fact, in 2021 the H2otel Congress & Medical Spa did see a recovery in visits to classic thermal spas, particularly among 45–74-year-olds, following the European health authorities' implementation of Clean & Safety measures. However, the HWT rebound was even greater. It is likely that the rapid recovery of demand can be attributed, in this particular region, to a new niche of clients interested in bringing HWT together with an appreciation of nature in a low population density region. Due to the current health context, said customers are thought to be changing their preferences and seeking out locations with plenty of nature and that are free of crowds, places that may offer them a safer, different experience (Gouveia & Seabra, 2022: 107). This may lead to a marked increase in tourism in this region post-COVID. What is not known is whether this trend will prevail now that WHO has declared the end of the global COVID-19 health emergency (5 May 2023). However, the current demand trend seems promising.

Moreover, Pinos Navarrete and Shaw (2021) predicted a growth in customer interest in medical mineral water, which may be indirectly linked with the values seen in Table 12.3. It shows that the 2021 estimated TRevPAR of €104.82 was almost the same as that of 2019 (€104.58), which might suggest that H2otel witnessed more resistance to demand shortfalls in its non-accommodation segment, including thermal treatments, spas and wellness services.

12.8 Conclusion

Unhais da Serra has a wealth of factors that contribute to its ability to be called a Wellness Village in the sense of Latif *et al.* (2019): its low population density (35 inhabitants/km^2); its setting within the extraordinarily exuberant landscape inside the Estrela UNESCO Global Geopark; and the economic contribution of HWT made by the H2otel Congress & Medical spa that directly employs 70 people, or roughly 7% of the local population of 1048 (Statistics Portugal, 2022). It takes advantage of natural resources, especially geothermal and landscape resources, and makes the most of them through the active involvement of the community, stimulating regional development, contributing to the quality of life of local residents and providing a high-quality, multidimensional tourist experience. These elements are important assets for stimulating a new trend of post-pandemic tourism demand. As posited by Gorretti *et al.* (2021), low density territories are indicative of the 'new desires' of visitors. This requires a novel approach to investments, both public and private, with the objective of augmenting the existing tourist offer while concurrently developing and publicizing a brand that can further increase demand. This new context may result in a shift towards more sustainable and health-orientated tourism practices, as well as the strengthening of non-tourism sectors to mitigate the potential economic impact that new health threats may bring.

Furthermore, Zhang *et al.* (2020) indicate that the rise in tourist demand for these locations can yield local advantages that extend beyond economic considerations, resulting in a mutually beneficial scenario. In addition to the increase in income, local residents can benefit from the social capital and cultural practices that visitors bring with them, thereby boosting the value of the territory's natural resources, particularly thermal water. In addition, visitors can help to introduce healthier lifestyles and improve preventive health practices. From this perspective, even the seasonal demand for wellness practices has the potential to transform these visitors into active participants in the local community. This can be achieved by taking advantage of the various forms of capital (social and cultural) to promote positive relationships and contribute to local development. This approach, advocated by Zhang *et al.* (2020), is innovative and was not covered in this study. However, it is an interesting avenue for future research.

It is possible to identify a number of limitations to this study. The demand indicators for the accommodation component (number of overnight stays and difference between TRevPAR and RevPAR) are the result of estimates, which are based on the assumption that factors outside the estimation model remain constant. It would be beneficial for future research to include input from local public and private actors, in order to provide a more comprehensive picture of the situation. In terms of tourism, it is essential that the region diversifies its attractiveness factors (Goretti *et al.*, 2021). This can be achieved by reinforcing the region's health tourism offer with nature tourism products and developing strategies to mitigate seasonal fluctuations and external shocks. Similarly, it is of significant importance to develop strategies that will encourage community participation in defining the primary elements of the local tourism offer. It is of the utmost importance to engage local residents in the process of tourism development. This ensures that they identify and value other forms of territory enjoyment with high potential, such as culinary tourism and geotourism.

Acknowledgements

The authors are grateful to Informa D&B Portugal (https://www.informadb.pt/pt/) for providing the unpublished statistical data on 4-star hotels in the city of Covilhã and for agreeing to respect national data protection.

Funding

This research was funded by national funds through the FCT – Foundation for Science and Technology, I.P., within the scope of the project UIDB/04084/2020.

References

Abranja, N., Almeida, A.E. and Almeida, M. (2020) *Gestão Hoteleira: O produto, o serviço e as técnicas*. Lidel - Edições Técnicas, Lda.

Antonovsky, A. (1979) *Health, Stress and Coping*. Jossey-Bass.

Araújo, A.R., Paiva, T., Ribeiro, M.P. and Coutinho, P. (2015) Innovation in thermalism: An example in Beira Interior Region of Portugal. In M. Peris-Ortiz and J. Álvarez-García (eds) *Health and Wellness Tourism: Emergence of a New Market Segment* (pp. 165–180). Springer International. https://doi.org/10.1007/978-3-319-11490-3.

Associação Termas de Portugal. (2022) *Travel BI Termas 2022 – Caraterização da Oferta e da Procura*. Turismo de Portugal. https://termasdeportugal.pt/noticias/travel-bi-termas-2022-caraterizacao-da-oferta-e-da-procura-ea53e06f-1089-4030-9266-b5696a1f6506.

Bauer, G.F., Davies, J.K., Pelikan, J.M., Noack, H., Broesskamp, U. and Hill, C. (2003) Advancing a theoretical model for public health and health promotion indicator development: Proposal from the EUHPID consortium. *European Journal of Public Health* 13 (3), 107–113. https://doi.org/10.1093/eurpub/13.suppl_1.107.

Buckley, R., Cooper, M., Chauvenet, A. and Zhong, L. (2022) Theories of experience value & mental health at tourism destinations: Senses, personalities, emotions and memories. *Journal of Destination Marketing & Management* 26 (2022), 100744. https://doi.org/10.1016/j.jdmm.2022.100744.

Costa, C., Quintela, J. and Mendes, J. (2015) Health and wellness tourism: A strategic plan for tourism and thermalism valorization of São Pedro do Sul. In M. Peris-Ortiz and J. Álvarez-García (eds) *Health and Wellness Tourism: Emergence of a New Market Segment* (pp. 21–31). Springer International. https://doi.org/10.1007/978-3-319-11490-3.

Cristobal-Fransi, E., Daries, N., del Río-Rama, M.C. and Fuentes-Tierno, M.G. The challenge of digital marketing in health tourism: The case of Spanish health resorts. *Qual Quant*. https://doi.org/10.1007/s11135-023-01744-2.

Croes, R., Ridderstaat, J. and Shapoval, V. (2020) Extending tourism competitiveness to human development. *Annals of Tourism Research* 80. https://doi.org/10.1016/j.annals.2019.102825.

Cunha, L. (2006) Turismo de saúde–conceitos e mercados. *Revista Lusófona de Humanidades e Tecnologias* 10 (10), 79–84.
Damijanić, A.T. (2020) Travel motivations as criteria in the wellness tourism market segmentation process. *Academica Turistica – Tourism and Innovation Journal* 13, 201–213.
Dillette, A.K., Douglas, A.C. and Andrzejewski, C. (2021) Dimensions of holistic wellness as a result of international wellness tourism experiences. *Current Issues in Tourism* 24 (6), 794–810. https://doi.org/10.1080/13683500.2020.1746247.
Dunn, H.L. (1959) What high-level wellness means. *Canadian Journal of Public Health/ Revue Canadienne de Sante'e Publique* 50 (11), 447–457.
Dunn, H.L. (1961) *High-Level Wellness: A Collection of Twenty-Nine Short Talks on Different Aspects of the Theme 'High-Level Wellness for Man and Society'*. R.W. Beatty Ltd.
Dwyer, L. (2022) Destination competitiveness and resident wellbeing. *Tourism Management Perspectives* 43 (2022). https://doi.org/10.1016/j.tmp.2022.100996.
Eisenhardt, K. (1989) Building theories from case study research. *Academy of Management Review* 14 (4), 532–550.
Fazenda, N., Ladeiras, A., Vieira, T. and Barbosa, D. (2009) *Programa de Acção de Enfoque Temático 'Turismo de Saúde e Bem-Estar' para o Porto e Norte de Portugal – Agenda Regional de Turismo*. Turismo de Portugal, I.P.
Fetscherin, M. and Stephano, R.M. (2016) The medical tourism index: Scale development and validation. *Tourism Management* 52, 539–556. https://doi.org/10.1016/j.tourman.2015.08.010.
Global Wellness Institute (2021) *Global Wellness Trends Report: The Future of Wellness 2021 with Mid-Year Update*. GWI. https://globalwellnessinstitute.org.
Goretti, M.M., Leigh, M.L.Y., Babii, A., Cevik, M.S., Kaendera, S., Muir, M.D.V., Nadeem, S. and Salinas, M.G. (2021) *Tourism in the post-Pandemic World: Economic Challenges and Opportunities for Asia–Pacific and the Western Hemisphere*. International Monetary Fund. https://doi.org/10.5089/9781513561905.087.
Gouveia, C. and Seabra, C. (2022) Impactos da pandemia COVID-19 nas viagens: O caso da Região Centro de Portugal. *RPER* (60), 105–115.
Guerra, R., Santos, N. and Gonçalves, E. (2022) Health and wellness tourism: Contributions to a local sustainable development strategy. In M.D. Vujicic, A. Kasim, S. Kostopoulou, J. Chica Olmo and M. Aslam (eds) *Cultural Sustainable Tourism. Advances in Science, Technology & Innovation*. Springer. https://doi.org/10.1007/978-3-031-07819-4_19.
Guo, C., Lu, X., Huang, S., Zhao, Y. and Zhao, D. (2024) Understanding the post-pandemic travel intentions among Chinese residents: Impact of sociodemographic factors, COVID experiences, travel planned behaviours, health beliefs, and resilience. *International Journal of Tourism Research* 26 (4), e2752. https://doi.org/10.1002/jtr.2752.
Gustavo, N.S. (2010) A 21st-century approach to health tourism spas: The case of Portugal. *Journal of Hospitality and Tourism Management* 17 (1), 127–135.
Hartwell, H., Fyall, A., Willis, C., Page, S., Ladkin, A. and Hemingway, A. (2016) Progress in tourism and destination wellbeing research. *Current Issues in Tourism* 21 (16), 1830–1892. https://doi.org/10.1080/13683500.2016.1223609.
Jennings, G. (2000) *Tourism Research*. Wiley.
Koskinen, V. (2019) Spa tourism as a part of ageing well. *InternationalJournal of Spa and Wellness* 2 (1), 18–34. https://doi.org/10.1080/24721735.2019.1668673.
Koskinen, V., Ylilahti, M. and Wilska, T. (2017) 'Healthy to heaven' – Middle-agers looking ahead in the context of wellness consumption. *Journal of Aging Studies* 40, 36–43. https://doi.org/10.1016/j.jageing.2016.12.006.
Kubo, J., Goldstein, B.A., Cantley, L.F., Tessier-Sherman, B., Galusha, D., Slade, M.D. and Cullen, M.R. (2014) Contribution of health status and prevalent chronic disease to individual risk for workplace injury in the manufacturing environment. *Occupational and Environmental Medicine* 71 (3), 159–166.

Lacalle, E. (2021) How TRevPAR can benefit your hotel and how to calculate this metric. *MEWS*, 5 May [hospitality platform]: https://www.mews.com/en/blog/trevpar-calculation.

Latif, R.A., Zubir, A.Y., Asbollah, A.Z. and Som, E.M. (2019) Development of wellness-village tourism: An exploratory study of a small town. *International Journal of Innovation, Creativity and Change* 6 (3), 417–432.

Lopes, R.P. (2016) Motivações e Práticas dos aquistas das Termas de Unhais da Serra. Motivações e Práticas dos aquistas das Termas de Unhais da Serra. Master's thesis, University of Coimbra.

Loureiro, I. and Miranda, N. (2010) *Promover a saúde. Dos fundamentos à ação*. Edições Almedina.

Medeiros, C. and Cavaco, C. (2008) *Turismo de saúde e bem-estar. Termas, spas termais e talassoterapia*. Universidade Católica Portuguesa. https://doi.org/10.34632/9789729045240.

Mota, A.M.M. (2022) O Turismo de Saúde e Bem-Estar na economia e desenvolvimento regionais. Uma análise ao território do Estrela Geopark Mundial da UNESCO. Master of Science dissertation in Tourism, Territory and Heritage. Universidade de Coimbra. https://estudogeral.uc.pt/handle/10316/104064.

Mota, M., Nossa, P. and Oliveira Moreira, C. (2023) The impact of health and wellness tourism in the regional economy of Estrela UNESCO Global Geopark, Portugal. *Sustainability* 15 (20), 15151. https://doi.org/10.3390/su152015151.

Nimrod, G. (2007) Retirees' leisure: Activities, benefits, and their contribution to life satisfaction. *Leisure Studies* 26 (1), 65–80. https://doi.org/10.1080/02614360500333937.

Nossa, P. (2020) Aging, financing, and innovation in the healthcare system: A necessary discussion to maintain the right to health. *Saúde e Sociedade* 29, e200081. https://doi.org/10.1590/S0104-12902020200081.

Nossa, P. and Caldeira, M. (2014) Turismo medicalizado: Um epifenómeno ou a consolidação de uma nova geografia dos cuidados de saúde? In CICS (ed.) *Trabalho em Saúde, Desigualdades e Políticas Públicas* (pp. 1–13). Centro de Investigação em Ciências Sociais (CICS-UM) Universidade do Minho Universidade do Minho.

Nunes, J.A. (2022) *Arquitectura Branca: Os sanatórios para a tuberculose em Portugal*. By the Book.

Peris-Ortiz, M. and Álvarez García, J. (2015) *Health and Wellness Tourism: Emergence of a New Market Segment*. Springer. https://doi.org/10.1007/978-3-319-11490-3.

Pine, B. and Gilmore, J. (2013) The experience economy: Past, present and future. In J. Sundbo and F. Sørensen (eds) *Handbook on the Experience Economy* (pp. 21–44). Edward Elgar.

Pinos Navarrete, A. and Shaw, G. (2021) Spa tourism opportunities as strategic sector in aiding recovery from Covid-19: The Spanish model. *Tourism and Hospitality Research* 21 (2), 245–250. https://doi.org/10.1177/1467358420970626.

Publituris (2020) Thermal spa at H2otel's 100,000€ renovation. *Publituris*, 2 October. https://www.publituris.pt/2020/10/02/termas-do-h2otel-foram-alvo-de-requalificacao-de-100-mil-euros.

Regina, C. (2021) H2otel wins the 12th consecutive Chave de Ouro. *A Notícia*, 17 June. https://anoticia.pt/2021/06/17/h2otel-recebe-chave-de-ouro-pela-12a-vez-consecutiva/.

Rolim, M., Malheiros, C., Gomes, C. and Santos, L.L. (2019) Determinantes do TRevPAR: Uma análise dos hotéis portugueses entre 2010 e 2017. In P. Almeida, M. Franco, J.P. Jorge (eds) *International Tourism Congress: The Image and Sustainability of Tourism. Proceedings Book* (pp. 244–253). Centre for Tourism Research, Development and Innovation (CiTUR).

Smith, M. and Puczko, L. (2009) *Health and Wellness Tourism*. Elsevier. https://doi.org/10.4324/9780080942032.

Statistics Portugal (2022) Censos da População 2021. https://censos.ine.pt/xportal/xmain?xpgid=censos21_main&xpid=CENSOS21&xlang=pt. Retrieved 4 January 2023.

Tavitiyaman, P. and Saiprasert, W. (2020) Medical quality and wellbeing perception of senior tourists. *Asia Pacific Journal of Health Management* 15 (2), 30–38.

Turancı, E. (2019) The use of Instagram as a public relations tool in health tourism: An analysis on 'health tourism Turkey' hashtag. *International Journal of Health Management and Tourism* 4 (1), 44–60.

UNWTO (2021) NEWS RELEASE - 2020: Worst year in tourism history with 1 billion fewer international arrivals. https://pre-webunwto.s3.eu-west-1.amazonaws.com/s3fs-public/2021-01/210128-barometer-en.pdf?VersionId=zMUGFEKuRN7RbuS5_atmiktM90Z_h4fM. Retrieved 8 January 2023.

Veiga, L. (2009) *Diário Económico* [Newspaper no longer published after 2016.].

Vellas, F. (2011) The indirect impact of tourism: An economic analysis. Paper presented at the Third Meeting of T20 Tourism Ministers, 25 October 2011, Paris, France.

Vieira, I.C. (2013) A Serra da Estrela e a origem do movimento senatorial português. *CEM*. 4, 91.

Vieira, I.C. (2019) A ilha da Madeira como centro de tratamento de doenças pulmonares em meados do século XIX. *Arquivo Histórico da Madeira, Nova Série* (1), 381–405.

WHO (World Health Organization) (1948) WHO definition of health [online]. https://www.publichealth.com.ng/world-health-organizationwho-definition-of-health/ Retrieved 4 January 2024.

WHO (World Health Organization) (1986) *Ottawa Charter for Health Promotion* (No. WHO/EURO: 1986-4044-43803-61677). World Health Organization Regional Office for Europe.

WHO (World Health Organization) (1997) The Jakarta Declaration on Leading Health Promotion into the 21st Century. See also *Health Promotion International* 12 (4), 261–264.

WHO (World Health Organization) (2015) *WHO Global Strategy on People-centred and Integrated Health Services: Interim Report* (No. WHO/HIS/SDS/2015.6). World Health Organization.

World Tourism Organization and European Travel Commission (2018) *Exploring Health Tourism*. UNWTO. https://doi.org/10.18111/9789284420209.

Yin, R. (1989) *Case Study Research. Design and Methods* (2nd edn). Sage Publications.

Zhang, Y., Lin, Z.X. and Lee, T.J. (2020) Wellness-oriented seasonal tourism migration: A field relationship study in China. *International Journal of Tourism Research* 23 (4), 491–503. https://doi.org/10.1002/jtr.2420.

13 Developing a Sustainable Tourism Energy Therapy Model in Nature: A Case Study of Mount Sabalan

Sonia Azhari and Mohammad Alizadeh

13.1 Introduction

Research on wellness tourism (WT) has recently seen rapid growth in the academic literature; indeed, the WT demand market is one of the economic megatrends globally. Wellness facilities and programmes became worldwide tourist attractions during the 20th century, and this trend shows little sign of slowing down (Erfurt-Cooper & Cooper, 2009). The wellness economy encompasses industries that enable consumers to incorporate wellness activities and lifestyles into their daily lives. One of the most important events that has accelerated the ascendance of wellness as a dominant consumer value all around the world is the COVID-19 pandemic:

> During the pandemic, many of us discovered that nature heals and nourishes both our physical and mental wellbeing. For many of us, being isolated at home has become a time for self-reflection and contemplation on our careers, family, and relationships, and even extending to deeper issues like our life purpose, gratitude, and compassion for others. (Global Wellness Institute, 2021: 15)

This renewed appreciation for nature has continued post-pandemic, and nature will be prominent in many wellness experiences in the future. Of course, there is a close connection between a love of nature and the protection of the planet. Additionally, tourists' physical and mental health are directly connected to social equity as one of the sustainability pillars (Buhalis *et al.*, 2023). In fact, WT is widely interconnected with sustainable development goals (SDGs) from social equity, economic viability and environmental protection viewpoints. Buhalis (2022) has argued that because of the global tourism management and marketing transformation, smart and knowledge-based sustainable tourism strategies should be considered. This practice considers stakeholders' value co-creation 'by adhering to ethical principles and ensuring that the welfare of all involved is considered – from academia to industry players, destination residents and consumers' (Buhalis, 2022).

A growing body of empirical evidence has revealed the value of experiencing nature for mental health. With rapid urbanisation and declining human contact with nature globally, important decisions must be made about how to preserve and increase opportunities to experience nature (Bratman *et al.*, 2019). Human wellbeing is connected to the natural environment in countless ways, and a practical understanding of these connections deepens various disciplines (Millennium Ecosystem Assessment, 2005).

In light of such concerns, comprehensive studies have provided a broad literature reviewing WT definitions, dimensions and components, motivations and tourist markets (Chatterjee & Dattaact, 2023; Demir & Zečević, 2022; Suban, 2023). Although these studies represent a majority of the research that has been done in the field of WT, few studies have directly addressed energy therapy destination (ETD) and its link with WT destinations. This chapter makes a research contribution by providing a model that brings pivotal determinations for ETD in the sacred mountain of Sabalan. In seeking to understand the effect that the presence of an energy vortex in a particular location has upon wellness, and exploring its healing power in human wellbeing, the study tackles an important theoretical and practical challenge and addresses a significant gap in the research.

13.2 Literature Review

13.2.1 Wellness and nature connectedness

There is a sense of nature-friendliness in human nature. Clear and abundant evidence demonstrates that interaction with nature affects not only wellbeing but also a healthy lifestyle. In principle, nature has its own ways of connecting and communicating its spirit to the human soul. Across the world, mental health and outdoor activities have always been linked to spirituality. Early research revealed that natural environments facilitate emotional and attention restoration (Kaplan, 1995; Wilson, 1984). Certain natural environments possess characteristics that are perceived in an automatic, almost unconscious way. These characteristics rapidly induce emotions, capture non-vigilant attention and block negative thoughts (Kaplan, 1995; Ulrich, 1993).

13.2.2 Wellness and spirituality

According to some researchers, spirituality can be understood through two dimensions: vertical and horizontal. The vertical dimension involves the relationship between humans and a higher power, while the

Table 13.1 Some philosophies relating humans to nature

Main concept	Description	Originator	Studies
Biophilia	Therapeutic benefits of taking people outdoors. Based on the biophilia hypothesis, human identity and personal fulfilment depend on their relationship with nature.	Edward O. Wilson (1984)	Wilson (1984); Brazier (2018); Ulrich, R. (1993); Fromm (1964); Jordan (2009); Antonioli and Reveley (2005); Richardson *et al.* (2015)
Attention Restoration Theory	Attention restoration theory (ART) posits that natural environments capture our involuntary attention, facilitating cognitive rejuvenation and reducing mental fatigue.	Rachel Kaplan & Stephen Kaplan (1989)	Van den Berg *et al.* (2007); Saegert and Winkel (1990); Collado *et al.* (2017); Kaplan (1995); Ulrich (1993); Wilson (1984); Hartig *et al.* (1991); James (1892); Kaplan and Talbot (1983)
Gaia Theory	The Earth's biosphere interacts with the atmosphere, lithosphere and hydrosphere to create planetary conditions that support life.	James Lovelock (1995, 2000, 2001, 2009)	Atkins and Snyder (2018)

Source: Author compilation, 2024.

horizontal dimension encompasses the relationship between individuals and their environment, as well as with other people. It is believed that the connection between humans and the divine occurs within the human experience and is deeply personal and mystical, varying from individual to individual (Vahedian-Azimi & Rahimi, 2013). Another perspective professes that spiritual tourists seek to connect with nature and enrich the non-material dimensions of their lives; furthermore, their spirit of adventure and exploration provides a foundation for a psychological experience (Hsu *et al.*, 2008). The followings are some philosophies and rationales that relate humans to nature (see Table 13.1).

13.2.2.1 Biophilia hypothesis

While some scientists believe in anthropocentric philosophies, others subscribe to a vision that is based on non-hierarchical interrelationships between humans and the environment. Edward O. Wilson (1984) describes the biophilia hypothesis as a genetic affinity for nature rooted in human evolution. Based on this hypothesis human identity and personal fulfilment depend on their relationship with nature. As a result, the human need for nature is linked not only to the material utilisation of the environment but also to the effect the natural world has on our emotional, cognitive, aesthetic and even spiritual development (Jordan, 2009).

13.2.2.2 Gaia theory

In the late 1960s James Lovelock (1995, 2000, 2001, 2009) studied the chemical balances of the atmosphere and discovered that they are maintained within the narrow limits necessary for life by self-regulating processes. Atkins and Snyder (2018) mentioned the earth as a whole entity and 'Metaphors of wholeness'. The entire planet is a self-regulating, synergistic, complex system. These are the hallmarks of a living system. Lovelock developed what is now called the Gaia hypothesis, and later put forward the Gaia theory, proposing that the Earth's biosphere interacts with the atmosphere, lithosphere and hydrosphere to create planetary conditions that support life.

13.2.2.3 Attention restoration theory: The theory of restorative environments

Nature has a positive impact on affect in more specific emotional states such as awe (Bethelmy & Corraliza, 2019; McMahan & Estes, 2015). Based on an analysis of unique properties of the natural environment, and extrapolating from William James' concept of fascination, Kaplan and Kaplan (1989) identified four properties that an environment must possess to provide restoration: fascination; being away; extent; and compatibility. An environment possessing these properties is considered to be a restorative environment. Thus, exposure to nature encourages effortless brain function, facilitating recovery from fatigue and positively-toned emotional reactions, which have a restorative effect (Collado *et al.*, 2017; Kaplan, 1995).

13.3 Energy

The concept of energy has a scientific denotation, and people often refer to subtle or astral energies, various dimensions of reality, holographic frameworks, and other pseudoscientific terminology. They are places where the power, vitality, or sheer otherness of non-human nature seem obviously present, places where the Earth seems to speak, relatively unobscured by the din of modern civilization. People believe such places harbour 'earth energies': energies that are thought to be beneficial and health-promoting in their effects and catalytic to spiritual growth. In the extensive literature discussing such power sites, these natural landscapes are often regarded as locations that facilitate personal transformation. Pilgrimages to these sites are viewed as a means of achieving such transformation (Ivakhiv, 2003).

13.3.1 Energy therapy

Energy therapy (ET) refers to various alternative medicine practices that improve physical, mental and emotional health by working with the body's energy fields or chakras. ET practices include reiki, acupuncture, meditation and aromatherapy. Believers of all faiths have contemplated the divinity of hilltops, mountains, rock landscapes, waterfalls, rivers, forests, lakes, trees, stones and other artefacts of nature, both in themselves or as part of the landscape (Singh & Singh, 2009).

13.3.2 Energy therapy tourism

A key aspect of wellness tourism is energy therapy tourism (ETT). Many of the ETT destinations emphasise a natural, holistic approach to wellness that promotes sustainable and eco-friendly travel. This aligns with the trend towards more mindful, responsible tourism (Goodrich, 1993). Moreover, the frequent connection between Gaia and energy discussions reflects the vast presence of alternative medical practices within New Age thought. A healthy body experiences an unrestricted flow of life energy.

Assuming the Earth is recognised as Gaia, it is rational to consider that life-energy flows through its body and that there exist specific locations known as 'chakras' or 'energy centres' where this flow is powerful and the energy is more focused than in other areas (Ivakhiv, 2003). The outpourings of energy associated with vortexes act as amplifiers; that is, they magnify what each individual brings to them regarding physical, mental or spiritual desires (Andres, 2000; Sanders, 1992). A vortex ultimately influences each person differently, based on their needs and desires.

13.3.3 Energy therapy destinations

Tourists seeking wellbeing and quality are looking for destinations that will satisfy their need for wellness in various and diverse arenas, from the physical to the psychic and from the spiritual to the cultural (Sirgy, 2019). The paradigm of this sector's overall vision has changed. In this regard, sectors that were not traditionally associated with wellness tourism are now tapped into; examples include areas such as culture and art (Fancourt & Finn, 2019), nature (Ohe *et al.*, 2017), sports (Smith & Kelly, 2006), the spiritual realm (Jiang *et al.*, 2018) and enogastronomy (Colombini, 2015).

Furthermore, one solution to many people's uneasiness has been a turn toward the New Age movement, which stresses the sanctity of nature, harmony of the cosmos, resurrection of ancient spiritual traditions, and self-improvement in the realms of spirit, mind and body. As Timothy and Conover (2006) state, four types of 'New Age tours or activities' can be identified: education; health; spiritual growth/personal development; and volunteering. Health holidays, or 'holistic tourism', focus on activities such as yoga and spa treatments, metaphysics, nature hiking, reflexology, crystal healing, meditation and aromatherapy (Smith, 2003; Timothy, 2002).

13.4 Study Area: Mount Sabalan

Mount Sabalan, an inactive volcano with an altitude of 4811 metres, is Iran's third-highest peak. The natural landscape of Mount Sabalan, located in Lahrood District, Meshkin Shahr County, Ardabil Province, was registered in the National Natural Heritage Attraction of Iran list in 2011. According to historians, the age of the area is related to the Eocene period. At the mountain's peak there is a crater lake of sweet water that is one of the highest sweet-water lakes in the world (UNESCO official website). There have been many studies of Sabalan and its different capabilities. Afkhami (2018) conducted an applied study with the goal of providing a comprehensive account of the cultural and natural values of Mount Sabalan for its inscription in the UNESCO World Heritage List (WHL). Indications are that registration of Mount Sabalan on the WHL is turning it into an international top brand, which will play a crucial role in conserving the Sabalan natural-cultural landscape and tourism development. There is also an ethno-botanical study on medicinal plants of Mount Sabalan, an area in which no earlier ethno-botanical research has been conducted. According to this study, an integrated approach for domestication, cultivation, conservation and isolation of active constituents for developing new therapeutics and standardising known herbal medicines is necessary (Panahy *et al.*, 2012).

Tabrizchi *et al.* (2020) designed a sports tourism developmental factor model for Mount Sabalan. The results identified seven factors as critical developmental factors in sports tourism. Infrastructural reinforcement and desirability were the most important factors in the developmental model for Mount Sabalan's sports tourism.

However, Sabalan (Savalan in Azerbaijani) mount is recorded in the UN tentative list because of its natural uniqueness, but its potential to have a power centre has been unrevealed. Mount Sabalan is considered holy by those who believe it to be where Zarathustra, the prophet of the Zoroastrian religion, was chosen. It was believed to be one of the seven holy mountains of heaven, and people would often climb the mountain to pray at the top. Respect for the mountain can still be seen in the way that people refer to it as 'Sultan Savalan' (Baba Safari, 1971). In general, from the locals' perspective (specifically Shahsavan nomads), and the mountaineers who permanently visit this mount, two places have specific and energetic focal points: Summit Lake and Mehrab Rock (Figures 13.1 and 13.2).

Figure 13.1 Mount Sabalan – Summit Lake
Source: Imanali Imani.

Figure 13.2 Mehrab Rock (Sang-e Mehrab)
Source: Imanali Imani.

The other dimensions that make Sabalan Mountain unique are as follows:

- *Cultural Attractions:* Shahsavan nomads (their customs and lifestyle), nomadic settlements (Alachigh) of about 100 families occupy the area between April and October, moving on to warmer places in the winter.
- *Natural Landscape:* Due to its location on the slopes of Savalan, the Moeil region has many important geological attributes, especially Iran's first geothermal field (Figure 13.3). Thermal and mineral springs are present in the heart of the rocks and by the Khiauchai river; specifically, the Qainarja spring, which, at 85°C, is among the hottest springs in the world (Noorollahi *et al.*, 2008).
- *Historical Attractions:* Moeil village is more than 3000 years old (dating based on historical monuments and fire temples around the village). The presence of the Moeil Soui hot spring in the center of the village is a sign of a several thousand-year-old civilization. Also, Moeil village has recently been included in the candidate list for the best world tourism villages.

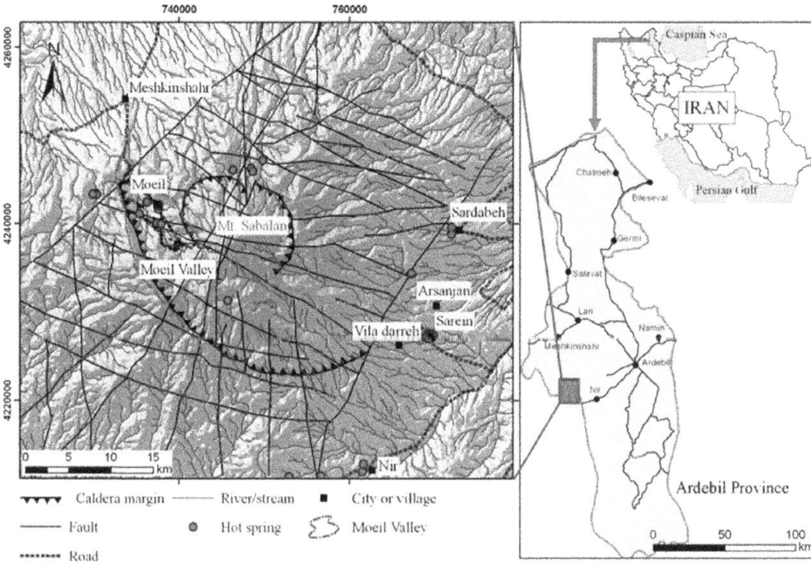

Figure 13.3 Location and geological structure maps of the Mount Sabalan area, northwest Iran

Source: Noorollahi *et al.*, 2008.

13.5 Research Methodology and Data Collection

This research takes a qualitative approach to grounded theory (GT), applying the community's viewpoint. This approach generates 'research methodology that gives understandings about how persons or organizations or communities experience and respond to events that occur' (Corbin & Holt, 2005: 49). The theory is formed during research through the successive interplay between data collection and analysis (Strauss & Corbin, 1998: 158).

13.5.1 Sample data

The landscape of Ardabil province is influenced by the presence of Mount Sablan, and more than 110 mineral water springs have been identified on the slopes of the mountain (General Directorate of Tourism, 2023). Local people developed tourism businesses such as eco-camps, hydrotherapy activities, and there is a local leader for mountain tours. The Shahsavan nomads have been moving on the slopes of this mountain for more than six centuries (from the beginning of the Safavid era) and, among the nomads, there is a senior member more than 90 years old who is able to recount how Mount Sabalan has been held a sacred place ever since he could remember? The driving factors of ETD were identified via input from eco-camp owners, local community guides, entrepreneurs,

Table 13.2 Demographic profile of the interview panel

Respondent number	Gender	Occupation	Age (years)	Years of association
1	Male	Eco-lodge owner (Durna)	40	15
2	Male	Eco-lodge owner (Valazir)	51	20
3	Male	Moeil hydrotherapy manager	48	12
4	Male	Qaynarje hydrotherapy manager	59	20
5	Male	Mountain tour guide	63	40
6	Male	Mountain tour guide	37	12
7	Male	Tourism expert	52	35
8	Male	Tourism expert	58	33
9	Male	Local entrepreneur	72	40
10	Female	Local entrepreneur	50	10
11	Female	Mentor	34	7
12	Female	Mentor	67	20
13	Female	Mentor	53	25
14	Male	Nomad expert	43	18
15	Male	Shahsavan nomad (veteran)	98	90

mentors, tourism experts, hydrotherapy managers and members of the Climbing Board of the Province (mountain tour guides) (Table 13.2). The research sample was determined using the snowball method (purposive sampling) until the study results were saturated (15 respondents). Data collection methods include in-depth and semi-in-depth interviews (Table 13.3), collaborative discussions, field observations, library studies, research records and documents and statistics.

The stages of data analysis and interpretation based on this method are as follows:

- Preliminary studies from Mount Sabalan and its surrounding area; preparation of data collection tools.
- Collect data from the Sabalan area using research tools and combine and adjust the obtained data.
- Data analysis.

13.5.2 Open data coding

In the first stage, necessary data and information were collected from residents and tourism experts in the research area. This information, obtained from interviews, conversations, observations and field studies, was converted into phrases or sentences. These phrases and sentences were obtained from field studies conducted in eco-camps near Mount Sabalan and Moeil village (Table 13.4). Part of these expressions were

Table 13.3 Questionnaire for the research sample panel on ETD in Mount Sabalan

Question number	Interview question
1	How do you explain the main motivation for tourists to visit Mount Sabalan? To what extent has the sanctity of Mount Sabalan influenced the tourists' motivation?
2	What are the tourists' experiences and feelings after visiting the Mehrab Rock and the crater and performing mindfulness?
3	To what extent does the presence of local and specialised mentors and tour leaders affect the quality of tourists' experiences?
4	Do the tourists of Mount Sabalan stay in the eco-lodges on the mountainside on the way back and forth?
5	What other attractions and complementary activities lead to extended stays or frequent visits to this site?
6	Do current facilities and services meet current ET demand? In your opinion, what facilities help improve the quality of mutual relations between the ET and the destination?
7	In what areas do the ET tourists affect the life of the local community (both positive and negative aspects)?
8	Has the government created facilities and equipment for mountain tourism in general and for energy therapy in particular? What essential facilities should be available in the region, the lack of which is a major obstacle for tourism development?
9	To what extent do you think Sabalan's registration in UNESCO and the registration of the world's best tourist village (Moeil) will help the development of the region's ETT?
10	Is the ownership and management of tourism complexes more facilitated by locals or investors from outside the region?
11	Is the development of tourism outside sustainable development, or is it clearly based on the guidelines and in accordance with the local conditions of the region?
12	Does the development of this type of tourism benefit the local community? To what extent is the development of this tourism based on sustainable development standards (practically)?

obtained through interviews (Table 13.3) with entrepreneurs, experts and local people and from a group discussion with them, marked with 'L' (local stakeholders); other parts are the result of field observations of the researchers of this research, note-taking and scientific reasoning. After combining the research records and scientific literature, the resulting phrases were indicated by the symbol 'S'. After summarising and removing incorrect data, 46 terms were extracted from the data collection stages.

13.5.3 Axial coding of data

The coding system is implemented again, resulting in the extraction of concepts from the expressions. At this stage, expressions are compared and placed in a category based on similarity and semantic connections. Each of these categories forms a concept. Finally, 22 concepts were extracted from the research terms (Table 13.5).

Table 13.4 Phrases and sentences from the research data

Gathering method	Statement	Statement	Gathering method
S	70 percent of energy therapies' tourists are mountaineers	The presence of numerous hot and mineral spas & hydrotherapy	L
S	Numerous health, wellness and hydrotherapy ecotourism complexes	Existence of the hot therapeutic spring of Qainirje	L
S	Dorna's unique Hobbit eco-lodge	Energy therapy in Mehrab Rock is desirable activity	L
L	Most tourists do not pollute the environment	The sanctity of a place and the perception of grandeur and awe	S
S	Adherence of the owners of eco-lodges to environmental norms	Existence of ancient history regarding the presence of Parthians	S
S	Lack of local guides to introduce attractions in a specialised way	Iran's first geothermal plant that is stimulating tourists' curiosity	S
S	Absence of a mentor to perform the activity of mindfulness	The presence of Shahsavan nomads as cultural tourism	L
S	Most of the eco-lodges don't use renewable energy	More than 80 % of native people are engaged in tourism business	L
S	High ecological potential of tourism in the village	Absence of rescue centres and well-equipped clinics	L
L	Empowerment of women through hospitality and handicrafts businesses	Improper access and the need to take care of the roads	L
L	Lack of vegan menu for satisfying ET food taste	Equipping the reconstruction and expansion of parapets (hut)	L
L	Establish a tourism information kiosk and provide postcards and advertising items from the symbol of Mount Sabalan	Locality of tourism activists in the village	L
L	Installation of boards (road information)/ signs indicating distance	Deploying a centre with helicopters, route equipment (GPS)	L
S	Increasing local income from selling products to tourists	Placement of telecommunications masts	L
S	Shahsavan nomad belief in Mount Sabalan's sanctity	Determining the access route to the attraction using signs	L
L	Weakness in tourism infrastructure	Introduction of Sabalan in the list of candidates for UNWTO	S
S	The short stay of tourists despite the presence of many attractions	Introduction of Moeil in the list of the Best Tourism Village	S
S	Low migration rate of youngsters & balanced population structure	Ascetic landscape and scenic view	S & L

(Continued)

Table 13.4 Phrases and sentences from the research data (continued)

Gathering method	Statement	Statement	Gathering method
L	The multiplicity of stakeholders for the development of Sabalan and the lack of agreement in advancing the goals	Lack of activities of travel agencies in providing specialised tourism packages	L
S	High level of local support for tourism development	Tourism development in cooperation with local entrepreneurs	L
S	The hidden motivation for ET and mostly covered by climbing	Applying the tastes of energy therapy tourists in the eco-camps	L
S	Nature-friendly development of tourism complexes	No destruction of the village due to tourism development	L
S	Development and revival of village houses compatible with environmental conditions	Providing creative investment packages with the aim of developing ETD	S

Source: Research findings, 2024.

13.5.4 Selective data coding

In this stage, the existing classes (22 sub-categories) are combined and integrated based on their nature to form a new research framework. The sentences and classes of the previous stage are compared, and the relationship between them is determined such that the concepts and classes become categories. Five sub-categories were obtained as macro categories (Table 13.5).

13.5.5 Preparation of a research model

The primary objective of basic theory is to develop a new theory or framework. However, analysing such data may not always lead to the development of a theory. Nevertheless, this approach can be employed to construct a research model or to identify the crucial dimensions and categories of an issue, ultimately aiming to achieve an ETD model (Figure 13.4).

13.6 Findings and Discussions

Surveys were conducted through multiple visits, observations of the study area, and interviews to identify and explain the main concepts of the ETD. Results confirmed that each of the categories corresponds to the critical United Nations sustainable development goals (UNSDG). In essence, the development of the ETD model, as a sub-category of wellness tourism overlapping with spiritual tourism, aligns with the SDGs. It meets the expected tourists' demand for spiritual healing, pleasure and peace and contributes to developing a sustainable destination.

Table 13.5 Axial and selective coding stage: Determination of macro categories of ETD

Micro-categories	Energy Therapy Destination Development Necessities	Energy Therapy Destination	Macro-categories
Axial Coding Stage	Strengthen infrastructure (SDG 9)	Investment in fundamental infrastructure	Selective Coding Stage
	Superstructure standardisation (SDG 9)		
	Accessibility facilitation (SDG 10)		
	Development of transportation facilities (SDG 9)		
	Inter-institutional interaction of bodies (SDG 17)	Destination management & marketing organisations' (DMOs) policies	
	Campaign for spiritual nature (SDG 8 & 9)		
	Registering Mount Sabalan on UNWTO (SDG 8 & 9)		
	Registering Moeil in BTV (SDG 8 & 9)		
	Allocation of treatment costs for 'prevention is more reasonable than treatment' (SDG 3 & 10)		
	Attraction promotion (SDG 11)		
	Enhancing community participation (SDG 10)	Empowering local community	
	Women's empowerment (SDG 5 & 4)		
	Active role of entrepreneurs (SDG 10)		
	Employing local tour guide (SDG 8)		
	Employing mentor (SDG 8 & 4)		
	The effect of energy therapy on wellness (SDG 3)	Establishing positive attitude towards life	
	The effect of energy therapy in creating meaning and setting goal for life (SDG 3)		
	Changing one's worldview and having a positive attitude towards life (SDG 3)		
	Enjoying mindfulness (SDG 3)		
	Increasing altruistic thinking (SDG 16)		
	Respect for nature as a gift from God (SDG 11)	Sustainable destination	
	Promoting public education on the restorative power of natural areas through energy therapy model (SDG 4)		

Source: Research findings, 2024.

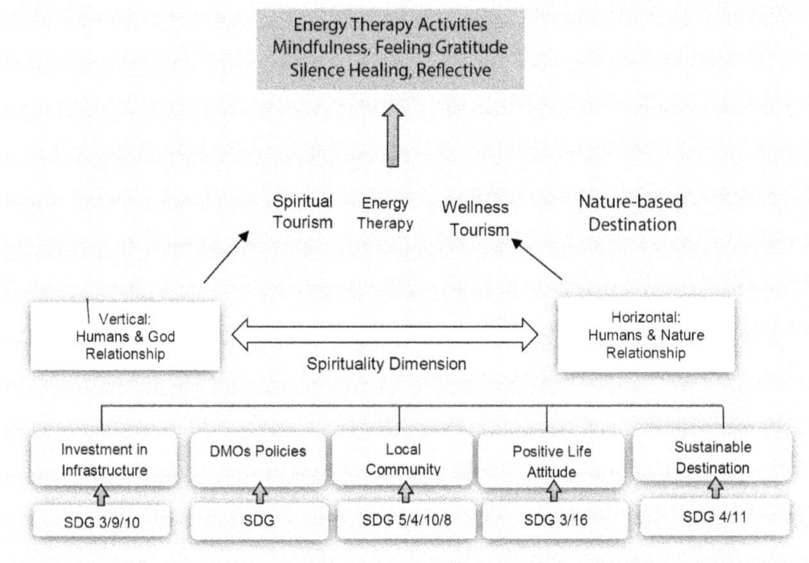

Figure 13.4 Conceptual framework for a sustainable model of energy therapy tourism destinations rooted in the natural environment

Source: The authors.

Health-oriented tourists prefer a skilled wellness workforce who perform local wellbeing practices (Tiwari & Hashmi, 2022), as evidenced by the numerous employment opportunities the wellness industry provides for women, minorities and youth and also for gender equality and women's empowerment. The wellness industry can help develop local infrastructure projects that are more sustainable and resource-efficient and reduce the industry's carbon footprint (Dwyer, 2022). Furthermore, health-oriented tourism can contribute to ending hunger by supporting local communities economically. The number of wellness travellers who prioritise locally grown food over fast-food chains continues to increase globally (Tiwari & Hashmi, 2022).

13.6.1 Investment in fundamental infrastructure

> Developing tourism infrastructure and superstructure has become an increasingly important consideration for investors and tourists.

So says the entrepreneur of Durna eco-camp. The worrisome issue regarding the tourism sector is the lack of facilities and infrastructure.

The Meshkinshahr tourism organisation manager and tour guide (also professional photographer) says:

> Although the basic infrastructure for arrivals is almost ready, but during holidays and tourism seasons, especially Sabalan Day [25 July], the number of tourists entering the region increases, while the facilities and services are not growing much, and the vehicles and safe access routes are not responsive to tourists.

The most important criticism expressed by Mount Sabalan tourists (inferred based on the words of local experts) is the lack of tourist information kiosks and rescue stations.

13.6.2 Destination management and marketing organisations' (DMOs) policies

Almost 70% of tourists are professional mountaineers who have visited Sabalan for the second or more than the second time. The owners of eco-camps have significant activity in promoting their accommodation on social networks, and as a result of these promotion activities, they receive favourable feedback. The Valazir eco-camp entrepreneur mentioned:

> another weakness in the management of tourism packages is primarily organized tours handled by out-of-province tour operators, which causes the local community to be unprofitable, How we could we connect with local tour operators while they don't focus on this area?!

Also, reserving vehicles in advance to climb the mountain is impossible, especially where the Mehrab Rock is concerned.

13.6.3 Empowering the local community

The region surrounding Mount Sabalan is renowned for its spiritual significance and the practice of silence, gratitude and worship. 'However, there is untapped potential for developing "silence tourism" and "ETT" in the area,' says mentor Zoleykha. According to tourism expert Mr Imani's observations, activities such as gratitude exercises, walking on the grass, meditation and offering vegan services could be incorporated into the tourism experience. To fully realise this potential, it is essential to empower the local community, provide training for local tour leaders and mentors, and update accommodation managers with the necessary information.

13.6.4 Establishing a positive attitude towards life

Many ET tourists strongly preferred staying in nomadic tents, particularly those of the Shahsavan nomads. According to a mountain leader with 40 years of experience, these tourists are drawn to the nomadic lifestyle and summer migrations, symbolising freedom and a detachment from material possessions. This way of life is seen as a powerful connection to nature, embodying a belief in its life-giving force and sanctity. The elder of the Shahsavan clan (90 years old) pointed out:

> Nomadic communities are perceived as free from illness and mental distress; heaven is not anywhere else except on earth and in the freedom and seeing the Prophet coming down from Mount Sablan. According to Sablan traditions, it is the place where Zoroaster appeared. Of course, the nomads know this sanctity from Sablan.

Additionally, the opportunity to interact with genuine individuals is cited as a key reason for tourists to visit these areas.

13.6.5 Sustainable development

Mount Sabalan is closely associated with the tourism industry, particularly as an energy therapy destination (ETD), which plays a vital role in the region's economy. The livelihood of local residents depends largely on this type of tourism, leading to the establishment of a wide range of eco-friendly accommodations that blend harmoniously with the natural surroundings. The local community has warmly embraced tourists from the outset (interviewee), so local residents predominantly hold tourism-related jobs. In addition, most tourism facilities in the area are owned and operated by local entrepreneurs.

Moreover, compelling evidence exists of climbers seeking out the energised Mehrab Rock on the mountain. Most incoming tourists are well-informed individuals or part of organised tours arranged by agencies. Sabalan's tourism market predominantly draws visitors from major cities such as Tehran, Tabriz, Urmia and Zanjan, as well as foreign tourists from Germany, France, the Netherlands, China and Turkey. These groups are well versed in tourism values and adhere to the fundamental principles of tourist destinations. As a result, environmental pollution is minimal, and experts believe that the development of ETT has had the least negative impact on this sector. Despite a threefold increase in tourist numbers over the last decade, no significant ecological changes have occurred, and the region's physical carrying capacity has been respected.

13.7 Conclusion

The findings of this study highlight energy therapy as an interdisciplinary field between wellness tourism and spiritual tourism. However, for ETT to grow into a sustainable and impactful tourism sector, various interconnected factors must be carefully considered.

These factors include the nature of the activities offered, the roles of spiritual and wellness tourism in shaping the visitor experience, and the broader frameworks required to foster long-term sustainability, such as infrastructure investment, policy formation, community facilitation and promoting positive life attitudes.

The core ETT activities are designed to harmonise the mind, body and the spirit. Practices such as mindfulness, feeling of gratitude, silence healing, and reflective exercises offer profound pathways to self-discovery and spiritual healing. Mindfulness allows participants to be present in the moment, fostering mental clarity and reducing stress. Gratitude, another essential component, encourages travellers to shift their focus towards the positive aspects of life, cultivating a mindset of appreciation and fulfilment. Silence healing helps individuals find peace in quietude, away from the distractions of modern life, while reflective practices enable travellers to delve into more profound spiritual or personal growth journeys.

Natural environments often enhance these activities. The tranquillity of forests, mountains, lakes and coastal regions creates the ideal conditions for participants to engage deeply with their inner selves. As nature acts as both a backdrop and a healing agent, travellers experience a profound sense of reconnection – not only with themselves but also with the surrounding world. This study concludes that the most critical element in ensuring energy therapy tourism's success and sustainability is appropriate infrastructure development. Tourism infrastructure should be built to support the natural environment rather than detract from it. This would allow destinations to maintain their ecological integrity while offering enriching energy therapy experiences. Additionally, investments should focus on creating immersive spaces – such as silent meditation halls, mindfulness gardens and gratitude circles – where travellers can engage fully in energy therapy activities.

Furthermore, destination management organisations play a central role in fostering the growth of energy therapy tourism by establishing policies that encourage sustainability. These policies should focus on preserving natural and cultural resources, promoting eco-conscious tourism practices, and fostering partnerships with local communities to ensure inclusive and beneficial tourism development for all stakeholders. In addition, DMO policies should promote ethical tourism, ensuring that both tourists and tourism operators treat sacred sites and natural environments with respect. By creating a framework prioritising sustainable tourism practices, DMOs can ensure that ETT destinations thrive harmoniously with nature and the local communities.

The findings also highlight the role of local communities in ETT. Community facilitation ensures that the benefits of tourism are shared equally among residents. By involving locals in the tourism process – through employment, business ownership and cultural contributions –

ETT can provide sustainable livelihoods while preserving the destination's cultural heritage. Local communities can also play a vital role in offering authentic energy therapy experiences by incorporating Indigenous healing practices, traditional spirituality, and local knowledge of the natural environment. When locals are empowered to take part in tourism management and decision-making, destinations become more resilient and sustainable, creating a mutually beneficial relationship between travellers and the communities they visit.

Energy therapy tourism is more than just a travel experience: it is a philosophy that encourages a positive life attitude. Travellers participating in energy therapy activities are guided towards developing mindfulness, gratitude and an appreciation for life's simple joys. When integrated into everyday life, these principles promote a healthier, more positive mindset. As travellers leave destinations with a renewed sense of wellbeing, they carry these lessons home, spreading positivity and mindfulness to their communities.

The long-term success of ETT depends on a commitment to sustainable development. Tourism activities must be designed to minimise their impact on the environment, conserve cultural heritage and contribute to the wellbeing of local populations. Sustainable practices such as using eco-friendly transportation, promoting local and organic products and reducing tourism-related waste are essential in maintaining the integrity of energy therapy destinations. By prioritising sustainability, energy therapy tourism can thrive as a model for responsible tourism that not only offers transformative experiences for travellers but also protects the planet and supports local communities for generations to come.

Acknowledgements

This chapter did not receive any financial or moral support.

Conflict of Interest

The authors declare no conflict of interest.

References

Andres, D. (2000) *What is a Vortex? A Practical Guide to Sedona's Vortex Sites, Sedona.* Meta Adventures.

Antonioli, C. and Reveley, M. (2005) Randomised controlled trial of animal facilitated therapy with dolphins in the treatment of depression. *British Medical Journal* (International ed.) 331 (7527), 1231.

Atkins, S. and Snyder, M. (2018) *Nature-based Expressive Arts Therapy: Integrating the Expressive Arts and Ecotherapy.* Jessica Kingsley Publishers.

Baba Safari, A. (1971) *Ardabil in Historical Transformation.* Omid Publications.

Bethelmy, L. and Corraliza, J. (2019) Transcendence and sublime experience in nature: Awe and inspiring energy. *Frontiers in Psychology* 10, 509.

Bratman, G.N., Anderson, C.B., Berman, M.G., Cochran, B., de Vries, S., Flanders, J., … and Daily, G.C. (2019) Nature and mental health: An ecosystem service perspective. *Science Advances* 5 (7).

Brazier, C. (2018) *Ecotherapy in Practice: A Buddhist Model*. Routledge.

Buhalis, D. (2022) Tourism management and marketing in transformation: Editor's statement and Introduction. In D. Buhalis (ed.) *Encyclopaedia of Tourism Management and Marketing* (pp. 1–18). Edward Elgar Publishing.

Buhalis, D., Leung, X.Y., Fan, D., Darcy, S., Chen, G., Xu, F., Wei-Han Tan, G., Nunkoo, R. and Farmaki, A. (2023) Editorial: Tourism 2030 and the contribution to the sustainable development goals: The *Tourism Review* viewpoint. *Tourism Review* 78 (2), 293–313.

Chatterjee, P. and Dattaact, S. (2023) Bibliometric and content analysis of literature on the role of healthcare hotel in medical and wellness tourism. *Acta Turistica* 35 (1), 7–42.

Collado, S., Staats, H., Corraliza, J.A. and Hartig, T. (2017) Restorative environments and health. In G. Fleury-Bahi, E. Pol and O. Navarro (eds) *Handbook of Environmental Psychology and Quality of Life Research* (pp. 127–148). Springer International.

Colombini, D.C. (2015) Wine tourism in Italy. *International Journal of Wine Research* 7 (1), 29–35.

Corbin, J. and Holt, N. (2005) Grounded theory. In B. Somekh and C. Lewin (eds) *Research Methods in the Social Sciences* (pp. 49–55). Sage.

Demir, M.R. and Zečević, M. (2022) Wellness tourism research: Bibliometric study of the scientific field. *Academica Turistica – Tourism and Innovation Journal* 15 (1), 53–63.

Dwyer, L. (2022) Destination competitiveness and resident wellbeing. *Tourism Management Perspectives* 43, 100996.

Erfurt-Cooper, P. and Cooper, M. (2009) *Health and Wellness Tourism: Spas and Hot Springs*. Channel View Publications.

Fancourt, D. and Finn, S. (2019) *What is the Evidence on the Role of the Arts in Improving Health and Well-being? A Scoping Review*. WHO Regional Office for Europe.

Fromm, E. (1964) *The Heart of Man: Its Genius for Good and Evil*. Harper & Row.

Global Wellness Institute (GWI) (2021) *The Global Wellness Economy: Looking Beyond COVID*. GWI.

Goodrich, J.N. (1993) Socialist Cuba: A study of health tourism. *Journal of Travel Research* 32 (1), 36–41.

Hartig, T., Mang, M. and Evans, G.W. (1991) Restorative effects of natural environment experiences. *Environment and Behaviour* 23 (1), 3–26.

Hsu, C., Killion, G., Brown, G., Gross, M. and Huang, S. (2008) *Tourism Marketing: An Asia-Pacific Perspective*. Wiley.

Ivakhiv, A. (2003) Nature and self in New Age pilgrimage. *Culture and Religion* 4 (1), 93–118.

James, W. (1892) *Psychology. The Briefer Course*. Holt.

Jordan, M. (2009) Back to nature. *Therapy Today*, 28–30 April.

Kaplan, R. and Kaplan, S. (1989) *The Experience of Nature: A Psychological Perspective*. Cambridge University Press.

Kaplan, S. (1995) The restorative benefits of nature: Toward an integrative framework. *Journal of Environmental Psychology* 15 (3), 169–182.

Kaplan, S. and Talbot, J.F. (1983) Psychological benefits of a wilderness experience. In I. Altman and J.F. Wohlwill (eds) *Behavior and the Natural Environment* (pp. 163–203). Springer US.

Lovelock, J. (1995) *The Ages of Gaia: A Biography of Our Living Earth*. W.W. Norton.

Lovelock, J. (2000) *Gaia: A New Look at Life on Earth*. Oxford University Press.

Lovelock, J. (2001) *Homage to Gaia: The Life of an Independent Scientist*. Oxford University Press.

Lovelock, J. (2009) *The Vanishing Face of Gaia: A Final Warning*. Basic Books.

McMahan, E. and Estes, D. (2015) The effect of contact with natural environments on positive and negative affect: A meta-analysis. *Journal of Positive Psychology* 10 (6), 507–519.

Millennium Ecosystem Assessment (MEA) (2005) *Ecosystems and Human Wellbeing: Synthesis*. Island Press.
Noorollahi, Y., Itoi, R., Fujii, H. and Tanaka, T. (2008) GIS integration model for geothermal exploration and well-siting. *Geothermics* 37, 107–131.
Ohe, Y., Ikei, H., Song, C. and Miyazaki, Y. (2017) Evaluating the relaxation effects of emerging forest-therapy tourism: A multidisciplinary approach. *Tourism Management* 62, 322–334. https://doi.org/10.1016/j.tourman.2017.04.010.
Panahy, J., Teymurzadeh, A. and Panahy, A. (2012) An ethnobotanical survey in southern slopes of Sabalan mountain. *Acta Hortic* 964, 13–21.
Richardson, M., Hallam, J. and Lumber, R. (2015) One thousand good things in nature: The aspects of nature that lead to increased nature connectedness. *Environmental Values* 24 (5), 603–619.
Saegert, S. and Winkel, G.H. (1990) Environmental psychology. *Annual Review of Psychology* 41, 441–477.
Sanders, P.A. (1992) *Scientific Vortex Information, Sedona*. Free Soul Publishing.
Singh, S. and Singh T.V. (2009) Aesthetic pleasures: Contemplating spiritual tourism. In J. Tribe (ed.) *Philosophical Issues in Tourism* (pp. 135–153). Channel View Publications.
Sirgy, J.M. (2019) Promoting quality-of-life and well-being research in hospitality and tourism. *Journal of Travel & Tourism Marketing* 36 (1), 1–13.
Smith, M. (2003) Holistic holidays: Tourism and the reconciliation of body, mind and spirit. *Tourism Recreation Research* 28 (1), 103–108.
Smith, M. and Kelly, C. (2006a) Holistic tourism: Journeys of the self? *Tourism Recreation Research* 31 (1), 15–24.
Smith, M. and Kelly, C. (2006b) Wellness tourism. *Tourism Recreation Research* 31 (1), 1–4.
Strauss, A. and Corbin, J. (1998) *Basics of Qualitative Research: Techniques and Procedures for Developing Grounded Theory*. Sage.
Suban, S.A. (2023) Bibliometric analysis on wellness tourism: Citation and co-citation analysis. *International Hospitality Review* 37 (2), 359–383.
Tabrizchi, S., Ameri, M.S. and Moharramzadeh, M. (2020) Designing sports tourism developmental factors model of Sabalan Mountain. *Journal of Advanced Pharmacy Education & Research* 10 (S4), 85–92.
Timothy, D.J. (2002) Sacred journeys: Religious heritage and tourism. *Tourism Recreation Research* 27 (2), 3–6.
Timothy, D.J. and Conover, P.J. (2006) Nature religion, self-spirituality and New Age tourism. In D.J. Timothy and D.H. Olsen (eds) *Tourism, Religion and Spiritual Journeys* (pp. 156–173). Routledge.
Tiwari, R. and Hashmi, H. (2022) Integrating concepts of destination image, travel motivations, expectation, and future behaviour to create a model of wellness travel intentions. *International Journal of Spa and Wellness* 5 (2), 185–206.
Ulrich, R. (1993) The biophilia hypothesis. In S.R. Kellert and E.O. Wilson (eds) *The Biophilia Hypothesis* (pp. 73–137). Island Press.
Vahedian-Azimi, A. and Rahimi, A. (2013) Concept of spirituality: A conventional content analysis. *Journal of Qualitative Research in Health Sciences* 2 (1), 11–20.
Van den Berg, A.E., Hartig, T. and Staats, H. (2007) Preference for nature in urbanized societies: Stress, restoration, and the pursuit of sustainability. *Journal of Social Issues* 63, 79–96.
Wilson, E.O. (1984) *Biophilia: The Human Bond with Other Species*. Harvard University Press.

14 Synthesizing Insights and Charting Future Directions in Wellness, Wellbeing and Tourism

Ranjana Tiwari and Timothy J. Lee

14.1 Theme 1: Integration of Cultural and Communal Dimensions

Under Theme 1, the cultural and communal dimensions, Chapters 2–6 have revealed how wellness tourism is deeply intertwined with cultural practices and communal wellbeing. From preserving culinary traditions in Kongunadu to integrating Indigenous knowledge in Malawi, these contributions highlight the importance of cultural authenticity and respect in wellness tourism and communal wellbeing.

In addition, the impact of wellness programs in enhancing student wellbeing and pastoral cultures further emphasize how traditional practices and communal values shape contemporary wellness experiences stressing the holistic wellbeing. Further, the ongoing development of new health diets and wellness solutions reflects a growing demand for novel and scientifically informed approaches to wellbeing.

This integration of culture with wellness practices highlights a crucial balance that tourism practitioners must strike. On the one hand, there is the desire to offer tourists novel, authentic wellness experiences; on the other, there is the need to preserve cultural integrity. These insights emphasize the importance of engaging local communities in tourism planning and implementation, ensuring they benefit from wellness tourism rather than becoming marginalized by it.

14.2 Theme 2: Innovation and Technology

Chapters 7–9, examining innovation and technology in wellness and wellbeing, have highlighted the transformative impact of technological advancements on the sector. The integration of neurosciences and computing, the design of personalized wellness experiences, and the application of calligraphy-based mindfulness therapies are examples of how technology enhances wellness practices. These innovations not only improve the quality and customization of wellness experiences but also drive new trends and opportunities within the industry. However, the continuous evolution of technology presents both opportunities and challenges for the sector. While innovations can elevate the quality of wellness services, there is also a growing need for ensuring that these technologies are accessible and inclusive. The risk of excluding certain demographics – such as older travelers, or communities with limited access to technology – must be addressed. Future research should continue exploring how technology can be used not only to enhance wellbeing but also to make it more equitable.

14.3 Theme 3: Destination Development and Management

Chapters 10–13, under the theme of Destination Development and Management, have highlighted the role of wellness tourism in fostering regional growth and sustainability. The potential for wellness tourism to stimulate economic development, as seen in Unhais da Serra, Portugal, and the benefits of thermal tourism in Europe, underscore its importance as a driver of regional prosperity. The case studies of energy therapy tourism in nature and exploring ethno-botanical practices in India demonstrate how wellness tourism can contribute to sustainable development and environmental stewardship for people in the society.

However, as wellness tourism grows, so does its environmental footprint. The sector must adopt sustainable practices to ensure it does not compromise the ecological balance of the destinations it promotes. Balancing economic growth with environmental conservation is essential for long-term success. Moreover, wellness tourism must contribute to local community development by creating equitable opportunities, fostering social inclusion and ensuring that tourism benefits are distributed fairly.

14.4 Implications and Future Directions

The exploration of wellness, wellbeing and tourism in this volume has revealed a number of important insights and implications, as summarized in Figure 14.1. To build on these findings and address emerging trends, future research should consider the following six areas.

14.4.1 Health and wellbeing trends in emerging markets

One of the key theoretical frameworks explored in this volume is the concept of transformative tourism experiences. Transformative tourism is characterized by powerful life moments that have the potential to elevate individuals' wellbeing. With the increasing emphasis on wellbeing (Huang *et al.*, 2024), it is crucial to develop a theoretical understanding of how transformative tourism experiences impact individual wellbeing.

Figure 14.1 Wellness, wellbeing and tourism: Implications and future directions

Future research should explore how wellness tourism is evolving in emerging markets outside traditional destinations, such as sub-Saharan Africa and Latin America (Global Wellness Institute, 2024). This investigation would involve identifying both the opportunities and challenges that arise in these developing regions. Additionally, it is important to assess how the growth of wellness tourism impacts public health outcomes (Kickbusch & Payne, 2003; Lehto & Lehto, 2019) across various regions. This research should evaluate the potential of wellness tourism to support broader health initiatives, helping to understand its contribution to public health on a larger scale.

14.4.2. Consumer behavior and preferences in wellness tourism

With growing demand for holistic, personalized and evidence-based wellness experiences, it is crucial to study shifts in consumer behavior, and preferences and expectations. The studies in the book have explored the dimensions of a healthy diet, forest therapy, aromatic plants and thermal baths and have laid out the framework to enable wellness tourism destination managers, governments, and restaurateurs to focus more on improving the products and services for wellness tourists.

Consumer behavior in wellness tourism reflects a growing desire for experiences that prioritize personal wellbeing, both physically and mentally (Luo *et al.*, 2018). Wellness tourists are increasingly driven by the pursuit of holistic health, seeking immersive experiences that range from spa therapies and mindfulness retreats to fitness programs and nature-based activities (Talukder *et al.*, 2025). A key trend in consumer behavior is the demand for personalized and evidence-based wellness services, with travelers expecting customized programs tailored to their unique health needs and lifestyle preferences (Tiwari & Hashmi, 2022).

Factors such as age, gender, socioeconomic status and cultural background significantly influence consumer preferences, with different demographics gravitating towards specific wellness practices – such as yoga retreats, detox diets or eco-friendly wellness escapes. Moreover, wellness tourists often value sustainability and cultural authenticity, preferring destinations that align with their values of environmental stewardship and respectful engagement with local traditions (Buzinde, 2020). As consumer expectations evolve, wellness tourism providers must stay attuned to these trends, offering innovative, culturally sensitive and sustainable wellness solutions that cater to diverse traveler profiles. Understanding these behavior patterns is crucial for the continued growth and competitiveness of the wellness tourism sector.

14.4.3 Cultural sensitivity and authenticity in wellness practices

One of the key challenges in wellness tourism is effectively integrating traditional wellness practices into modern offerings without compromising cultural authenticity or engaging in cultural appropriation. This book sheds light on pastoral community practices, calligraphy and traditional gastronomical practices for wellness and wellbeing.

As wellness tourism continues to grow, there is a risk that traditional practices – such as Indigenous healing methods, spiritual rituals or herbal medicine – could be commodified or misrepresented (Viale & Vicol, 2023). This raises ethical concerns and could harm the practices' integrity and the communities that rely on them (Kaldjian, 2019). Future research should focus on identifying best practices for integrating these traditional wellness elements in ways that respect and honor their cultural origins. This may involve collaborating directly with local practitioners and communities to ensure that wellness tourism offerings are authentic and provide tangible benefits to the local culture. Moreover, the research could explore frameworks for responsible tourism development that allow for cultural preservation while meeting the expectations of wellness tourists. The goal is to create wellness experiences that are both enriching for travelers and empowering for local communities, ensuring mutual benefit and sustainability.

Moreover, cultural representation in wellness tourism is a complex issue that has the potential to shape how tourists perceive and engage with different cultural heritages. Misrepresentation or superficial portrayals of cultural practices can lead to stereotyping, perpetuate misconceptions and alienate local communities (Puddifoot, 2021). Therefore, research should examine how various cultures are portrayed within the wellness tourism sector, assessing the effects of these representations on both local populations and tourists. Studies could investigate whether the commercialization of cultural elements has led to the dilution of traditional practices or, conversely, whether respectful representation can foster greater appreciation and understanding of diverse cultures. Additionally, there is a need to explore how wellness tourism can promote meaningful and respectful engagement with cultural heritage, encouraging tourists to deepen their understanding of the history and values behind the wellness practices they experience.

14.4.4 Technological innovations and wellness and wellbeing offerings

Emerging technologies like virtual reality (VR), artificial intelligence (AI), and wearable health devices are reshaping the wellness tourism landscape by offering new ways to enhance experiences and improve health outcomes (Baran & Karaca, 2023). Virtual reality, for instance, can provide immersive relaxation environments, guided meditations, or virtual wellness retreats, making wellness experiences more accessible and engaging. AI and machine learning can optimize wellness programs by analyzing vast amounts of data to provide personalized recommendations for tourists, such as suggesting specific spa treatments, fitness regimens or mindfulness practices based on individual health profiles (Ahmed *et al.*, 2020). Wearable health devices, such as fitness trackers and biometric monitors, allow tourists to track their physical activity, sleep patterns, and other vital metrics in real-time, encouraging more mindful and health-conscious travel experiences.

The implications of integrating these technologies into wellness tourism are significant. By making wellness services more customizable and data-driven, tourism providers can enhance the personalization of the tourist experience, improve customer satisfaction and promote better health outcomes. Moreover, technology enables a broader range of tourists to access wellness experiences, potentially reaching those who may not traditionally engage in wellness tourism. However, these advancements also raise questions about data privacy, the potential loss of cultural authenticity, and the risks of over-reliance on technology.

14.4.5 Sustainable development and wellness tourism

As wellness tourism grows, so understanding and mitigating its environmental footprint becomes increasingly essential. As discussed in detail in this book, wellness tourism often occurs in pristine natural settings such as coastal areas, forests, mountains and rural regions – particularly vulnerable to environmental degradation due to high tourist traffic. The environmental impacts may include over-use of natural resources, increased carbon emissions from travel, pollution, habitat destruction and strain on local water and energy supplies. Research in this area should focus on measuring the direct and indirect environmental costs of wellness tourism activities, such as the construction of wellness resorts, transportation emissions, and using resources like water and energy in spas, wellness retreats, and other facilities.

Furthermore, as the book's chapters demonstrate, wellness tourism has significant potential to contribute positively to local community development, promoting economic growth, social equity and environmental sustainability. It can be crucial in revitalizing rural or underserved regions by creating employment opportunities, supporting local businesses and generating revenue.

Future studies should also investigate how wellness tourism can align with environmental sustainability principles (Mathew, 2022). This might involve evaluating how wellness tourism can support local conservation efforts by promoting ecotourism practices, reducing waste, and fostering environmental stewardship among tourists (Becken & Kaur, 2021). Research could further assess how wellness tourism businesses can collaborate with local governments and organizations to protect natural resources and biodiversity, ensuring that wellness tourism remains a positive force for both the environment and for local populations.

14.4.6 Policy and regulatory frameworks

The current policies and regulations governing wellness tourism vary widely across regions and countries, and their effectiveness in supporting sustainable development and protecting cultural and environmental resources is not yet fully understood (Zhong *et al.*, 2021). Wellness tourism intersects with various policy areas such as environmental protection, public health, cultural heritage preservation, and tourism management, making it essential to evaluate how existing regulations align with wellness tourism's objectives. Some policies may prioritize economic growth over environmental sustainability (Eisenmenger *et al.*, 2020). In contrast, others may fail to adequately address the cultural implications of tourism (Frey & Briviba, 2021), particularly in destinations that rely on Indigenous knowledge and local traditions as part of their wellness offerings.

Research in this area should focus on analyzing the effectiveness of these existing policies. For example, how well do current environmental regulations reduce the ecological footprint of wellness tourism activities? Are cultural heritage laws effectively protecting Indigenous wellness practices from commercialization or cultural appropriation? By identifying gaps and shortcomings in existing policies, researchers can provide insights into where improvements are needed to ensure that wellness tourism grows in a way that is both economically beneficial and environmentally and culturally sustainable.

***

The findings presented in this book underscore the transformative potential of wellness tourism. It not only enhances individual wellbeing but also contributes to regional development and cultural preservation. However, the continued success of wellness tourism will depend on how effectively the sector can navigate the challenges of cultural integration, technological innovation, and sustainability. By addressing these challenges and focusing on future research areas, wellness tourism can evolve into a truly inclusive and sustainable industry, promoting wellbeing for travelers and host communities alike.

This book sets the stage for future exploration in the global wellness tourism industry, encouraging scholars and practitioners to continue advancing the field while ensuring it remains grounded in cultural respect, innovation and sustainability.

References

Ahmed, Z., Mohamed, K., Zeeshan, S. and Dong, X. (2020) Artificial intelligence with multi-functional machine learning platform development for better healthcare and precision medicine. *Database* 2020, baaa010.

Baran, Z. and Karaca, Ş. (2023) Next-generation technologies in health tourism. In O. Doğan (ed.) *Global Perspectives on the Opportunities and Future Directions of Health Tourism* (pp. 138–164). IGI Global.

Becken, S. and Kaur, J. (2021) Anchoring 'tourism value' within a regenerative tourism paradigm – A government perspective. *Journal of Sustainable Tourism* 30 (1), 52–68.

Buzinde, C.N. (2020) Theoretical linkages between wellbeing and tourism: The case of self-determination theory and spiritual tourism. *Annals of Tourism Research* 83, 102920.

Eisenmenger, N., Pichler, M., Krenmayr, N., Noll, D., Plank, B., Schalmann, E., Wandl, M.-T. and Gingrich, S. (2020) The sustainable development goals prioritize economic growth over sustainable resource use: A critical reflection on the SDGs from a socio-ecological perspective. *Sustainability Science* 15, 1101–1110. https://doi.org/10.1007/s11625-020-00813-x.

Frey, B.S. and Briviba, A. (2021) A policy proposal to deal with excessive cultural tourism. *European Planning Studies* 29 (4), 601–618.

Global Wellness Institute (2024) *Sub-Saharan Africa Wellness Tourism Economy*. GWI. https://globalwellnessinstitute.org/industry-research/wellness-tourism-africa/.

Huang, X., Wang, P. and Wu, L. (2024) Wellbeing through transformation: An integrative framework of transformative tourism experiences and hedonic versus eudaimonic wellbeing. *Journal of Travel Research* 63 (4), 974–994.

Kaldjian, L.C. (2019) Understanding conscience as integrity: Why some physicians will not refer patients for ethically controversial practices. *Perspectives in Biology and Medicine* 62 (3), 383–400.

Kickbusch, I. and Payne, L. (2003) Twenty-first century health promotion: The public health revolution meets the wellness revolution. *Health Promotion International* 18 (4), 275–278.

Lehto, X.Y. and Lehto, M.R. (2019) Vacation as a public health resource: Toward a wellness-centered tourism design approach. *Journal of Hospitality & Tourism Research* 43 (7), 935–960.

Luo, Y., Lanlung, C., Kim, E., Tang, L.R. and Song, S.M. (2018) Towards quality of life: The effects of the wellness tourism experience. *Journal of Travel & Tourism Marketing* 35 (4), 410–424.

Mathew, P.V. (2022) Sustainable tourism development: Discerning the impact of responsible tourism on community wellbeing. *Journal of Hospitality and Tourism Insights* 5 (5), 987–1001.

Puddifoot, K. (2021) *How Stereotypes Deceive Us.* Oxford University Press.

Talukder, M.B., Hossain, S.E., Al Ferdous, F. and Khan, M.R. (2025) Exploring the rise of wellness tourism: Trends, benefits, and market potential. In K. Wongmahesak and R. Rillera Marzo (eds) *AI Technologies and Advancements for Psychological Well-Being and Healthcare* (pp. 351–378). IGI Global.

Tiwari, R. and Hashmi, H. (2022) Integrating concepts of destination image, travel motivations, expectation, and future behavior to create a model of wellness travel intentions. *International Journal of Spa and Wellness* 5 (2), 185–206. https://doi.org/10.1080/24721735.2022.2057714.

Viale, M. and Vicol, M. (2023) Conserving traditional wisdom in a commodified landscape: Unpacking brand Ayurveda. *Journal of Ayurveda and Integrative Medicine* 14 (1), 100667.

Zhong, L., Deng, B., Morrison, A.M., Coca-Stefaniak, J.A. and Yang, L. (2021) Medical, health and wellness tourism research: A review of the literature (1970–2020) and research agenda. *International Journal of Environmental Research and Public Health* 18 (20), 10875.

Index

Affective Computing xiii, 4, 99–101, 103, 113
Aging Population 81, 83

Biophilia 218
Body–Mind–Spirit Connection 67

Calligraphy Therapy xiv, 138–9, 142–6, 148–50
Chinese Wellness Tourism 5, 80, 84–6, 93
Co-Design 117, 119, 122, 126, 128, 131–2
Community Empowerment xii, 4, 75
Community Engagement 3, 14, 16, 20, 23, 33, 169
Community Participation 212, 228
Community Wellbeing 9–10, 14–18, 20, 25, 43, 48, 159
Consumer Behavior in Wellness Travel 4, 19, 103, 112, 228–9
Creative Expression 140, 144
Culinary Heritage ix, 3, 9–10, 12–16, 18–20, 22–4, 41, 86
Cultural Authenticity 3, 236, 239–40
Cultural and Ecological Conservation 159
Cultural Identity 9–10, 13, 17, 22, 32, 39, 43–4, 61
Cultural Sustainability 11, 14
Cultural Wellness Experiences 14

Destination Management and Stewardship xii, 106, 228, 230, 232
Destination Stewardship 3, 155–62, 164, 166, 168–70

Energy Therapy Tourism (ETT) 220
Ethics in Artificial Intelligence x, 101, 106, 240
Ethno-botanical Wellness Tourism (EWT) 156

Factorial Correspondence Analysis (FCA) 107
Food Therapy 83
Food Tourism viii–ix, xiii
Forest Bathing 117, 122, 124–5, 127–8, 132

Gaia Theory 218–19
Grounded Theory Methodology 223

Health and Wellness Tourism xiii, xv–xvii, 84, 105, 186, 191, 197
Health Promotion 158, 177, 185, 192, 195, 201
Health-Conscious Consumers 86–8, 240
Healthy Diet Trends 89
Heritage Preservation 14, 241
Higher Education Institutions (HEIs) 48
High-Level Wellness Framework (Dunn) 2, 62, 67, 75
Holistic Health xix, 2–4, 75, 117, 181, 239
Holistic Wellbeing viii, 17, 33, 62, 170, 236
Holistic Wellness Frameworks 3, 50–1, 185

Indigenous Knowledge xix, 5, 28–30, 32–5, 40–1, 43, 62, 67, 236, 241
Integrative Health Practices 83, 197
Interpretivist Qualitative Research 57

Japanese Tourists 5, 117, 121, 125–30

Local Gastronomy xvi, 129

Medicinal and Aromatic Plants (MAPs) 156
Mindfulness xiv, 1, 4–5, 67, 71, 137–8, 40–6, 48–9, 225–6, 228, 232–3, 237, 239–40
Modern Thermalism 175, 177, 182, 184, 187

Nature-Based Wellbeing Tourism 117, 119, 122
Neuroscience Methods (EEG, fMRI, Eye-tracking, etc.) 101–3, 110–14
Neurotourism 101
Non-Bovine Milk 2, 62, 64–5, 68–9, 74–5

Pastoral Communities xii, 62–7, 68, 72, 74–5
PERMA Model 30, 32–7, 39–40, 43–4
Preventive Health 197, 211

Regenerative and Sustainable Practices viii, 13, 62–3, 103, 233, 237
Regenerative Tourism xv
Regional Development xvi–xvii, 5, 191, 194, 198–9, 202, 211, 242
Restorative Environments 219

SaimaaLife 4, 119, 121–31
Similitude Analysis and Graph Theory 107, 110, 114
Six Dimensions of Wellness 49–51, 54
Socio-cultural Identity 9–10, 13, 17, 22, 32, 39, 43–4, 61
Spa Industry 179
Spiritual and Holistic Wellbeing viii, 17, 33, 62, 170, 236
Student Awareness and Participation 58
Student Wellness 49–54, 56–8
Sustainability xi, xiii–xiv, xvi, xviii, xix, xxi, 1–2, 5–6, 11, 14, 18, 32, 80, 86, 99–101, 103–4, 106–9, 111–14, 119–22, 129, 170, 194, 198, 216, 232–3, 237, 239–42
Sustainable Business Models 4, 119–20, 122, 127, 129–32
Sustainable Development 1, 99–100, 111–13, 119, 160, 194, 198, 216, 225, 227, 231, 233, 237, 241
Sustainable Development Goals (UNSDGs) 99–100, 119, 216, 227

Thermal Spas 182–3, 192–3, 210
Thermalism xvi, 3, 175–80, 182–7, 193, 204–5
Tourism Experience xiv, xx, 4, 63, 67, 74, 83, 87, 93, 106, 113–14, 117–19, 122, 126–30, 230, 237
Tourism mSMEs 121, 127, 132
Traditional Chinese Medicine (TCM) 80, 87
Traditional Cuisines 30–1, 40–1
Traditional Ecological Knowledge (TEK) 156
Traditional Healing 66–7, 69–70, 74, 168
Traditional Healing Practices 69, 74
Transformative Experiences viii, 105, 233

Wellbeing 1, 4–5, 9–10, 28, 32, 48, 99, 103, 106, 108, 111–12, 117, 140, 183, 196, 236
Wellness and Nature Connectedness 217
Wellness Destinations 87, 145, 156, 158, 176, 192
Wellness Economy 117, 140, 156, 193, 216
Wellness Programmes 48–9, 51–4, 56–8
Wellness Tourism vii, xiii, xv, xvii, xix, xxi, 1–6, 61–2, 64–5, 67, 69, 71, 74–5, 80–5, 87–9, 92–4, 105, 113, 117–19, 121, 130, 137–40, 142–3, 145–6, 148–9, 155–8, 160–1, 165, 169–70, 175, 185–6, 191, 197–8, 216, 220, 227, 231–2, 236–42
Work Placement Learning 52

For Product Safety Concerns and Information please contact our EU Authorised Representative:

Easy Access System Europe

Mustamäe tee 50

10621 Tallinn

Estonia

gpsr.requests@easproject.com

www.ingramcontent.com/pod-product-compliance
Ingram Content Group UK Ltd.
Pitfield, Milton Keynes, MK11 3LW, UK
UKHW021828100926
8556IPUK00003B/219